ALSO BY JULIAN RUBINSTEIN

*Ballad of the Whiskey Robber: A True Story of Bank Heists,
Ice Hockey, Transylvanian Pelt Smuggling, Moonlighting
Detectives, and Broken Hearts*

THE HOLLY

THE HOLLY

FIVE BULLETS, ONE GUN, AND
THE STRUGGLE TO SAVE
AN AMERICAN NEIGHBORHOOD

JULIAN RUBINSTEIN

Farrar, Straus and Giroux
NEW YORK

Farrar, Straus and Giroux
120 Broadway, New York 10271

Printed in the United States of America
First edition, 2021

Library of Congress Cataloging-in-Publication Data
Names: Rubinstein, Julian, author.
Title: The Holly : five bullets, one gun, and the struggle to save an
    American neighborhood / Julian Rubinstein.
Description: First edition. | New York : Farrar, Straus and Giroux,
    2021. | Includes bibliographical references.
Identifiers: LCCN 2020057989 | ISBN 9780374168919 (hardcover)
Subjects: LCSH: Gangs—Colorado—Denver. | Gang prevention—
    Colorado—Denver. | Violent crimes—Colorado—Denver—
    Prevention. | Community development—Colorado—Denver.
Classification: LCC HV6439.U7 D3978 2021 | DDC 364.106/60978883—dc23
LC record available at https://lccn.loc.gov/2020057989

Our books may be purchased in bulk for promotional, educational, or
business use. Please contact your local bookseller or the Macmillan
Corporate and Premium Sales Department at 1-800-221-7945, extension
5442, or by email at MacmillanSpecialMarkets@macmillan.com.

www.fsgbooks.com
www.twitter.com/fsgbooks • www.facebook.com/fsgbooks

10   9   8   7   6   5   4   3   2   1

For my mom, Diane Rubinstein

And in memory of:

Ernestine Boyd (1936–2018)

Lauren Watson (1940–2019)

Bishop Dennis Leonard (1949–2018)

Ngor Monday (2000–2019)

Contents

Cast of Characters
ix

Maps
xiii

PROLOGUE
3

ACT I
13

ACT II
143

ACT III
217

EPILOGUE
341

A Note on Sources
363

Notes
365

Acknowledgments
379

Cast of Characters

THE ROBERTS FAMILY

TERRANCE ROBERTS: Former Blood gang member known as ShowBizz; later an anti-gang activist, founder of Prodigal Son and the Colorado Camo Movement

GEORGE ROBERTS: Terrance's father, funeral preacher

ERNESTINE BOYD ("GRANNY"): Terrance's grandmother, owner of A&A Fish, one of the first African Americans to live in Northeast Park Hill

HOLLY REDEVELOPMENT PLAYERS

AARON MIRIPOL: President and CEO, Urban Land Conservancy, which bought Holly Square in 2009

PHILIP ANSCHUTZ: Denver-based billionaire; his family foundation became the largest investor in the redevelopment of Holly Square, funding the Boys & Girls Club

JOHN ARIGONI: President and CEO, Boys & Girls Clubs of Metro Denver

PATRICK HORVATH: Director, Denver Foundation's Strengthening Neighborhoods Program, later director of economic opportunity for the foundation

MIKE JOHNSTON: Colorado state senator, shared an office with Terrance, married to an assistant district attorney, 2020 candidate for the U.S. Senate

LAW ENFORCEMENT

COMMANDER MIKE CALO: Head of District 2, longtime gang officer working the Holly

ROBERT WHITE: First African American Denver police chief, from 2011 to 2018

JAMES COMEY AND TIM KAINE: Former FBI director and current U.S. senator, first to implement Operation Ceasefire in Richmond, Virginia, as managing U.S. attorney and mayor, respectively

REGINA HUERTER: Former executive director of Denver's Crime Prevention and Control Commission, in charge of Denver's anti-gang effort under Mayor Hickenlooper

PAUL CALLANAN: Former probation officer, became director of the Gang Reduction Initiative of Denver (GRID), which coordinated Denver's anti-gang effort beginning in 2011 after Mayor Hancock was elected

ACTIVISTS

LAUREN WATSON: Leader of Denver's Black Panthers

BISHOP ACEN PHILLIPS: Head of the Northeast Denver Ministerial Alliance and an ally of the Black Panthers; his church was in northeast Park Hill

REV. LEON KELLY ("REV"): Anti-gang activist with the oldest program in Denver, Open Door Youth Gang Alternatives

BROTHER JEFF FARD: Owner of Brother Jeff's Cultural Café in Denver and a well-known African American activist

BRYAN BUTLER: Terrance's childhood friend and later an outreach worker for Prodigal Son

ALEX LANDAU: Beaten nearly to death by Denver police in 2009, has become a leading voice in northeast Denver

AQEELA SHERRILLS: Former Crip from LA, nationally recognized anti-gang activist

GERIE GRIMES: Longtime northeast Denver activist, mother of "Brazy" Grimes, president of the Holly Area Redevelopment Project (HARP)

HASIRA "H-SOUL" ASHEMU: Northeast Denver activist, son of Lauren Watson

JEHRIN "J HOOD" CLARK: Former Gangster Disciple from Chicago, joined the Colorado Camo Movement when he met Terrance

KAMAO "KTONE" MARTINEZ: Denver DJ and a leader of the Colorado Camo Movement

THE MAYORS

BENJAMIN STAPLETON (1923–31 and 1935–47): Longest-serving mayor of Denver, KKK member

JAMES QUIGG NEWTON (1947–55): First to call for a "purposeful integration" of Northeast Park Hill (including the Holly)

THOMAS CURRIGAN (1963–68): Mayor during Denver's tumultuous civil rights movement in the Holly; empowered the "Group of 15" activists

FEDERICO PEÑA (1983–91): First Denver mayor to confront the city's gang problem

WELLINGTON WEBB (1991–2003): Mayor during Columbine shooting and national leader of the anti-gun movement, intimately involved in Denver's African American community and anti-gang efforts

JOHN "HICK" HICKENLOOPER (2003–11): As mayor of Denver, worked with Terrance on the anti-gang effort and the redevelopment of Holly Square; became Colorado governor in 2011; elected U.S. senator (D) in 2020

MIKE HANCOCK (2011–present): Current mayor, participated with Mike Asberry in Rev Kelly's Red Shield program as a kid; worked with Terrance and later funded the group that replaced Prodigal Son

LAWYERS

BILL RITTER: Denver district attorney, 1993–2005, then Colorado governor, 2007–2011; prosecuted Terrance as a Blood

MITCH MORRISSEY: Denver district attorney, 2005–17; prosecuted Terrance as a Blood, recognized him with awards as an anti-gang activist, prosecuted him again for the Holly Square shooting

HENRY COOPER: Assistant district attorney, co-prosecutor of Terrance's case

ALMA STAUB: Assistant district attorney, co-prosecutor of Terrance's case

MARSHAL SEUFERT: Terrance's public defender

LISA ARNOLD: Terrance's public defender

ORIGINAL GANGSTER (OG) BLOODS

CARL "FAT DADDY" McKAY: Park Hill Blood, owner of car wash/computer shop in the Holly; later an anti-gang activist

ISAAC "ICE"/"ICEMAN" ALEXANDER: Legendary Park Hill Blood, father of Hasan "Munch" Jones, grew up with Terrance

JOEL "WAY OUT" ALEXANDER: Park Hill Blood, operated car wash/computer shop with Carl McKay

PERNELL "P. LOK" HINES: Powerful Park Hill Blood; later an anti-gang activist

SHERIA "DRETTIE" HICKS: Park Hill Blood, Pernell's so-called PR man; later an anti-gang activist

AARON "BRAZY" GRIMES: Cousin of Terrance's childhood friend Bryan Butler, son of the HARP president Gerie Grimes

OTHER BLOODS

BARRY "LIL TEK 9" JOHNSON: One of Terrance's closest friends

RICARDO "BOONEY" PORTER: Another Blood, also one of Terrance's closest friends

HASAN "MUNCH" JONES: Second-generation Blood; son of Ice Alexander

AUNDRE "AD" MOORE: Key neighborhood Blood

"L SHADY": Blood, married to Terrance's cousin

CRIPS

MICHAEL "PSYCH" ASBERRY: Founder of Denver's first Crips gang, the Rollin 30s Crips

DERRICK "LIL CRIP" WILFORD: One of Terrance's most-feared enemies, he would later help change Terrance's life in the Denver Jail

GERALD "HOOP RIDE" WRIGHT: Crip who later joined forces with Terrance and the Camo Movement

DARYL "DG" GIVENS: Crip who befriended Terrance in jail and testified against a fellow Crip

ORLANDO "LIL O" DOMENA: Crip who worked with Asberry on an ill-fated anti-gang program in the 1990s, later convicted of killing a Blood

ORGANIZATIONS

PRODIGAL SON INITIATIVE: Founded by Terrance in 2005 to do gang-prevention work

OPEN DOOR YOUTH GANG ALTERNATIVES: Denver's first major anti-gang organization, founded by Rev Leon Kelly in 1988, described as a community-based, non-law enforcement effort

DENVER FOUNDATION: Colorado's oldest and largest community foundation, a nonprofit organization founded in 1925; a partner in the Holly redevelopment

ANSCHUTZ FAMILY FOUNDATION: Family foundation of billionaire Philip Anschutz, the wealthiest man in Colorado; a partner in the Holly redevelopment and funder of the Boys & Girls Club

URBAN LAND CONSERVANCY (ULC): Founded in 2006 by Sam Gary, a wealthy Colorado oilman, ULC was formed to preserve community assets for urban communities. In 2009, one of the first properties it bought was Holly Square. ULC's CEO and president is Aaron Miripol.

GANG REDUCTION INITIATIVE OF DENVER (GRID): City office that sits under the Department of Public Safety and coordinates the city's anti-gang effort; run by Paul Callanan

HOLLY AREA REDEVELOPMENT PROJECT (HARP): Steering committee set up by Aaron Miripol of the ULC and Terrance Roberts, to coordinate a neighborhood vision for the new Holly Square

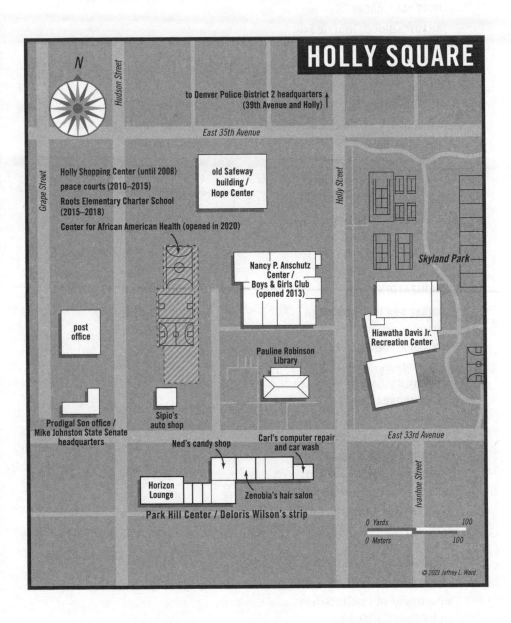

HOLLY SQUARE

N

Hudson Street

to Denver Police District 2 headquarters
(39th Avenue and Holly)

East 35th Avenue

Grape Street

Holly Shopping Center (until 2008)
peace courts (2010–2015)
Roots Elementary Charter School
(2015–2018)
Center for African American Health (opened in 2020)

old Safeway
building /
Hope Center

Holly Street

Skyland Park

Nancy P. Anschutz
Center /
Boys & Girls Club
(opened 2013)

post
office

Hiawatha Davis Jr.
Recreation Center

Pauline Robinson
Library

Prodigal Son office /
Mike Johnston State Senate
headquarters

Sipio's
auto shop

East 33rd Avenue

Carl's computer repair
and car wash

Ned's candy shop

Ivanhoe Street

Horizon
Lounge

Zenobia's hair salon

Park Hill Center / Deloris Wilson's strip

0 Yards 100

0 Meters 100

© 2021 Jeffrey L. Ward

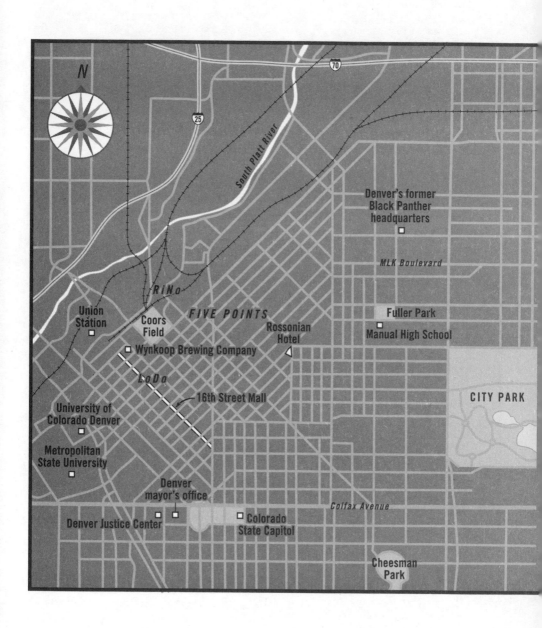

NORTHEAST DENVER

I-70

Denver Police District 2
headquarters

NORTHEAST
PARK HILL

MLK Park

Station 26 Brewing,
opened 2013

East 36th Avenue

Dahlia Square

Holly Square

East 33rd Avenue

STAPLETON/
renamed
CENTRAL PARK
in 2020

MLK Boulevard

Ernestine Boyd's home

Colorado Boulevard

A&A Fish

East 29th Avenue

Denver police
gang unit

East 23rd Avenue

GREATER
PARK HILL

Monaco Parkway

Quebec Street

Colfax Avenue

Driftwood Motel

0 Miles   .5   1

0 Kilometers   .5   1

© 2021 Jeffrey L. Ward

The Holly

Prologue

September 20, 2013

Denver, Colorado

Terrance Roberts took off his shirt and climbed up to the roof of the small building that housed his organization, Prodigal Son. Under one arm, he carried a sledgehammer.

Across the street in the sun, next to a pair of basketball courts, a group of Blood gang members watched. "Climb like Tarzan," one of them sneered.

Terrance, who had big eyes and a trim beard, tried to ignore the taunt. Now thirty-seven, he'd spent the last nine years of his life working to end the gang violence he'd once been a part of. Prominent activists, influential clergy, two Denver mayors, even law enforcement had all praised his efforts. Not that any of it came easily.

The roof was only one story up. Once on top, Terrance looked out at the young gang members, several of whom he knew. He had grown up in the neighborhood and had been a Blood. Tattooed on his left arm, in ornate cursive, was "ShowBizz," his former gang name; across his muscled chest was "Damu Rida"; *damu* was Swahili for "blood."

Terrance had never been on the building's roof before. It offered him a commanding view of Holly Square, a 3.6-acre space about five miles east of downtown Denver. The Holly, as it was known, was legendary in Denver's African American community. For decades it was the site of a shopping center and served as the community hub. In 1968, a police shooting in the parking lot became the pivotal moment in Denver's civil rights movement. In the 1980s, the square became an open-air drug market, and the headquarters of Denver's first Blood gang. Now it appeared to be finding a new identity.

A high-profile redevelopment of Holly Square was coming to fruition, and Terrance had been an integral part of it. In the middle of the square was a new Boys & Girls Club that he had campaigned for. Terrance had planned a peace rally for that evening, in advance of its official opening. He wanted residents to come together to promote gang unity and an end to the violence that had flared again in recent months.

The day, however, had begun inauspiciously. When Terrance got to the Holly, he had run into Aaron Miripol, the white CEO of the local nonprofit that bought the square in 2009. As they greeted each other, two men rattled the chains around the club's front doors. "It's not open yet," Terrance called out.

"Gentrifiers!" they yelled back.

As Terrance turned and headed back toward the Prodigal Son office, he had his first encounter of the day with the Bloods. Five of them were under the gazebo next to the basketball courts, smoking "spice," a synthetic marijuana, and acting rowdy. "I already told you, you can't be over here if you're going to be like that," Terrance told them. He had a lease to maintain and operate the courts. Drug use wasn't permitted.

"Whatever, snitch," said Hasan "Munch" Jones, getting up from the table. Terrance looked at him. Hasan was twenty-two, thin but wiry. He had a long face and two big front teeth, from which he got his gang name. "These are *our* courts," Hasan said. He tugged a front pocket of his pants, showing Terrance the butt of a knife that was clipped inside.

Watching from outside the Prodigal Son office, Bryan Butler, one of Terrance's gang outreach workers, called out to Terrance. Bryan had also grown up in the neighborhood, and knew Hasan. He couldn't hear the threat Hasan had just made, but he could feel the tension.

"T!" Bryan yelled. "We gotta go." Bryan wanted to get Terrance out of the Holly to let things cool down. Prodigal Son's board had raised a couple thousand dollars for new office furniture and they planned to go to Ikea. After the peace rally, they would move the Prodigal Son office across the street and into the Boys & Girls Club.

But when they returned to the Holly a few hours later, the group of Bloods milling around the courts had grown. One of them pointed to a bulky camera on the roof of the Prodigal Son building and accused Terrance of collecting evidence for the police.

Oh, yeah? Terrance thought. *I'll show them.* And so there he was on the roof, with a sledgehammer. He walked over to the camera, which looked like an old battleship gun. As far as Terrance knew, it had never worked. As the Bloods watched, he took a deep breath and swung the heavy hammer into the camera, again and again.

ACROSS THE STREET, a working police HALO surveillance camera—Denver's first—sat atop a utility pole. At 5:50 p.m., ten minutes before the peace rally was to begin, Hasan entered the frame, on a low-rider dirt bike, looping in and out of light traffic, his oversized white T-shirt puffing like a parachute behind him.

Hasan was a second-generation Blood. His father, Isaac "Ice" Alexander, was a legend in Denver's underworld, and one of the first Bloods in the city, an "OG," or Original Gangster. Terrance grew up with Isaac a few blocks from Holly Square.

Hasan had become a key figure in the Holly, and in Denver's gang war. He was the Bloods' so-called YG Regulator, a designation bestowed by the OGs. It meant that among the Young Gangsters, Hasan was a field general, feared and revered. Law enforcement called this type of gang member the "trigger puller" and claimed they were responsible for as much as 90 percent of a gang's violent crime.

Terrance felt duty-bound to keep the neighborhood's violence at bay. He had recently emerged as the charismatic founder and leader of the Colorado Camo Movement, a citywide gang unity initiative. In fiery speeches, he challenged warring gang members to become community activists. Denver's gang violence began to decline for the first time. More recently, the city of Denver had selected

Terrance's organization to be part of its prestigious federal Project Safe Neighborhoods effort, America's premier anti-gang program. Denver hoped to become a national model for combatting gang violence, and Prodigal Son was fighting the battle on the front line.

Terrance spoke to Hasan every chance he could, hoping to show him another path. Recently he'd taken Hasan to a Denver Nuggets game in box seats. Hasan was an especially personal project for Terrance. Not only did he know Hasan's father, but Terrance also saw himself in Hasan. Terrance, too, had been the YG Regulator.

AFTER CLIMBING DOWN from his roof, Terrance went home to get ready for the rally. He showered and shaved his head and, though he wasn't particularly religious, he got down on his knees. He'd had a couple of visions involving the Holly. One was about putting up a youth center. That one had come true. The other was one he hadn't told anyone about. It was that he would end up having to shoot someone there. The threats he faced earlier in the day had not come out of the blue. Terrance feared there were others behind Hasan's threat, in particular the OGs, guys he'd known most of his life. Several of them hung around a new shop at the other end of the block. Terrance had become suspicious of the place and wondered about these men's motivations. But even for an insider like him, it had become difficult to know what was really going on, who was pulling the strings. The neighborhood was changing quickly. The associations and entanglements among politicians, funders, developers, police, gang members, and informants were more complex than ever. He had recently acquired a 9 mm pistol. He prayed for no one to get hurt.

He put on a pair of jeans and a camouflage Nuggets hat, and placed the gun in the trunk of his SUV. As Terrance knew, calling someone a snitch was a threat that had to be acted upon—even or especially on a day that was supposed to symbolize peace and progress. On his way back to the Holly, he called his father, George, a street preacher. "Pops, I need you up at the Holly," he said. "I think something's going to happen to me."

At about 5:45 p.m., he pulled into a parking spot next to the "peace courts," the basketball courts he'd built over the ruins of the old shopping center. "Sa-whoop," he heard when he got out. It was the Bloods' alert call. "The snitch is back," he heard one of the Bloods say.

Hasan appeared, on his low rider. He stopped in front of Terrance. "On Bloods," Terrance heard Hasan swear, "I'ma be back over here in a minute to fuck you up." He pedaled away.

Terrance looked around. It was a cloudless evening. The sun was slowly sinking over the Rocky Mountains. On the courts, young men waited their turn to play. Across the street, State Senator Mike Johnston, an Obama education adviser with whom Terrance shared office space, was hosting an event to support a public school funding initiative.

To some, nothing appeared amiss. To Terrance, it seemed that the threat he feared was about to unfold. He watched Hasan swing onto 33rd Avenue. Terrance went to his SUV, to get his gun.

Minutes later, Senator Johnston's event ended and attendees streamed out of the office. Next to the courts, about a dozen Bloods, including Hasan, moved toward Terrance. "This is *our* neighborhood," one of the Bloods said.

Three gunshots pierced the air. People ran out of the square while others ran in. Another shot came, and another. The courts were suddenly empty and quiet. Next to them, Hasan Jones lay faceup on the ground. Terrance walked backwards, holding the gun in one hand. He could hear his own breathing. Gang members he recognized scampered for cover behind parked cars. Others raced toward Hasan, with a hand over their waist as if they had a weapon. Senator Johnston appeared on the courts, near Terrance. "Put the gun down," Johnston told Terrance. "They'll think it was you."

Terrance heard footsteps coming from 33rd Avenue. Two Denver police officers charged into view. Their guns were trained on him.

Terrance's other vision had come true. "Drop your weapon!" a police officer shouted. "Drop your weapon!"

AT THE TIME of Terrance's arrest, I had long ago left Denver, where I'd grown up, for the East Coast. I was living in Brooklyn, where housing costs continued to rise, and neighborhoods like Bedford-Stuyvesant that once had been considered dangerous were gentrifying. Some of these communities would also receive Project Safe Neighborhoods grants, about which there was little public reporting.

I had been raised in south Denver in the 1970s and '80s. My only impressions of the Holly came from an occasional story about drugs or gangs that made the local media. I felt like I'd been forewarned not to go there, and I hadn't. But on September 27, 2013, a *New York Times* story caught my eye: "After Violence Interrupts Progress, a Struggle Ensues in Denver."

Terrance Roberts, an anti-gang activist, had reportedly shot a gang member, Hasan Jones, in Holly Square, at his own peace rally. Hasan had survived but was paralyzed from the waist down. Terrance faced attempted murder and assault charges, as well as possession of a weapon by a previous offender, which carried a mandatory prison sentence.

The *Times* had published Terrance's mug shot. He stared out from behind a yellow jumpsuit like tomorrow was gone. "I swept up the glass. I swept up the bullet shells. I swept up the people when I needed to," Terrance told the *Times*. "And sometimes they swept me up. I hope I don't get hurt when I go back. But I'm going to go back one day."

I was intrigued by the redevelopment effort at the Holly—it involved Denver's African American mayor, Colorado's oldest and largest community foundation, and the prominent billionaire Philip Anschutz—and puzzled by why an anti-gang activist would shoot someone at his own peace rally. I found Terrance's email on the Prodigal Son website (it was terrancerobertsloveslife@yahoo.com) and sent him a note. He had bonded out of jail, and replied. When we spoke by phone, he sounded incongruously upbeat. He told me he was working on taking his "movement" to other cities. I didn't know what to think, but I asked if he would meet me in Denver.

TERRANCE CHOSE AN International House of Pancakes on the opposite side of town from the Holly. When I arrived, he was sitting in a booth in the back. He wore a sleek black-and-white track sweatsuit and a Denver Broncos hat with the decal on. He sprang up to shake my hand. "Wassup!" he said. His beard was neatly trimmed and he wore a stylish ultrathin mustache. In each ear was a diamond stud.

I had read closely the voluminous local media coverage of the shooting, which suggested that Terrance had fallen back into gangster life and become enveloped in neighborhood beefs. Witnesses had reportedly told police that Terrance had shot Hasan five times, including twice while he was on the ground.

It was easy to see that Terrance carried some of his past with him. The edges of tattoos on his forearms were visible. On his neck was another tattoo I didn't understand, BIP Lil Tek 9.

Terrance was a powerful presence. Talking to him felt like entering a force field. He could talk for hours, about hip-hop or Black history or gang history. All of it seemed to come back to the Holly. He was a third-generation resident of the neighborhood. He said that except for his decade in prison from 1995 to 2004, he felt like he'd spent his whole life there. "I love the Holly," he told me. "I've been shot for the Holly. Twice. All the energy you see coming out of me—I got that in Holly Square."

Terrance had a much different story about what had happened the day of the peace rally. Over the course of our first few meetings, he intimated that he believed he had been the target of a plot to remove him from his position in the neighborhood. He took issue with developers, police, city hall, and gang members he suspected were informants. The information wasn't very coherent, at least to me, but it was clear that whatever happened cut deep, and I wanted to know more. Many of the players had known one another for years. Terrance's grandmother, who owned a soul food restaurant in the neighborhood, had become one of the first African Americans to live there, in 1960.

I MOVED BACK to Denver, and over the next seven years, as the Black Lives Matter movement grew, I sought to understand what had gone wrong that September day, why Terrance had shot Hasan. The stakes were high. Youth violence in the neighborhood, and across America, was rising. Aqeela Sherrills, a well-known Los Angeles anti-gang activist, who described Terrance as a "rock star for the peace movement," told me that anti-gang activists around the country were watching Terrance's case closely. As were people in northeast Denver, who were suspicious of local media reports about Terrance and suggested to me that there were political reasons behind what had happened. "I knew [Terrance] was in danger the day he started marching," Bishop Acen Phillips, one of Denver's most prominent African American clergy members and activists, told me. "The beauty of it was, he knew he was in danger."

As a white man attempting to gain trust in a historic African American community, I faced certain challenges. At first, many residents didn't want to talk to me. I persisted, eventually finding my way to the people at the heart of this story. I never imagined how entangled in the case I would become. Eventually, by luck or by effort, I managed to bear witness to an extraordinary series of events that illuminated some of the questions I had, and why people were afraid to talk about them. I pulled court cases and police records and filed open-records requests. Some of these documents provided startling revelations—about Terrance's case and how America's effort to fight gang violence is waged.

Some truths remained beyond my reach, while other evidence continues to hide in plain sight. I came to think of northeast Denver's gang neighborhoods as "invisible Denver." No matter how striking or consequential, little that took place there seemed apparent to anyone outside the community.

I hope this book will contribute to changing that. It would not be possible without the dozens of residents who shared that hope and came forward to me. Their bravery and trust enabled me to tell an alternate history of why Terrance Roberts shot Hasan Jones, and to examine how a historic neighborhood could be fighting an invisible war in a major American city, for decades.

ACT I

Terrance's grandmother, Ernestine Boyd, was nineteen when she decided to run away. It was 1955. The eldest of ten, she was living with her parents and nine siblings in a small cabin on a cotton plantation in Bradley, Arkansas, where the family worked. She had just been promoted to cook, which seemed to be a blessing. She hadn't enjoyed picking cotton in the baking sun, for two dollars a day. In the kitchen, she'd make three dollars, and the plantation owner and his wife, on whose property she'd lived since she was six, loved her cooking.

But a few days into the new job, Mr. Pearson, the plantation owner, came into the kitchen and grabbed Ernestine from behind. He tried to kiss her. When she pushed him away he said something that kept her up all night. He asked if she would like to see the "nigger" who'd recently come by on his bike to pick her up "lying in a ditch."

Ernestine wasn't sure yet if she was in love with the man on the bike. Tall, lithe, and spirited, she had many suitors. But by morning she was sure of one thing: she couldn't bear to be the cause of someone else's death.

She had an aunt who had recently uprooted from Mississippi, where Ernestine was born, to a place called Denver. Ernestine knew nothing about Denver except for a postcard from her aunt, depicting a line of snowcapped mountains marching across a sunny horizon. Without telling her family for fear of retribution against them, Ernestine skipped work the next day and made her way to the town bus. Carrying $110 and a small bag, she was leaving home, for good.

Her journey out of the South was solitary but hardly unique.

Nearly five million African Americans left a former slave state between 1940 and 1979, the largest migration of the American populace in the twentieth century. As her bus rode north and west through the empty prairies of Missouri, Kansas, and eastern Colorado, she would have been hard-pressed to imagine the overcrowding that Black neighborhoods in Chicago, Los Angeles, and Oakland already faced, a burgeoning housing crisis that would help spark the civil rights movement.

Denver was the largest city within a radius of several hundred miles, a regional hub with a population of about 450,000. It had no professional sports teams. Vail Ski Resort was still seven years from opening. A rodeo and stock show were the capital city's biggest event.

But for Ernestine, Denver appeared full of promise. When she arrived at the downtown bus station, vendors of different races were selling flowers and newspapers, and a line of taxicabs waited, accepting customers of any race. She got into one, without any idea where to tell the driver to take her.

Her unfamiliarity with the city was of no consequence. There was only one place for "Negroes" in Denver. Located about a dozen blocks northeast of the capitol, the Five Points neighborhood was established about a decade after William Larimer, a land speculator from Kansas, founded Denver City in 1858.

In 1879, Five Points grew during the "Exoduster Movement," in which approximately forty thousand former slaves headed west to Kansas, Oklahoma, and Colorado. By the turn of the century, following the gold and silver mining boom in the nearby Rocky Mountains, Five Points had its own cable car—Denver's first—and was said to have more Black-owned businesses than anyplace west of Harlem.

The neighborhood's most famous establishment, the Baxter Hotel, sat on its namesake corner, where five streets came together. Renamed the Rossonian in 1929, it was frequented in the 1920s by Duke Ellington. Later, it hosted Ella Fitzgerald, whose late-night performances there after playing Denver's white venues gave Five

Points its moniker, "Harlem of the West." Like Harlem, Five Points was open to anyone, though few from outside the community visited. One who did was Jack Kerouac, who memorialized Five Points in his 1947 book *On the Road*, describing a walk through the neighborhood on a redolent "lilac evening . . . with every muscle aching among the lights of 27th and Welton in the Denver colored section, wishing I were a Negro, feeling that the best the white world had offered was not enough ecstasy for me."

When Ernestine arrived, Five Points' population was about twenty-two thousand. Most of the two-story Victorian-style homes had been divided into apartments. Vacancies were hard to come by. Discriminatory zoning and mortgage-lending practices, known as redlining, prevented Blacks from living in other neighborhoods.

Denver's segregation was rooted in the 1920s, when both the governor, Clarence Morley, and the mayor, Benjamin Stapleton, were members of the KKK. Stapleton served five nonconsecutive terms, more than any other Denver mayor.

"Negroes are holed up in a small area which is getting worse and worse," Mayor Quigg Newton, who defeated Stapleton in 1947, said when he took office. "They are victims of an unwritten law. Sooner or later there must be a breaking through." But, as Ernestine got into a taxi that day, it still hadn't happened.

Ernestine's taxi driver, who also was African American, told her that he'd heard of a place that had a vacancy and took her. It was a two-story, eight-unit building. Ernestine waited on the porch. "Susie?" she heard a woman's voice call. Susie had been Ernestine's childhood nickname in Mississippi. She turned to see her aunt, whom she hadn't seen since her aunt left the South several years earlier, standing at the entrance. She was the building manager.

FOR $11 A week, Ernestine got her own one-room apartment down the hall from her aunt. She answered a classified ad in *The Denver Post* to be a cook for a wealthy white family, and was hired, for $20 a day. Soon she had saved enough to buy burial insurance; she wanted to be sure no one in her family would be stuck raising money for her funeral. Then she began making a series of bus trips, back and forth to Arkansas, until she'd brought all nine of her siblings with her to Denver.

In Chicago and Los Angeles, massive public housing complexes such as Cabrini-Green and Jordan Downs were becoming temporary answers to overcrowding in Black neighborhoods. For its part, Denver slowly loosened the boundaries of Five Points. Some of its African American residents moved eastward toward the city's grandest public space, City Park. But the neighborhood that Mayor Newton had singled out for an experiment in "purposeful integration" was on the other side of the park. Allowing Blacks to "jump the park" meant giving them passage to one of Denver's most venerable neighborhoods, Park Hill.

Settled in 1887 by Allois Guillaume Eugene von Winckler, a Prussian baron and soldier, Park Hill had gun violence in its DNA. During the Spanish-American War, von Winckler hosted U.S. Army battalions, who fought mock battles there. A few years later, according to an account in *The Denver Times*, von Winckler drank enough strychnine to kill six men and shot himself in the chest, a suicide the newspaper called "one of the most remarkable on record."

Von Winckler had begun creating a neighborhood for well-heeled industrialists and statesmen, and after his death, a group of investors who bought the land—including David Gamble, whose family owned Procter and Gamble—were careful about curating Park Hill's development. It had wide boulevards separated by tree-lined medians and featured large Victorian and Tudor homes with carriage houses for the horses. Country living just outside town, according to its marketing.

But one last tract of Park Hill, the far north piece, remained undeveloped until the late 1940s. Denver's new residents then included many military families relocating after the war to Lowry Air Force Base. Some became the first residents of the 2,600 small brick ranch houses that comprised Northeast Park Hill, just a few miles from the base. The neighborhood was also just across Quebec Street from Stapleton International Airport, named for the former mayor.

In 1956, the Federal-Aid Highway Act facilitated construction of the two major interstates that run through Denver, I-70 and I-25. A rapid development of the city's suburbs began. Bigger homes with large backyards went for as little as $20,000. Young military families and other white residents were enticed to move out of the city.

While the federal Fair Housing Act wasn't signed until 1968, Denver's Association of Real Estate Brokers agreed by 1960—more than a decade after Mayor Newton's appeal—to start showing properties in Northeast Park Hill to African Americans. One of the first was Ernestine Boyd.

She was shown a three-bedroom brick house on Pontiac Street. The price was $8,500. She loved it. She and her new husband, Richard, who sold fish at the city markets, had recently started a family. The people Ernestine cooked for helped with the down payment and connected her with a bank. She was approved for a thirty-year mortgage, at $112 per month. At twenty-four years old, a grandchild of slaves, Ernestine was a Denver homeowner.

NORTHEAST PARK HILL was alluring to Blacks in Denver. Its stand-alone homes, for sale and rent, had backyards and were walking distance from City Park. But the neighborhood's most distinctive feature was a pair of shopping centers—still a new phenomenon in America—that had opened in the mid-1950s. What was particularly unusual about "The Dahlia" and "The Holly," as they were eventually known, was that they were located not on a busy boulevard but on a narrow neighborhood street—33rd Avenue—five blocks from each other.

The Dahlia, owned by the local businessman Bernard Bernstein, had two strips facing each other across a wide parking lot. Businesses included a Miller supermarket, a tailor, a barbershop, and a bowling alley, the Dahlia Lanes. The Dahlia Lounge offered dinner and dancing, and was where Ernestine occasionally went to meet friends.

The Park Hill Shopping Center, soon renamed the Holly Shopping Center, was owned by Robert J. Main, a former FBI special agent. It had a department store, a dress shop, a pharmacy, and a hardware store. On the east side of the expansive parking lot was a Dar-E-Delight ice cream stand. A separate building on the north side of the square housed a Safeway supermarket.

For the neighborhood's growing number of Black residents, the shopping centers became magnets for their civic and social life. Ernestine could always find a friend in the Holly or the Dahlia to catch up with, or to watch her young daughter, Suzanne. At night, the parking lots became gathering spots for African American youth, who listened to music and danced. Many felt an intense pride in their neighborhood. It was a place unlike any they had experienced.

AS MORE AFRICAN Americans moved into Northeast Park Hill, Denver's "bold experiment" in racial integration earned Greater Park Hill the nickname "the conscience of the city." President Lyndon Johnson, during a trip to Denver in 1966, directed his motorcade from the airport to stop so he could get out and see it for himself. "It would be difficult to believe that those were Negro homes if you hadn't seen them standing there," Johnson remarked. "When [people] ask 'How can these cities handle some of their problems?' The first thing I would say is, 'Go and see Denver.'"

And yet Denver's mayor, Tom Currigan, who grew up in Park Hill and was with President Johnson that day, knew the neighborhood's reputation was misleading. While the city promoted Park Hill as a "model" of integration, the part of the neighborhood that had been the experiment in integration—Northeast Park Hill—had in fact become one of the nation's most dramatic cases of white flight. Real estate brokers, looking to spur a wave of new sales, warned white residents that the arrival of "Negroes" would begin a downward spiral in home values. One flyer warned that Park Hill was becoming "Dark Hill." Northeast Park Hill, which had been about 98 percent white in 1960, would be about 90 percent Black by decade's end. Its schools were already badly overcrowded, and its unemployment rate was significantly higher than the city's as a whole.

The Watts Riots of 1965 in Los Angeles, sparked by a drunk driving arrest, had exploded because of frustrations in the African American community about housing, overcrowded schools, and a lack of jobs. Five days of mayhem, broadcast on national news programs, saw helmeted police with batons beating Blacks; looting; burning cars; and bodies in white sheets loaded into ambulances. Thirty-four African Americans died, nearly a thousand were injured.

Mayor Currigan had assured Denver residents that "Denver is not Watts," but he knew that racial tensions in northeast Denver were growing. While the KKK no longer held political office, a white supremacist organization that called itself the Minutemen—an offshoot of a Los Angeles group that terrorized Blacks—had announced its presence. Several members of Denver's District 2, the police substation that patrolled northeast Denver, were said to be members.

Ernestine began to see racial epithets on driveways and sidewalks. A religious woman, she shied away from politics and found solace in radio preachers. But other African Americans in the neighborhood were galvanized. Rachel Noel, a sociologist from Virginia, led a group of activists to bring their concerns directly to Mayor Currigan.

Soon after LBJ's visit, Currigan agreed to commission Noel's group, which became known as the Group of 15, to independently monitor the Dahlia. That summer, the Group of 15 witnessed a racially charged environment ruled by District 2 officers. Rattling nightsticks around the windows of cars in which youth were eating takeout from the hamburger stand, they addressed them with racial epithets, including "nigger." According to a report the group submitted, this often provoked youth to respond with their own insults. Sometimes they also threw rocks and bottles at the police. Their resulting arrests were carried out in brutal fashion. Some youth suffered severe head wounds.

Noel's commission reported that riots were barely averted. "Police action in Dahlia could have provoked serious complications if intelligent people who had knowledge of the problems that exist for these young people had not intervened," the scathing nineteen-page report delivered to Mayor Currigan stated. "The major problem facing minority youth is employment," the report stressed, a conclusion the Kerner Commission report on the Watts Riots reached the following year. Job prospects, the Group of 15 wrote, were severely hurt by the heavy policing of the neighborhood, and the many arrests for petty offenses like jaywalking or "using filthy language." Some youth were charged with false robbery or assault charges. "Police records are used to slam the doors of employment shut," the Group of 15's report said.

Urgent needs recommended by the report included job training—and a youth recreation center.

CURRIGAN CONSIDERED HIMSELF a civil rights advocate and supported LBJ's Great Society effort to end poverty and strengthen at-risk communities. Armed with the Group of 15's report, he assembled his most progressive political strategists, and for months they worked on grant applications for the new federal Model Cities and War on Poverty programs.

Denver's Model Cities proposal addressed the requirement for "citizen participation" through a process it described as "shared power." Elected community representatives from northeast Denver, it said, would help decide the future of their own communities. The proposal was singled out, and Denver won the designation of a "demonstration city," receiving extra funding.

Denver also won a War on Poverty grant, which Currigan directed toward a jobs initiative. As the summer of 1967 began, a mobile job-placement office rolled into the Dahlia Shopping Center parking lot. W. Gene Howell, the president of Denver's NAACP, manned the "Denver Opportunity" trailer in a three-piece suit and top hat.

That year also saw the formation of Denver's two most storied activist groups. On the west side of town, where most of the city's Latinos lived, the mustached Rudolfo "Corky" Gonzalez, who was thirty-nine, created the Crusade for Justice. A graduate of Manual

High School, Corky was a poet, activist, and former professional featherweight boxer who had entered politics in 1947 campaigning for Quigg Newton. Corky's efforts to highlight injustices in the Latino community took hold, making him a national icon, "the fist of the Chicano movement."

And in Whittier, a mostly African American neighborhood between Five Points and City Park, home to the upscale after-hours club Pierre's, Lauren Watson was forging a political identity.

Watson, who was six feet two, was a Manual High School graduate twelve years Corky's junior. He was born in San Francisco in 1940 and came to Denver with his mother at the age of nine. After graduating from Denver's Metro College in 1964, he worked as an actor, playing the lead in several stage productions. But he wanted to get more involved in the civil rights movement and felt that Denver wasn't politically active enough. He moved to Los Angeles and worked construction until he was fired when his employer found out he had lied about a juvenile arrest. He was unemployed when the Watts Riots broke out.

Watson, then twenty-five, walked up and down Central Avenue, where the apocalyptic scene of burning cars and storefronts was accompanied by its own soundtrack, the voice of Malcolm X, who had been assassinated in New York six months earlier. Activists blared his speeches over loudspeakers. "Stop singing and start swinging!" Malcolm implored, a swipe at MLK's nonviolent protest strategy.

Watson moved back to Denver and began organizing protests. In 1967, he was part of an anti–Vietnam War rally in Oakland where he encountered several members of a new group that called itself the Black Panthers. Huey Newton, the group's co-founder, was then in jail on murder charges that the Panthers believed were falsified. Watson returned to Denver and went to the editor of the *Blade*, then the city's lone major Black publication. He proposed a story on Newton and returned to Oakland with a press credential. During his jailhouse interview of Newton, Watson asked what he could do for the cause.

Watson had a tufty beard and large afro, which was in vogue

with many activists, including the Panthers. He and Newton also shared a political philosophy. They wanted to provide mentorship and education to youth, so that they understood and appreciated their own history of overcoming oppression and their rights as citizens. Watson also agreed with the Panthers that in the streets, they needed to start defending themselves against racist aggression with the same weapons that they were threatened with. Newton sent Watson to see the Panthers' co-founder Bobby Seale, who gave his blessing for Watson to open a Denver chapter of the group.

Watson rallied several dozen of his trusted allies for a meeting on the second floor of his home, which would become the group's Denver headquarters. Like other Black Panther chapters, among the group's first regular activities was a free breakfast program to feed and educate Black youth.

One of the first youth to join the breakfast program was George Roberts, who years later would marry Ernestine's daughter and father a son they named Terrance. But in 1967, George was just a boy of ten who lived with his mother and three brothers in a triplex condo around the corner from Lauren Watson. Georgie, as he was known, was a street-smart social butterfly who had never met his father. His mom worked several part-time jobs—dishwasher, airport baggage handler, department store clerk—and was rarely home. Watson, with his leather jacket and black beret, became Georgie's role model.

In 1967, due to the heavy police presence at the Dahlia, Denver's African American youth relocated their regular gathering spot to the Holly. The shift was noted by federal law enforcement. The U.S. attorney for Denver's judicial district requested daily reports on activity at the Holly.

On Saturday, July 29, as a city-sponsored free youth dance let out, a young Black man was ticketed and arrested in front of his friends, for jaywalking. The crowd recongregated at the Holly, agitating for a fight. Some threw rocks through storefront windows.

"Disturbances are becoming increasingly serious and police are becoming increasingly concerned," the police chief, Harold Dill, said at a press conference the following day.

That night Watson and the Panthers split into groups and circled the neighborhood as Rachel Noel rounded up community members. More than a hundred youths, including George Roberts, gathered in the Holly Shopping Center parking lot. Soon sixteen District 2 police cars and two paddy wagons arrived.

"About fifty youths coming toward us with bottles," came an officer's voice over police radio at 10:30 p.m. "They're starting to throw."

Chief Dill, who was on site, gave the order. Three dozen officers in riot gear got out of their cars, nightsticks in hand. Some had dogs, who barked and lunged as the officers marched toward a crowd around the Dar-E-Delight ice cream stand. A voice over a police megaphone directed them to disperse. Instead, garbage and glass bottles came flying. One youth grabbed a policeman's nightstick and was wrestled to the ground. Another tried to photograph the incident but was beaten back. The Denver media was not exempt; in what would become a concurrent campaign against the city's white-owned media, a car driven by a newsman was chased and pelted with rocks. By night's end, three youths were in custody and windows in four police cruisers, and several stores, were broken.

The Group of 15—which included Colorado's first African American state senator, George Brown, and the Denver Broncos running back Cookie Gilchrist—got a meeting with Mayor Currigan the following morning. They had a bold request. They asked the mayor to leave the policing of the Holly to them.

The following night, the city braced for what many expected would be a spectacle. "Dozens of private cars cruised through and around the Holly Shopping Center," a front-page story in *The Denver Post* reported. "There was an air of expectancy as persons stood by their cars parked on the perimeter of the shopping center and watched the crowd milling on the parking lot."

District 2 officers positioned themselves on the edge of the lot while neighborhood activists went in and spoke to the youth. Scattered incidents of vandalism took place in other parts of Denver that night, but in the Holly, nothing. According to an assistant professor of social work at the University of Denver, who was at the scene, "Had not the citizen's patrol intervened on the night of August 1, there was the strong possibility that the shopping center could have been burned to the ground."

"Denver is at the crossroads," Mayor Currigan told the media the following day. "We do not want to be listed among those cities where these tragedies have occurred." He announced an investigation into police brutality and extended the duties of the Group of 15 to the end of the summer.

More than one hundred American cities saw rioting in the summer of 1967. Denver was not among them. In November, Currigan was reelected. Among his first acts was to ask for the resignation of his police chief.

But the defining moment of Denver's civil rights era was yet to come. On April 4 of the following year, Martin Luther King, Jr., was assassinated in Memphis. Currigan, who had personally escorted King around Denver during his 1964 visit to the city, was devastated. Rioting broke out in more than one hundred cities, though not in Denver, at least initially. Lauren Watson and Corky Gonzales, who had become friends, co-led a march on the Colorado state capitol, demanding civil rights legislation and police reform. Then they took to the road, co-piloting what became known as the "western caravan" of activists to the Poor People's Campaign in Washington, D.C., the mass protest and tent city MLK had organized before his death.

The PPC's mass protest was entering its second month when Watson returned to Denver in June. Days later, Robert Kennedy, who many in the Black community saw as their best hope to defeat the Republican Richard Nixon in the upcoming presidential election, was assassinated. Watson felt the tenor of northeast Denver shift.

The evening of June 24, 1968, was cool and clear. Hundreds of young men and women were gathered in the Holly Shopping Center parking lot, their elongated figures silhouetted by the moon. Some discussed jumping the Skyland Rec Center's fence across the street to go for a night swim in the pool. When a District 2 patrol car drove past along 33rd Avenue, some threw bottles after it that shattered across the asphalt.

For fifteen-year-old Alvin Jones, it was his first night out since being in a car accident in which two of his classmates were killed. Both of his arms were in a sling. Alvin's mother had asked his older brother Nathan, who was seventeen, to look after him.

Nathan and his friends were drinking gin and getting rowdy. When other friends pulled up in a car and flashed a fake gun, Nathan thought it was hilarious and grabbed it. He went around, waving the toy pistol in people's faces and howling with laughter. Alvin didn't like it. "You're gonna end up shot," Alvin told him.

Across the street, four men, including two plainclothes District 2 police officers, watched the scene from an unmarked car. Around 1 a.m., when a skirmish over a girl broke out near the Dar-E-Delight ice cream stand, Officer Arthur Hutchinson, who would become one of Denver's first gang unit officers, decided to move in.

His partner, Officer Robert Moravek, called out to Nathan, whose shirt was unbuttoned. Moravek saw the butt of what appeared to be a gun protruding from Nathan's belt. Seconds later, gunshots pierced the night.

Alvin, who was on the other side of the shopping center, hustled toward the noise. A group of people stood around a man on the ground. Alvin saw it was Nathan. He was bleeding from his neck and abdomen. "You shot him in cold blood!" Alvin heard someone shout as the unmarked car went into reverse and sped off. Hutchinson radioed dispatch. His partner had been shot, he said. They were headed to the hospital. Reinforcements were needed at the Holly.

Squad cars barreled toward the shopping center. Out of one stepped Chief George Seaton, unmistakable in his thick glasses and tailored suit. "Civil rights!" one of the youth yelled, as a group charged him. Seaton pulled his pistol, halting them in their tracks.

By the time Lauren Watson, and Georgie and his brothers, and other residents who'd heard shots and sirens arrived, the Holly was barricaded. Watson and the Panthers circled side streets, weapons pointing from their car windows, taking witness accounts. Meanwhile, angry and drunken youths spilled across City Park, delivering the news. Soon, the Rossonian in Five Points was the site of a clash with police and looting. The Welton department store lost 1,400 shirts and 1,000 pairs of pants.

The night came to an end when police used tear gas in two locations. One was on Welton Street next to the Rossonian Hotel in Five Points, the future home of Denver's first Crips gang. The other was the Holly Shopping Center, the future home of the Bloods.

"I AM APPEALING at this time to the entire community to remain calm," Mayor Currigan said in an address that interrupted local programming. With Governor John Love by his side, Currigan urged residents to stay inside; Love declared a state of emergency, activating National Guard troops. "I'd like to point out that only a very small percentage of our population has been involved," Love said.

According to *The Denver Post*, "several FBI agents and deputy U.S. marshals were known to be circulating in parts of the city." Chief Seaton assembled the media. "He [Nathan] raised the tail of his shirt with his left hand, drew the pistol with his right hand and fired at

Moravek all in one motion," Seaton told Denver's press corps. Officer Moravek, according to Seaton, was recovering.

Meanwhile, at Lauren Watson's home, Black Panthers and clergy crowded into the living room, facing multiple crises. In Washington, police in riot gear were swarming the Poor People's Campaign. And at Denver General Hospital, Nathan Jones clung to life, his legs cuffed to the bed, a police officer seated outside the door. Two bullets from Moravek's gun had passed straight through him. One had gone through his abdomen and colon and out his back; the other entered from the back of his neck and exited his chin.

NORTHEAST DENVER REMAINED in a perpetual state of emergency for the remainder of the summer. Firebombings of houses, stores, and churches became so common that the fire department couldn't keep up with the calls. Some of the targets were white-owned, others not. Rev. Acen Phillips, the head of the northeast Denver ministerial alliance, whose church sat between the Holly and the Dahlia, watched a Molotov cocktail come through his church window. He told Watson, who had become a friend, that the Panthers could keep their weapons in the basement. He felt he needed protection.

The Jones family also felt under siege. They were a Gold Star family; Nathaniel Jones, an Air Force pilot, had been killed during a training exercise. Now the family regularly received threatening calls from men identifying themselves as Minutemen, sometimes demanding that Nathan drop his insistence that he didn't have a real gun on him that night.

But many in the community believed Nathan. W. Gene Howell, of Denver's NAACP, demanded the formation of "an impartial citizen's review committee" to investigate the Nathan Jones shooting. "There are too many eyewitness accounts that dispute the findings of the police," Howell said. The police's decision to use tear gas had also drawn condemnation. "The lack of sufficient warning of its use to residents of the area is an indication of a tendency to use excessive and unwarranted force," the Colorado ACLU wrote in an open letter to the police.

The former Colorado governor Dan Thornton called the unwillingness of white employers to hire African Americans "sickening." "This is the most serious human relations problem that Colorado has ever faced," Thornton said.

George Roberts joined about five hundred northeast Denver residents on the city's largest civil rights march, from the state capitol to the steps of the City and County Building. "This demonstration is to show white Denver that we are united as one and seek immediate redress of our grievances," Joe Santifer, a student activist, said on the steps. The list of demands presented by the community included an investigation into the shooting of Nathan Jones, an end to the Denver Police Department's "stop and frisk" policy, the removal of white cops from Black neighborhoods, and more "responsible and accurate" media coverage of their community.

Additional demands included a ban on the use of mace or tear gas, and a promise from the city to spend "as much money preventing riots" as it does stopping them. "War weaponry equipment, tanks and the National Guard mobilization poised to move in and encircle our community—this makes our community even more a concentration camp and builds on the feelings that we are the enemies of the total society."

DENVER'S MODEL CITIES effort kicked off that summer. Watson noted that the schedule for public hearings included an initiative to improve "Police-Community Relations." He built a coalition that included the NAACP and the Student Nonviolent Coordinating Committee (SNCC). Together they drew up a proposal for an armed citizen patrol to replace the District 2 police.

On the day of the hearing, community members showed up in force and voted to approve the $179,000 proposal, which included plans for training, uniforms, and staffing. But, city officials later announced, the measure needed the approval of the police chief. Seaton vetoed it.

The incident was a turning point for Mayor Currigan, who had championed allowing Denver's Black community to determine its own future. Currigan had begun to get briefings not just from Seaton but from Denver's FBI officials, about the danger posed by alleged "black militants" in the city. Chief among them was Lauren Watson, whose phone was already tapped. And so, instead of the elimination of District 2, Currigan and Seaton announced that they would increase patrols in Five Points and Northeast Park Hill.

Weeks later, after the white owner of a dry cleaner's on Welton Street allegedly chased a young Black youth out of his store with a lead pipe, the Panthers were on the scene to protest. Some of the protesters set fire to the dry cleaner's. District 2 showed up and arrested Watson, alleging he had instigated the arson.

As word spread of Watson's arrest, George Roberts was among a group of youths from the breakfast program who broke into an army supply store and stole cargo pants and boots; some took guns and ammunition. Denver's "Dry Cleaner Riot" lasted two days, ending only after Rev. Acen Phillips convinced Mayor Currigan that the way to stop it was to let Watson out of jail to speak to the protesters. Sheriffs escorted Watson out the back. He called off the demonstrators before being taken back to a holding cell.

WATSON, WHO WAS engaged to be married to the activist and Panthers minister Marylou Brooks, beat the charge of inciting a riot, but his legal troubles were only beginning. Chief Seaton told the Denver media that the city's Black Panthers were plotting to overthrow the city government before the November presidential election. "I would assume that the police department intelligence division has such information," was all Currigan would say.

Watson was arrested nearly two dozen times over the next year, so often that his apparent persecution became the subject of

America's first televised trial documentary, which aired on PBS. The program concerned charges stemming from an incident on November 6, 1968, the morning after Richard Nixon was elected. Watson had stepped outside, and a District 2 cop he knew greeted him by saying, "White power." When Watson got in his car, the cop followed him. A white lawyer, Leonard Davies, had become Watson's personal attorney, and Watson pulled into a 7-Eleven to call him, but police entered the store and arrested him for resisting arrest. At trial, Watson was acquitted in less than two hours.

On another occasion, after bullets shattered the windows of his home, Watson told me he saw two police officers jump into a squad car and take off. In December, the night he married Marylou, they returned home to find their belongings strewn across the house and a search warrant on the table. Another raid days before Christmas resulted in the seizure of their holiday and wedding gifts. Being an activist, at least for Watson, meant being a target.

IN THE AFTERMATH of 1968, northeast Denver community activists struggled to find signs that their efforts had achieved something. Of the eight demands made following Nathan Jones's shooting, only one was met, partially. The district attorney's office had announced a new policy that any police shooting would prompt an automatic investigation. But the process would be run by the DA's office, despite what appeared to be a conflict of interest; the DA's office represented and defended the police in court.

The first test of the policy was the Nathan Jones case itself. A grand jury was convened to consider whether Officer Moravek was justified in shooting Jones. No clear evidence was presented that Nathan had a gun, but the jury cleared Moravek.

The jury was also asked to consider whether to charge Nathan for shooting Officer Moravek. The jury handed up charges of assault with a deadly weapon; an arrest warrant was delivered to Nathan's hospital room.

Nathan was determined to fight the case. Alvin had found the plastic gun at the Holly and brought it to the district attorney's office. But at trial in January 1970, prosecutors accused Nathan of shooting Officer Moravek with a gun they said was never found. Nathan's friend Donald Chapman testified that he had given Nathan a toy gun that night. Nathan testified as well. According to *The Denver Post*, Moravek testified that he heard a gunshot and felt a "concussion," but not that he had been shot. Despite this, Nathan was convicted and sentenced to one to five years in prison.

IN THE EARLY 1970s, oil shortages shook the country and America's economy suffered, but in Denver, companies like Halliburton opened regional offices and began prospecting. The city's economy prospered. Some African Americans saw a way forward that didn't involve protesting the system. Elvin Caldwell, a businessman whose light skin almost meant he could be mistaken for white, successfully campaigned for city council on the promise to support increased police patrols in northeast Denver.

Watson branded Caldwell an "Uncle Tom" and held a mock "people's tribunal" to prosecute him for "failing to serve the needs and desires of the people." Caldwell was not amused. "So far as I am personally concerned," he wrote in a letter to Chief Seaton, "I won't be satisfied until every Black Panther is run out of Denver."

Indeed, the Panthers would not last much longer in Denver, or nationally. Documents stolen from an FBI office in 1971 revealed Director J. Edgar Hoover's FBI COINTELPRO (Counter Intelligence Program) operation. The program's goal was to "expose, disrupt, misdirect, discredit or otherwise neutralize the activities of black-nationalist, hate-type organizations and groupings, their leadership, spokesmen, membership and supporters." The Black Panthers, Hoover believed, were "the greatest threat to the internal security of the country."

Covert operations to dismantle leading Black activists often relied on infiltrators. Fred Hampton, the charismatic leader of the Chicago Black Panthers, was victimized by his own head of security, twenty-year-old William O'Neal, an FBI informant. O'Neal provided a layout of Hampton's apartment before the Chicago police broke in and killed Hampton in bed. Stokely Carmichael, the charismatic New York–based leader of the SNCC, was the target of an elaborate FBI operation that involved framing Carmichael as an informant. The FBI planted fake materials in the cars of Carmichael's associates that were made to look like FBI dispatches from Carmichael. Carmichael was expelled from the SNCC, and left the country, fearing for his life.

In Southern California, FBI informants were instructed to foment conflict between leaders of the Los Angeles Panthers and their fellow activists, the San Diego–based Organization Us. On January 17, 1969, after months of manufactured threats against them, US members assassinated an influential leader of the Los Angeles Panthers, Bunchy Carter, along with another LA Panther, in broad daylight, on the UCLA campus. The Los Angeles Police Department then arrested dozens of the LA Panthers for conspiring to retaliate, effectively eliminating the group.

The Manhattan district attorney's office charged twenty-one members of the New York Black Panthers chapter with plotting to bomb police stations. One of the so-called Panther 21 was Afeni Shakur, who would give birth to her son Tupac shortly after being released from jail.

The New York Panthers' eight-month trial, then the longest in New York history, revealed that the informant at the center of the case—a Black New York City police officer named Gene Roberts—had been the one to promote the idea of bombing police stations. Roberts's unmasking as an undercover cop was particularly devastating because he had also been Malcolm X's bodyguard, including on the day in Harlem in 1965 that Malcolm was assassinated. Many in the community now believed it was the reason Roberts hadn't successfully protected Malcolm that day.

In Denver, some of Corky Gonzales's Crusade for Justice members were charged with attempting to bomb police stations. The cases, which were built on an informant who had suggested committing the crimes, did not result in convictions. But the economic hardship, and mistrust, that took hold helped to destroy the group.

Watson and the Denver Panthers also became suspicious of people they had once trusted. One day in August 1969, two Panthers from Oakland's HQ arrived in Denver to meet with Watson. He was told he was being removed from his leadership role; he was never sure why.

Mayor Currigan unexpectedly left office as well. He resigned at the end of 1968 when the Denver City Council refused to give him a pay raise from his $14,000 per year salary. William McNichols, his former assistant, became mayor. Like many of his peers, the cigar-smoking McNichols was interested in "urban renewal," the large-scale demolitions of what were deemed blighted areas and their replacement with new buildings or, as downtown Denver would soon see, even parking decks. Urban renewal soon became suspect in the Black community, including to Lauren Watson, who in 1970 was elected to be one of northeast Denver's Model Cities representatives.

As THE BLACK freedom movement split and lost momentum, America's anti-poverty efforts took on a new focus. Model Cities shifted from community empowerment to urban development. President Nixon moved the program to the Department of Housing and Urban Development (HUD), run by George Romney, the former chairman of American Motors and governor of Michigan.

In Denver, Lauren Watson quickly became opposed to McNichols's idea of urban renewal. In particular, he questioned the incentives that were being offered to African Americans to move to Montbello, a new community farther east. Montbello had virtually no trees; it was next to a former chemical weapons manufacturing site. At meetings, Watson voiced his disapproval but found that he was simply ignored. Soon, he realized, meetings and votes were being held without him. He rounded up dozens of residents for the next meeting, and when their questions were ignored, they kicked over chairs and climbed onto tables. A photo of Watson, wearing sunglasses and being restrained from going after a regional Model Cities administrator, ran in *The Denver Post*.

The incident did not go unnoticed by federal law enforcement. In September 1970, Director Hoover of the FBI asked HUD to undertake an "inquiry" into Lauren Watson. George Romney dispatched his undersecretary to Denver. "All of our information confirms the reports of Mr. Watson's militant and anarchistic activities," Floyd Hyde, the undersecretary, reported back. "We would view his continuation in the Denver program as an extremely dangerous and intolerable situation."

Romney wrote to Hoover, assuring him that "both Mr. Hyde and the Mayor of Denver are undertaking to bring about a termination of Mr. Watson's association with the program."

BLACK OWNERSHIP WAS on the minds of many in the community. In 1969, the Dahlia Shopping Center was put up for sale and Rev. Acen Phillips decided to take action. He gathered a group of northeast Denver residents—and one white man, the future Colorado governor Roy Romer—who decided that the way they would uphold MLK's legacy was to buy the shopping center and turn it into a community-owned cooperative. "From Protest to Production" was their motto.

They got a loan from the Presbyterian Economic Development Corporation (PEDCO), an organization that had a partnership with the Office of Economic Opportunity, then run by future secretary of defense Donald Rumsfeld. With the loan, Phillips's group bought the Dahlia for $1.1 million. The sale made national news. According to reports, the Dahlia Shopping Center was now the largest Black-owned shopping center in the West. Governor John Love attended the ribbon cutting. "It was necessary to protest a few years ago to awaken the conscience of America," Rev. Phillips said at the ceremony. "Now we must move on to the next step—the step of production. This is what we are hoping to do here in this center. We are not interested in profiteering. This community center belongs to the community."

African Americans from around the country visited. The King Soopers supermarket, which had a year earlier threatened to leave, expanded. And Phillips started selling stock in the center to residents, with the goal of paying off the loan.

But PEDCO, which financed 93 percent of the project, did not appear interested in funding a cooperative. When PEDCO's executive director, Milton Page, was next in Denver for a board meeting of the ownership team, Rev. Phillips told me that Page gave him the wrong address. By the time Phillips found the meeting, nine of the eleven board members had been removed, himself included. The two remaining board members were white. "We are studying our legal recourse and what reaction the community will take," Phillips told the *Rocky Mountain News*. Many in the community saw the wresting away of the opportunity to retain African American ownership of their community as pure racism. Phillips was told there was little he could do legally.

Garbage began to pile up in the Dahlia parking lot. Leaks sprang in store roofs. Residents protested that there appeared to be no management of the center, which PEDCO continued to own and operate from New York. In 1974, a fire burned the Dahlia Lanes to the ground. Residents couldn't get anyone to clean up the debris. The charred structure, with the collapsed roof, sat, leaving community members to wonder if such an eyesore would be allowed to linger in a white community. Both of the center's gas stations, the hamburger stand, and the supermarket all closed.

Questions about invisible forces in the neighborhood began to surface. To the people living there, the civil rights movement had seemingly won them nothing. Alvin Jones stopped going to church. Lauren Watson and Marylou divorced.

Like many former Black Panthers, Watson, who moved into a rental a few blocks away from his family, struggled to find work. Government jobs were among the biggest employers of African Americans, but they were not easy to come by for former members of an organization that the government considered an enemy of the state. In Denver, law enforcement and city officials were well aware that FBI Director Hoover had demanded Watson's removal from Model Cities. And media coverage of Watson's disagreements with the city council president Elvin Caldwell and over the direction of Model Cities did not help his reputation with whites in Denver. For a while, Watson found work as a bar bouncer and at a record store. Eventually, he resorted to selling drugs.

The city of Denver as a whole entered an era of employment growth in the 1970s that outpaced all American cities but Houston. Thanks to the city's U.S. mint, the Air Force base, and growing regional federal law enforcement offices, Denver had more federal employees than any city but Washington. And as oil companies grew their Denver-based operations, Mayor McNichols demolished sections of "blighted" downtown areas to build parking lots and to begin to create the city's modern skyline. Construction began on Denver's most iconic structure, the so-called Cash Register building, designed by Philip Johnson as part of a master plan by I. M. Pei.

In 1972, the U.S. Supreme Court took up the case *Keyes v. Denver School Board*, in which the Northeast Park Hill activist Rachel Noel had advocated on behalf of nine families, claiming that the neighborhood's overcrowded schools were not equal. The following year, in one of its most consequential school desegregation rulings, the high court ruled 5–4 in favor of the Park Hill families, writing that the city of Denver had covertly created a de facto system of segregation that was "intentionally created and maintained."

GEORGE ROBERTS WAS then in the eleventh grade at Manual High School. He was illiterate, though he didn't mind. With no male role models in his life, and no hope to find a regular job, he saw opportunity in becoming a young con man in northeast Denver.

At seventeen, and without a driver's license, George cruised town in a '65 Lincoln. He'd got the car for $200 plus a stolen car stereo. He also had a pistol, which he used to stick up hippie pot

dealers. School was a thing of his past. He'd been expelled for playing dice in the bathroom. His mother wasn't happy about it, but she
did appreciate that he could contribute to the family expenses.

In 1975, seeking lower rent, Carrie Odessa Roberts and her four
sons moved east across City Park into a two-bedroom house in Northeast Park Hill. It had an apple tree in the backyard that produced
such delicious fruit that kids climbed the fence to get them. One
day, George looked out the window and saw a girl who looked like
Diana Ross. She was the prettiest girl he'd ever seen. Her name was
Suzanne. She was sixteen, a junior at George Washington High
School. Her mother was Ernestine Boyd.

George began to court Suzanne, who lived only a few blocks
away. Ernestine was dubious. George, who'd had two teeth shot out
by a BB gun in sixth grade, looked like a street hustler. He had platinum implants. He didn't appear to be in school or to have a job.
But George's charm worked on Ernestine. Suzanne, who became
pregnant, said she loved him. She dropped out of school, and in
February 1976 she married George in their local church. At thirty-
eight, Ernestine was going to be a grandmother.

With gifts from friends and family, the teen newlyweds moved
into a small apartment near City Park. By May, the relationship was
over. According to Suzanne, George hit her. George said Suzanne
hit him first. Whatever the truth, Suzanne called Ernestine, who
grabbed her husband's Colt 45 and drove to her daughter's apartment. When George opened the door, she pointed the pistol at his
head. "Get out," she told him. Her daughter needed time to pack.

Ernestine helped Suzanne look for a place back in Northeast
Park Hill. She found an opening in a small public housing project,
Elm Park. It was on 33rd Avenue, directly across from the burned-out
Dahlia. The complex, which had six two-story brick buildings, would
soon be famous in Denver's underworld as a nest for the neighborhood's gang leaders. On August 9, 1976, Suzanne gave birth to one
of them. She named him Terrance Terrell Roberts.

It would be hard to imagine a better vantage point from which to witness life in Northeast Park Hill than the picture window of the first-floor apartment little Terry Roberts shared with his mom. Directly across the street was the Dahlia Shopping Center.

After two long years, the debris from the former bowling alley had finally been cleared. In its place opened Fast Eddie's, a roller rink, as well as some shops and an after-hours "dice shack." The center's vast parking lot became a gathering place again, featuring folding chairs, chess tables, and an occasional sofa. Terrance, who wore a tall afro and rode a plastic tricycle, paid close attention to the men playing chess and talking politics. "Don't ever forget you're from Park Hill," they told him.

"Park Hill Pride" was a mantra many in Denver had heard. A 1974 study commissioned by the Colorado Civil Rights Commission, "The Park Hill Experience," described the neighborhood as "one of the few, perhaps the only, ethnically and economically diverse 'stable' communities in the United States." The false narrative of the community's successful integration continued. South Park Hill remained a wealthy, mostly white neighborhood. Northeast Park Hill was neither diverse nor economically stable, but despite this, its pride was something to behold. In the 1960s, the neighborhood was home to Pam Grier, who in 1974 became the iconic justice avenger Foxy Brown, star of the eponymous blaxploitation film. Many, including Ernestine, kept their lawns meticulously groomed, and bushes and trees shaped.

Eventually Terrance was exploring the neighborhood by tricycle. He rode down 33rd Avenue, where he passed, in alphabetical order, Elm and Forest and Grape, until he arrived at the neighborhood's

other capital, between Hudson and Holly, the Holly Shopping Cen
ter. Along with the low-slung shopping strip on the south side of
33rd, and the Skyland Rec Center across Holly Street to the east, the
area was simply known as "the Holly."

In his travels, Terrance encountered Vietnam vets and former
Black Panthers. Many wore traditional Ghanaian kente cloth or
T-shirts in red, green, and black, the colors of the African liberation
movement. Some spoke of the government's plan to keep Black
people in poverty, and how America's first police force was created
to catch runaway slaves. "Got that young blood," one said to Terrance, using a term of endearment that, along with *cuz*, would
eventually signal violent division in the community.

Terrance was precocious and he intuited early that there was a
code in his community one shouldn't violate: an intolerance of disrespect. Perhaps it was generated by years of oppression, perhaps by
more recent slights, like PEDCO leaving the Dahlia Lanes a burned-
out shambles.

One day in the summer of 1979, age three or four, Terrance was
walking in the common area of the Red Bricks apartments when
he was goaded into a circle of boys from the complex. An older kid
pushed him around and asked if he was a "punk." Terrance tried to
throw a punch but was too small.

The bigger kid appeared angered by Terrance's gall and picked up
a stick from the ground, threatening to whack him. Terrance ran. But
as soon as he got to his apartment, he knew he had to go back. He was
no punk. He found a loose brick and marched toward the group with
his little arm cocked and ready. For the others, the sight was enough.
From that point, Terrance was accepted as part of the group.

A couple dozen kids his age lived in and around the Red Bricks.
Most of them had single, working mothers, including the three Alexander brothers. Isaac, the oldest, was one of the neighborhood's
toughest and cockiest kids.

When the snow fell heavily, they gathered at Chauncey Billups's
house on 29th and Poplar, around the corner from Ernestine's place.
The city's plows would pile the snow high on Chauncey's corner,

and the kids would climb the snow mound and see who could stay on top longest by pushing others off. It was called "King of the Hill," as in Park Hill. Chauncey, a future NBA superstar, had the name of the game tattooed on his arm.

In the summers, music blared from boomboxes as the Holly and Dahlia parking lots were transformed into break-dancing venues. Terry, as some called Terrance, refused to let his diminutive size and age prevent him from being part of the neighborhood troupe. To gain acceptance, he rounded up cardboard boxes to create dance floors.

Terrance's favorite tune was "Rapper's Delight" by the Sugarhill Gang. Terrance had an impressive windmill, spinning on his shoulders with his feet splayed in the air, and a pushup-style move in which he held himself aloft with one hand while twirling in circles. The troupe spent entire days practicing for dance-offs against other neighborhoods. Their biggest rival was Five Points, against which they faced off at City Park, as relatives and neighbors cheered.

ERNESTINE WAS STILL cooking for the same family, but in 1980 she decided to take her chance at a lifelong dream. A restaurant on a small commercial block near her home was closing. She negotiated to take over the lease and, working nights and weekends, she opened a soul food restaurant, A&A Fish.

The two jobs kept her going from dawn to dusk, but she had help from her huge extended family, who cooked, waited, and hosted. Early each morning, Ernestine went to the Asian fish markets on the west side of town. When her vegetable truck made its deliveries, she called Rev. Phillips and the other clergy to tell them to come get what they needed.

A&A became a neighborhood institution. Denver Broncos players and other prominent community members—including the future first Black mayor of Denver, Wellington Webb—were regulars. At six feet five, Webb was easy to spot. When Ernestine saw him come in, she didn't have to wait for his order. She began making the fried catfish and black-eyed pea plate.

Terrance would often stay all day at the restaurant, talking to customers and playing the Centipede video game. When he got bored he'd go across the street to hang out in the barbershop. The local economy benefitted from being almost its own system; money changed hands within the neighborhood multiple times.

And yet the neighborhood's poverty rate, already well above that of the city, was rising. Denver's environmentalism had made it the first city to turn down an Olympic Games, in 1976. But the mostly progressive city remained a particularly segregated one; many employers remained unwilling to hire African Americans. One that did was Stapleton Airport, just across Quebec Street. Suzanne worked for Hertz. George's mother took a job on the janitorial staff. Terrance's grandmother on his father's side worked as a baggage handler. The other big employer was Safeway. The regional supermarket chain's distribution center was located in the northern industrial edge of the neighborhood. Chauncey Billups's dad and Terrance's mother's boyfriend, and many others, worked there.

Despite the lack of resources, the occasional Rolls-Royce or custom Cadillac found its way onto the streets. For the kids, the excitement of spotting such a car became a game they called *That's My Car!* One day Terrance spotted a tricked-out Mercedes-Benz coming toward them. "That's my . . . ," he began to call out until he realized who was waving from the passenger seat. "That's my . . . dad! *That's my dad!*" Terrance yelled, running over.

George saw Terrance a few times a year, always unannounced. He was living between Denver and Oakland, where he also had family, and his gregarious nature led him through many circles, including that of the former Black Panthers. He had photos of himself with Huey Newton, who he was often mistaken for in Oakland, due to their similar light complexions and soft features.

George made no pretense about being an activist. He was a street hustler and good at it, living off of robberies and scams. At the time, this was something that former Black Panthers like Lauren Watson had come to appreciate.

George had no bank account or savings, sometimes nothing in his pockets but a pair of weighted dice. Lithe and handsome, he dressed in silk shirts, alligator boots, and gold chains. He was a ladies' man and an entrepreneur who started a side business doing pedicures for the beautiful women he befriended on the street, Black and white alike.

Gangsters had many friends in the neighborhood. They spread the wealth and kept up the cheer. Terrance loved it when his dad came around, and slipped some money in his pocket and asked if all was cool in the hood. Terrance thought he had the best dad in the world.

Suzanne did not share her son's opinion. When George did show up, he and Suzanne inevitably wound up in a shouting match. Once she took a bike chain and beat on George's car. "Don't ever be like him," Terrance's mom told him.

THOUGH GEORGE WAS mostly absent, Terrance's family—like many in Denver's African American community—was large. Because of Ernestine and her nine siblings, it was particularly so.

One of Terrance's favorite things to do was go to Five Points to visit his aunt Marsha and her four kids, who lived in a two-bedroom apartment in the Arapahoe Projects. It was one of the few public housing blocks the city had erected in the 1950s. Terrance loved to curl himself into a ball and sit on his cousins' feet so that they could cannonball him into the air. Whenever Terrance and his mom got back home from a visit, she made him shake his clothes out because roach egg sacks would hang from his pants and shirt. They had roaches, too, Terrance and his mom joked, but at least theirs ran when the lights went on.

While the fires burning in the Bronx became the national

symbol of late '70s urban decay, Five Points became Denver's. The historic "Harlem of the West" was no longer welcoming or safe to outsiders. With few jobs and high poverty rates, robberies, such as the basic stickups that George and his friends committed, were common. Most of the original Welton Street shops and restaurants closed due to lack of business. Elvin Caldwell, the Black city councilman who Lauren Watson had pilloried, purchased the Rossonian Hotel in the hopes of refurbishing it, but it failed to attract investors. Instead it burnished a new reputation as the boarded-up backdrop for sex workers, drug dealers, informants, and police stings.

On one of Terrance's visits to his cousins' apartment, they were heading to the nearby candy store when Terrance saw a body facedown in a grassy area between buildings. The man's head was turned to one side, his eyes and mouth open. The area was cordoned off with police tape, but Terrance saw that no one seemed to care. A group of kids played hopscotch nearby. His eleven-year-old cousin grabbed his hand and they kept on to the store.

Though gun violence was not yet common, arguments and fights in northeast Denver were regular. As he lay in bed each night, Terrance heard shouts and screams from the north end of the Dahlia, near the after-hours club. The place was operated by the Sons of Darkness, a motorcycle club whose founders included Nathan Jones. Nathan had never fully recovered from being shot. He told his brother Alvin he felt like he'd died that day. He wore black leather jackets and had scars on his neck from Officer Moravek's bullet. He openly despised the police and believed they targeted him for being a "cop shooter." Nathan's long arrest record included drug possession, forgery, and littering. He was angry and often drank to excess. In 1993, while on bond for a cocaine case, he killed his girlfriend with a punch. Nine years later, he died in prison, after falling ill and begging for medical help. A staff nurse told Denver's alternative weekly newspaper *Westword* that Nathan would have lived if he'd received care. He was fifty-two.

Anger was a problem in northeast Denver. Lauren Watson, who had been arrested thirty-three times without a conviction, frequently quoted James Baldwin, who said that "to be a Negro in this country and to be relatively conscious is to be in a rage almost all of the time." He and his wife named their first child Hasira, Swahili for "righteous rage."

Watson partially blamed the failure of the city's civil rights movement on other Blacks—informants working for the government and "sambos," or traitors, like Elvin Caldwell, whom he felt had sold out their roots for their personal gain. One day in 1980, Watson drove to the Holly to play volleyball at the Skyland Rec Center and encountered a man he considered to be part of the problem. He went back out to his car, got a gun from the trunk, and returned to the weight room, where he shot the man, hitting him in the arm. Watson's resulting criminal case would be the only one he ever lost; he took a plea that enabled him to serve less than a year in prison.

THE DISMANTLING OF America's most influential civil rights groups and leaders accompanied a new phenomenon that was of immediate interest to police departments across the country: an explosion in the number of street gangs.

Gangs of all races had existed for decades. As the Black population of Los Angeles soared in the post–World War II years, racist white gangs such as the Spook Hunters threatened to hurt Blacks who crossed certain streets in the city. In reaction, Black gangs like the Slausons—named for Slauson Avenue, which traverses Central LA— formed in self-defense. Soon, some of the city's Black neighborhood groups—car clubs, dance groups, and street fighters— developed their own rivalries. But, with the onset of the Watts Riots, those conflicts eased as many LA gang members recognized they were on the same side of a bigger fight. Some formed civil rights groups. Bunchy Carter, a member of the Slausons, became a leader of the LA Black Panthers. Other former gang members drafted a plan to rebuild Los Angeles.

Bunchy's assassination on the UCLA campus four years later devastated the youth of his community, who looked up to him.

Among them was Raymond Washington, a fifteen-year-old high school sophomore, who had been one of the youngest members of a group allied with the Black Panthers, the Avenues. After Bunchy's death, Washington felt the city change. Unemployment in South Los Angeles was rising, and the streets were increasingly dangerous. Washington asked his friends, Who is left to protect and defend the neighborhood? They agreed a new organization was needed.

Washington founded the Avenue Cribs. For short, they were the Cribs or the Baby Avenues, a claim to be the new generation. But Washington didn't want his group to represent only their own neighborhood. He wanted it to become a movement, like the Panthers. The Cribs distinguished themselves by wearing leather jackets and earrings and carrying embossed canes as a fashion accessory. Eventually they began calling themselves Crips.

On March 20, 1972, a group of new Crips committed a murder that captivated the city and set the gang on an unexpected course. On that night, the Black soul musician Curtis Mayfield, known for the civil rights anthem "People Get Ready," was playing at the Palladium theater in Hollywood. After the show, about twenty Crips were watching the crowd leave when they spotted an African American teen in a nice leather jacket. Several Crips jumped him and attempted to steal the jacket. Seeing this, sixteen-year-old Robert Ballou, Jr., a high school football star, came to his aid. The Crips turned on Ballou, stomping him to death as a crowd watched.

Ballou's murder made front-page news and gave the teenaged members of the Crips something they craved: notoriety and respect. Some made death threats to witnesses.

The specter of tragedy loomed. At Ballou's funeral, the priest officiating the ceremony had a heart attack and died at the pulpit. LA mayor Sam Yorty decided to take $250,000 out of his Model Cities funding to create a Parent Power program, in hopes of providing more responsible role models.

But nothing was able to thwart the appeal of the Crips, who offered family, protection, and even infamy to thousands of youth in South LA who sought it. The gang's recruitment soared.

But not every neighborhood group wanted to become Crips. Some youths had begun to form gangs in the name of their own neighborhood. And in a world in which pride and ego were sometimes all that they had, the Crips took offense. "We morphed into the monster we were addressing," Stanley "Tookie" Williams, who joined Washington in 1971 as a leader of the Crips, later said.

The Crips killed several gang members from other neighborhoods and the rising threat the gang posed prompted the leaders of a gang from Compton called the Piru Street Boys to call what would become a historic meeting of non-Crip gangs. Those who attended agreed to form an alliance to protect one another; in solidarity they decided to refer to one another as "blood," short for "blood brother." It was a term widely used within the Black Power movement, and by Black soldiers in Vietnam.

As with the Crips, being a Blood was an affiliation. Each individual group or "set" maintained its neighborhood identity. Despite law enforcement claims, they did not have centralized leadership. To identify themselves, Bloods wore the color red, symbolizing their blood bond. Bloods also respectfully called themselves *damu*, Swahili for "blood."

For many elders, watching Black neighborhoods go to war with one another was devastating. Some saw it as a grotesque outgrowth of generations of trauma, this time fueled by tribalism, PTSD, and self-hatred. Some believed it was because of the leadership vacuum that had been created by the loss of the previous generation of activists. Others felt that without role models or historical context for decades of struggle, the youth were left with only the same implicit societal bias that America generated, that Black lives didn't matter.

But for the young men in the streets—streets that felt increasingly like battle trenches and which delineated new borders—the reason for the violence was simple: attacks demanded retaliation. They weren't punks.

Raymond Washington, the Crips' founder, was an old-fashioned street fighter and disliked guns. But he'd quickly been caught and convicted of a robbery, and spent several years in prison in the early to mid-1970s, as Los Angeles's gang homicide tally rose into the hundreds per year; nearly all of the killings were gun-related. The old-fashioned street fight had become a relic of a bygone era.

When Washington got out of prison, Crips hid their firearms when he was around, but that would not be for much longer. In 1979, Washington was shot on the street and died in surgery, age twenty-five. Like many gang-related homicides, his murder remains unsolved. Tookie Williams was taken off the streets for good as well. While maintaining his innocence, he was convicted in 1979 of killing four people in two separate robberies, and sentenced to death.

Yet despite the losses of the gang's leaders, the Crips had too much momentum. "Crips don't die, they multiply," became the gang's motto. Indeed they would grow faster than anyone could have predicted.

By the late 1970s, Denver police were tracking a few dozen street gangs, most of which had recently appeared. Some were Latino, some Asian, but the majority were African American and located in northeast Denver. Among them, two clear rivals had emerged: the Brick Cities, from Five Points, and the BOYZ, from Northeast Park Hill.

The BOYZ had formed in part to replace the aging Sons of Darkness, many of whose members had been locked up or were incapable of providing the kind of physical defense needed. While the Sons of Darkness were still headquartered in the Dahlia, the BOYZ claimed the Holly Shopping Center, which was Black-owned for the first time. In 1983, Johnny Copeland, the well-dressed owner of one of northeast Denver's most popular after-hours club and a legend of the invisible city, bought the Holly Shopping Center for $800,000.

Terrance started to see the BOYZ. They wore Members Only jackets, and B on their hats for BOYZ, or P for Park Hill. Ranging in age from fourteen to twenty-four, some spoke to Terrance, and occasionally slipped him a dollar. With hundreds of members, the BOYZ were believed by Denver police to be the biggest of Denver's gangs, though members explicitly called the group an organization.

Every few weeks the BOYZ had a showdown with another Denver gang. Sometimes it was a dance-off. Increasingly, when it involved the Brick Cities, it featured a brawl.

By the early '80s, animosity between the gangs from Denver's most storied African American communities grew to the point that Terrance could no longer visit his aunt Marsha and his cousins; the Brick Cities were named for the Arapahoe and Curtis Park brick housing projects where they lived. Terrance, a resident of the rival neighborhood, was no longer welcome. From that point forward, Terrance's idea of family began to change.

BY THEN, TERRANCE and his mother had moved into a rental house on 29th and Olive, around the corner from his grandmother. Terrance's new best friend was Bryan Butler, part of a well-known Northeast Park Hill family. One day Terrance and Bryan were throwing a Nerf football when some older kids came and stole it. Terrance gathered Bryan and some of their other friends over to the shed in his grandmother's backyard. Terrance suggested that for protection they form their own gang, the Park Hill Ninja Club.

Terrance, age nine, was the bossy leader, hatching plans and ordering missions such as ripping tiles from roofs and fashioning them into dangerous Chinese stars, or stealing bikes. Emulating the BOYZ, if the Park Hill Ninja Club members saw kids who weren't from their hood, they tried to fight them.

Like much of the youth in Northeast Park Hill, Terrance and Bryan wanted to be accepted by the BOYZ. They hoped one day to be the defenders of the hood. There was no higher honor.

One day, word came that the Brick Cities were coming for a showdown at the Dahlia. Terrance and Bryan scoured the neighborhood, collecting sticks and bike chains, and brought them to the parking lot. "Right on," some of the BOYZ called out.

Around dusk, a group of cars appeared on 33rd Avenue from the west. Members of the Brick Cities stepped out, four and five to a car, some carrying bats. Terrance watched in awe as northeast Denver's toughest teenagers faced off in the parking lot, about twenty a side. The BOYZ's best puncher started the battle by knocking down a member of the Brick Cities with one swing. The melee that ensued involved bats, sticks, bike chains, knives, and Chinese stars. No one called the police and none came. Finally, with few left standing, the fight ended, a draw.

There were no deaths that day, but months later, in the spring of 1983, four gang-related homicides marked Denver's passage to a new era. One of the murders that featured prominently in the local news was that of seventeen-year-old William Berrien, a Five Points resident and member of the Brick Cities. William had gotten in a dispute at a party with members of a rival gang. He was clubbed in the head with a baseball bat and stabbed in the back. He bled out on the floor. His fourteen-year-old brother, Eric, witnessed his death.

At the funeral, reporters crowded his mother, asking what she knew about her son's gang. "You all keep saying, Gang, gang, gang," she said, according to *The Denver Post*. "What is a gang? A group of boys hanging together? All I know is my child is dead."

William's brother Eric appeared dazed. "First, we was just dancing," he told the *Post*. "It was a dancing group."

As DENVER BEGAN to peer into a violent abyss, the city's gang progenitor, Los Angeles, had entered an unprecedented era. The dramatic rise in LA's shootings accompanied a flood of cocaine into the city. The kingpin was a slender twenty-something who lived in a Crip neighborhood by the freeway. But "Freeway" Rick Ross wasn't a gang member. He had an aversion to violence after, as a five-year-old, he witnessed his mother shoot and kill her brother as he stabbed his wife.

Ross wanted to be a businessman but couldn't get hired. He was illiterate and unable to even fill out a job application. Around 1980, he found a cocaine connection and began to sell small bags of what he'd previously thought of as a "Hollywood drug." A couple of years later, someone showed him something called "ready rock." It was smokeable cocaine. People would pay fifty dollars for a pebble of it, which could be put into a pipe. Later called crack, it was made by adding water and baking soda to powder cocaine and boiling it in a jar until it formed a waxy substance that could be cut up. Smoking it produced a brief euphoric high. Ross could see that many of its users immediately wanted more. He saw a huge market for the new drug and was determined to find the biggest cocaine supplier he could. Soon he was introduced to a Nicaraguan, Danilo Blandón, who was flying in cocaine by the ton.

Blandón became like a second father to Ross, selling him as much as 500 kilos (or 1,100 pounds) per week. He also provided guns, ammunition, and even bulletproof vests. Ross decided to work mostly with Blood and Crip leaders, who offered him protection in exchange for the opportunity to sell his product in their neighborhoods.

By 1983, Ross was becoming the biggest drug dealer in South LA, selling around one million dollars' worth of rock every day. He became a hero in his neighborhood, where he put up the money to build basketball courts and sponsored a community Easter egg hunt.

In 1986, the planes carrying Freeway's product were still flying when ten-year-old Terrance Roberts was leaving the YMCA one afternoon. He was startled by what turned out to be his first glimpse of the man who would become Denver's greatest underworld legend. Several kids ran toward Terrance, calling out something he couldn't hear. Another group followed behind. "Michael Asberry is coming!" he heard them shout. "Michael Asberry is coming!"

Michael Asberry, the teen king of Denver's underworld, was born in northeast Denver in 1969, the youngest of four. His father, Hubert, a classmate of Lauren Watson's at Manual High, had been absent from Michael's life since before Michael could remember. His mother, Josie, was a cook at a south Denver bar, among other jobs, and was rarely home.

When Michael was in elementary school, it was another former Manual High student who became one of his father figures, a man he called "Uncle Georgie": George Roberts, Terrance's dad. In 1980, George had taken an apartment next door to the Asberrys.

Michael, then eleven, was having an identity crisis. At his school, an integrated facility that was about half Black, he felt looked down upon by white kids. At night he lay awake cycling through feelings of self-hatred and praying to wake up white.

Uncle Georgie, boundlessly optimistic and oozing gangster cool in a fedora, pinstripe suit, and fresh cologne, could see Michael lacked male role models. He told Michael he could always come "chop it up" with him—discuss things man to man. For Mike, it was easy to tell if Uncle Georgie was home: a huge black limousine would be parked in the alley. George, who was by then a crack addict, had taken a job driving hearses for northeast Denver's busiest funeral home, Pipkin Mortuary, and kept one of the company cars.

Michael wanted to escape the poverty and anonymity of being Black in Denver. He hustled jobs mowing lawns and shoveling driveways. George didn't let on that he supplemented his income by driving around the Midwest with two prostitute friends who drugged and robbed their johns. Those parts of his life were ugly, even to himself. He told Michael that he would have opportunities. "Everyone has to find their path," George told him. Soon they would both be transformed.

A FEW YEARS later, Michael was in Los Angeles visiting his aunt when he was challenged by a group of older kids and asked where he was from. They beat him. Mike saw that the kids, who were only a few years older than he was, had the respect of the hood. They wore blue plaid button-down shirts and blue handkerchiefs hung from their back pockets, which he learned signified their association with the Los Angeles supergang, the Crips.

Michael went home and tested his own street toughness. He won a few fights with members of the Brick Cities. The following year, two new kids Michael's age showed up in the neighborhood. The families of Phillip Jefferson and Albert Jones had both relocated from Los Angeles. Jefferson and Jones were both Crips. Soon they were hanging out with Michael in Fuller Park behind Manual High School, where they were enrolled but rarely showed up for class.

In 1985, Asberry, Jefferson, and Jones, along with another LA transplant, Matthew Vick, decided they were going to start Denver's first Crip gang. Mike, the Denver native, didn't care what neighborhoods the Brick Cities or anyone else claimed. He wanted their gang to represent all of northeast Denver.

In honor of the numbered streets where they lived, they christened themselves the "Rollin' 30s" Crips. Fuller Park was the gang's secret birthplace, but its holy mecca was ten blocks west, on Welton Street from 27th to 28th, the heart of Five Points, the block that Jack Kerouac had memorialized, where the dilapidated Rossonian stood empty, where Denver's civil rights movement had been tear gassed into submission. All of its ghosts would now rise.

WHETHER BY DESIGN or by providence, one man in Denver had a real-time vantage point on this development. The local branch of the Salvation Army, located around the corner from Fuller Park, ran one of the few free youth rec programs in northeast Denver, called the Red Shield. In the spring of 1986, the Red Shield got a new director, Leon Kelly, a thirty-three-year-old ex-con for whom the city's looming gang war would become an obsession and a livelihood.

Leon, who was six feet five and had a deep Barry White voice, was born in northeast Denver in 1953. From the corner of the Red Shield, "Rev," as he soon became known, could see Asberry and his crew in Fuller Park. Cars pulled up and off. Rev knew a drug operation when he saw one. He was only two years removed from a life as a high-flying cocaine dealer in a downtown penthouse, a world that crashed around him when, he said, he was nabbed for selling drugs and sentenced to prison. A few years later, he took a Bible class and considered following in the footsteps of his preacher father. Instead he applied and was offered the job at Red Shield, which he'd attended as a kid.

Rev was an oversized presence at Red Shield. He had a winning rapport with the kids, occasionally joining their basketball games, where he dunked the ball—instant respect. One day, Rev introduced himself to Asberry and his crew and suggested they come into the gym. They did, and soon it was full of young gang members, hooping with other kids, most of whom didn't yet know who the Crips were.

Asberry became friends with a diminutive teen his age, Mike Hancock, who had had a hard-knock childhood. Asberry and Hancock became known as "the two Mikes." It was a friendship that wouldn't last. Mike Hancock would become mayor of Denver. "Psych" Mike Asberry was on another path.

DENVER'S TWO DAILY newspapers, the *Rocky Mountain News* and *The Denver Post*, took an interest in the gang. Rev's folksy charm and proximity to its members made him the go-to source. "I feel I'm the only one who has rapport with the Crips," he told the *Rocky*, as the *Rocky Mountain News* was known, in 1986. "I may be the only one who can reach them."

Within the African American community, where Rev still had a reputation as a drug dealer, some questioned whether he was using his connection to the gang for illicit activity. But Asberry, whose willingness to speak to the Denver media distinguished him among gang members, backed Rev. "He tells us we're hard heads and that we don't listen," Asberry told the *Rocky*. "He tries to get us to change. Other adults try to get us high."

But, week by week, Fuller Park became more crowded with young Crips, wearing blue, smoking pot, and helping introduce rock cocaine to Denver.

Denver's recently formed gang unit had only two officers. One was Arthur Hutchinson, the patrolman at the wheel of the car from which Nathan Jones had been shot. Hutchinson, who had tufty reddish hair, was well-known within the Denver police for his style in training new cadets. He berated African Americans recruits as "tree swingers," "chimpanzees," and "niggers." Once, during a training session that was videotaped, he ordered them to perform the minstrel tune "Camptown Races." "All you fucking niggers tap dance!" he yelled as they sang.

In the spring of 1986, Hutchinson realized that what he saw in Fuller Park was an outpost of the Los Angeles Crips. Denver immediately became a city of interest to law enforcement around the country. It was the farthest east the Los Angeles street gang had been seen.

"Due to increased gang activity in District Two, we will begin compiling information on gang members and their activities . . . Our immediate concern is with the 'Rolling 30 Crips' or 'Rolling 30s.' They are drug dealers and have access to hand guns and shotguns," read an internal Denver police memo of May 25, 1986.

"We got a pretty extensive list [of identified gang members]," Hutchinson told a Denver news station. "The second thing we're doing is putting a lot of police officers into the problem area, to contact as many gang members as we can for as many violations as we can." Flooding gang neighborhoods with police patrols would be the de facto response to gang tensions in northeast Denver for decades.

THE YEAR 1986 was a watershed for the federal anti-gang effort. In June, the University of Maryland basketball star Len Bias died of a cocaine overdose two days after he was drafted by the Boston Celtics. Misreported as a crack overdose, Bias's death made him the Archduke Ferdinand in the war on drugs, by some accounts. President Reagan declared crack "an uncontrolled fire," and signed a landmark crime bill. It included a 100:1 disparity in the amount of powder cocaine versus crack that would be required to trigger a mandatory minimum sentence. And it included the provision for the 5K1.1 motion, which could be filed by prosecutors to help a defendant avoid such punishment, if they agreed to provide "substantial assistance" to the government in the "investigation or prosecution of another person." Hundreds of millions of dollars were allocated for federal undercover drug operations in gang neighborhoods. In Los Angeles, a Ricky Ross Task Force was formed.

Crack was big business, and not just for the dealers. The U.S. government had declared a "war" on drugs. To fight it, thousands of new law enforcement jobs were funded. Some officers saw additional perks. The 1986 bill expanded civil forfeiture laws, enabling police to keep up to 80 percent of proceeds from raids. A single bust could be worth millions. One LAPD officer later said that priorities began to change, as some cops saw they could skim off the top. "The focus went from getting the drugs off the street to bringing money in," LA Sheriff Deputy Robert Juarez, who worked drug task forces, said years later. "Pretty soon I'm buying a vacation home, I'm going to Hawaii. The greed came in. We had gone from being cops to being crooks."

The supply of the drug remained abundant. In fact, in Los Angeles, a surplus had driven prices down and helped spur an eastbound micro-migration of Crip and Blood crack dealers. One migrant was Kinshasa Cooley, a wide-faced, light-skinned "Crenshaw Mafia Gangster" Blood from Inglewood. A high school dropout, he'd come to Denver in 1985 looking for a better return on his investment. He was seventeen.

Cooley found he could get $80 a rock, four times more than he got in South Central. But, he quickly realized, he had a big problem. He'd set up his operation in a neighborhood that was claimed—by the Crips. Mike Asberry had overseen a rapid expansion. In short order, nearly all of Denver's Black neighborhoods were flying blue flags. All but one.

Cooley soon found his way to the Holly, where he couldn't miss the BOYZ. In Los Angeles, the Bs and Ps on their hats meant Bloods and Pirus, the original Bloods.

Cooley gained their acceptance in part because of a shared hatred of the Crips. The BOYZ had recently squared off with Asberry's crew in an already legendary rumble in City Park that ended only after police in riot gear arrived. One thing was sure: the BOYZ were never going to join a gang from Five Points. But Cooley didn't have luck convincing them to become Bloods either. Many of the BOYZ were in their late twenties or older and weren't interested in disbanding to join a gang from LA.

But Cooley found others his age who were interested. One was Terrance's childhood neighbor Isaac Alexander.

Cooley got permission from his OGs in Inglewood for Park Hill to become the first Crenshaw Mafia Gangster (CMG) Blood gang outside of LA. They would call themselves the Park Hill CMG Bloods. Not "Northeast" Park Hill. They were laying claim to all of Park Hill, the "model of integration," "the conscience of the City." But there was no question about the gang's sacred headquarters. It was the Holly Shopping Center, where Nathan Jones lay bleeding in 1968. Its ghosts, too, would rise.

"What up, you know Michael Asberry?" "Ty Bud" Lockett said to Terrance on the block one day. Ty Bud, then eleven, was wearing a red shirt and a red San Francisco 49ers hat that was too big for his head.

Terrance, who was roughly Ty Bud's age, hadn't seen Asberry since that day outside the YMCA. "Why you wearing those blue shorts?" Ty Bud asked. He lifted his shirt. Terrance could see the butt of a pistol in his waistband. "Don't be wearing no blue," Ty Bud warned Terrance.

Another day at Skyland Park, Terrance was playing basketball when a kid was nearly beaten up for using the word *cuz*, a common term of endearment. "We don't say that no more," he heard the kid get warned.

Terrance could feel something was changing in the neighborhood, and one day, he was walking with Bryan when it took shape in a stampede of kids, perhaps dozens, who charged down the middle of the street. They were dressed in red—shoes, shirts, hats; some wore bandanas over their faces. "Ma-fi-as, MA-FI-AS!" they chanted as they ran past. Terrance recognized several of them, including Ty Bud and Bryan's cousin, Aaron, who was thirteen. Terrance heard others calling Aaron "Brazy."

Terrance and Bryan went to the shed in his grandmother's backyard. Bryan explained that his cousin and the others were Bloods now. *Mafia* was short for Crenshaw Mafia Gangster Bloods, the LA gang they were associated with. Bryan told Terrance that Asberry and the Crips were their enemy. The level of disrespect Northeast Park Hill had for them was so great that the Bloods would never again use the letter C. Thus the unusual spelling of Aaron's new nickname.

"POLICE IN DENVER and elsewhere have offered a variety of explanations for the appearance of the Crips and Bloods—including the theory that they might be the advance guard of a Los Angeles invasion force plotting the takeover of the cocaine trade in black communities throughout the West," read a 1987 story in the *Los Angeles Times*.

The Denver police teamed up with the FBI to gather intelligence on the city's Crips and Bloods. The district attorney's office made gang-affiliated youth eligible for "direct file," meaning they could be charged as adults. As gang arrests soared, Rev Kelly began putting Crips who were part of the Red Shield program over the gym loudspeaker when they called from jail. "Be cool, don't do nothing wrong," the voice of Matthew Vick, who had shot at a District 2 cop, warned the group one day. "The police are not playin'. They want us any way they can get us . . . Chill, get a job, be cool."

But in Denver, as elsewhere, it was too late. Gangs were becoming a political movement supercharged by music out of LA's gang neighborhoods. A new rap genre lionized life on the streets, on the run from the police. "Six in the morning, police at my door . . . ," begins Ice-T's 1986 song "6 'N the Mornin'," widely considered to mark the birth of gangster rap.

Another LA group, N.W.A, began its 1988 debut album, *Straight Outta Compton*, with the words "Crazy motherfucker named Ice Cube. From a *gang* called Niggaz with Attitudes." N.W.A didn't even call themselves a group. They were a gang.

Straight Outta Compton, according to *Newsweek*, "introduced some of the most grotesquely exciting music ever made." It was banned from radio, public libraries, and some retail chains due to profanity but N.W.A's tour sold out arenas, as white fans loved the fearless, untethered performances.

Fuck the police comin' straight from the underground . . .
Fuckin' with me 'cause I'm a teenager
With a little bit of gold and a pager

ON JUNE 25, 1988, two months after N.W.A's sold-out show at Denver's McNichols Arena, Michael Asberry led a dangerous mission into Northeast Park Hill. The incursion would finally launch Denver into the war for which Los Angeles had created the mold.

Soon after midnight, Asberry and four other Crips, riding in a stolen station wagon, slipped across Colorado Boulevard into Bloods territory, heading to an address they all knew. The house, two blocks from Ernestine's, was home to the three Lockett brothers, as well as Ty Bud. They were all Bloods.

Around 1 a.m., Clarence Lockett, who went by "Basper," was on his sidewalk when he saw Asberry, whom he recognized, leaning out the window of the approaching car in an LA Dodgers baseball cap. Basper was caught slippin'; he didn't have a weapon. "What's up, cuz," Asberry said, and squeezed the trigger of his gun.

The station wagon hit two parked cars as it screeched off. Basper lay on the ground, shot in the torso. Doctors were unable to remove the bullet, which was lodged next to his spine, but he survived.

The following night, a group of Bloods drove across Colorado Boulevard, toward Fuller Park. As they approached, a figure in blue appeared on the sidewalk. The Bloods opened fire. Delontay Carolina, a seventeen-year-old Crip, was hit and killed, becoming the first homicide in Denver's LA-style gang war.

The second came less than twenty-four hours later—another Crip. This time the gunman was an undercover police officer, Bernard Montoya. He had come to secretly surveil a gathering of Crips to mourn Delontay. Believing he saw a gun, Montoya fired from behind a thicket of bushes. Rasheen Riley, who was eighteen, was killed instantly. No gun was found. Montoya, who had earlier been suspended for kicking and beating a drunk driving suspect, was not charged or reprimanded.

The two quick casualties shocked Denver's most powerful gang and made one thing painfully clear: it was only a matter of time before Northeast Park Hill would mourn its first victim. That day came on November 3, 1988, five days before Reagan's vice president George H. W. Bush defeated Michael Dukakis to become president.

Around midnight, Cameron Smith left his girlfriend's house and began riding his bike home along Colorado Boulevard. The north-south Denver artery that runs along the east side of City Park once formed an invisible border that African Americans were not to cross. It was about to become for all intents and purposes the front line in the city's gang war. To the west was Crips territory; to the east, Bloods.

Smith, who was a high school senior, lived in Northeast Park Hill and had just received a scholarship to the University of Oklahoma. He would be the first in his family to go to college. He wore a red Oklahoma Sooners baseball cap but was not a gang member.

It was mostly quiet until a car pulled up next to him. In it were several young Crips, looking to prove themselves and gain stature. Elliot "Hollywood" Raibon, who was eighteen, was told to get out and deal with Smith.

Raibon called Smith a "Slob," a derogatory term for a Blood. Smith wasn't a Blood, but he also wasn't a punk. He stopped. The two young men faced off. But Raibon had a pistol. According to police, he shot Smith in the head. Smith died in the street. Raibon said the others had fired the shots, but he was convicted at trial after two other Crips in the car, who were given immunity to testify, broke the gang code and took the stand. Raibon was sentenced to life in prison.

DENVER'S MAYOR, Federico Peña, a Latino lawyer and state representative who had ended the fifteen-year run of Mayor McNichols in 1983, became the city's first chief executive to address the gang problem. "I am not going to tolerate a situation in which citizens have to worry about what color clothing they are wearing for fear of being shot," Peña said. He directed the Denver PD to increase its gang unit to one hundred officers, who were sent to Los Angeles to train with the LAPD gang unit.

He also created a Crack Task Force. According to police, several Northeast Park Hill homes were functioning as dope houses. Peña instituted what he called a "zero tolerance" policy for known gang members. "That means if they're caught jaywalking, they're arrested," he said.

Terrance, then twelve, was an honor student in middle school. He was proud and outgoing, and wore his long hair in Jheri curls. But anytime he left his neighborhood, he was taunted or pushed around. Anyone from Northeast Park Hill was considered to be affiliated with the Bloods, who were not only the smaller gang in northeast Denver but the lesser known nationally. Most of the best-known national rappers, from Ice-T to members of N.W.A to Snoop Dogg, were Crip-affiliated. The two hit gang movies *Colors* (1988) and *Boyz n the Hood* (1991) both featured Crip protagonists; the young *Colors* star Don Cheadle was from northeast Denver. Some girls teased Terrance by calling him "off-brand."

So, after school, Terrance and Bryan went by the Holly Shopping Center parking lot, where they felt safer and were close enough to feel the energy of a new movement in the name of Park Hill taking shape along the wall behind Johnny Copeland's liquor store. There, the young defenders of the neighborhood could be found. Among them was Terrance's childhood neighbor Isaac, now known as "Iceman." All of fifteen, Iceman wore gold chains and his braided hair in a ponytail.

Cars pulled in and out of the parking lot. Crackheads wandered through like zombies. "Hood rats," or girl packs, strutted in tight jeans and high heels, some with red streaks in their braided hair, some looking for a john from whom they might get twenty dollars for a blow job. Other men and women, secretly cooperating with law enforcement, tensely mingled among them, their conversations monitored a few blocks away by Denver police and DEA and FBI agents in vans.

Terrance began working for an older Blood as a runner. White guys in suits and ties, Mexicans in pickup trucks, neighborhood crackheads on bikes were all his customers. Terrance took their money and ran through the alleys to wherever the dope house was located that week, and back. It didn't pay well, and it was risky.

But he and Bryan hoped to impress the older Bloods. One night, Terrance stole his granny's pistol, and he and Bryan ran through City Park to a house where they knew a Crip lived. Terrance shot the house up, then they ran back to Bryan's cousin Brazy's house. They were almost to the front porch when two beams of light illuminated the yard. Bryan and Terrance were ordered onto the ground and searched. Terrance, who was fourteen, had the pistol on him.

POSSESSION OF A weapon, Terrance's first offense, landed him at Denver's Gilliam Youth Services Center, where he had to sleep on the floor because the facility was out of beds. Ernestine came to visit. "God is not happy with this," she scolded Terrance. But she went to see his judge and said she would be intervening at home. Terrance got probation.

Gilliam was in Crip territory. Terrance managed to be released without his ride. While he waited at the bus stop, three Crips appeared. One put a gun to his head and asked what he was doing there. Terrance was sure he was going to die, but the bus pulled around the corner. "If we catch you over here again, we'll kill you," he was told. And so, following his release for possession of a weapon, Terrance concluded he needed to acquire a gun, immediately.

Terrance's arrest had the opposite effect on Bryan. He kept reliving the moment the lights flipped on in his cousin's yard, and thinking about the cops, hiding in the dark to apprehend them. He feared he was already known to the police, and he may well have been. The Denver police had compiled an extensive gang database, so extensive that it raised the alarm of the local NAACP, because it included two in three African American youths in the city. "They ought to call it a blacklist," an NAACP official told *The New York Times*. "It's not a crackdown on gangs; it's a crackdown on blacks." But Denver's police chief, Jim Collier, was unapologetic. "If it walks like a duck and talks like a duck, the chances are it's not an antelope," he told a Denver City Council inquiry into the matter.

The next time Bryan and Terrance met up in the back of Ernestine's house would be the last for some time. Terrance was late; he said he'd just come from Cherry Creek mall, where a fight with the Crips had broken out after a screening of *Boyz n the Hood*. He was amped up and talking about revenge.

"So you doin' this?" Bryan said.

"The hood needs us," Terrance said. "People like Granny need us."

"I dunno," Bryan said.

"Well, you're in or out," Terrance said, "but they gonna get you one way or another."

"I guess I'm out," Bryan said.

"Then that's it," Terrance said. "We move in a different way now."

"A'ight, fam," Bryan said. "I'ma see you."

THAT FALL, TERRANCE was at Metro South, an alternative school for at-risk youth, his third high school in two years. He had been expelled from the first two for fighting. He and a few other Park Hill Bloods were skipping class and smoking a joint in the back of the schoolyard when one of his friends, known as Lil Tek 9 for the machine gun he carried, said, "You know, Terrance ain't been put on yet." Getting "put on" meant being initiated.

The conversation came to a halt. "Really?" said "Mafia Mike" Robinson, one of the OGs, approaching Terrance with a finger to his chest. "You ain't been put on?"

Terrance stared back. "You gotta fight Scrappy," he was told.

Scrappy, who was standing with them, was one of the Bloods' best street fighters, someone Terrance would never want to fight. But he knew if he backed down, he'd never have the respect of the hood.

Terrance handed the joint to Mafia Mike and squared off with Scrappy. Terrance swung first, glancing Scrappy's cheek. Scrappy moved in, his long arms and large fists swinging wildly into Terrance's face and body. Terrance kept swinging, but Mafia Mike and Lil Tek 9 jumped in and forced him to the ground. They crouched over Terrance, punching and kicking him until he was gasping and spitting blood.

"Now you're from the hood," they told him. Black-eyed, bloody, and barely able to get off the ground, Terrance Roberts was finally an official member of his neighborhood's elite armed militia, a Crenshaw Mafia Gangster Blood.

The concrete wall that was the back side of the Holly Shopping Center now carried the same bulbous-lettered graffiti that was being authored in Los Angeles by the Crips and Bloods, as they marked their territory. On one section, spray-painted in yellow with a black outline, were the oversized letters *CK*, short for Crip Killer; on another, *No Crabs*, a derogatory term Bloods used for Crips.

Preening and politicking beneath the stark pronouncements—"bickin back being bool," as they put it—were America's teen soldiers, "billin'" at the base. Fat marijuana blunts passed through their fingers. Music from N.W.A and DJ Quik, the first nationally known Blood rapper, thumped from car stereos, as empty malt liquor "40s" clanked along the pavement.

They rooted for the city's perennial NFL contender Denver Broncos, who wore blue and orange, but they dressed in gear stocked specially for them in stores along Colfax, from the Kansas City Chiefs and San Francisco 49ers, whose colors were red. Some wore Boston Red Sox hats, with the red *B* on the crown. Paisley red handkerchiefs, or "flags," hung from their back pockets; on their feet were red Converse or Nike sneakers that floated the hop to their step. Their love for the hood was greater than ever because, they believed, they were the chosen ones to protect it.

Many of the OG Bloods were already serving prison time. Others, like Iceman Alexander, who had convictions for driving with fake plates and possession of a concealed weapon, were "on paper," meaning parole or probation, a condition that typically required them to stay away from other Bloods, and from the Holly.

This left Terrance's crew—the so-called YGs, the Young Gangsters—to fill their shoes. They were a couple dozen strong, mostly aged fourteen to seventeen. Many had known one another for years. Billy Wooton lived across the street from Terrance, Kenny Greenwood lived a block away from Ernestine. They began referring to one another as "rellies" or "fam." They would be there for one another, inside the pen or out, for life. The bond was both personal and political. They were willing to die to defend the neighborhood. When a District 2 or Gang Unit squad car passed, they hollered and flipped it off. They had made a complete surrender, and it felt as if they had been saved.

Like many of his fellow gang members, Terrance was determined to make money. His mother was away at work all day, and he easily hid from her that he had stopped going to school. At night he snuck out to sell crack from inside of a dumpster in the alley. He was never tempted to try the drug. It was purely business. He kept his hair carefully braided and used cologne. He spent his money on Dickies khaki pants and Ben Davis button-down shirts, which he ironed and folded. At fourteen, he had a reputation to protect. Many knew his dad was a certified gangster with Oakland ties. And everyone knew his grandmother's restaurant. Few could boast as much neighborhood credibility.

With many of the OGs away, Terrance asserted his leadership skills. At that time, they all carried pagers. He paged everyone and instituted a 4 p.m. roll call at the Holly. No excuses. Crips were coming through the neighborhood shooting at cars and people every day. They weren't just needed at the Holly to represent. They needed to "politic" about the day's developments and share intelligence. Information was the coin of their realm as much as it was law enforcement's, and their sources were good. The eyes of the hood were all-seeing. Crackheads, young community members, storekeepers, and guys coming out of jail all talked—about shootings, cases, snitches, and the movements of their enemies.

When the sun fell, they moved on to discuss more serious business. Sometimes that meant the back of MLK Park, next to the abandoned fire station at the far northeast end of Northeast Park Hill. Other times, it was Ernestine's house, on 29th and Pontiac. Granny, as the Bloods called her, worked long hours. With her home's central location and stocked refrigerator, the Bloods called her place simply the "Launching Pad." Terrance and the YGs kicked it in her living room, teens on a couch, counting their guns and ammo, and plotting.

They saw their most important mission as a basic one: defend the hood from attack by the Crips. This wasn't easy. Unlike gang neighborhoods in housing projects of Los Angeles, designed with few roads leading in, Northeast Park Hill was porous. Roughly the shape of a square, it comprised 520 blocks. Every street was an artery. Every alley was a vein.

Greater Park Hill's southern border was Colfax Avenue, Denver's most notorious street, a place of prostitutes, small-time drug dealers, and cheap motels. The west side of the neighborhood was Colorado Boulevard, which ran north-south along City Park. Quebec Street formed the east side and separated the neighborhood from Stapleton International Airport, which in 1995 would be replaced by a larger airport farther northeast. The northern border was the warehouse district on either side of I-70.

Patrolling this, or any, area posed the fundamental challenge that Eazy-E sang about on N.W.A's hit song, "Boyz-n-the-Hood." "It's all about making that GTA," Eazy-E said, or Grand Theft Auto. None of them owned a car. Terrance's crew had some success stealing Wagoneers, a popular four-wheel drive in Denver that had a flaw: one could break the steering column and hot-wire it. But stolen vehicles could only be used for a few days before they became high risk, requiring fake plates or to be wiped down and dumped.

There was one group of Bloods who were experts at stealing cars. It was a crew of girls, about half a dozen of whom had been officially put on the hood. Terrance and Billy Wooton, his neighbor, were always asking one of the girls if they could borrow a car, but the girls were skeptics. Terrance had respect, but it was partly because he was wild and unpredictable. If he ran into someone he didn't know, or didn't like what someone said, he was in their face fast, calling for a fight or pulling out a pistol. It was a continuous drama. The girls started calling him "Show Business." Terrance didn't like it but it stuck, and his gang name was settled: "ShowBizz," or for those closest to him, "Biz" or "Bizzy Bob."

Billy's personality was different. Outwardly quiet and calm, he was inevitably into something deep, a high-profile shooting or a messy robbery. One night the girls let Billy and ShowBizz take a car. As they were riding, a District 2 squad car appeared behind them, and on came its lights. Billy swerved down an alley but hit a fence. He hopped out and ran one way, Terrance another. Billy was caught, and the car impounded, creating weeks of stress for the girls about whether they would be implicated.

Billy kept his mouth shut and managed to get off with a minor juvenile offense, but the mishap led to his gang name: "Too Much." His little brother Chris, fourteen, who had also just been put on, became "Lil' Too Much."

With a safety pin and ink, one of the girls tattooed Terrance's and Billy's new names on their left arms. ShowBizz and Too Much would now live forever, they thought.

As THE NUMBER of Denver's gang members rose from the hundreds to the thousands, Rev Kelly left Red Shield to open an anti-gang organization, Open Door Youth Gang Alternatives. During a television special on gang violence, he appeared in an embroidered Open Door shirt, looking chastened. "You've been a prophet and sadly a correct prophet," the local journalist Peter Boyles said, "telling me and people: Violence is coming, gangs are going to escalate, the narcotics trade is going to grow larger. And now, you're correct. That's gotta make you the saddest man in the city."

"Well, I sympathize with the prophets of the days of old," Rev said. "Nobody listened."

But Rev cut a different figure in the Holly. He regularly pulled up in an oversized GMC conversion van, bouncing on its suspension wheels, subwoofer speakers blasting rap music. Because of his close relationship with Mike Asberry, many Bloods had initially considered Rev a Crip affiliate. But more recently Rev had developed relationships with several of Park Hill's OG Bloods, including Iceman, or Ice, Alexander and Carl "Fat Daddy" McKay. Rev's ability to cross into many worlds without being pinned to one would prove to be his special power.

To Terrance, Rev acted neither like an anti-gang activist nor a reverend. He didn't have a church. And word was that Rev was helping the district attorney's office; he was frequently an expert witness. In the gang world, to help law enforcement, including the prosecutors' office, was to "snitch."

The term, which meant to "inform," had historical connotations that highlighted the deadly divisions within the Black community. During the civil rights movement, informants from within the community helped dismantle and destroy leaders; in slave times, a deadly eighteenth-century Virginia law, the Meritorious Manumission Act of 1710, enabled slaves to gain their freedom by informing their master about a revolt or escape plan.

Turning on one another to side with the system that had enslaved and imprisoned them had proved both tempting and severely damaging to Black communities. Terrance and the Bloods were becoming aware of the phenomenon, as drug stings in the neighborhood became common, and Denver police or federal agents making the arrests told them there was in fact one way to help themselves out of their criminal charges.

Terrance didn't trust Rev. Whenever he saw him in the Holly, Terrance stared him down. *What are you doin' coming here like this?* he thought, his muscled arms crossed, long hair braided in cornrows. He didn't let Rev approach, and Rev didn't try. It was the beginning of a rivalry that would permanently alter the city.

IN LOS ANGELES, the gang war was entering its third decade. The physical and emotional toll had become staggering. Several hundred young men were murdered every year. Hundreds of others, maimed, rode the streets in wheelchairs, veterans of a war from which there was no being sent home.

Some of the LA OGs began to organize. They were ready to change. Instead of going to strip clubs, they began to hold meetings about ending the violence. In the fall of 1989, the Nation of Islam leader Louis Farrakhan visited LA, where he invited gang leaders to a meeting at a hotel. Farrakhan spoke to them about self-empowerment. "When you're underrepresented, and those that represent you don't represent you, then, my brothers and sisters, your natural aggressive tendencies degenerate into what they call gang activity," he said. Three months later, Farrakhan returned to LA for his "Stop the Killing" lectures. Hundreds of LA gang members flocked to the Los Angeles Memorial Sports Arena. It was an electric evening. The crowd stayed on its feet. "Why can we take the trigger and pull it at each other?" Farrakhan said. "We are killing ourselves."

In the audience was the former NFL star Jim Brown, who had since retired and moved to Los Angeles, where he was acting in Hollywood films and trying to find a way to help the city's gang problem. He had begun meeting with the brothers Aqeela and Daude Sherrills, former Grape Street Crips who were determined to build mentorship programs. Together, they had founded one of the first big "anti-gang" programs, Amer-I-Can, which offered job training and life skills classes to gang members looking to leave the life.

After Farrakhan's lecture, Brown invited Farrakhan to his house in the Hollywood Hills. The Sherrills brothers and other peace-seeking OGs joined. They wanted to start a peace movement but saw the police as an impediment. Few in their communities trusted the police. They resolved to push an effort that was all their own.

As word spread, a mural in the Nickerson Gardens projects in Watts went up, depicting several sets of bandaged fingers holding up peace signs. In the center, two hands clasped each other, draped by a braided rope of red and blue. "Nobody Can Stop This War But Us," read the inscription. When Aqeela came upon the scene of a shooting, he would say to gang members standing around, "See this? Who's getting paid here? Are you?"

The night after Thanksgiving 1991, an electrical blackout at the Imperial Courts, one of Watts's biggest housing projects and a Crip stronghold, triggered a police response. When LAPD officers arrived, according to their account, they were fired on by residents. The police fired back, killing a twenty-eight-year-old resident, Henry Peco, who was trying to help children take shelter. No gun was found on Peco, who had just begun to mentor his nephew Dewayne Holmes, a young Crip who wanted out of the gang life.

Jesse Jackson flew in to speak at a memorial for Peco, making him a symbol of the fight not just to stop violence by gang members, but the threat of the police, none of whom were charged in Peco's death.

Dewayne Holmes joined the Sherrills brothers and others, adding momentum to the peace movement. In the spring of 1992, the group's leaders produced a peace agreement. The language had been adopted from the 1949 agreements that formally ended the Arab-Israeli war of the time and established armistice lines. To the former Crip and Blood leaders, the land rights conflict between the Jews and Arabs seemed comparable to the neighborhood beefs at the heart of gang violence. The "Truce of Nine-Deuce" was signed by members of the Crips and Bloods on April 28.

Two DAYS LATER, four LAPD officers who had been caught on video beating the African American motorist Rodney King nearly to death were acquitted. South LA exploded in protest. Crips and Bloods wanting justice for Peco were among them. Not since the Watts Riots in 1965 had LA seen such unrest.

In the midst of the mayhem, a white truck driver, Reginald Denny, who'd taken a wrong turn, found himself trapped in an intersection. Four young African American men pulled Denny out of his cab. As a news helicopter hovered above, one of them flashed Crip gang signs as the group beat Denny nearly to death, fracturing his skull in ninety-one places

The grisly scene made national news. In Washington, Congressman Henry Hyde implored Congress to approve the formation of a national gang database, comparing the threat of the Bloods and Crips to that of the Nazis. "I would be more comforted knowing that our intelligence services knew who the Nazis were back in, say, 1941, 1940, 1939," Hyde told the Judiciary Committee.

And so, only weeks after the historic Truce of Nine-Deuce, law enforcement began its biggest gang crackdown yet. Emergency federal and state funds were allocated to create dedicated gang squads. The FBI in Los Angeles boosted its number of special gang agents to one hundred. The LAPD added forty additional gang officers. The LA County district attorney's office increased its force of dedicated gang prosecutors and investigators to eighty-two.

Meanwhile, as had been the case in the aftermath of the Watts Riots, many of LA's gangs remained unified. Some submitted a proposal to the city to repair the damage from the riots. "Give us the hammer and the nails, we will rebuild the city," it said. It was rejected.

Peace meetings continued, this time with police helicopters hovering overhead. In some cases, participants emerged to find police waiting to arrest them, citing a city injunction prohibiting them from gathering with other gang members. Congresswoman Maxine Waters, an African American who represented the district and attended some of the meetings, reported that the police were harassing peace activists.

As tensions between the gang members and police rose, the LAPD announced that it had received threats from gang members against its officers, justifying its harsh measures. Members of gang communities, including Northeast Park Hill, took this as a commonly falsified allegation against them.

The historic summer concluded tragically. During a community dance at Imperial Courts, police responded to a report of a robbery. Dewayne Holmes, well-known as one of the movement's leaders, was working at the event.

Police had received a call about ten dollars being stolen at the event. Holmes, who had two five-dollar bills in his pocket, was arrested and ultimately convicted. At his sentencing, Congresswoman

Waters and former California governor Jerry Brown spoke on Holmes's behalf. But, due to prior felonies, the judge sentenced him to seven years in prison.

"I want to live like everyone else," Holmes told the *Los Angeles Times*. "But every time I try to do right, it seems like wrong is always going to be there because of my past." He would not be the last anti-gang activist left to wonder whether his activism had made him a target.

In Denver, where many of the city's Original Gangsters had LA connections, a corresponding Truce of Nine-Deuce was attempted, and failed. In fact, Denver's homicide tally in 1992 was ninety-five, the most since 1980. A majority of the deaths were gang-related. Among the dead was eighteen-year-old Jennifer Manchego, shot in a Colfax motel by Bryan's cousin Aaron "Brazy" Grimes, who was seventeen.

It was only a matter of time before Suzanne figured out what Terrance was up to. One day, thinking his mother wasn't home, Terrance came out of his bedroom with his shirt off. His mom was at the top of the split-level stairs. She couldn't help but see "ShowBizz" emblazoned on his left arm.

Terry had been her little star. She had tried to support him, worked multiple jobs, moved around the neighborhood seeking lower rents. "You're in the gang?" she yelled. She told Terrance he would end up dead.

The neighborhood churches had been passing around pamphlets for parents who wanted to talk to their kids about gangs. Suzanne called Billy Wooton's mother. They reached out to other mothers; together they would host meetings that their kids were required to attend.

But one day, Billy's mom called Suzanne. The police had a warrant for Billy's arrest. As Terrance knew, "Too Much" had shot a Crip on Colfax. An older man witnessed the shooting and followed

Billy's car. He went to one of the girl Bloods' houses. Soon District 2 was at her door. Billy escaped out the back, but the girl and her mother were called in for questioning.

They claimed ignorance. But when suggestions were made that they could be charged as well, the mother broke down and gave a statement. Billy, sixteen, was arrested. The mother, once well-liked in the neighborhood, was now a "snitch." Soon afterward, her daughter arrived home to find her mom hanging from a belt in the shower. She had killed herself. Suzanne began using drugs. Terrance ran away.

THE DENVER THAT Terrance escaped into was undergoing its biggest redevelopment project yet, the "revitalization" of LoDo, or Lower Downtown, a section of mostly empty factory buildings. Chic loft apartments and offices opened, as did bars and restaurants, including the city's first craft brewery, the Wynkoop, started with an economic-incentive loan from the city. One of its owners was the laid-off oil worker John Hickenlooper. Construction was also under way for a taxpayer-funded classic brick baseball stadium, where the city's new Colorado Rockies would play.

In 1991, Mayor Peña, who had been instrumental in pushing to develop LoDo, and in getting the approvals for Denver's new international airport, decided not to run for a third term. The city's mayoral race unexpectedly came down to two African American candidates, District Attorney Norm Early and City Auditor Wellington Webb, a regular at A&A Fish; Webb narrowly won the race.

The election of a Black man stirred racial tensions in a city where white supremacist groups were still alive and dangerous. In 1984, members of the white supremacist group the Silent Brotherhood assassinated the liberal Jewish Denver radio host Alan Berg. And in January 1992, on the first Martin Luther King Day after Webb took office, about a hundred KKK and White Aryan Nation members disrupted the traditional "marade," or march, down Colfax. Terrance Roberts, then fifteen and newly a Blood, and George Roberts were both there. Dozens were injured and police paddy wagons filled with arrestees.

Mayor Webb, who was another Manual High graduate who grew up in northeast Denver, also faced the specter of a growing gang war. In the spring of 1993, the battle exploded from the shadows with a series of shootings that killed and maimed innocent victims. One day the Crips shot up Webb's house and car. A *Denver Post* columnist described the city as "teetering on the edge of a murderous abyss." "Under Siege: Living with Barbarians at the Gate," read a headline in the *Rocky Mountain News.*

That summer, Mayor Webb was scheduled to host Denver's largest-ever international event, World Youth Day. It would feature visits by Pope John Paul II and President Clinton. As the event approached, Denver's highest-ranking Catholic leader, Archbishop J. Francis Stafford, implored the city's residents "to pray that we will be violence-free, at least for the next three weeks."

The youth summit went off without incident, nor any mention of the youth war that had led the Denver media to christen the summer of 1993 the "Summer of Violence." But Mayor Webb made a point of pulling aside President Clinton, who was beginning to formulate a sweeping crime bill, to talk about the problem.

TERRANCE WAS OBLIVIOUS to the pope's visit. He was a runaway, though he hadn't run far. He was living out of a Colfax motel called the Driftwood, ten minutes from his mom's house. The two-story motel had become something of a barrack house for the Bloods. It was set back half a block from the street and had a front-facing balcony, a tactical advantage. The weekly rates were cheap. They paid cash, and on good nights, gave the night manager extra.

Terrance, now seventeen, had a girlfriend for the first time. Clarice, sixteen, whose brother and friends were Bloods, was also a runaway who had recently dropped out of school. Like Terrance's mother, Clarice's mom had a drug dependency. Clarice fell for Terrance, who commanded the respect of his peers and seemed unshakable in the face of their distress. Terrance had found a way out of trouble so many times he believed God was watching over him. When he was too broke to afford food, "Mama San," the owner of Chow's Kitchen, a Chinese food counter in the strip of stores across the street from the shopping center, fed him hot wings. Once she even hid him in the back when a District 2 cop came in looking for him, then drove him back to his grandmother's house.

In the middle of the Summer of Violence, Terrance found one of his prayers answered. He met a neighborhood crackhead, Paula, who had a house she was willing to let him use in exchange for free drugs.

Terrance brought in Ricardo "Booney" Porter, one of the toughest Bloods who joined the gang while in juvenile detention, and Lil Tek 9 and a few others. They alternated nights. Paula was in her forties and epileptic. She gave them a key and stayed in her room watching TV sitcoms.

One hot night, Terrance was working. A line of "baseheads" snaked out the back. One by one he let them in, keeping the butt of his gun visible and his eyes on their hands. Some talked, others said nothing. If the police or feds came, he could be out the back in seconds, down the alley in any of several directions.

He usually sold only fifty-dollar rocks, but he was in a good mood and willing to cut it up. What did they want? Twenties? Forties? He even agreed to a few tens. Within a couple hours, he was sold out. He had promised Clarice they would meet up later that night, and he went to the living room and got low on the floor to count his earnings by the light of the moon.

It was almost $1,200. He was stuffing it into his underwear and pockets when he heard a noise. Without thinking, he flipped on a light. A fusillade of bullets tore through the front and side windows. He ran toward the kitchen but was hit. *Play dead*, he told himself. He waited. Blood seeped from his abdomen. He crawled along the floor, but the gunfire resumed, blowing out the windows. He couldn't move. He didn't know how many times he'd been hit.

Paula appeared. "Call 911," Terrance tried to say. Paula had a special phone with oversize buttons. As she grabbed it, her arm began shaking and she seized up. The phone crashed to the floor, scattering the numbers.

A noise came from the back and someone appeared in the kitchen doorway. It was Barry, Lil Tek 9. He'd heard the shots. Terrance was barely conscious. Paula was on her knees, fists and jaw clenched. Lil Tek felt his way over to the phone and dialed 911. "Someone's been shot," he said.

"The money," Terrance said, pulling at bills. Lil Tek 9 grabbed what he could from Terrance's blood-soaked pockets. Sirens became audible. Terrance looked at Lil Tek 9, not knowing if it was for the last time. "Go," he said, before falling unconscious.

Clarice waited for Terrance's call, but her page went unreturned. By morning it seemed the whole neighborhood was looking for Show-Bizz. Finally Clarice called Ernestine. Granny said she'd pick her up.

They headed to University of Colorado Medical Center Hospital, on Colorado Boulevard, the war's front line. So many gang shooting victims were admitted that the Denver PD opened a sheriff's station in the emergency room. For the paramedics who brought in Show-Bizz that night, it was hardly a surprise that he was in the police gang database. As per regulation, Terrance was admitted under an alias.

When Ernestine and Clarice arrived, tubes sprouted from Terrance's nose, machines whirred and beeped. He had been hit by just one bullet, a .45 caliber. It had entered the right center of his back at an angle, missing his spine by a centimeter. It traveled into his spleen, which ruptured, and then into his gut, shredding his upper and lower intestines and cracking his pelvic bone.

Doctors were able to remove the shell. But there was cartilage damage too close to his spine to safely attempt a repair. It remained to be seen if his injuries would be permanently debilitating.

TERRANCE'S VISITATION WAS restricted to family. He saw his mother for the first time in almost a year. Suzanne was living in a drug treatment facility, a condition of a drug court conviction. For her, seeing Terrance laid out from a shooting triggered the anger she'd turned to drugs to escape. Wasn't this exactly what she'd warned him about? He was too weak to argue. She didn't visit again.

George was in the midst of a crime spree with two prostitute friends somewhere in Kansas when he got word. He drove straight back. He hadn't seen his son since Terrance had been put on the Bloods, but he knew all about ShowBizz. Everyone knew about ShowBizz. George was proud of his son.

He was also worried. He knew Terrance was in deep and prayed Michael Asberry hadn't been involved. The last time George had seen Michael, the Crip leader had asked George if ShowBizz was his son. *Tell him we're cousins*, Michael said. George realized he'd never relayed the message.

He arrived in Terrance's room in gold chains and a fedora, and showed Terrance his gun. He spotted an armchair in the corner. "I'll sleep here," he said. Terrance nodded. They both knew the Crips were probably just finding out he hadn't been killed and were liable to show up at the hospital. One employee had been injured in gang crossfire in the parking lot.

George spent the next few weeks chatting with the nurses and entertaining Terrance and Clarice with stories of his escapades. At night, he settled into the chair with the remote control. One night the door opened and a hulking man appeared. George got up and put his gun to the man's head.

"It's okay, Pops," Terrance groaned. It was Lizard, one of Terrance's homeys. Biz and Liz, they were called.

George put his hand on his new friend's shoulder and laughed. "But you could tell I wasn't joking," he said. "Ain't *nobody* messin' with my son." Terrance was destined for greatness, George was sure.

Another friend who found his way past the security desk, and George, was Bryan Butler. He and Terrance hadn't seen each other in a minute, as they said. They couldn't remember the last time. Bryan was heavier and had a beard. He'd started attending the small Nation of Islam outpost in the Dahlia. Farrakhan's speeches about the white-controlled system that was set up to ensnare them resonated with him.

"So what are you thinking?" Bryan asked his oldest friend.

"Don't even go there," Terrance said.

Bryan dropped it. It was as he'd suspected. Getting shot in invisible Denver was rarely the wake-up call one might imagine. It was a major rite of passage, as it was in Baltimore or Ramallah or South LA, or any neighborhood where an underground war was being waged. Terrance had just earned a big stripe. He'd been shot for the Holly. Now he was a Gangster with a capital G, a real one.

HE WAS RELEASED on bed rest and moved into Ernestine's house. As did Clarice and George, who was between places, and one of Terrance's friends, Krystal, who was homeless.

Ernestine counted herself blessed to have a place big enough for them all. She stocked the refrigerator with baloney and Wonder bread. But when she got Terrance alone, she had stern words for him. He was the oldest of her grandchildren. All lived within the boundaries of the war. "I didn't bring this family to Denver to die," she told Terrance. She reminded him that all of his cousins looked up to him. Some had recently become gang members. "God has a plan for you," she said. She flushed his pain meds down the toilet. The stuff was addictive, she said.

Terrance didn't want to dishonor her. She fed community members who couldn't afford to eat. She held the community together. "I'm going to turn my life around," Terrance told her. "You watch."

But it was only lip service. Soon the YGs were deep at the Launching Pad again. When Lil Tek 9 first saw Terrance, he hugged him so hard his stitches almost ripped out. "On Bloods, I'd be dead," Terrance told Lil Tek. "On Bloods" roughly meant, "I swear to God."

George befriended the guys with stories of life on the streets from Kansas City to Oakland, where he was known as Diamond G, and of the old days in Park Hill—when Granny pulled a gun on him. They kept the curtains pulled for safety and hid guns in the flowerpot on the porch. For them, the war was only just beginning. They made a list of every Crip they knew who hadn't yet been shot, and made a pact: *Everyone gets touched.* The scars would cut them all.

PUBLIC FUNDING FOR anti-gang programs was almost nonexistent in Colorado, but following the Summer of Violence, Governor Romer championed a ten-year, $7.6 million bill aimed at steering youth away from street gangs. "Colorado's not going to become another Los Angeles," Romer promised.

Rev Kelly, the city's most prominent anti-gang activist, was flooded with invitations to corporate events and fundraisers. He attended in purple zoot suits and alligator hats, talking in his soothing bass voice about a world many in Denver had never imagined.

"He's charismatic," Jean Galloway, a Denver socialite and vice president for community relations for 9News, the city's leading news station, said. "He can walk into a room and just cover it. It's not just his physical presence; it's his personality. He knows of what he speaks. Let's face it. He makes good TV." Executives from companies such as Coors and AT&T, and from the Denver Broncos and Nuggets pro sports teams, partnered with him. The Kiwanis Club made him its first African American president.

Rev positioned his organization as a faith-based initiative. In the gang world, "faith-based" importantly meant "no police." Rev said he wanted to do prevention work, which meant cutting off gang recruitment, by providing alternatives and support for prospective new members. "It's easier to mold and build a kid than to repair an adult," he liked to say. But he also allowed his organization to be steered by powerful law enforcement interests. His board of directors included the Denver police chief, David Michaud, and the FBI's Denver bureau chief, Bob Pence.

Galloway also joined Rev's board, and together they spearheaded the creation of the Metro Denver Gang Coalition, an umbrella organization to discuss anti-gang strategy and funding. At a press conference announcing the coalition, Galloway referred to its members as "soldiers." Indeed, a new army was entering the war. While it marched under the banner of social services, it would work with, and receive most of its funding from, law enforcement.

MAYOR WEBB EMERGED from the Summer of Violence as "a national leader in the fight against urban violence," according to the Associated Press. President Clinton appointed him to lead a national conference of mayors on youth and urban violence.

The homicide tally for Denver's most infamous year wound up at seventy-four, a significant drop from the ninety-five the previous year. But things in Denver had forever changed. Ernestine put a shotgun behind the counter at the restaurant. When Mayor Webb arrived, he had an aide enter first and check the bathrooms. The restaurant was so ensconced in Bloods territory that a new Bloods set, called the Deuce Nine Family Bloods, named themselves for its corner, at 29th and Fairfax. They were one of six Bloods sets that followed the Crenshaw Mafia Gangers Bloods in Park Hill.

For many in northeast Denver, shame took hold. "The KKK doesn't even have to rally," one mother told *The Denver Post*. "We're taking our own lives."

Once the proud center of the city's civil rights movement, the Holly was now a symbol of danger and despair.

"A battle over the Holly: It's Residents vs. Drug Dealers for Control," read a front-page headline in the *Post*. A photograph depicted a young Blood handcuffed on drug charges behind Ned's, the candy and convenience store in the small shopping strip across the street from the shopping center. The story described the Holly as "an urban sore that won't heal."

"One look at the blighted area during the daytime is enough to persuade most to stay away. After nightfall, locals offer simple advice—enter at your own risk . . . No one is sure exactly when and how The Holly succumbed to such despair, but it's a common enough tragedy in big cities." The owner of Ned's, a Palestinian who had emigrated from the Gaza Strip, said the violence was similar to what he'd faced there.

WITHOUT A FORMAL education or mentors, Terrance had a worldview that was informed by the rappers whose lyrics he knew by heart. His favorite was Tupac Shakur, who was gestated in a New York jail cell when his mother was being held in the Panther 21 case.

> *They claim that I'm violent*
> *Just 'cause I refuse to be silent . . .*
> *Envious because I will rebel against*
> *Any oppressor—and this is known as self-defense*

Tupac's raps critiqued systemic racism in America and often featured violence, including against police officers. Vice President Dan Quayle called on his record label, Interscope, to withdraw his 1992 album *2Pacalypse Now* due to lyrics that Quayle said threatened law enforcement. Many of the elders in northeast Denver, including Rev. Acen Phillips, didn't like the new genre either. They felt it glamorized the violence that was destroying the community and killing their children.

Tupac, who befriended both Crips and Bloods, said he felt obligated to talk about the violence. "What we're doing is using our brain to get out of the ghetto any way we can," Tupac said. "So we tell these stories. And they tend to be violent because our world tends to be filled with violence."

Northeast Denver's gang war produced young male bodies almost weekly. Many of the gang funerals were held at Pipkin Mortuary, where George Roberts, who drove the hearses, knew the grieving families. Terrance and the Park Hill Bloods attended the memorials flamed up, as they said. Not with emotion. They went flamed up in red, ceremonially, saluting those who died for the cause. There was no bigger rite of passage. The dead were martyrs, heroes whose names and likenesses were emblazoned on silk-screened T-shirts and tattooed on their bodies. B.I.P., they said, their loving farewell.

Often, lives of the fallen were celebrated with house parties. One night Terrance and Clarice were dancing at a memorial for Billy Mac, a Blood OG who had been shot and killed on Colfax. They all knew who did it. Word on the street was fast, and uncannily accurate. Revenge was coming. But for now, they partied like there was no tomorrow—until suddenly the music switched off.

"Some Crabs just ran over Lil Tek," Booney said.

"What?"

"Lil Sexy just called," Booney said. "She said some Crabs just ran him over on Colorado Boulevard, and on Bloods, he's dead."

Terrance felt his face go flush. He was only alive because of Lil Tek 9. He headed to the hospital. Others followed. They pushed past the emergency room nurses and found Barry's room. His face was so distorted and discolored it was barely recognizable. Terrance went to Barry's side. His eyes were open. Barry and Terry, they were called back before they were Bloods. Barry looked like he was trying to say something but no sound came.

Soon the room was filled with Bloods. Barry didn't move. As they watched, his breathing stopped and the bedside monitor transitioned to a single solemn tone.

Terrance went out. A Crip who must have been visiting someone else was in the hall. Terrance knocked him to the floor and busted his knuckles on his face until the nurses pulled him off.

In September 1994, President Clinton signed into law the Violent Crime Control and Law Enforcement Act. Mayor Webb, who had consulted on the bill, was on the East Lawn of the White House for the ceremony. Clinton called him out by name.

The bill, the largest crime legislation in American history, put a new army of 100,000 police officers on the streets of America's cities. It also added an assault weapons ban and some money for drug treatment. A "three strikes" provision mandated life sentences for criminals convicted of a third federal felony, even a nonviolent one. And the 100:1 disparity in sentencing for crack vs. powder cocaine, instituted in the Reagan era, was extended, disappointing criminal justice advocates. Studies showed that a disproportionate number of people charged with drug offenses were Black, and most were not significant dealers.

Colorado was among the states that began building new federal and state prisons to accommodate demand.

TERRANCE MOVED OUT of Granny's and back into the Driftwood Motel. He was back in the crack trade. His first customer was his father. When Clarice realized Terrance was selling to George, she confronted him. "It's not like he was always there for me," Terrance said. Clarice dropped it. She could see the situation they were all in. It was a survival mindset. The Crips had shot up Terrance's grandmother's house. He feared for his life every time he had to go to a pay phone to return a page, exposed to the road. George's survival was about finding crack, which he called dope or rock. If Terrance wouldn't have sold to him, George knew he would probably try to steal it. They all had their priorities.

In his own way, Terrance saw selling to his father as an example of his focus. He needed money—every dollar he could get if he was going to move up in the drug game and find suppliers who would sell him powder cocaine. Now he was lucky to make a grand a week. He needed guns, ammo, food, clothes, and ideally a real cell phone so he didn't have to use the pay phone. It would be more profitable if he could make the rock himself, and soon he accomplished his goal.

The process, which required a friend with a kitchen, took a couple of hours. He used baby food jars to mix the cocaine with water and baking soda. Then he dropped the jars into a pot with a couple of inches of water. He boiled the water, let the substance cook for a few minutes, then removed the jar and shook it. The substance eventually hardened like wax. Sometimes it was chalky and needed to be scraped out. Other times it dropped out like a solid piece, a rock. He carved it up with a pocket knife and weighed the pieces on a scale.

He bought a '65 Impala with a maroon interior, like the one Eazy-E sang about in "Boyz-n-the-Hood." He got silver Dayton wheel rims for it. When Clarice rode around the neighborhood with Terry, as she called him, she felt like royalty. One day he had almost $30,000 on him. People called out to them from the street. If Terrance took too long in a store, a younger Blood would often show up to check on him, "Just making sure you're boo," which meant "cool."

Life with ShowBizz also had its downside. His Impala didn't last long; the Crips dropped large rocks through his windshield and shot it up twice, once when Terrance and Lizard were in it, leading to a shootout. Clarice waited each night for Terrance at the Driftwood, hoping he would return. Most of Terrance's drug sales were done between two and five in the morning. At the motel, women came and went, and Bloods carrying guns had access to all of the rooms. For any teen girl, hanging out with the Bloods in a Colfax motel always carried the memory of eighteen-year-old Jennifer Manchego, who was killed by Brazy.

One day Terrance returned to the Driftwood and told Clarice they were clearing out. He'd gotten into it with Ice Alexander and another OG Blood at a house party over whether Ice was disrespecting some Bloods from LA that Terrance had invited. Terrance and Ice had nearly come to fisticuffs. Later, other Bloods warned Terrance that he was "in the hat." Any of the younger Bloods who hurt or killed Terrance would be rewarded for it. As an OG, Ice was one of a handful of Bloods with enough stature to make such a call on someone like Terrance, who had significant clout himself.

Terrance and Clarice moved back in with Granny. He showed her where he kept a gun hidden in the flowerpot. If they needed to go to the store, it was with the loaded Mac 11 automatic pistol on Terrance's lap. About a week later, Terrance's pager went off. He went to a pay phone and called the number. "Who's this?" he said.

Ice himself was on the line. He laughed and said the hit was off. But for Clarice, the stress had become too much. Terrance tried to talk her into staying, but she was done. She didn't know yet that she was pregnant.

Terrance hopped into his car. He wasn't going to let any woman bring him down. That, too, was part of the code of the hood. "MOB" was one of the acronyms the Bloods often used. It was even the name of a Tupac Shakur song. Some took it to mean "Money Only Bloods," others interpreted it as "Money Over Bitches." It was a male-dominated world.

When Terrance reached the Dahlia, he saw a group of OGs in the parking lot and pulled in, making a wide circle. He got out and set the butt of his long gun on the ground. Everyone knew the hit had been lifted. ShowBizz wanted to make a point that would later haunt him: he didn't care if he wasn't an OG. He was determined to become a Park Hill legend of his own.

The Denver County Jail was a series of grim concrete buildings surrounded by concertina wire, ten minutes from Ernestine's house. In March 1995, Terrance, #449863 in the gang database, was hauled in for the first time. It was because he'd had such an explosive argument with his mother that a neighbor called the police. Terrance had left but was apprehended nearby. He had a semiautomatic weapon on him.

He put on the green jumpsuit and headed, he assumed, toward Building 8, the notorious scene of riots, fires, beatings, and stabbings. It was where the city housed most of the Bloods and Crips. Instead, Terrance was diverted into a gymnasium, where rows of cots sat. The jail was over capacity. Mayor Webb had requested an emergency $3.2 million to expand the grounds.

Terrance looked around. A couple dozen new inmates occupied the cavernous room. He saw a few "baseheads," or crack users, he had sold to, and a handful of Crips. Worse, staring at him was "Psych Mike" himself, Michael Asberry.

The two had come face-to-face only once, about a year earlier. Terrance and another Blood were picking up a friend at East High School, where Mike and a group of Crips jumped them. District 2 pulled up minutes later and they all ran.

Terrance looked at Mike, in his matching jumpsuit. He was average height, with a thick neck, a wide face, and a twitch in his cheek. He had recently been in the news again. As money poured into the city's coffers from Governor Romer's anti-gang bill, Denver's first publicly funded programs had begun. One of them was an experimental effort that was supposed to employ former gang members to stop gang disputes before they escalated. It had employed none other than Mike Asberry and his top deputy, Orlando "Lil' O" Domena, two of the city's most feared men.

Within Denver's gang communities, the program was a joke. Whether to counter any perception that they were working with the police, or because they thought they had immunity, Mike and Lil' O seemed to only step up their criminal activities. Mike was arrested for drug sales. Domena was charged with shooting two Park Hill Bloods, one of whom died. The program was canceled.

As Psych approached, Terrance kept one eye on the guys behind him.

"I'm Michael," Psych said, extending his hand.

"Terrance," ShowBizz said.

"We know who you is," Mike said. He looked over his shoulder. "Ain't no one gonna do something to you here."

DENVER'S JAIL OVERCROWDING left judges with no choice but to set bonds lower. Terrance's was $25,000. He needed only 10 percent in cash, or $2,500, for a bail bondsman to spring him. If he showed up to court, that would be all he owed. Granny put up her house as collateral and gave Terrance an earful. But he was arrested again in a matter of days. A passenger in a white Cadillac Seville had shot a Crip, hitting him in the hip. An informant had told police Terrance was one of the Bloods in the car. Terrance denied it, but this time the judge set his bond at $250,000, annotating in long-hand on the order, "suspect in many other cases involving guns and shootings."

This time, as he entered the jail, he was led to an office in the administrative wing. Framed photos and awards were on the wall. A man peered at Terrance from behind his desk, right down to his red Converse shoes. Somehow Terrance had managed not to give them up on intake. "Do you know who I am?" the man asked.

"Yes, sir," Terrance said. Terrance had never met his grandfather, Sheriff "Big John" Sanford, but he knew about him. He was George's father. George hadn't even met him until he was sixteen. Big John had known that one day Terrance would show up.

Like several of the older African Americans who worked the jails, John looked out for his family and kept quiet about it. Whenever George was inside, he tried to see he was assigned to Building 22, where the amenities were better, and arranged to slip McDonald's cheeseburgers to him via the guards. But he wasn't one for long speeches.

"You know there's a gang war going on in there," Big John said, eyeing Terrance's shoes.

"Yes, sir."

"Well, be careful."

AT LAST SHOWBIZZ entered Building 8. It was a full block long and three stories high. Each floor was lined with small cells containing metal bunk beds and holes for toilets. Crips down one side, Bloods the other. For much of 1994 and 1995, as O. J. Simpson led police down the LA freeway and Timothy McVeigh blew up the federal building in Oklahoma City, Terrance resided in Building 8, awaiting charges in multiple cases, unable to make bond.

One advantage to being a gang member in jail or prison was that you always had family to protect you. In Building 8 that was crucial. On the hour, between 6 a.m. and 6 p.m., the cell doors would slide open, allowing inmates to go in or out for sixty seconds. The small opening was also exploited by other gang members to gain access to an adversary's cell.

Terrance found himself in the same pod—a group of cells that shared a common area—with Kinshasa "Benny Lok" Cooley, the founding member of the Park Hill Crenshaw Mafia Gangster Bloods. Benny Lok had spent most of the last several years locked up. One day they were sitting in the television room when highlights of a Los Angeles Lakers game mentioned the NBA team's arena, in Inglewood, California. "That's your home," Cooley said to Terrance, referencing the birthplace of the Crenshaw Mafia Gangster Bloods, formerly known as the Inglewood Family.

Terrance knew his gang history. He knew about "the Bottoms," as the original CMG hood was called, and about 104th and Crenshaw, the sacred corner. But Park Hill also had its history.

"I'm not from Inglewood," Terrance said. "I'm from Park Hill."

Cooley took offense. ShowBizz was gaining a reputation for having a bit too much of an independent streak.

IN FEBRUARY 1995, Ernestine visited with news: Terrance was a father. He was eighteen. He didn't know how he was supposed to feel. He hadn't even known Clarice was pregnant. Granny told him she was taking in Clarice and Javon, Terrance's new son. Clarice's family and friends were homeless or in jail. They had nowhere else to go.

Another day, Terrance was summoned to a room in the administrative wing. Big John was there, as were his mother and father, both in jail jumpsuits. Terrance couldn't remember when he'd last seen his mom. He'd fallen out with his father about a year earlier, when George admitted selling one of Terrance's best machine guns for $50; it was worth about $750. George had been desperate to score.

Big John asked if they had anything to say to one another. They didn't.

THE JAILHOUSE REUNION didn't faze Terrance, but George went back to his cell and was overcome with despair. He had friends and family all over Denver. All he'd done was ruin his life because of a drug addiction.

He was facing a potential prison sentence for robbing a dope house in Denver's Capitol Hill neighborhood. Along with two friends from St. Louis, George had kicked in the door and yelled, "If there's a God in heaven, he'll save everybody in this house. If not, you can kiss the babies goodbye."

Five people, most of them white, were sitting at a table full of razor blades and cocaine. George and his friends taped their mouths and tied them to chairs. But instead of getting out quickly, they proceeded to smoke and snort the supply. Until the front door came down and police rushed in.

George's bail was low. After the meeting with his family, he cobbled together enough money from friends to get out. He went to stay with a friend in Aurora but ended up on another crack binge. When the supply was gone he nearly came to blows with his friend, a scene witnessed by his friend's wife, Sherri. "Please help me," George asked her. Smoking crack used to make him feel like he was floating. Now he hallucinated that he saw rocks of cocaine everywhere. "I'm losing this battle," he told her.

Sherri took him to Now Faith Christian Center, a congregation that had relocated from Northeast Park Hill to Montbello, the predominantly Black subdivision north of I-70. George sat in the last row, afraid he stank.

"Preacher, come here," called the pastor, Leon Emerson, during the service. "God says he's about to change your life."

He can't be talking to me, George thought. *I'm no preacher, I'm a crackhead.*

"Come on," a man said, motioning toward George.

George went to the front. Pastor Emerson held out his hand. "Man of God, you're bound by crack cocaine and God's about to deliver you."

"Who's telling you my business?" George said.

"Brother, don't fear. God's about to deliver you." Emerson turned to face the congregation. "Everybody who's been delivered from drugs, stand up." George watched as about a dozen people stood.

"All the jailbirds who've been delivered from incarceration, stand up." Another group stood.

"Everybody who's been delivered from something, stand up," Pastor Emerson said.

Most of the congregation stood. George began to cry. Then he vomited there on the dais. Demons, he could feel, were leaving his body.

AFTERWARD, GEORGE HAD no craving for the drug. He went to the church every day. His life was in God's hands, he believed. One day District 2 picked him up on the street on an outstanding warrant, and back he went to Building 22. A member of Now Faith visited and brought a Bible.

One night, a female jail guard who knew George came by his cell. "Roberts, you're not allowed to have a hardback in here," Officer Tracy Jones said. She noticed he was looking at the book strangely. "Roberts, do you know how to read?"

"No, ma'am," George said.

Jones taught George to read each night after her rounds. The first thing he learned was Ezekiel 37. Letter by letter he sounded it out, until he heard God's voice.

> The hand of the LORD was on me, and he brought me out by the Spirit of the LORD and set me in the middle of a valley; it was full of bones. He led me back and forth among them, and I saw a great many bones on the floor of the valley, bones that were very dry.
>
> He asked me, "Son of man, can these bones live?"
>
> I said, "Sovereign LORD, you alone know."
>
> Then he said to me, "Prophesy to these bones and say to them, 'Dry bones, hear the word of the LORD! This is what the Sovereign LORD says to these bones: I will make breath enter you, and you will come to life. I will attach tendons to you and make flesh come upon you and cover you with skin; I will put breath in you, and you will come to life. Then you will know that I am the LORD.'"
>
> So I prophesied as I was commanded. And as I was prophesying, there was a noise, a rattling sound, and the bones came together, bone to bone. I looked, and tendons and flesh appeared on them and skin covered them, but there was no breath in them.

Then he said to me, "Prophesy, son of man, and say to it . . . 'Come, breath, from the four winds and breathe into these slain, that they may live.'" So I prophesied as he commanded me, and breath entered them; they came to life and stood up on their feet—a vast army.

George felt his spirit rise. As he awaited the outcome of his case, he told other inmates about the valley, which was the jail they were in, and the dry bones, which were them. They needed to breathe and come back to life, he said. One day he was called down to admin. He was free to go, he was told. His charges had been dropped. He never knew what had happened, only that it was the first of many miracles he would experience.

MEANWHILE, IN BUILDING 8, a series of violent fights in the so-called Thunderdome—the common space inmates had to go through to get to the yard—had led the sheriffs to try an experimental approach to quashing gang tensions that had been attempted in California. They would commingle the Bloods and Crips.

Into Terrance's pod came Darryl "DG" Givens, a high-ranking Crip who was the second alleged perpetrator, along with Orlando Domena, of the shooting that had killed one Blood and wounded another. At first, Givens and Terrance stayed away from each other. But, as time went on, they began to talk. Givens, tall and thin with a quick wit, was about the same age as Terrance. They both had just had their first kid. They bonded over the crazy things they'd been through and their public "pretenders," or defenders, who they saw as part of the system, cajoling them to take a plea deal.

Terrance was facing multiple charges in two cases. In one, he'd allegedly beaten up and robbed another Blood who'd claimed he was going to form his own gang in Aurora. In the other, he'd allegedly pointed a gun at his cousin's friend's head and threatened to kill her, because she was dating a Crip. He wasn't taking a deal because he was sure the witnesses wouldn't show up for trial.

Givens was in a worse predicament, facing a potential life sentence for first-degree murder. One afternoon, he came into the Thunderdome and called Terrance over.

"I just got back from court," Givens said. "They offered me a three."

"That's a *great* deal, brother."

"But there's something else," Givens said. "If I testify, I walk." Terrance knew he meant taking the stand against Domena, one of his best friends and one of the most powerful Crips in the city.

"I don't know," Terrance said. "I'd take that three."

"My girl's pregnant," Givens said.

"I ain't seen my kid yet," Terrance said. "I think you better talk to your homeys."

But Terrance could tell Givens had made up his mind. That night, Building 8 went on security lockdown. The sound of a cell door opening and an inmate being led down the hall echoed through the building. It was Givens.

THAT YEAR, DENVER'S gang problem entered the mayoral race, as Wellington Webb sought his second term. Mary DeGroot, a forty-three-year-old white city council member representing south Denver, called Webb's administration "the most corrupt in the country," in part because Denver's new airport had gone $2 billion over budget, prompting a federal investigation. She also accused the mayor of coddling gang members. "There is no way a group of gang members would take over the mayor's office under my administration as they did under this administration," she said, referring to the failed program that employed Asberry.

DeGroot promised to fight Denver's gangs with a strategy she called "maximum harassment." And she stopped just shy of accusing the police of corruption, promising to shut down six well-known crack houses in her first week on the job, all of them in northeast

Denver. Both of Denver's daily newspapers endorsed DeGroot, but Webb narrowly won.

CITY POLITICS WERE of no consequence to Terrance. He didn't vote. To him, Northeast Park Hill was a country of its own. The north end of the neighborhood was barren; the warehouses were empty, the firehouse had been closed for years, and MLK Park was a place few felt safe going.

The night he was released, after nearly two years, Terrance was there with a large group of Bloods. He had eventually pleaded guilty to felony robbery and "menacing," a charge often used for a drive-by shooting in which no one was hit. Boomboxes blared. Terrance felt alive again. Tucked into his jeans was a Mac 90 long rifle with a thirty-round clip. The gun was long enough that he couldn't sit down. He could take down a helicopter, he thought, which was what one gang member in LA had done.

Denver's Crips and Bloods were engaged in heavy fighting again. Shootings and firebombing of each other's cars and homes were regular. The meeting that day was the kind at which any of the OGs could say to any of the younger Bloods something as simple as "I've seen some guys over by X, Y, or Z location," and those guys were as good as dead.

The OG who took charge of the meeting that day was Pernell "P. Lok" Hines. Terrance had just met him in prison, where they had briefly overlapped.

P. Lok called out ShowBizz, "the homey," who P. Lok said would be running the "car" as the gang's new YG Regulator. The position, held by a younger gang member, was akin to field general, arguably the most important role in the gang. In the car were the riders, the trigger men, who carried out the bidding of the OGs, who were the "shot callers."

Terrance accepted, but as many there knew, ShowBizz had already been the de facto YG Regulator. It was nothing new. Only now there were informants among them.

The message today to the Bloods, the Crips, to every criminal
gang preying on the innocent is clear: We mean to put you out
of business, to break the backs of your organization, to stop you
from terrorizing our neighborhoods and our children, to put you
away for a very long time. We have just begun the job and we do
not intend to stop until we have finished.

—President Bill Clinton, May 13, 1996

The violent crime rates had been steadily dropping since 1993. The
White House credited stricter sentencing, enhanced law enforcement, and the Brady Bill, which required background checks for
gun buyers. But gang violence was a growing concern.

"Twenty years ago, fewer than half of our cities reported gang
activity," Attorney General Janet Reno said, before President
Clinton's remarks. "A generation later, reasonable estimates indicate that there are now more than a half a million gang members in
more than sixteen thousand gangs on the streets of our cities."

African Americans were more than six times more likely to die
by gunshot wounds than whites. Indeed, the leading cause of death
for Black men aged fifteen to twenty-four was homicide. Thousands were dying every year. Beat cops could see that most of the
deaths were gang-related, but the official toll was always lower than
the actual numbers for various reasons, including the legal pitfalls
of having to prove in court that an alleged perpetrator was a gang
member, and even public relations concerns. Whether or not people wanted to hear about it, many of America's neighborhoods were
also the scene of deadly battles fought by teen soldiers.

Clinton and Reno announced a change in the way the government would prosecute gang members. The Department of Justice would now regard street gangs as "organized crime" groups, making it easier for law enforcement to obtain search warrants and phone taps and allowing prosecutors to use the threat of longer sentences to get cooperators on board.

In Chicago, several members of the Gangster Disciples—a gang formed in the late 1960s on the South Side—were charged with running a $100-million-a-year drug business, based on evidence obtained by informants within the gang. States were also beginning to go after gangs as crime syndicates. In Denver, a joint FBI and Denver police investigation had been ongoing for almost a year, led by two informants inside the target organization, the Park Hill Bloods.

"BOONEY'S SNITCHIN'" CAME the whisper from the grate in the door separating two jail pods. Terrance recognized the voice on the other side. It was Carl "Fat Daddy" McKay, one of the Park Hill OGs.

Terrance was back in jail yet again, this time in Arapahoe County, southeast of Denver. He'd been identified as one of the assailants who beat a Crip in the parking lot of the Aurora mall. It was a violation of his parole.

Terrance didn't want to believe what he'd just heard. Booney was one of Terrance's closest friends. They'd shared a crack house, pulled robberies and shootings together, things he didn't want to remember.

The next day, he and others fought for the newspapers, both of which carried the story on the front page. "DA Slams Bloods Gang," read the oversized type across the top of the *Rocky Mountain News*. "It is the first time in Colorado history that prosecutors have used the state's hardline racketeering statute—known commonly as the Colorado Organized Crime Act—to go after a street gang," noted *The Denver Post*.

"Drug trafficking was the focal point of the Crenshaw Mafia Gangster's activities, and from that, extreme acts of violence emanated through Denver," read a letter in the court file from Captain Steve Shepard of the gang unit. "Quite simply, these criminals have very nearly ruined Park Hill."

The nineteen-count indictment against ten Blood leaders included allegations of drive-by shootings and of an ongoing crack distribution ring. But the centerpiece charge, which five of the defendants faced, was conspiracy to murder the top-ranking Crip Eric "E-Baby" Thomas, who'd been killed in October 1993. The alleged trigger man was Ice Alexander, whose bond was set at $1 million.

According to *The Denver Post*, "two confidential informants" were key to the investigation, which included secretly recorded audio from Blood meetings.

For America's gang communities, it was a time of paranoia and fear. In September 1996, Tupac Shakur, who had become the world's most famous rapper and a Blood affiliate, was murdered in a drive-by shooting in Las Vegas. He was twenty-five. Tupac had tried to stay out of gang life, but as he had risen to stardom, he had been drawn ever deeper into the world he rapped about. Two years earlier, he had been shot five times in the lobby of a Manhattan recording studio in what appeared to be a robbery. Tupac believed the theft was just a cover story, and that the rapper-producer duo of Biggie Smalls and Sean "Puffy" Combs were behind the shooting. Tupac, who lived in LA, and Biggie and Puffy, who lived in New York, had developed a much-discussed East Coast–West Coast rivalry that had begun to mimic the gang war and included thinly veiled threats against each other on awards shows and in their music.

Tupac also believed he was a target of law enforcement. In November 1993, he was charged with sexual assault in a case he believed was a setup, and went to trial. Though he was acquitted at trial of all the more serious charges, he was convicted of forcibly touching a woman's buttocks and sentenced to eighteen months to four years in prison. Then twenty-three, he was broke from his legal battles, and trying to help his mother save her house, which she couldn't afford, when he was contacted with an offer. The CEO of Death Row Records, Suge Knight, a much-feared "Bompton" Blood from Compton, offered to pay the $1.4 million bond to get him out while he awaited his appeal, if he signed with Suge's record label. Tupac—who would soon have a MOB tattoo, associated with the Bloods—accepted the offer.

The night Tupac was killed, he was with Suge Knight in Las Vegas, attending a Mike Tyson fight. After the match, Tupac got into a fight of his own, with a member of the Compton Crips, in the casino of the MGM Grand Hotel. The Compton Crips were rivals of Suge's "Bompton" Blood gang. Some of them had also befriended Tupac's rival Biggie Smalls, and worked security for him.

Later that night, Tupac was on the Strip, in the passenger seat of Suge's BMW, when a white Cadillac pulled up alongside and someone inside started shooting. Tupac was hit four times and died in the hospital six days later.

Many in the gang world came to believe that Orlando Anderson, the Compton Crip who had fought with Tupac only hours earlier, pulled the trigger. The case was never solved, partly because Anderson, who was twenty-three, was killed in a shootout at a car wash two years later.

Christopher "Biggie Smalls" Wallace—who also went by Notorious B.I.G.—had also been drawn into the gang world, and after Tupac was killed, he knew he was a marked man. Many Bloods believed Biggie had paid Orlando Anderson to kill Tupac. In March 1997, six months after Tupac's death, Biggie was in Los Angeles to attend the Soul Train Music Awards. Afterward, he was a passenger in a two-car convoy when another car pulled up alongside at a stoplight. Four shots were fired. Christopher Wallace was dead at twenty-four. His murder is also unsolved.

THE DRIVE-BY SHOOTINGS of the world's biggest rap stars would fuel books, films, and conspiracy theories for decades to come. But it was yet another story that would fuel the biggest conspiracy theories and shape attitudes about the American government in gang communities. "For the better part of a decade," an August 1996 investigative series by Gary Webb in the *San Jose Mercury News* began, "a San Francisco Bay Area drug ring sold tons of cocaine to the Crips and Bloods street gangs of Los Angeles and funneled millions in drug profits to a Latin American guerrilla army run by the U.S. Central Intelligence Agency."

It turned out that in the 1980s, unbeknownst to him at the time, Ricky Ross's Nicaraguan drug supplier had been funneling his profits to the CIA-backed Contras, an opposition group that was fighting to overthrow Nicaragua's Soviet-backed Sandinista government. America's illicit support for the Contras through arms sales to Iran had already gotten Lt. Colonel Oliver North indicted, and had threatened to bring down President Reagan.

In the African American community, many believed the reporting was evidence of a government effort to destroy it. The cocaine sales made by Danilo Blandón, Ricky Ross's supplier, were made in Los Angeles gang neighborhoods in mass quantity beginning in the early 1980s, fueling the gang war. In 1986, President Reagan signed new drug laws that incarcerated tens of thousands of people, a disproportionate number of them Black. "It is unconscionable that the intelligence community or the CIA could think so little of people of color that they would be willing to destroy generations in an effort to try to win the war in Nicaragua," Congresswoman Maxine Waters said. The CIA eventually acknowledged that some of the drug profits made by Blandón and his partner Edward Meneses went to support the Contras. But an inspector general report released in December 1997 described Gary Webb's *San Jose Mercury News* series as "exaggerations of the facts." The inspector general did identify "troubling aspects" of the case, including that Blandón had improperly received a U.S. green card, but the report concluded that the irregularities "fall far short of the type of manipulation and corruption of the criminal justice system that the articles suggested."

By the time the story broke, Freeway Ricky Ross had discovered

another side of it, the hard way. After leaving LA ahead of the efforts to catch him, he ended up being convicted on drug cases in
Ohio and Texas, for which he served nearly five years. Soon after
his release in 1994, he was approached by none other than his old
friend Danilo Blandón, who proposed doing another deal. Ross was
reluctant. Blandón told Ross that he only needed him to be the go-
between, for which he would be paid $300,000. Ross, who was broke,
agreed.

This time, however, Blandón was officially working for the US
government. In order to avoid a long prison sentence, he had agreed
to become a DEA informant. The first target the DEA gave him was
Ross. The sting resulted in Ross's third felony conviction. Under
Clinton's three-strikes provision, Freeway Rick, then thirty-six, was
out. He was sentenced to life.

By 1995, America's prison population had surpassed one and a half
million, more than any country in the world. America's incarceration rate was also the highest, at six in one thousand people; in
gang communities it was far higher. Criminal defense advocates began to campaign for alternate sentencing. In Denver, Mike Asberry
became the guinea pig in a high-profile experiment to see whether
a hardened gang member could be rehabilitated outside the prison
system.

In 1995, Mike was facing drug and assault charges that could have
gotten him ten years behind bars, but the judge in his case, Lynne
Hufnagel—whom Asberry affectionately called Judge Homegirl—
signaled she was willing to consider an option presented to her by
Rev Kelly. Rev had reached out to Jim Brown of Amer-I-Can, and
Brown offered to take Mike into his program in lieu of a prison
term. "He has to learn how to control his temper," Rev said, in a
hearing covered by Denver's media, "but I've never felt so strongly
about a youth's rehabilitation."

The Denver police vehemently opposed the idea. In a letter to
the court, District 2 Officer Paul Baca described Mike as a violent

"chameleon" who was skilled at fooling people into thinking he was salvageable. Mike had spat at police and kicked out a squad car window. And, according to Baca, the police had a letter from another top Crip saying Asberry had called on his gang to "start a war on the police." Mike denied it.

In court, Mike said he had been trying to escape gang life but had been unable. "This might save my life," he said.

"If he [Mike] indeed has the potential Jim Brown and Rev Kelly say he has, he may be able to use it in Los Angeles," Judge Hufnagel said in her ruling. "He is beyond that here." She handed him a six-year suspended sentence, requiring him to enter Amer-I-Can, and begin its counseling and job-training programs.

TERRANCE, MEANWHILE, WAS headed to prison. He pleaded guilty to second-degree assault for the Aurora mall incident, a violation of his parole, and was sent to Territorial, a prison in Cañon City, about two hours south of Denver.

The Cañon City area, then home to seven prisons, was "the corrections capital of the world," according to T-shirts sold in the town's museum. Among the facilities were America's highest-security federal penitentiary, known as "Supermax," in nearby Florence, where inmates included Tupac Shakur's stepfather, Mutulu Shakur, a former Black Panther, and the "Unabomber," Ted Kaczynski. (Future inmates would include the Oklahoma City bomber Timothy McVeigh and the 9/11 plotter Zacarias Moussaoui.)

As Terrance was being checked in, other inmates passed in the hall. To his surprise, one of them was Booney, his friend and one of the alleged informants in the ongoing 1996 racketeering case.

"Most of what they're saying ain't true," Booney called out.

Terrance couldn't believe it. *Most?* Now he felt sure that what Fat Daddy told him was true.

Territorial had three tiers, with cells on either side. Booney was somewhere down the hall. Whenever the guards weren't around, he loudly whispered to Terrance. He said he had been in the Denver County Jail when he was called into an interrogation room. He said investigators played him recordings taken at Blood meetings in MLK Park, and at the home of Joel "Way Out" Alexander, another OG, who claimed to be the brother of Ice. The home was another secret Blood meeting spot; Terrance had been there many times.

Booney said that detectives told him they had evidence that he, Booney, was in the car that killed E-Baby, and that they wanted the name of the trigger man or else he would face murder charges. Booney offered them other information instead—but quickly realized he had made a mistake. "I can't believe I did some busta shit like this yo," he said to Terrance. "Tell the homeys. I ain't taking the stand."

Booney had good reason to give Terrance this assurance. Taking the stand against your own gang was perhaps the most egregious type of snitching. As if to underline the point, news had just spread through the prison that Darryl Givens, the Crip that Terrance befriended in jail who had testified against fellow Crip Orlando Domena, was dead. Givens had been shot and killed in his car. He was twenty. No arrests had been made, but there was no question in the gang community that, thinking he would save himself, Givens had paid the ultimate price for cooperating with law enforcement against a member of his own gang. He left behind his wife and two kids.

Terrance became feverish. He filled out a "kite," or request to see the nurse. Finally he was taken to the infirmary and told a stomach bug was going around. He was sent back to his cell. He hadn't had a bowel movement in three days. That night he threw up a black mucusy bile. "I'm dying," he called out. He lay down on the cold floor, sweating and shivering.

In the morning he didn't get up. When Booney passed by on the way to breakfast he saw Terrance on the floor, his cell door open. "This nigga's dying," Booney yelled. "Someone help! This nigga's dyin' here!" Two other inmates ran over and helped Booney carry

Terrance to the infirmary. Terrance woke up the next day in a hospital. Scar tissue from his bullet wound had caused a bowel obstruction. He'd had emergency surgery. Booney had saved his life.

THE BLOODS RACKETEERING case meandered through the Denver County Court while a few blocks away in the federal courthouse, Timothy McVeigh stood trial for the biggest act of domestic terrorism in U.S. history.

Lawyers for Ice Alexander claimed the prosecution "was trolling for jailhouse snitches," and alleged prosecutorial misconduct. Defense lawyers for the Bloods also challenged the district attorney's right to shield the identities of its informants. At least one of them had become known. The person was placed under law enforcement protection after they began receiving beeper messages simply saying "187," a reference to the statutory citation for homicide in California's penal code.

The defense's attempt to learn the informants' identities went all the way to the Colorado Supreme Court, which ruled in favor of the DA's office. Thousands of pages of documents were sealed for ten years. Their cover sheet included a mug shot of Ice Alexander and a red stamp, "Confidential."

Despite the procedural victory, the DA's office still needed the informants to testify, at which point their identities would have to be revealed. Their credibility would also be assailed. In the end, none of the cases went to trial and no one pleaded guilty to the main charge of murder.

Joel Alexander, who was twenty-five, pleaded guilty to racketeering and received the longest sentence, twenty-four years. Ice also pleaded guilty to racketeering, and got fourteen years. Pernell, who spent almost a year on the run from arrest, eventually turned himself in and pleaded guilty to drug distribution. He got twelve years.

"It's not the sentences we had hoped for, to be sure," Tim Twining, deputy district attorney, told *The Denver Post*, "but breaking up the gang has been achieved."

THE TAKEDOWN OF the leaders of the Bloods changed life in Northeast Park Hill. The infamous crack houses that had become a liability for Webb in the 1995 mayoral election were finally shut down. The presence of the Bloods at the Holly was diminished. More residents were willing to go to the shopping center again.

For others, the end of the case brought a stark new reality.

"I am the mother of Isaac two little girls," wrote Vandy Harper, Isaac Alexander's girlfriend, in half-printed, half-cursive pencil, to the judge. "Isaac is a man that cares, is loveing and works hard for his family's happyness. Since his be away my 3 year old wets the bed and haves nightmare wakeing up yelling for her daddy and when she sees he's not home she crys herself back to sleep. I ask you to please let him come home to his family. We need him so much."

Isaac's parole was denied.

The sister of Carl "Fat Daddy" McKay, who got five years for a separate drug distribution case and another five for burglary, asked the court for its reconsideration: "Life for all of the McKay children was tough," she wrote, "but Carl probably suffered the most . . . My mother was verbally and physically abusive . . . Carl was exposed to violence, drugs, alcohol, crime and neglect. My mother was and still is a cocaine addict. Carl for many years before he turned 18 barely had a roof over his head."

The file on Carl, who had a wife and two children, also included a letter from Rev.

"I have worked with youth who are in the eyes of the public, unsalvageable," Rev typed on Open Door Youth Gang Alternatives (ODYGA) letterhead. "I have known Carl McKay for over seven years and I have been aware of his ups and downs . . . I see Carl as a young man full of potential . . . ODYGA will overwhelmingly be there to support Carl in any way that we can."

MEANWHILE, MIKE ASBERRY wasn't doing well in Los Angeles. He had started out living in Jim Brown's Hollywood Hills mansion but he didn't get along with Brown's twenty-four-year-old son, who helped run the program. Brown was concerned about Mike's mental health, particularly his anger.

Mike moved out and soon stopped attending the counseling and skills sessions that were the core of Amer-I-Can's program. He spent a few weeks in a homeless shelter then got a job as a warehouse stock boy. He worked the graveyard shift. Without a car, he had to walk more than an hour to work through neighborhoods where robberies, assaults, and shootings were regular. One day, according to a LAPD report, he was spotted wearing blue in a well-known Crip neighborhood, and searched. He was carrying a loaded .38 Special, a violation of his probation.

"Street Thug a Legacy of Leniency" was the headline of a column by Ken Hamblin, an African American columnist for *The Denver Post*. "Who among us truly believed the Asberry saga would end differently?" wrote Bill Johnson, the *Rocky Mountain News*'s lead African American columnist.

Mike was brought back to Denver and to Judge Hufnagel's courtroom. The negative publicity surrounding Asberry's arrest had come at a bad time for Hufnagel. She had become one of the few judges in Colorado history to be voted off the bench. The hearing in Mike's case would be one of her last as a judge.

Mike, who was now twenty-seven, sat to her left in a red jumpsuit, hands shackled.

"He was given a generous opportunity earlier," the prosecutor Tim Twining told the court. "There is no indication he is going to do anything but continue on his path as a career criminal." The district attorney's office asked that Mike get ten years, the max, for his original charge.

Rev Kelly rose on Mike's behalf. "He, like a lot of others, would rather be stopped by police with a gun than by a gang without a gun," he said. Jim Brown agreed. "Michael has not attacked anyone, he has not stolen anything," Brown told the Rocky *Mountain News*. "He made a mistake based on fear. That's all. They don't understand the conditions these kids live in. You have gangs, you have threatening situations. You have a choice of putting a gun in your pocket or putting your life in danger."

Mike spoke only briefly. "I can't make no excuses," he said. "I should get my punishment."

Holding back her emotions, Hufnagel gave Mike four years. As bailiffs led him from the courtroom, she called out to him. "Good luck, Mr. Asberry," she said.

"You too, ma'am," he replied.

As America's gang war continued to grow, three major efforts that would shape the understanding of why gang violence happens, and how it should be combatted, emerged. The first began in 1995 at Harvard's Kennedy School of Government, when David Kennedy, a staff writer in the school's case-writing office, began looking into shooting patterns in Boston. He found that essentially all youth homicides in the city were being committed in just a few neighborhoods, which were predominantly Black. Once Kennedy began to speak to police and outreach workers in the neighborhoods, as well as looking at ballistics reports, he learned from them that among the gang members, only a tiny number were involved in carrying out violence. He called them the "impact players," people either pulling the trigger, or older gang members who had enough stature in the gangs to call for it.

The findings shattered the notion of the Black superpredator.

But the solution wasn't easy. In the community, many people knew who the most dangerous people were, but lack of trust in law enforcement and fear of retribution enabled these men to stay on the street. With funding from the National Institute of Justice, Kennedy helped bring stakeholders to the table—outreach workers, community groups, and local and federal law enforcement. Beginning in 1996, Operation Ceasefire and the Boston Gun Project aimed to stop gang violence by reaching out directly to gang members, letting them know how much their own community needed the violence to stop, offering them immediate services and support, and spelling out what law enforcement would do if the violence continued. In addition, the effort sought to disrupt the illegal firearms market, which was mostly white. In the first two and a half years of the programs, youth homicides in Boston dropped by 63 percent and all homicides by half. The project got the attention of President Clinton and Attorney General Janet Reno.

Another influential program was developed around 1999 in Chicago by Gary Slutkin, an epidemiologist who had traveled the world battling infectious diseases. When he returned to Chicago, homicides in the city had soared. Slutkin was inspired to examine map-based data of the violence. He reached a similar conclusion to Kennedy. The maps showed clusters, which was a familiar sight for Slutkin. It was the way infectious diseases spread. He postulated that the way to stop the violence was to interrupt its transmission.

Slutkin's program, which he also named Ceasefire (and was later renamed Cure Violence), was in essence a street-outreach approach, involving "violence interrupters," or community members who were close enough to the people committing the violence that they could intercede. Often the best interrupters were former gang members, some of whom turned out not to be fully out of the life. It was a similar challenge faced by experimental anti-gang programs for years, including in Denver with Mike Asberry. In Slutkin's program, potentially violent gang members would be brought into discussions with social workers and with law enforcement, who warned them of the consequences of their actions. The program was piloted in 2000 in the West Garfield neighborhood, then one of the city's most violent. In its first year, Ceasefire reported a 67 percent drop in shootings. Slutkin began to get foundation grants, and expanded into other neighborhoods and cities.

The third major effort, Project Exile, an anti-gun program, was funded in part by the Department of Justice and piloted in 1997 by the U.S. attorney's office in Richmond, and run by James Comey, then a managing assistant U.S. attorney for the Eastern District of Virginia. Situated on I-95, Richmond was a major drug transfer point that averaged a hundred murders a year. The FBI ranked it the second most dangerous city in America. "Most violence in Richmond is what I call 'happenstance homicides,'" Comey said at the time. "It's what would have been a fistfight or a stabbing 15 or 20 years ago but like all altercations, it ratchets up to the most lethal available weapon. And because the gun is there, it's a shooting."

Project Exile was a federal law enforcement program that created partnerships with local law enforcement agencies in the hope of reducing violent crime by taking guns off the street. The program's name was meant as a warning to lawbreakers: if convicted in federal court of illegally carrying a gun, one could be exiled to any one of America's prisons, far from home. Exile's strategy included a media campaign warning that possession of a gun was punishable by five years. Richmond's mayor, Tim Kaine, a future senator and vice presidential candidate, was a key ally and supporter of the program.

Officials said crimes involving guns plummeted 65 percent in the program's first three years. But Exile was not without detractors. The Richmond public defender's office decried Exile as racist; more than 90 percent of those arrested were Black. The National Rifle Association (NRA) became a surprising supporter of Exile, donating $100,000. Some activists suggested that if the goal was taking guns out of the hands of young Black men, the NRA was in favor of it. The NRA said its support was based on Exile's premise of enforcing existing gun laws rather than creating new ones.

In March 1999, President Clinton ordered Attorney General Janet Reno and Robert Rubin, head of the Treasury Department— which then housed the Bureau of Alcohol, Tobacco, and Firearms (ATF)—to come up with a comprehensive federal plan to get guns out of the hands of criminals. Richmond's Project Exile and Boston's Ceasefire would be the templates. The ATF, which would soon undergo a major expansion, would be the lead agency.

TERRANCE RECOVERED FROM bowel surgery and was reassigned to another prison, Four Mile. He was determined to stay out of trouble for just a few months to get a parole hearing. But he was also well known as a Blood and with that came provocations from Crips. He soon got into a fight and was transferred to a higher-security prison,

Buena Vista, known in Colorado's gang community as "Gladiator School." It housed the highest number of Bloods and Crips in the state.

One section of the prison included a metal shop, where inmates worked. The shop was also a supplier of improvised weapons. Like many of the inmates at Buena Vista, Terrance made sure he was armed with handmade shanks from the shop. The environment was dangerous and unpredictable. Terrance walked around with a thick *Vibe* magazine under his shirt as a protective vest. One day, he and another Blood chased some Crips around the yard because they owed $25 on a drug buy. When Terrance got back to his cell, the police were there. They found a shank behind his ceiling light fixture.

The Chaffee County District Attorney charged Terrance with a felony, for possession of contraband. ShowBizz almost never cried, but when he arrived in a new locked-down wing of the prison, he cried for days. It had been a tough ride through the penitentiary system, and he'd been only weeks from a mandatory release date. Now he was facing up to six additional years. With little option, he went to court in his jumpsuit and pleaded guilty. The judge sentenced him to two more years, with a three-year "tail," a long parole.

He was reassigned again. This time it was to the one place no convict in Colorado hopes to see, Colorado State Penitentiary, or CSP, the state's only Level 5 maximum-security prison. Most inmates serve under Administrative Segregation, or solitary confinement. Terrance was no exception.

For the next twenty months, he lived in a seven-by-thirteen-foot cell, with no window. His meals were delivered though a slot. He did not see the sun. Three times a week, his wrists and ankles were shackled, and guards led him to the shower. *I'm in literal bondage*, he thought.

The one thing he looked at all day was the inmate directly across from him. George White was a member of the Black Guerrilla Family, a politically active gang formed at San Quentin in the late '60s during the Black Power movement.

George knew Swahili and sign language and offered to teach Terrance. It would enable them to speak freely. They practiced every day. George would write a word on a piece of paper and hold it up. Then they would practice the sign, and then the Swahili word. Terrance learned hundreds of Swahili words and became fluent in sign language.

The pod, an oval-shaped unit, housed sixteen convicts on two floors. Sometimes one of them went crazy, and screamed and bashed his head into the wall. To get by, they collected old fruit, bread, and yeast and took turns making it into hooch. They would put the fruit into a pillowcase, add water, and smash it flat and let it ferment under the bed. The smell was strong, so it had to be "burped" frequently, for which they used the toilet. They had fishing-type lines made from the threads of their bedsheets, and when the hooch was ready, everyone got their empty shampoo bottles filled and sent back to them on the fishing line. Together they got drunk and felt crazy and free for a few hours. Other times Terrance thought about killing Crips. Every other day he did a thousand push-ups. He jogged in place.

A MONTH AFTER President Clinton unveiled Project Exile, some of his cabinet members flew to Denver for the 1999 National Conference of Black Mayors. Mayor Webb, a close ally of the administration, was the body's vice president. For Webb, it was a precarious time. He was weeks away from an election he hoped would give him a third term, but some northeast Denver residents had threatened to disrupt the conference if Webb would not agree to discuss issues "that concern the masses of black people." Prominent members of Denver's Black community had withdrawn their support, among them Dr. James "Daddy-O" Walker, the owner of the influential KDKO community radio station that had helped Webb get elected the first time, in 1991.

Just as the conference was beginning, on the morning of April 20, 1999, it was abruptly derailed. Webb received word that two students at Columbine High School in the affluent southwest Denver suburb of Littleton were barricaded inside the school. They had killed twelve classmates and a teacher with military-grade machine guns, which they ultimately turned on themselves. Mayor Webb led conference attendees on a march from the hotel to a church to pray. The "Columbine Massacre" was then the deadliest school shooting in U.S. history.

Just as Len Bias's noncrack death galvanized Congress to pass new criminal laws used primarily in low-income neighborhoods with gang activity, Denver's suburban high school shooting turbocharged national efforts to pass stricter gun laws—laws whose enforcement efforts would focus on African American gang neighborhoods, through Project Exile.

Colorado's new U.S. attorney, Tom Strickland, was sworn in the day after Columbine. A former corporate law partner at Denver's political powerhouse Brownstein law firm, Strickland had never tried a criminal case. He announced that he would make Colorado one of the first places in the nation to run Project Exile.

Webb won a third term as mayor with a record 81 percent of the vote. And like Jim Comey and Tim Kaine, he and Strickland formed a partnership to test the new federal anti-gun program. *USA Today* deemed Colorado "a new ground zero for gun control politics."

A DEPARTMENT OF Corrections van dropped Terrance at the bus station in Pueblo. He was given a hundred-dollar bill. He was twenty-four years old, and free again after nearly four years, pursuant to the conditions of his parole, which included a stipulation that he not go to the Holly or associate with gang members.

Ernestine picked him up in LoDo near Denver's Union Station, where she'd arrived forty-five years earlier. She thought Terrance looked older, more serious. His hair was long and in two tight braids on either side of his neck. She told him he could stay with her but that there were some things going on. "You need to keep your head on a swivel," she said. They turned into the small parking lot at A&A

Fish. Outside Vick's barbershop across the street, a cluster of cars blocked the road. Ernestine had hoped it wouldn't be the first thing Terrance saw.

Vick, the barber whom Terrance had known since childhood, had been killed by the Crips the previous night. He was shot three times while driving home from a bar with three other Bloods. Age twenty-eight, he left behind his wife and two kids.

Within hours, Terrance had met up with some other Bloods and acquired a semiautomatic rifle. He spent the night cruising past Project Exile billboards—"Pack an Illegal Gun, Pack Your Bags for Prison"—looking for Vick's killer. The Bloods knew who it was. Three witnesses were in the car with him. But they wouldn't be going to the police. In this jurisdiction, justice was meted out in the streets.

A rash of shootings and firebombings ensued, claiming several lives. The *Rocky Mountain News* coverage made reference to the Summer of Violence. Soon Vick's killer would come face-to-face with ShowBizz.

A WEEK LATER, the District 2 police captain Joseph Bini led a SWAT team through Five Points. Colorado's Project Exile included some high-profile corporate partnerships. On that day, the force included the Colorado Rockies' star second baseman Mike Lansing, doing a ridealong.

Around 2 p.m., Bini's team pulled up outside a multilevel home of an alleged drug dealer. Using a battering ram, they charged through the door of a second-floor apartment. Kneeling on the bedroom floor was their apparent target. Within minutes he was dead.

But Ismael Mena, who was forty-five, wasn't a drug dealer. He worked a night shift at a Coca-Cola bottling factory in north Denver, and on the streets of his neighborhood he sold corn, strawberries, and flavored ice. He sent much of his earnings home to his wife and nine children, who were still in Mexico.

Inside invisible Denver, anger over Mena's death grew until months later, word reached a local television reporter, who uncovered an internal police department complaint. A District 2 officer said she was pressured to forge documents about nonexistent drug complaints at Mena's address. Officer Bini, apparently acting on the word of an informant, had led his team into the wrong house.

Over the course of the 1990s, Denver police had shot 126 people, killing 35 of them. No officer had ever been charged, and though this case seemed clear cut, it, too, resulted in no charges. To the dismay of many in northeast Denver, Mayor Webb agreed with the district attorney's decision. "If Mr. Mena didn't have a gun and wasn't pointing it at police officers, he'd be alive today," Webb said.

U.S. Attorney Strickland hailed Colorado's Project Exile as a success. Gun prosecutions tripled. But the effect on violent crime was inconclusive. During the program's three years, youth homicides rose from thirteen in 2000 to twenty-four in 2002. Though official statistics underrepresented the gang connections to the deaths, it was plain to residents of northeast Denver that most of Denver's homicides were connected to the gang war. And the majority of them remained unsolved. The botched, deadly raid of Mena's home deepened the community's mistrust of law enforcement.

Nationally, opponents of Exile put their objections on the record. "Project Exile has transformed our court into a minor-grade police court," the federal judge Richard Williams of Virginia wrote in a 2001 letter to then U.S. Supreme Court Justice William Rehnquist. "More than 200 gun-possession cases totally lacking in federal significance have been processed through our court. Not only does this do violence to the concept of federalism, but the cost to national taxpayers is at least three times more than if the state handled these cases."

But in May 2001, President George W. Bush announced a $450 million expansion of Exile, which he rebranded Project Safe Neighborhoods.

.   .   .

Reentry into the community was difficult for Terrance. Many of his old friends were in prison or dead. Clarice and his son, Javon, had moved to Sacramento. Terrance was required to attend anger management classes; he showed up carrying a gun, which, as a convicted felon, he was forbidden to carry, for life. He didn't care. To him, there was no choice. Armed Crips were in the class and out on the street. He needed protection.

He also needed money and kept an ear out for a good drug connection, and accepted a friend's referral to work at a call center for Sportsman's Warehouse, a clothing superstore in south Denver. Soon he had enough money to put down a first payment on one of Ernestine's cars, a Fleetwood Cadillac that she sold him for $1,200. He bought custom gold rims. In order to put them on he borrowed a specialized Dayton hammer from a younger Blood, Kelly "Lil Spliff" Glasper.

A few days later, Lil Spliff, the younger brother of a Blood Terrance knew, returned to Ernestine's house and accused Terrance of damaging his hammer. "Get the fuck off my property," Terrance told him. He was sure he hadn't done anything to the hammer, and in Terrance's world, his seniority and position in the gang meant that Lil Spliff had no right to talk to him like that. Lil Spliff, who was six feet six, went back to his car and, it seemed to Terrance, was acting like he was getting a gun from under his seat. ShowBizz reached for the Mac 11 in the flowerpot. Lil Spliff sped off as Terrance fired at his car. An hour later, Terrance heard footsteps on the roof. A SWAT team had Ernestine's house surrounded.

This time when Terrance entered Building 8, it was on lockdown. Inmates had been fighting guards, who had shut off the water. By the second day, the place smelled like a sewer, and dehydration was setting in. Terrance, who was on the bottom floor, whispered up to a gang member above him who had a lighter. "Light this motherfucker up," he said. A flaming pillow landed on the floor.

Others followed. An uprising that sent several guards and inmates to the hospital ensued.

Terrance and five other Bloods were accused of starting the riot. They were sent to Building 6, the infamous "dungeon," where they were locked down twenty-three hours a day. One day the guards told them they could go back—so long as they agreed to be commingled with the Crips. Terrance knew that if they refused, the guards would tell the Crips. Terrance and Cedrick "Baby Brazy" Watkins cut their long hair off in preparation. They would be outnumbered about twenty-five to five. And one of the Crip inmates was the barber Vick's killer, Derrick "Lil Crip" Wilford.

They didn't even make it down to the yard. As soon as they got downstairs, they were fighting. Lil Crip and Terrance were among the few still standing by the end of the hour. Terrance quickly headed inside to the second floor, where a Blood he knew handed him a shank. He hid behind a wall waiting for Lil Crip. When he saw him, he leapt out and drove the homemade knife into Lil Crip's neck.

Lil Crip screamed and fell. He pulled out the shank and ran toward Terrance, knocking him down. Others gathered along the rails as two of the city's most powerful gang members faced each other. Terrance got up and kicked Lil Crip in the nose. They squared off again but police in riot gear appeared and they split like nothing had happened. Terrance walked back to his cell. When he saw the police were gone, he went back to the second-floor railing and climbed over it, dropping himself down to the main floor, where everyone on the rails could see him. "Y'all a bunch of bitches!" he yelled to the Crips. "That's why your homey got fucked up."

TERRANCE RAISED HIS bail money and got out, but Granny wouldn't let him back into the house. His attitude was making people think he had a death wish. One day he went to pick up his son, Javon, at Clarice's cousin's house and found a Crip he recognized sitting on the couch with Clarice's cousin. He went outside and got a rifle, and headed back. "I'll shoot your guts out and dump you in the dumpster," he said.

Then, according to Clarice's cousin, Terrance pushed her down and choked her, ripped the phone out of the wall, and told them that if they called the police, someone would be killed. But they did call the police, and Terrance was picked up. This time, on his way into the jail, he asked one of the sheriffs to place him anywhere but Building 8. "I could get killed in there," he said.

FOR THE FIRST time, Terrance entered Building 22, where he knew his father had been saved. He saw the carpeted floors and went to the phone bank in the dayroom but had to quickly hang up. Passing by one of the entrances was someone he didn't expect to see: Lil Crip. Nearby was a broom. Terrance grabbed it, and backed up against the wall.

He heard footsteps from another direction. Terrance turned to see Lil Crip, who pulled a book from behind his back and set it on the table. "Bible study, every day," he said. Terrance watched as Lil Crip walked out.

Terrance started to see the group in the yard. The leader was an older former Crip from LA called Brother Doug. He knew Raymond Washington and Tookie Williams, who was writing children's books and preaching peace from Death Row in California.

One day Terrance was playing basketball and ended up on a team with Brother Doug. He told Terrance he wasn't against gangs, but gang violence, Brother Doug said, was "demonism." "If it ain't about God, it ain't about nothin'," he told Terrance.

Terrance joined the Bible group. One night he called his mom, but she wouldn't talk to him. Every time he opened his mouth, she said, "*When* is it going to stop?" He went to the TV room, where a documentary about the life of Martin Luther King was on. Terrance realized he didn't know much about MLK. He sat down.

The program covered how King had been a target of the FBI's COINTELPRO effort. And it included black-and-white footage from the church gymnasium in Memphis where King gave his "Mountaintop" speech.

"*I don't know what will happen now,*" King said to a group of supporters. "*We've got some difficult days ahead. But it really doesn't matter with me now. Because I've been to the mountaintop.*

"*Like anybody I would like to live a long life, longevity has its place. But I'm not concerned about that now. I just want to do God's will.*

"*And he has allowed me to go up to the mountaintop and I've looked over and I've seen the Promised Land. I may not get there with you but I want you to know tonight that we as a people will get to the Promised Land.*

"*So I'm happy tonight. I'm not worried about anything, I'm not fearing any man. Mine eyes have seen the glory of the coming of the Lord.*"

Less than twenty-four hours later, King was assassinated.

Terrance went back to his cell and cried all night. King had overcome and accomplished so much in his thirty-nine years, Terrance thought. He couldn't think of one good thing he'd done in his twenty-four. He was determined to make something of his life.

The next morning on the breakfast line some of the guys greeted him. "What's up, Biz?"

"Don't call me that no more," he said. "My name is Terrance."

They laughed. "Okay, Biz."

"Okay," Terrance said. "We'll just see, then." He sat alone at another table.

The DA's office muscled Terrance on the case of shooting at Kelly Glasper's car. In addition to three felony charges—attempted murder, first-degree assault, and possession of a weapon—District Attorney Bill Ritter added the discretionary "habitual criminal" charge to each count, the "big bitch," as it was called on the street. It added an enhanced and mandatory sentence. If convicted on all counts, Terrance could die in prison. His public defender strongly advised he seek a plea. Terrance refused. He was sure Glasper wouldn't show up to testify. It was against the gang code. And without him, Terrance knew, the case would be weak.

Indeed, Glasper was already ducking investigators, and the DA's office faced a familiar dilemma: whether to subpoena someone to testify when doing so would likely place them in danger. Darryl Givens, the Crip who testified against Orlando Domena and was later assassinated, would never be forgotten in the Denver DA's office. And so, days before Terrance's trial, the DA's office informed Terrance it would recommend a two- to six-year sentence if Terrance pleaded guilty to two felonies, for menacing with a gun and illegal possession of a gun.

Terrance took the deal, hoping for two. The judge gave him seven.

At "DRDC," the diagnostic center where inmates went for evaluation and prison assignment, Terrance told his social worker and case manager he was no longer a gang member. They had heard it before. Even from him.

He researched his charges in the law library and discovered he had 180 days to file a motion for reconsideration. He enrolled in a computer skills class and filed the motion himself. "This defendant wants the court to know that he has re-structured his thinking about his past gang involvement . . . and that given my past history, that I could be a huge influence in the lives of many young children who might make some of the same mistakes that have caused me to be incarcerated today . . . I hope you won't view this as just another jailhouse conversion," he wrote.

The motion was denied.

TERRANCE WAS SENT to his seventh Colorado prison, Fremont, another heavily gang-affiliated facility. Terrance was assigned to a cell with his childhood friend Cedrick "Baby Brazy" Watkins.

"I ain't a Blood no more," Terrance told him. Baby Brazy asked for a transfer. It wasn't safe to be around Terrance. Blood In, Blood Out, was the saying. Terrance was liable to get beaten for leaving the gang.

One day in the yard, a Blood Terrance trusted nodded toward the back fence, where a group of Bloods were huddled. Terrance had already felt the tension at breakfast. He headed straight toward them.

"I know what y'all are talkin' about," Terrance told them. "I've never disrespected the hood, I've never snitched on anyone. I've been having y'all as a crutch my whole life. I just want to do this on my own." The group, which included Pernell Hines's younger brother Leland, looked at Terrance. "If something happens to me," Terrance said, acknowledging he would no longer have their protection, "then I don't know. But I'm asking you, don't sneak up on me, or cut my neck in the chow line, or jump me out here. Just let me do me."

THE PRISON WARDEN approved Terrance's job request to be a janitor, which paid $1.50 a day and enabled him to be out of his cell, traveling to all the buildings. In his first week, sirens went off and the prison was locked down. In New York, the twin towers had just come down.

But most of the time, the outside world did not exist. Still, Terrance felt his life expanding. As he walked the prison, he interacted with Latinos, Muslims, Sureños, Norteños, none of whom he would have talked to before. "Don't even go there," he responded if they asked him to transport drugs or a weapon. Once people saw that he was serious, he recognized that he gained their respect. Some gang members confessed to him that they, too, wanted out. Terrance became certain he could make a difference.

WORD OF SHOWBIZZ's conversion spread, all the way to Ricky Ross's Texas federal prison cell, which he shared with a Montbello Crip. Terrance got letters from people inside and outside the system. One of them was Lil Crip.

"I write this letter with a heavy heart," Lil Crip wrote in pencil from the Denver Jail.

> Our brother Robert ('Lil Loco') was found guilty today and he's in the hole now because he threw the water pitcher and they say a chair at the jury.
>
> I wanted to let you know so that you could send him some words of encouragement. Because he needs to hear from the body that it's not over and that God has the last say so on all matters . . . I know he's hurting. The whole building just seems darker.
>
> We don't know how truly blessed we are. After all we've done and been through we've still got another chance at life. They've offered me a deal for 5 years. Can you believe I thought about not taking it? Well I'm trying to get in court so I can take it and get out and allow God to use this life for His glory. Because you know and I know that could easily be one of us in Robert's shoes.
>
> I want to thank you for walking with integrity and the character of a man of God right in the belly of the beast.

Terrance continued to receive news from all over Denver's gang world and decided to start a newsletter. He called it *The Way*. He got the computer class teacher to let him use one of the stations every two weeks. He wrote the newsletter with a pencil in his cell then typed it up twice a month. It offered two to four pages of updates from the community and proverbs from the Bible that Terrance found helpful. He emailed it to a woman he had been dating on the outside, Desirée Mayberry, who distributed it in the Holly and the Dahlia, and at Ernestine's restaurant.

Black-owned media was virtually nonexistent in Denver. It consisted of two small publications, the weekly *5 Points News*, published by the activist Brother Jeff Fard, and the monthly *Urban Spectrum*. James "Daddy-O" Walker's flagship community radio station KDKO was shutting its lights. In its heyday, Daddy-O had used the station to discuss social justice issues and question lawmakers. But few could afford to pay for advertising. In April 2002, he got a call from a representative of an unlikely source, the Denver billionaire Philip Anschutz. Anschutz made Daddy-O an offer for the station of $2.2 million. Daddy-O, who was seventy-two, couldn't turn it down. "KDKO has been silenced," announced the station's former website. "The Afro-American community of Denver is mourning the loss of their voice." Anschutz changed the station's call letters and turned it into a news talk radio channel. A year later, he shut it down altogether.

TERRANCE READ Martin Luther King's biography, and *Soul on Ice*, the autobiographical essays of Eldridge Cleaver, which Cleaver had written from California's Folsom State Prison. They told of Cleaver's transformation from a street criminal and rapist to a revolutionary and adherent of Marxism. And he read *The Autobiography of Malcolm X*; Terrance learned that Malcolm had been known as Detroit Red back in the mid-1940s, when he was hustling and selling drugs in his late teens in Harlem and Boston.

Terrance kept notes. "We can no longer allow our past to destroy what God has for us in the future," he wrote. He was determined to address injustices, and started a Bible group.

The prison chaplain, Gary Pritt, agreed to baptize Terrance. Over the next few weeks, on his rounds, Terrance invited his friends to be his witnesses. When the day came, inmates filled the chapel and flowed into the halls. Terrance nearly cried. Baby Brazy came, as did many of the Bloods.

The prison staff were concerned. No one of Terrance's gang stature had publicly renounced their affiliation in prison.

One day, Terrance was in the yard when a riot was brewing. In a show of force, the Crips and Bloods had joined together against a powerful Mexican gang who they said owed them money on heroin deals. Terrance could see that it was the younger guys in front, as usual. The older guys used them like pawns. Terrance went straight between the two sides and called out to the OGs in the back. "If you all want to fight," Terrance said, "why don't you just fight me?"

No one moved. "You're such fighters but you won't fight me?" Terrance said.

The tension fizzled and the groups dispersed. The following day Terrance was called in to his caseworker's office and asked about the incident. He explained what happened but was told that a decision by the warden had already been made. If he was able to stop a riot, he says he was told, he could also be able to start one. He was transferred to another facility.

In the fall of 2004, George drove to the Way Way—or halfway house—to pick up his son. His south Denver home was only a short ride away. Like many from northeast Denver, George had moved to the suburbs seeking lower rent.

He'd also found full-time work, gassing up planes for United Airlines on the tarmac of Denver's new airport. It paid $23 an hour, and George's boss let him slip out to do an occasional funeral. Everyone who ran into George could see his transformation was real. Funeral home owners recommended the former Pipkin hearse driver to grieving families. George's sermons quickly became known for their emotion and flair. "When a person dies they leave for a new address," George often preached, to shouts of Amen and That's right. "Home ain't where I live," George called out. "Home is where I'm going!"

George's father, Big John, helped him get accredited to preach at the Denver County Jail. George's favorite sermon was also his most requested. It was his version of "The Valley and the Dry Bones." George called it "The County and the Dry Bones." Tears flowed regularly. "Come on, somebody," he beckoned until at least one person came forward to accept Jesus.

George was proud that Terrance had been saved. He had read every issue of The Way and distributed it at the funeral homes and churches where he preached.

Terrance's halfway house was in a partially developed suburban office park. He shared a large room with seven others, in bunk beds. They could leave during the day on approved purposes such as for a class or job.

When George pulled up, Terrance was outside in wireframe John Lennon glasses, looking righteous, George thought. Terrance noticed that George had put on some weight. He wondered if his dad could still do a backflip on the sidewalk. They embraced and had a short laugh. "We're blessed to even be standin' here," George said.

They drove around southeast Denver, where Terrance filled out job applications at fast food chains and retail stores, checking yes, he was a convicted felon, wondering who would hire him.

They both had the activism bug. George had been preaching at the funerals of gang members; the unrecognized pain of their mothers had gotten to him. He wanted to organize a march in their honor. Terrance said he wanted to start a gang prevention program for kids. "I'm calling it Prodigal Son Initiative," he said. As George knew, the prodigal son was a parable from Luke in the New Testament, about a young man who abandons his family and wastes his fortune only to return home for redemption.

TERRANCE APPLIED FOR and was accepted into a leadership course at the Community Resource Center, an established Denver organization that fostered nonprofits. Most of the students were middle-aged, well-off white women for whom Terrance was something of a novelty. The ornately tattooed ex-con was handsome, humble, and well-spoken, with a southern-inflected accent they didn't recognize. "I'm just here to learn, y'all," he said. He kept his ankle bracelet hidden beneath his pants.

They told him they had no idea there were gangs in Denver. After his presentation, one of his classmates wrote him a check.

George was well aware of Terrance's leadership skills, and he invited his son to a planning meeting for his march. At the meeting, Terrance was annoyed by the lack of progress and threatened to leave. "Are we just talking or are we going to do something?" he said. That was why George had brought him. Terrance helped get a consensus in favor of George's idea of marching in honor of the mothers who had lost children to gang violence and police shoot-ings. "Not Another Mother's Child," they called it. The route would run from Five Points to the Holly.

Terrance asked his parole officer if he could participate. The an-swer was no: he wasn't allowed near the Holly. But on the day of the march he couldn't help himself. He had George drop him off near the shopping center, where he would try to join the march's final leg.

It had been almost five years since he'd been in the Holly. It looked the same. Some Bloods whom Terrance didn't recognize came toward him.

"What's up," he said.

"Who the fuck are you?" one responded.

Terrance cleared out and found his way to the Dahlia, where he waited for what turned out to be about 100 participants to arrive on their way to the Holly.

ONE DAY, TERRANCE was at the Way Way when a call for him came in. The voice on the other end was unmistakable. It was Rev Kelly.

Terrance had never spoken to Rev, nor had he wanted to. But he was trying to shed his old negative mindset. Whatever Terrance thought about Rev, Rev was the most prominent anti-gang activist in the city. Rev told Terrance he'd heard that Terrance had become a Christian and invited him to visit his after-school program.

Terrance arrived at an old cavernous bus garage in Cole, a mostly African American neighborhood adjacent to Five Points. A huge metal door clanked open. About thirty kids, ages eight to fifteen, were running around the large industrial space. Along the rail outside the office were two high-ranking OGs Terrance knew. He couldn't believe it. It was a violation for him even to be near them.

One was Rodney "Big Rod" Jackson, a Park Hill OG Blood and a close associate of Carl "Fat Daddy" McKay. He was a crack dealer, recently out of prison. Terrance was disturbed. In his view, they were not role models. Terrance decided not to tell Rev that he was planning on starting his own program.

AFTER A YEAR at the Way Way, Terrance was permitted to leave. He had continued seeing Desirée even while in prison, and he moved into her three-bedroom house in Aurora. She was the manager of a dental office, making about $40,000 a year. She'd saved up and got a mortgage on her own.

Terrance had landed a minimum-wage job at Einstein Bros. Bagels. His outgoing personality helped him move quickly from the kitchen to the register, where he loved chatting with customers, mostly white people he'd never had a chance to meet before. In the afternoons, the restaurant, which was near Cherry Creek High School, filled with latchkey kids of all races. With the permission of his boss, Terrance created an after-school program in the store. At 3 p.m., they moved the tables around, changed the music, did homework, and played games.

Terrance was obsessed with making up for lost time. Desirée gave birth to their first child, a girl, Trinity. And Terrance called his ex-girlfriend Clarice in Sacramento and convinced her to send Javon to Denver to live with him and Desirée. He wanted to be a father to Javon.

Terrance's mother had overcome her drug problems and become a successful real estate broker. She gave Terrance a car. Desirée taught him Excel and QuickBooks. He opened a bank account for the first time and recruited a board of directors for his anti-gang organization that included Laquita Taylor, of Taylor Mortuary, an old friend of his father's, and Michelle Wheeler, president of the Northeast Park Hill Coalition, who had seen Terrance speak at a school and was impressed.

Desirée was proud of Terrance, but concerned. She was from Northeast Park Hill and she knew that trying to take on the Bloods on their own turf could be dangerous. Sometimes Terrance sounded like he was prophesying his own downfall at the hands of an as-yet-unknown enemy. He told Desirée he was going to do everything by the book because "one day, I already know, someone is gonna try to come for me."

The strategic plan Terrance wrote for Prodigal Son included his own story of going from honor student to gang member, and how there were thousands of kids just like him in northeast Denver with nowhere to go after school. Northeast Park Hill mothers had already told him they would enroll their kids if a free program existed. All Terrance needed was a place to host the youth.

He took his proposal to Hallett Elementary School, one of the schools that had been integrated following the 1973 Supreme Court case. Terrance had graduated from Hallett in 1986, as the neighborhood's gang violence was beginning. Administrators and teachers at the school were taken with Terrance, who exuded positive energy and had deep connections to the neighborhood. They let Terrance use the premises.

That fall Terrance enrolled thirty-five youths, the maximum his insurance would allow. They met in a classroom where Terrance began each day with a pledge he made them memorize. "This is my life, my most valuable possession . . . I will always respect myself, my family, and all others . . . I am strong and my value cannot be measured." He wanted them to have pride and self-discipline. If any of the kids fought each other, they were suspended. He arranged math and writing tutors. And they took field trips to the mountains, places he'd never been. Once some Denver Nuggets players came to speak to them.

Javon, who was nine, had moved back to Denver to live with his dad and Desirée. He remembered wondering if his dad would ever get out of prison. Now he was a local celebrity.

"Prodigal Son Leaves Jail, Starts Nonprofit for Kids," read the headline in the *Rocky Mountain News* on February 6, 2006. A front-page photo depicted Terrance with three kids in his program holding up their report cards. It was all A's and B's. "[Terrance's] personality and the way that he approaches children, and him living that life is the value of it," Lazette Ray, an administrator at Hallett, said. "It's real. It's not pretend."

Rev was also quoted. "I feel like a Moses and I'm looking for a little Joshua to come forward and take my place here," he said. "I've heard so many people try to do what I do, but they're not prepared for it . . . [Terrance] has been consistent. He certainly has the potential to be the Joshua."

IN 2003, THE LoDo brewery owner and raconteur John Hickenlooper, who hadn't voted in the previous mayoral election, was elected Denver mayor after a campaign *The New York Times* called "remarkable in modern American politics, one nearly devoid of rancor, mudslinging and negative advertising."

Twelve years of Wellington Webb had left some Denverites frustrated with the basic workings of local government. Hick, as Hickenlooper was called affectionately, appeared in a series of folksy campaign ads, wearing cowboy boots and a hat, and offering spare change to aggravated motorists trying to feed broken parking meters. "Making change" was his pledge. He termed the effort a "movement" aimed at taking on "the fundamental nonsense of government."

In 2005, Hickenlooper, who had lived in LoDo, moved to Park Hill. He and his wife purchased a $1.6 million estate, built in 1905, a dozen blocks south of the Holly. The mean streets of northeast Denver would never be far.

Two weeks before Hickenlooper assumed office, District 2 police responded to a call half a block from the Holly. It was the Childses' home. The family had lived there for decades. The youngest son, Paul Childs, was mentally disabled. Paul's mother had called 911, because Paul was threatening her with a knife. Seven officers surrounded Paul, tasers aimed. Then Officer James Turney—who the previous evening had threatened his own mother-in-law—opened fire with his primary weapon. Paul was hit four times and died in front of family and neighbors.

Park Hill activists spread the word, and within a week, the celebrity defense lawyer Johnnie Cochran was holding a press conference on the Childses' lawn, demanding justice. Officer Turney was not charged, but Cochran was able to get the City of Denver to pay $1.3 million to the family in a civil suit. It was the last case Cochran handled before his death from a brain tumor.

Hickenlooper saw the development of northeast Denver as key to the city's economic growth. He created a Five Points Business Improvement District with incentives for new development. And in 2005, with the media in tow, he donned a hard hat and hopped aboard a tractor to celebrate the demolition of the Dahlia Shopping Center. After years of empty promises and false starts under Mayor Webb, not to mention the discovery of methane gas leaking from the site, the shopping center was finally going to begin a major redevelopment.

The Dahlia's owner, Verne Harris, a friend of Webb's and one of Denver's most prominent African American landowners, agreed to sell the site and let the city set the rules for its redevelopment. The Denver Urban Renewal Authority (DURA) sent out a request for proposals. Bidders were required to provide a mix of single-family housing and senior housing with a health clinic and fifteen thousand square feet of mixed-use commercial space. Only two bids came in. One was from Wellington Webb, whose team included Steven Farber of the national law firm Brownstein, Hyatt & Farber. Objections were raised about cronyism and the fact that Webb had no experience as a developer, but DURA selected Webb's bid. Harris sold the historic site to Webb's group, for $3.4 million.

Seeing this, the owner of the Holly Shopping Center, Johnny Copeland, put the center up for sale after owning it for twelve years. A white developer, Michael Bullock, offered $1.1 million. Copeland, who was sixty-nine, took the deal.

With new ownership, many in the neighborhood expected improvements. Instead Holly Square became the scene of increased police activity as the city adopted "Broken Windows," the policing strategy that Hickenlooper had championed and with which Rudy Giuliani had claimed success in New York. The Broken Windows theory held that a crackdown on small offenses like public drunkenness and vandalism would create an environment that rewarded positive behavior and discouraged serious crime. Critics charged that the program was implemented in a racially biased manner and caused needless arrests for people who couldn't afford the fines.

The police presence in the neighborhood was also reinforced by the addition of a new $6 million taxpayer-funded building three blocks up Holly Street from the square. After decades on Colorado Boulevard, the District 2 substation was moving into Northeast Park Hill.

WORD SPREAD ABOUT Terrance. He was asked to speak at churches and schools as well as at the metro area's juvenile detention facilities. He wore khaki pants and a Prodigal Son shirt with long sleeves to cover his tattoos. He told his own story, sometimes lifting his shirt to show the large zipper scar up his abdomen from the Summer of Violence. Principals and administrators gave him standing ovations; kids lined up to high-five him.

One day, Rebecca Hea, executive director of the Denver Children's Home, asked him to consider applying for a position as a community education liaison, helping kids who were going through the youth justice system. He got the job. The Children's Home let him work three-quarters time, so that he could also continue Prodigal Son. Terrance quit his job at Einstein Bros. Bagels. Fresh off parole, he had a $40,000-a-year social services job, and his own office inside one of the state's best-known and well-connected charities.

That winter, Oprah Winfrey donated a warehouse full of clothing to the home. Terrance volunteered to give it out. He rode around northeast Denver like Santa Claus, stopping at every barbershop and community center. His fervor to help the community was also about healing himself. Privately he struggled with memories of the destruction he'd wrought and the trauma he'd witnessed.

On his rounds he ran into old friends and former adversaries. As they caught up, they couldn't help but feel the presence of those who had lost their lives. Survivor guilt caused some to turn to drugs or alcohol; some told Terrance they wanted out. One day Terrance ran into Mike Asberry. They locked arms and hugged. Terrance noticed that Mike's eyes were hollowed out, his gaze distant. He carried a Bible that George had given him.

Mike said he was out of the game. Rev Kelly had helped him get a job at a Starbucks owned by Magic Johnson, who'd opened several stores in the Denver area, hiring primarily minorities and ex-cons. But Mike's job didn't last. He kept catching cases—seventeen of them between 2004 and 2006, including five assaults. "Hang in there, brother," Terrance told him. But he left feeling shaken. He wondered if his own past would catch up to him.

IN THE EARLY hours of New Year's Day 2007, Denver finally had its own Columbine moment, a shooting that would define the city's efforts to fight gang violence. Several members of the Denver Broncos and Nuggets celebrated the new year at a downtown nightclub, where they had an altercation over spilled champagne with members of the "Elite Eight" Crips, a powerful subset of Denver's Crips. The athletes left in a Hummer limousine. At a stoplight, a GMC Suburban pulled up alongside in the snow.

Shots were fired into the Hummer. One of them hit twenty-four-year-old Darrent Williams, a starting defensive back for the Broncos, in the neck, killing him instantly.

The drive-by murder of a Bronco shocked the city. At Williams's televised funeral his three-year-old son asked his mom if his father had his cell phone; he wanted to call him. Many waited impatiently for Mayor Hickenlooper to speak out.

"Mayor All Quiet on the Gang Front," read the headline in a series of pointed columns by the *Rocky Mountain News* sports columnist Dave Krieger. "All anyone is asking him to do is his job," Krieger wrote. "Provide leadership, acknowledge the problem, talk to affected community groups, tell them what he's doing, offer to coordinate those trying to help."

State senator Peter Groff, an African American whose district included Park Hill, said that the city's effort to be image-conscious needed to stop. The Denver PD had not even categorized Williams's murder as gang-related. "Let's make it clear we have gang problems," Groff said, "even though the actual crime data doesn't show that."

The city council went around Hickenlooper and approved an emergency $350,000 for the district attorney's office to hire more gang investigators. And the Department of Justice awarded Denver a Project Safe Neighborhoods grant. It would be spearheaded by the ATF, whose new regional headquarters had just opened in Denver, staffed by 130 agents.

PROJECT SAFE NEIGHBORHOODS grants gave cities and federal prosecutors wide latitude to determine how they would be run. It was Denver's first, and the city hoped to pull ideas from all three of the major anti-gang efforts formed in the 1990s. The ATF and the Denver police formed a task force to handle undercover operations, targeting the illegal possession and sale of weapons. Intervention workers would work in the community to quell tensions and meet with gang members recently released from prison. The city also planned to offer social services and counseling, and it would use the momentum from the prestigious award to raise additional funds from local foundations and other partners to support additional work, including media relations and events to build community relationships.

To manage its efforts, the city revived the Metro Denver Gang Coalition, which had shut down in 2002, when the ten-year funding from Governor Romer's anti-gang bill ran out. This time the city kept the organization under its own umbrella. Regina Huerter, whom Hickenlooper had appointed director of the Crime Prevention and Control Commission, was in charge. Her office would administer the funding and coordinate the city's effort.

Terrance was one of several former gang members invited to

attend the commission's meetings. The role he could play excited Huerter, and others. "I think there needs to be intervention that is a true partnership between people like Terrance Roberts who have walked this path and professionals like social workers or psychologists that know that piece of it as well," District Attorney Mitch Morrissey, whose father had grown up in Park Hill, told *The Denver Post.*

Terrance wasn't sure what to expect but soon found himself feeling uncomfortable at meetings. Whenever there was a gang shooting, "Reggie," as Regina went by, wasn't shy about asking the group about the "word on the street." The meetings, often held at the City and County Building, had a few dozen people. Terrance didn't know who all of them were. Some, he assumed, including Reggie, were connected to law enforcement. Her office was at police headquarters. Terrance felt that what was really wanted from his participation was information. Gang members usually claimed their hits, and Terrance was still close enough to the streets that he often heard such information. He wasn't trying to protect gang members who were committing crimes, but he also wasn't going to talk about that kind of thing to people he didn't even know. Assuming they were connected to law enforcement, that was snitching. People were killed for it.

From his own life experience, Terrance believed the best way to stop gang violence was to cut off recruitment. Once you're in, it's hard to get out. Many don't. Terrance wondered sometimes if he would have been a professor or a lawyer if he had had positive male role models. He believed in the "prevention" model—mentoring and activities for at-risk youth. At the same time, in northeast Denver, he was becoming known as the person gang members called on when tensions flared. But he did that intervention work on his own, without involving law enforcement. Mistrust of the police was so high in the neighborhood that it was dangerous to be seen as working with them. During one meeting, when Huerter asked about word on the street, Terrance decided it was time to let her know the potential consequences of her question. If word got around that he answered the question, he was a snitch, and could have to pay the price. "Hold up a second there, Reg," Terrance said. "Don't get anyone shot in the head."

DENVER USED PART of the grant to support a series of community events for a "Summer of Peace." Six organizations had been chosen as official sponsors. They were all city agencies or Latino organizations, and Prodigal Son. Terrance was surprised when he read about it in the paper. He hadn't even been asked.

He showed up to the kickoff march with his bullhorn and warmed up the crowd for Mayor Hickenlooper.

"Whose community is it?" he shouted.

"Our community!"

Firing up crowds came easy to Terrance. He went to every event, barbecue, and rally, stopping cars passing in the street. "Summer of Peace, man," he said. "Everybody's on board—*everybody*. After this we're doing 'Keep the Peace'!"

Whenever possible, he brought a friend to record his interactions with a video camera. He wanted to make sure his community's voices were heard. He approached mothers, kids, Crips, Bloods, and Latino gang members. "What's it going to take for a summer of peace?" he asked. Some talked about jobs; others worried about kids whose parents were gang members. One young man, with a black LA Raiders hat, introduced himself as a Crip. "But I'm not banging anymore," he said. "I'm twenty-two, you know. That shit get old."

"Can you see yourself doing what I'm doing?" Terrance asked.

The guy paused . . . "Yeah."

Terrance hugged him then held up his fingers in a peace sign. "Metro Denver Gang Coalition!" he said to the camera.

By the end of the summer, Terrance wasn't as effusive. He discovered that he was the only regular participant who hadn't received any funding. Meanwhile GRASP, a Latino anti-gang organization that Regina Huerter had helped start on the west side, had received several hundred thousand dollars. At a meeting with Hickenlooper present, Terrance accused Huerter, the head of the city's anti-gang effort, of misdirecting funds. "Most of the violence is on the East Side," Terrance said in front of the group. "You're funding a *Latino* organization with East Side violence." His seemingly explosive charge was met with silence, as if it had not been heard. He quit the coalition.

A FEW MONTHS later, George Roberts was asleep when his phone started "blowing up." This was how he was awakened a few times a week, by calls or texts. Usually it meant someone had been shot. The spirit world, so he believed, was with him in these moments. Still, George was unprepared for the news this day. The legendary Crip founder Michael Asberry was dead.

George had just seen him. "Call me Brother Michael," he'd told George. He was carrying the Bible George had given to him, but his sadness was apparent.

George knelt to pray but the tears came, only briefly. There was work to do. He got dressed. The address he had been given, a townhouse complex off Colfax in Aurora, was one he knew well. A former girlfriend had lived next door. It was also where Mike's older sister, Star, was living.

It was about 9 a.m. when George arrived. A dozen police cruisers and squad cars were parked around the complex. Yellow police tape surrounded one of the homes. Clusters of young men and women huddled together outside it, hugging and sobbing. George spotted some of Mike's family. Hubert, one of Mike's older brothers, was wheezing loudly and clutching Star. They all knew Uncle Georgie, and he made his way over. Few in invisible Denver had more access to word on the street than George. Over the next hour, he learned what had happened.

Sometime after midnight, Star was looking to score some dope from a neighbor. She didn't have any money so she struck a deal to put up her television as collateral. But she realized she'd been taken. The stuff was "woo"—fake crack. Star called Mike, who was only a few blocks away at Wolf's, a motel and dive bar on Colfax.

He got to Star's place around 3:30 a.m. and soon was inside the dealers' apartment. They were two young African Americans. Mike didn't know them and it didn't seem that they knew him. Mike took the first swing, hitting one of the guys in the face. He turned to the other, who had a gun. Mike swiped at it, but two shots came, hitting him in the torso.

The dealers ran. Star rushed in. "I can't breathe," Mike said to her. An ambulance arrived, but by the time it reached the hospital Mike was dead.

George saw people were streaming toward the area. The crowd was growing, well beyond the usual size. Dozens of Crips, wearing blue bandanas and shirts, stood in the street, blocking traffic and banging on windshields. Whether Asberry was still running Denver's Crips didn't matter. He would always be the founder and king. Now the king was dead. George knew as well as anyone— vengeance was coming.

Some of the police officers who knew George from the funerals they patrolled asked for his help clearing the street. "Anyone who's a Code Five, we're arresting them," they told him. Code 5 meant people with warrants.

George called his boss at the airport and told him he wouldn't be able to come in. He waded into the groups of familiar and unfamiliar faces. "Code Five," he said. "Code Five."

BEFORE DAWN THE following morning, Terrance's phone woke him. Something was going on at the Holly. He pulled on some clothes and got in the car. When he got close, the streets were blocked by fire trucks and police vehicles. He got out, smelling smoke, and walked toward the shopping center. It was engulfed in flames. From the roof over the liquor store to the Family Dollar in the middle of the center, flames lashed forty feet into the night sky.

Neighborhood residents began to gather, some in pajamas, as firefighters on ladders high above the shopping center blasted water onto it from thick hoses. When daylight began to break, and the fire still was not out, the extent of the damage became visible. The building's roof had collapsed, leaving only naked steel beams. Store windows and doors were shattered, revealing wiring and the burning remains of products and shelving. After more than half a century, the Holly Shopping Center was gone.

ACT II

Terrance paced up and down 33rd Avenue, the taste of smoldering metal on his tongue. People he hadn't seen in years were on the block, dazed. They'd never experienced a loss like this. The sixty-year-old shopping center was part of their identity. Around mid-morning, the fire engine ladders finally came down and white smoke rose from the charred remains.

Before long, word on the street provided a possible explanation for what had happened: Michael Asberry had been murdered the previous night. Revenge by the Crips seemed likely.

Terrance began working his phone. He needed to know if any of the Bloods were claiming Psych Mike. But he made call after call and the answer was no. Finally he reached his father. George told him it wasn't the Bloods who had hit Mike. But Terrance could see that that critical fact no longer mattered. The Bloods were sure the fire was the work of the Crips. "This is worse than 9/11," one of the Bloods gathered outside Ned's candy shop said. "They burned down our hood."

YG Regulator cars began to pull into the Horizon Lounge's parking lot, next to Ned's candy store. The Crips had avenged their leader's killing by destroying the most sacred thing to Denver's Bloods. Like 9/11, it would never be forgotten. One regulator car headed to the Park-n-Ride in Five Points, a Crip hangout. Another was said to be headed to firebomb Crip homes.

Denver's assistant fire chief told reporters the department was "not suspecting it's criminal, contrary to some of the rumors that are going around." But in fact the city had conclusive evidence of arson. By lunchtime District Attorney Morrissey was watching the grainy black-and-white footage captured by a security camera on the back of the small library in Holly Square. At 3:40 a.m. the previous night, eight figures walked into the camera's view, each holding a flaming bottle. One by one they hurled the Molotov cocktails onto the shopping center's roof and ran.

TERRANCE WAS AMONG those called to Mayor Hickenlooper's office for an emergency meeting on Monday morning. The City of Denver's public safety office was deep into planning with federal law enforcement for the 2008 Democratic National Convention, to be held in August. Regina Huerter wanted to coordinate a public response to the events of the weekend.

She suggested that it wasn't clear if the Holly fire had anything to do with Michael Asberry's death. Terrance couldn't believe it. He'd also noticed that Rev Kelly had already appeared in news reports, trying to "dispel rumors" that there was any connection between Asberry's death and the Holly fire. Terrance was beginning to see the machinations behind the city's official falsehoods about his community.

"With all due respect," Terrance interrupted, "the Holly fire was a gang arson. I don't have all the details on Mike [Asberry], but we're gonna say what we're gonna say. I have my own board and my own community to answer to."

As in the past, his comment was met with an uneasy silence. This time it cut deep. His phone hadn't stopped ringing. Former and active gang members on both sides were calling. Some were angry, some were fearful. They were looking to him for leadership; they'd never heard of Regina Huerter.

Terrance attended the following day's meeting but stood in back so he could leave early. The pastor at New Hope Church on Colorado Boulevard had given Terrance the space to hold his own meeting later that day; the community needed to come together to grieve. Terrance was getting ready to leave when Huerter and Rev Kelly approached him. They had heard about Terrance's meeting. Huerter was concerned about what might be said.

Terrance lost it. Did she expect him to take directions from city hall or the police on this?

"This is *our* time," he told her. "This is not *your* time. Don't tell me how to talk about peace in my community." He said he hoped gang members *would* speak to the media. "They should say what they want," Terrance said. "Whatever comes out of us is what it is." He left.

When he got to New Hope, dozens of former and active Crips and Bloods were in the gym, along with neighborhood pastors, his father, and a few journalists. Many of the gang members were older and knew Mike Asberry personally. They embraced. Many cried.

Terrance led a discussion that resulted in three goals being agreed: to spread word that Mike's killing wasn't a gang hit; to find alternatives to gangs for young men and women; and to try to enforce a forty-day truce so that Mike could be buried in peace and the invisible city could avert a summer of bloodshed.

News reports that day contradicted one another. *The Denver Post* quoted a police spokesman who inaccurately claimed they had seen no retribution since Asberry's death. But Fox 31, who had a reporter at the New Hope meeting, began its newscast with the words no one in Hickenlooper's administration wanted to hear. "It's been fifteen years since Denver's so-called Summer of Violence," announced the longtime anchor Ron Zappolo, leading off the ten o'clock news. The story disputed police and fire department denials about retaliatory violence and connected the Holly fire to Asberry's murder.

MIKE'S BODY WAS at Pipkin Mortuary in Five Points. George got a call from Rev, asking him to meet there.

George had known Rev for years. He knew Rev was controversial in the hood because of his work for the DA's office and his close association with gang members. But George had no beef with Rev. In George's work, everyone was equal. And he knew Rev was mourning. No one had been closer to Mike.

When George arrived, he saw Rev had bought the most expensive coffin Pipkin offered, fit for a bishop or a president. He went to Mike's side. The twitch in his cheek was finally gone. He seemed at last at peace, George thought. Mike wore a blue suit but George noticed that he had no shoes on. George had just bought a pair of blue alligator loafers and he told Rev he'd bring them. Rev in turn asked George if he would officiate the funeral. George agreed.

Soon others arrived, including "OG Phil" Jefferson, one of the Crips co-founders. Phil, now thirty-nine, was disabled from a bullet lodged in his head and walked with a cane. Several Denver and Aurora police officers arrived as well to discuss security. Crips from Los Angeles to Louisiana were said to be flying in.

George raised another security issue: what to do about Terrance. Normally no Blood would attend a Crip's funeral, especially not the funeral of the gang's founder. But several Crips had asked Terrance to deliver a eulogy. Some of them had their kids in Prodigal Son.

"Ain't no one gonna hurt him," Phil promised.

The group left for Fuller Park. Rev had called his own press conference in the spot where twenty-three years earlier he'd met a teenaged Mike. Terrance and other former and current gang members came, as did the Denver media. Rev, visibly holding back his emotions, announced that there had not in fact been a truce, but a cease-fire. "With a truce, you sit down and ask the question: 'What does it take for us to stop?'" Rev said. "None of that happened here. We have a cease-fire. It means it is over. Finished."

FOR TERRANCE, MIKE's murder and the Holly fire felt biblical, a sign. He knew he needed to change Prodigal Son's strategic plan. Gang prevention traditionally meant after-school programs or mentorship. Terrance believed it needed to include community redevelopment. That would bring actual jobs, which young men in the neighborhood needed, and it would bring honor back to the community. He was determined to redevelop the Holly.

He called for a march against gang violence. Later that week, about sixty people gathered in the parking lot of the gutted shopping center. Terrance wore a white T-shirt and khaki pants, and carried his bullhorn. The group fanned into a circle, linking hands. "I got love for all these gang members," Terrance said. "I'm not going to act like I don't. But I—don't—like—what's—happening—to my community. And if I gotta get killed or if I'm wrong for saying I don't want to come to the Holly and look at this—when I grew up buying candy from these candy stores."

"Yeah," some in the circle cheered. Overhead, a Denver police helicopter hovered.

Terrance walked toward a young girl, who was holding an older girl's hand. "Look at this little girl . . ." he said. "She told me she's scared . . . This is a war zone, guys. No! I don't like what Bloods and Crips are doing to my community."

People cheered.

"But I love you though," Terrance responded.

"We can stop it!" a man yelled.

"I love you though," Terrance repeated.

"Stop the violence!" another person yelled.

They joined arms and marched through the neighborhood, singing "We Shall Overcome." As they passed residents, Terrance called out to them. "We're doing it for you," he said. "Come on, we're doing it for the Holly." People ran from their porches to join.

REV HAD FOUND a church outside the war zone for Mike's funeral. When Terrance pulled up, police and Crips were everywhere. One of them was Derrick "Lil Crip" Wilford. He and Terrance hadn't seen each other since they were together in Building 22. They embraced.

Inside, George waited at the podium in a double-breasted pinstripe suit. His sermon was called "Thank You Lord for Changing Me." It was based on the book of Job, chapter 14. "If a man dies," George said, "he will live again. Wait—for change to come. This man wanted to change his life. My message today is to put down your guns and colors and receive the blood of Jesus. *Somebody*," he said, calling out, "needs to change today. Can I hear somebody?"

People cheered and cried. Mike's sister Star walked to the foot of her brother's coffin and curled into a fetal position. After a slideshow, Terrance went to the stage. He wore dark pants and a tan button-down shirt.

"I don't want anybody to get o-ffended," he began. "If you're from LA or Atlanta or Dallas and all these other beautiful places. But I gotta speak to my brothers and sisters who grew up with me in Denver."

People clapped. "There's a brother who's in here right now, who I thought was my enemy," Terrance said. "All the stuff you see me doing in the newspapers—I wouldn't be doing none of this if it weren't for a brother they call Lil Crip, who's my friend . . . Come on up here, brother, come on, man."

Cheers accompanied Lil Crip's walk to the stage. "This brother right here saved my life," Terrance said. "It wasn't a Blood, it wasn't no big homey. I went to Building 22 and this brother right here said: 'God's good to you, Terrance, all the time.'

"Y'all need to read some of these articles and blogs—what people saying about East Denver African Americans," Terrance continued. "They're saying we're nothing but a bunch of crackheads . . . Talking about we're stupid, we're illiterate, thank God for gentrification now that people are taking the properties. Them are some nice brick houses on the Five Points and Park Hill."

He paused. "But: we want to kill each other."

The room clamored and cheered.

"You're my people," Terrance said. "I love y'all." He added, "If you need something to do with your children, give me a call and we'll work it out. I just don't want to see nobody else get killed."

TERRANCE WASN'T THE only one interested in redeveloping Holly Square. Two weeks after the fire, City Councilwoman Carla Madison, who was white, held a public discussion on the future of the Holly.

Madison, who had red hair, had rubbed some in the Black community the wrong way because, for a newsletter put out by the powerful Denver Foundation, Madison said that the fire "may have been the best thing that could have happened to this community."

The meeting was held in the community room at the new District 2 police headquarters. More than 125 people showed, about half of them white people who Terrance was sure didn't live in the neighborhood.

Madison disclosed that the city was in negotiations with Michael Bullock, the Holly's owner, to acquire the property. She referred to Bullock as the shopping center's "longtime owner" and an "ally" of the community. Terrance didn't know what she was talking about. Bullock, who was white, had barely owned the place two years. Terrance had never met him.

Madison proposed building a charter school on the site, consistent with the Neighborhood Plan that the city council had quietly ratified eight years earlier. She opened up the room for feedback, noting that she had brought a mediator.

Terrance proposed building a workforce training center. Michelle Wheeler of the Northeast Park Hill Coalition suggested a drug and alcohol treatment center. Some wanted a supermarket, as they'd been promised for decades. One white attendee proposed an incubator for startups.

Terrance felt compelled to speak again. "The Holly is the hub of the community," he said. "And to many African Americans in northeast Denver, this is 'home.'" What needed to be addressed first, he said, was a cleanup of the site. "It's like a dead body now that needs to be buried," he said.

BUT THE RUINS of the center remained untouched, just as the burned-out ruins of the Dahlia Lanes had years earlier. Mayor Hickenlooper had appointed Terrance to the Denver African American Commission, and Terrance went to every event he could, seeking out city officials who could tell him when the remains of the shopping center would be cleared. He was like a broken record no one heard. Finally someone got him a private meeting with Hickenlooper.

The mayor had never had a conversation with Terrance, but he'd witnessed Terrance's no-nonsense style in meetings and hoped he was prepared.

"Let me just ask you something," Terrance said to Hickenlooper. "In a white community, would you ever see a burned-down shopping center rotting in the middle of the neighborhood?"

Hickenlooper had no answer.

"Let me just tell you what I'm seeing every day," Terrance continued. "There are Bloods pointing to the Holly and telling the little homeys, 'They burned down our hood.' That fire was the best recruiting tool the Bloods ever had."

Hickenlooper told Terrance that the economic reality was not in their favor. The 2008 housing crash and ensuing recession had hit Denver hard. The city was operating at a deficit. Michael Bullock, the Holly's owner, said his insurance wouldn't pay for the cleanup. And the city, Hickenlooper said, just didn't have the funds.

But Hickenlooper had an idea. He introduced Terrance to the director of his Office of Housing and Neighborhood Development, Terrance Ware. Ware, who was African American, soon realized that Terrance was George Roberts's son. Ware and George shared a close friend growing up back when George was a fast-talking, karate-fighting, drug-dealing con man. Ware liked George. He also knew Ernestine.

Ware met with Terrance and told him he agreed the Holly had to be cleaned up and that it should get city development money. But finding funding and the right partners took time. He promised Terrance he would work on it.

In August, Denver hosted the Democratic National Convention. Thousands of journalists from around the world converged for what appeared to be confirmation of America's progress on race relations. None of them mentioned that just beyond the klieg lights, the host city's most famous civil rights site was literally a pile of mangled metal and ashes.

In November, Terrance voted for the first time in his life, for Barack Obama. That night he took his three-year-old daughter, Trinity, to an election night party at Brother Jeff's Cultural Café in Five Points. The place was operated by Brother Jeff Fard, publisher of *5 Points News*, who had become perhaps the most prominent northeast Denver activist. As Obama clinched the historic victory, a *Denver Post* reporter interviewed Terrance. "This is one of the best nights of my life," Terrance said. "Change is here. It's not coming. It's here." Terrance's photo, in a silkscreened "Change" T-shirt, ran on the paper's front page.

Weeks later, Terrance was eating a plate of fried fish and fries on the small concrete patio outside his grandmother's restaurant when a car pulled up. A Blood whom Terrance knew called Panther got out.

"Niggaz is talkin'," Panther said.

"About what?" Terrance asked.

"About you, what you're doing."

Gang members were well practiced in circular dialogue. Terrance didn't know exactly what Panther was referring to, but the Bloods had no shortage of reasons to be unhappy with him. Among them was the fact that he'd spoken at Psych Mike's funeral, where he'd hugged Vick's killer, Lil Crip, onstage.

Panther told Terrance he needed to speak to P. Lok, Pernell Hines. Terrance hadn't seen Pernell in years. His style was always to be "low"—behind the scenes. But across northeast Denver, people reported that Pernell was still calling shots for the Bloods.

"Tell him I'm waiting," Terrance said. Let them try something right in front of Granny's restaurant, he thought. For better and perhaps also worse, Terrance had remained as fearless as ever.

Three cars pulled up. Out of one hopped Pernell, wearing Spike Lee glasses and a black tracksuit. The others waited in their cars. Pernell sat down across from Terrance. He said he'd seen Terrance in the media.

Terrance didn't even know which story Pernell was referring

to. After the photo on the front page of *The Denver Post*, Terrance and his program had been featured in another front-page story, in the *Rocky Mountain News*. One of the kids in his program told the paper she ran into the street and cried for joy when she heard Obama had won. "Now I know for sure I can do anything," she said. Opportunity, Terrance knew, was the biggest threat to the Park Hill Bloods.

"I'm not a Blood no more," Terrance said. "I don't answer to you or no one."

But this is the hood, and we run the hood, Pernell told him. So Terrance needed to keep in touch with him about what he was doing, he said.

"Well, this is what I'm doing," Terrance said. "This is what the community needs. If it goes good, it's positive attention and attention we need."

They parted, without agreement.

ON DECEMBER 17, after a seven-month grand jury investigation, nine members of the Crips—"the Holly 9," the media would dub them—were indicted on conspiracy and arson charges for burning down the shopping center. The motive, according to district attorney Mitch Morrissey, was retaliation for the murder of Michael Asberry.

"That is one of the older shopping centers," Morrissey said at a press conference. "It is kind of the heart there, with the police station down the street . . . It is our theory that they were targeting the shopping center. I don't think they really cared much about the businesses. The statement they were trying to make was to the Holly itself. I think it was an attack on the community."

As the charges against the Holly 9 were announced, the American Planning Association, the country's largest urban planning group, named Park Hill one of America's "10 Great Neighborhoods." The citation, heralded by the Denver media, noted Park Hill's "tolerance and openness toward others" and its "progressive integration, diversity and memorable character." No mention was made of the burned-out shopping center and erstwhile home of the Bloods that no one could afford to clean up.

Fall came and went. The first African American president was sworn in. And the mangled remains of the shopping center sat. Everywhere Terrance went, community members asked him what was being done—Bloods; grandmas like Ernestine; parents who had to walk past the site every day and try not to let it affect them. "If you can't get it cleaned up, what's the point of being on TV?" one of the "aunties" Terrance knew admonished him. "We don't support you to make you famous but to make our community better."

Terrance knew the community was wary of upstart politician types who did nothing but get in the media. He was honored to be held to a higher standard. But he didn't know what else to do. Then one day, Terry Ware, from the city's Office of Housing and Neighborhood Development, called him back. There was someone he wanted Terrance to meet.

ACROSS THE COUNTRY, low-income neighborhoods like Five Points and Northeast Park Hill were the hardest hit by the subprime mortgage crisis, an early indication of the changes coming to the area.

Denver's population was growing, and Mayor Hickenlooper was interested in utilizing hybrid public-private funding models to get more out of its development projects. He had cultivated relationships with nonprofit executives from the Anschutz Foundation, run by Phil Anschutz, and the heavily endowed Denver Foundation, which had operated under several mayors as a quasi-government agency and was also helping fund the anti-gang effort.

Hickenlooper had also begun to partner with a tiny new organization on the scene, the Urban Land Conservancy. The ULC was founded as a nonprofit real estate corporation that would buy community assets in distressed neighborhoods and develop them in partnership with the city. The ULC's founder, Sam Gary, was a former oil "wildcatter" who had a long philanthropic relationship with the city. Efforts he had funded included the ill-fated anti-gang program that had employed Michael Asberry.

Ware had met with the ULC's only employee, CEO Aaron Miripol, to discuss the Holly. Miripol was interested.

SOON AFTER MEETING with Ware, Miripol called Terrance to invite him to his office, downtown on the fifty-third floor of the city's tallest building. When Terrance got out of the elevator, he was at the headquarters of Gary-Williams Energy Corporation, Sam Gary's company. Miripol, who wore a sports jacket and shirt with no tie, greeted Terrance. Miripol didn't look like a business executive. He had an unruly shock of brown hair and a five-o'clock shadow. Ware had briefed Miripol on the politics of Northeast Park Hill, and about Terrance, the former gang member who had become something of a community representative for the Holly redevelopment.

They went to Miripol's office, where, outside a window, the city lay beneath them. Terrance knew he would have to live in two worlds if he wanted to get the Holly redeveloped. He was ready.

Miripol, who was forty-four, told Terrance about his childhood in a rough neighborhood in Chicago. His best friend was an African American kid whose brother was killed during a robbery. Miripol had watched his friend endure the trauma of violence. "The Holly is the reason I'm doing what I do," he told Terrance.

"I figured there was a reason I was here," Terrance said. "People are asking me what's going on."

Miripol told Terrance the ULC was in negotiations to buy the Holly. He said he would need Terrance's help.

"I just want to be part of the process," Terrance said, leaving many things unsaid. The depth of the Bloods' ties to his community was something few would understand. The neighborhood's youth football coach was Aaron "Brazy" Grimes, Bryan Butler's cousin. At thirty-seven, Grimes wore red hats and bandanas to practice; the kids called him "Coach Brazy."

Miripol, whose salary was $190,000 a year, had his own vantage point. He had proposed to the ULC's board of directors that he grow the nascent organization's holdings to a $75 million valuation in five years. He had just bought another property in Northeast Park Hill, the Dahlia Apartments. It was a small housing project next to the Red Bricks, where Terrance grew up. The Dahlia Apartments were also part of Bloods lore, known as "Up Top," because it sat on a small bluff.

For all of their differences, Aaron and Terrance had at least one thing in common. Redeveloping the Holly was what they believed they were meant to do. In anticipation, Miripol formed an LLC for the property's management. He named it Holly Grail.

UNLIKE THE WELL-CHRONICLED negotiations over the Dahlia, discussions around the Holly sale were kept out of the Denver media. Miripol had filled the ULC's board with influential people, including a vice president of the Denver Foundation, which agreed to become a partner in the redevelopment of the Holly, offering $100,000 and ongoing support. Hickenlooper pledged financial support from the Office of Economic Development.

With funding lined up, Miripol offered Bullock $650,000 for the Holly, about half of what Bullock had paid for it. It was a terrible offer. Johnny Copeland had paid twice as much in 1983. But Bullock's hands were tied. The City of Denver had its preferred buyer, and with the center lying in ruins, it could declare the site blighted at any moment, invoke eminent domain, and seize the property. Bullock accepted the offer.

"Shopping Center to Face Wrecking Ball, Renewal," read a *Denver Post* headline on April 23, 2009. Almost twelve months after the arson, the wreckage would finally be removed, and the Urban Land Conservancy would own the city's 2.2-acre civil rights landmark. Miripol, the only person quoted in the story, noted that future plans for the property had already been discussed with the community. "There's a lot of motivational pieces to this," he told the *Post*. "We're going to ensure whatever ends up there has a long term public benefit."

Terrance's phone and email blew up. Despite what Miripol told *The Denver Post*, few in northeast Denver had heard anything of the plans, Terrance included. "Are you involved in this?" one high-profile activist, Lisa Calderon, wrote to Terrance, forwarding him the story.

No, he replied. Miripol hadn't told him anything. But he was excited. The Holly was back.

WEEKS LATER, MAYOR Hickenlooper, in a baseball hat and tie, stood at a podium in Holly Square. Behind him, the lot was empty. All that remained of the shopping center were twelve steel stanchions that had once supported the awning.

City officials and reporters filled the folding chairs. Terrance, who wore shorts and a Prodigal Son shirt, kept his eye on cars rolling past. He didn't know what the Bloods' response might be.

What had happened at the Holly, Hickenlooper told the crowd, was "all of our faults." Leaving unmentioned the millions the city was pouring into the residential development of the old Stapleton Airport site across the street, Hickenlooper said that the city had to "scratch together" funds to help the Urban Land Conservancy purchase the property. With his folksy optimism, Hickenlooper implored residents to let the city know their dreams for the site, declaring "a new day at the Holly."

"Empty Lot Is Full of Promises" was the headline of *The Denver Post*'s coverage, written by its staff columnist Bill Johnson. "Count me as a skeptic," wrote Johnson, an African American who grew up in LA. "I have lived long enough in poor, mostly black neighborhoods laid low by violence to never believe a politician until the first bulldozers arrive."

Johnson asked Miripol whether the community should believe the promises. "I do know that this is a community that deserves to be treated with respect," Miripol told Johnson. "Keep my feet to the fire. I welcome it."

"I promised him I would, indeed," Johnson wrote.

He didn't. Johnson, who left the *Post* two and a half years later, never wrote about Northeast Park Hill again. Nor did Denver's other daily newspaper. After 150 years of publication, the *Rocky Mountain News* had shut its doors three months earlier. The paper's newsroom, once a downtown landmark, was purchased by the City of Denver, and quickly leveled. Steel and other building materials were repurposed for use in the construction of the $376 million Denver Justice Center—comprising a new jail connected by an underground tunnel to a thirty-eight-room courthouse—set to open the following year.

TERRANCE SUDDENLY HAD access to a part of Denver he never imagined he could enter. Hickenlooper named him one of Denver's 150 Unsung Heroes. He was invited to cocktail hours and functions with Denver's movers and shakers. Miripol just called him "T."

One day, Aqeela Sherrills, co-negotiator of the LA's Truce of Nine-Deuce, called. Terrance and Aqeela had met in 2007, when Regina Huerter had flown Aqeela to Denver to speak after Darrent

Williams's murder. Aqeela was in a new documentary, *Crips and Bloods: Made in America*, which had an upcoming Denver premiere. He asked if Terrance would host a panel after the screening. The film, Aqeela said, included interviews about police misconduct, and COINTELPRO.

Terrance knew that few of the young boys and girls in the neighborhood understood this part of their history. He agreed to host the event and bought tickets for all the kids in his program.

Among those who saw Terrance's Facebook posts promoting the film was Captain Mike Calo, head of the gang unit, one of the few Denver police officers who had participated in devising the city's 2000 Northeast Park Hill Neighborhood Plan. Calo, who had a broad face and thick dark hair, had known Terrance back when he was ShowBizz. Calo wrote to the film's publicity contact, describing Terrance as a friend, and asked if the police would also be invited to speak.

Terrance began to see Captain Calo regularly around the neighborhood. They became cordial, but it was hard for Terrance to overlook what he felt was racism in the police department. The Denver PD averaged more excessive force complaints per capita than the average American city; a Black man in Denver was three times more likely than a white man to be shot by a police officer.

One day, while Terrance and Calo waited for Rev to arrive to discuss a three-on-three basketball tournament with the police, Terrance says Calo suggested he run for city council or school board. The machine will back you, Terrance remembers Calo telling him. Terrance couldn't help but feel that Calo was also making a statement about what it would be like to go against the machine. Terrance didn't scare easily. If going against the machine was what his work required, he thought, that was what he would do.

In the spring of 2009, Terrance and Calo were both in the District 2 community room. State senator Peter Groff, a longtime Northeast Park Hill resident and the first African American president of the Colorado Senate, had accepted an offer from the Obama administration to head a faith-based-initiative office at the U.S. Department of Education. Colorado's legislative body would be left with only one Black representative.

Groff's replacement would be decided by a ballot of party officials. In the audience was one of the hopefuls, the school principal Mike Johnston, whose campaign was being run by a friend of Terrance's. It had been more than fifty years since the seat was held by anyone but an African American. Johnston, who was thirty-four, was white.

After the meeting, Michelle Wheeler, who was on Prodigal Son's board, introduced Terrance to Mike. The two appeared to have little in common. Johnston, who was thin with wispy blond hair and wire-frame glasses, grew up in room 300 of the Christiana Lodge in Vail, which his parents bought when the resort was still in its infancy. His father later became Vail's mayor. Mike went on to attend Yale, as well as Yale Law School, and then Harvard, receiving a master's degree in education. In 2008, Obama named him an education adviser for his presidential campaign. Mike lived with his family in Stapleton, which featured large homes and its own town center.

Terrance was impressed by Johnston's credentials, and Johnston by those of Terrance, whose Facebook page listed his college as "Pen" State, as in the penitentiary. They were both looking for office space in the Holly and agreed to scout locations together. There were few. The only commercial strip was Mrs. Wilson's on the south side of 33rd Avenue. One of the storefronts looked empty, and Terrance went to speak to Deloris Wilson at the Horizon Lounge, to see if she would consider renting it to them.

Deloris, who was sixty, had owned the strip for almost four decades. The idea of having an up-and-coming white politician and an anti-gang organization move into the Bloods' last stretch of the neighborhood didn't seem advisable to her. She liked Terrance but told him no. Terrance understood.

That left only one possible place. It was a small abandoned building on the southwest side of the Holly, next to the post office.

Terrance remembered it from his childhood as Red's, a soul food restaurant even before Granny's place opened. Large weeds sprouted from cracks in the asphalt outside.

Terrance inquired and found the building was owned by the Union Baptist Church, a few blocks away. The church was willing to rent the space to them for $700 a month, if they took care of the rehab. Terrance, Mike, and his campaign manager went to check it out. When they got inside, the stench was hard to take.

"It's gonna take some work," Terrance said, and they all laughed. Mike had won the balloting to become the area's next state senator. They felt the excitement of working at the heart of an experiment in community redevelopment. They took the place.

TERRANCE PULLED HIS white Dodge Ram pickup truck up onto the sidewalk and started hauling out garbage. He posted on his Facebook page for volunteers, and each day new people arrived. Ethiopians from the west side, student volunteers from a class at Metro. They said they were moved by Terrance's story of the Holly and wanted to help.

They pulled out the old banquettes and benches and ripped out the kitchen, finding dead rats, squirrels, and birds. They spent a week just scrubbing the floors and walls. A friend of Terrance's mom's, a contractor, laid down a carpet. Others donated chairs, a leather couch, and a flat-screen television.

Mike took the larger office suite to the left. Terrance's side had two small offices and a storage room. Mike's rent would be $400; Terrance would pay $300.

He fit a small desk into his office. There was no window, but he got a bench and chair so that people could come in. An artist Terrance knew from Five Points, Thomas "Detour" Evans, came by with a portrait of Biggie Smalls. They hung it on the wall in the wood-paneled front room.

Terrance's obsession with his work wasn't going over well at home. Desirée felt he'd put Prodigal Son over everything. He was rarely home. Terrance felt she was jealous that he was starting to get recognition. He seldom drank, but he did start enjoying his new-found friends and the nightlife scene. Desirée soon discovered he was cheating on her.

Terrance moved out and into his mom's basement. Suzanne's commercial real estate career had continued to thrive, and she now had a three-bedroom house in a suburban Aurora cul-de-sac. Terrance's two stepsiblings, Chris and Shavon, slept upstairs.

In August, the office was ready, and Terrance and Mike held a community barbecue. Desirée brought over Trinity, Terrance's daughter. He was thrilled. He missed her. She wore a white dress and pigtails, and climbed around on his shoulders.

Terrance and Mike were charming hosts, taking turns working the grill. Terrance wore a camouflage shirt with the Denver sky-line on it. Mike wore khaki pants and a blue oxford button-down. Batman and Robin, one local news station would soon dub them. When it came time for the dedication, Terrance introduced "our honorable senator," drawing cheers and whistles.

"It's appropriate that I come *after* Terrance," Johnston said. "Be-cause the purpose of us being here is that we know we literally stand on the shoulders of giants . . . And when we saw this big vacant lot across the street," he said, pointing to the former Holly, "what you see is a big hole where there used to be a shopping center. What you see is an absence where there used to be a presence. But what that absence gives us is a chance to reimagine what this neigh-borhood's going to be about. It gives us a blank canvas to say, 'What are we gonna put there that is gonna describe what we're about and what this place is going to stand for?'"

As Mike spoke, Terrance heard a commotion out front. Some-one was yelling for help. He handed Trinity off and got a friend. They went to the front, where he saw several young Bloods trying to force another kid into the back seat of a Caprice Classic. Terrance grabbed one of the Bloods, who was thin but strong. The kid pushed Terrance away, and they locked arms.

"Who da fuck 'r you?" the Blood said. He was about five feet eight and no more than eighteen years old. His face had tight, small features, and when he spoke Terrance saw he had two big front teeth. Terrance had never seen him before.

"Who the fuck are *you?*" Terrance said back.

He pushed him away and helped the other kid out of the car.

"Whatever, Blood," the young Blood said, watching as Terrance took the Crip inside.

Terrance spent the following morning chopping it up with the neighborhood "crackheads," as he affectionately called them, and the old men at Sipio's auto shop, which occupied a small garage on the south side of Holly Square that wasn't part of the Urban Land Conservancy's purchase. The men had witnessed the altercation the previous day and knew the parties.

Terrance learned that the Blood he had grabbed by the neck was called "Munch," because of his long front teeth. He had just been released from juvenile detention, where he'd spent several years. He was new to the streets of Northeast Park Hill, but his reputation preceded him. His real name was Hasan, and his father was Ice Alexander, the Denver gangworld legend who'd once put a hit on Terrance.

Across America, as gang membership rose, it was common for young gang members to be second generation, born into a war the country barely acknowledged. Hasan had never even met his father. Ice was still in prison.

Terrance started to see Munch around. He and his crew stood on the corner across the street, representin', their baggy shirts suggesting to Terrance concealed weapons. One day, Terrance was walking across the Horizon parking lot to Ned's candy store, when Munch was coming out. "I know who you are," Munch said to Terrance.

It wasn't hard to learn Terrance's backstory. A few times a week someone called him ShowBizz. For Terrance, his past was both his biggest asset and greatest threat. Blood In, Blood Out was the code, as he well knew. He was supposed to get beaten for leaving the gang. On the other hand, the fact that guys like Hasan knew he had walked in their shoes gave his efforts extra potency.

One cold day, Terrance saw Hasan and his crew shivering on the corner. He brought them sandwiches and cookies left over from an event. They grabbed the food like they hadn't eaten in days. "What you want to do this for?" Terrance asked them. "You're pushing a Los Angeles street gang—you ain't ever even been to Los Angeles."

Senator Johnston was rarely around. He had another office in the capitol. Terrance was sure he was afraid. Shootings on the block were regular. Since they'd moved in, two bullet holes had gouged the side of their building, just outside where Johnston's desk sat.

Terrance made sure to get in by 9 a.m. Most days he sat at the slatted wood tables on the front patio, in jeans and pressed button-down shirts. He told anyone who walked by about the new office, which he was calling the Park Hill Community Center. Some came in for a tour. Others asked if they could partner with him. Soon the lobby was host to weekly women's health classes and a financial literacy course, teaching adults how to budget and manage their money. One day he posted on Facebook for a muralist. Dan Levin-son, a white artist, came. Terrance took him across the street to the asphalt parking lot and had him draw the image of a phoenix rising from the ashes. That was how it felt to Terrance.

When it was quiet, he got out a laptop and worked on a donor and outreach database, and sent emails to grant givers and founda-tions. His misspelled words and incorrect syntax reflected his lack of formal education, but did little to dampen his message. Three days a week, the kids in his after-school program came. One was a cousin of Munch's. They worked on homework and, if the weather was nice, played chess and games outside.

But it was the other "kids," the young Bloods across the street, to whom Terrance couldn't help feeling drawn. Whenever he could, Terrance brought a friend with a video camera when he spoke to the young Bloods. They were the most voiceless people in the city, he thought. He wanted to give them a microphone.

"I'm Terrance," he said one sunny afternoon, holding out his hand to four Bloods in the empty Holly lot.

Seventeen-year-old Montea Tyree Davis, or Baby AD, was one of them. Montea was tall, thin, and handsome, with broad shoulders and a devil's smile. He wore a red bandana around his forehead and a bright red T-shirt. Terrance had known his mother for years.

"He da damu, he da big homey, dawg," Baby AD said of Terrance.

Terrance acknowledged the camera. "Say whatever you want to say," he told Baby AD. "Let 'em know how we livin' over here."

Baby AD looked into the lens. "We really getting active in these streets, and that's all we do, homey," he said. "We gotta eat. Our families gotta feed, homey. So, its my life—or your life. You feel me? Shit, dis is Park Hill, Denver, Killerado, Blood, get it correct." He twisted his fingers into a series of gang signs that he threw down like he was keeping the beat.

"My name is Terrance, by the way, man," Terrance said, bringing in another of the guys.

"I'm Bully B," he said. He was nineteen. His thick arms bulged from a white tank top. "We get active, you know what I'm sayin', but hey, sometimes we gotta put the word on some dudes. It is what it is . . . What I do, is benefit me and my family, you know."

Terrance turned to the camera. "This is real life, the Holly Shopping Center," he said, though the center itself was gone.

"Show them what they did to the block," Baby AD said, nodding to the camera operator. He pointed to the emptiness where the shopping center had been. "Ey, nigga—this used to be stores. That," he said. "That used to be a liquor store. Down there used to be a daycare. You feel me? Right here used to be a Family Dollar."

"Police involved with that shit," Bully B said.

"That's what I said," Baby AD responded. They locked arms and threw gang signs. Baby AD did a hop-step. Though the rumor was unproven, many in the community had come to believe that the Crips who burned down the Holly were put up to it by the police or the city, so that the local authorities could regain the land for their own purposes.

"Everyone's talking about increasing the peace, stopping the violence," Terrance said. "But, let me ask this to you: If I found you a job, would you work?"

"Hell, yeah," Baby AD said.

"You would work a job?" Terrance repeated.

"Hell, yeah," they all said.

"Niggas out in these skreets is *strug*-gling, nigga," Baby AD said. "We gotta feed *our* family, nigga. *Our* moms, and *our* sisters, Blood. We ain't got dads, nigga. And if we do, Blood, where dey at? Prison or dead, nigga, or runnin' around."

Bully B stepped back into the frame. "Shit, nigga," he said, holding up one finger. "Y'all give us *one* strike and expect us to do something, Blood? What we supposed to do but gangbang?"

"Period, Blood," Baby AD said.

"Well, that's our office over there, Park Hill Community Center," Terrance said. "I'm on the block. I'm a Hillsider, y'know what I mean. We gon' holler at y'all brothers. Watch and see. We gon' have a voice over here."

THAT FALL, Robert Mueller, director of the FBI, flew to Denver. The city was about to become home to a $100 million regional FBI headquarters, housing more than six hundred employees. The 100,000-square-foot facility, set to open the following year, would be located in Stapleton, minutes from the Holly.

While terrorism remained the top concern for American law enforcement, Mueller's priorities included countering the dramatic rise in America's gang population, which now rivaled the size of the American military. "By some estimates, these one million individuals account for upwards of 80 percent of the crime in some areas," Mueller told Denver law enforcement. "How can we best attack these gangs?" he asked. "We must continue to work with you and with our partners . . . But, we must also continue to work human source and surveillance angles . . ."

In Denver, the FBI gang unit was always recruiting informants. In fact, complications involving some of those gang members' cases had unexpectedly slowed the city's highest-profile gang case, the investigation into the murder of the Bronco star Darrent Williams, which was going on two years. "We know who was in the car, we know who allegedly pulled the trigger," Rev Kelly, who was privy to the machinations, told *The Denver Post*. "But even the witnesses that have to testify on that side of it—things have to be worked out with them."

Terrance expressed concern about the case, and cutting deals with people. "I'm not going to knock the prosecutors for doing their job and trying to get people . . . to say, 'I was there and this is what I seen,'" he told the *Post*. "But I don't always agree with that tactic, because sometimes the main perpetrators of these crimes are the leaders of some of the most heinous gangs and groups, the masterminds, and they're getting off."

ONE OF PRODIGAL Son's new programs was a free weekly yoga class, held at the Denver Museum of Nature & Science, in City Park. It was there that Terrance met Jillian, or Gigi, a twenty-five-year-old Colorado native whose African American family had settled in Henderson, a small town about half an hour northeast of the city. Gigi was a religious person who worked at her church. She was inspired by Terrance's life and work.

Terrance had never been in a relationship with someone who hadn't grown up in the confines of the gang war. His relationship with Desirée, which had always been volatile, had come to a violent end. They ended up in a fight that resulted in each of them bruised and charging the other with domestic violence. The charges against Desirée were dropped. Terrance went to trial and was acquitted. He was ready to move his life in a new direction. After dating for six months, he asked Gigi to marry him. She agreed, and later that day, George performed the ceremony in the Holly.

To save money they moved temporarily to Gigi's childhood home in Henderson. On his drive to work each day, cruising down the industrial corridor north of Denver, Terrance's mind raced with ideas about how to redevelop the Holly.

At Miripol's suggestion, he had formed a steering committee for the redevelopment effort, HARP, the Holly Area Redevelopment

Project. Terrance, the founding member, was joined by his Prodigal Son board member Michelle Wheeler, and by Gerie Grimes, who had been involved in social services and city planning for years. Terrance had known her and her two sons, Aaron ("Brazy") and Troy (who had become an activist), since childhood.

The Urban Land Conservancy also hired an outside group, Community by Design, to facilitate a series of public events and report on its findings. Terrance brought all the kids in his program to the "Holly Fair," where sketched proposals for the site were put on display. Some included a school, others a mixed-use building to house start-ups. Coverage of the "visioning process" appeared in the *Greater Park Hill News*, though not by a journalist but by Patrick Horvath, manager of the Strengthening Neighborhoods program of the Denver Foundation, which was the ULC's partner in the Holly redevelopment.

One night, in the bedroom Gigi grew up in, Terrance jolted awake. In his mind's eye was a vision of a new Holly Square, featuring a big youth center. Terrance knew Northeast Park Hill had about nine thousand residents, perhaps twenty-five hundred of them children. His after-school program couldn't handle even close to the demand. Like the Group of 15 had concluded in 1967, Terrance saw the need for a youth center.

When he got to the Holly, he walked around the site, imagining a gym, classrooms, offices. There was more than enough space. He called Dan Levinson, the mural artist. Levinson created a sketch based on Terrance's idea. Terrance got a frame and hung the drawing in the lobby of his office, so everyone would see it.

The next time Miripol came by, Terrance showed him the sketch.

Looks great, Miripol said. But who's going to pay for it?

Terrance realized there was one possible source that was almost too obvious: the Boys & Girls Clubs, which operated primarily in underserved communities, where they offered after-school activities and mentorship. The national organization already had five clubs in the Denver area, the most recent one in Montbello. It was dedicated to the fallen Bronco, Darrent Williams. Terrance looked up the number for the Denver Metro Boys & Girls Club CEO, John Arigoni, and cold-called him.

Arigoni, who was sixty-one, was a well-known figure on the Denver political and philanthropic scene. He had spent more than twenty years with the Boys & Girls Club, becoming president and CEO of Denver's clubs in 1993, just as the Summer of Violence began. He had recently moved back to Denver, after a six-year stint in Atlanta at the national headquarters, as a senior vice president.

Arigoni invited Terrance to his office, where Terrance told his story about going from honors student to gang member, and how he had to turn away dozens of mothers who were begging him to let their kids into his program. "There's nowhere for these kids to go but to the Bloods," he said.

Arigoni looked up the stats on the neighborhood. It was the prototype of the community the club tried to serve, where a majority of families earned less than $25,000 a year, and most children were in single-parent homes. It was also a gang community. Since the 1990s, Boys & Girls Clubs had developed educational partnerships with the FBI in gang communities.

Arigoni told Terrance he'd like to visit. When he did, Terrance showed him the vacant lot and took him to his office, where he pointed to the drawing on his wall.

TERRANCE DIDN'T MENTION his meetings with Arigoni to Aaron Miripol. Terrance understood he had to hedge his bets. He could see that HARP was a token committee with no real power. Terrance did ask Miripol for a meeting to discuss what could be done with the Holly while the visioning process crawled along. "There's twenty-two thousand square feet of space doing nothing," Terrance told Miripol. Terrance proposed putting in some basketball courts, a gazebo, and tables, and turning the old steel columns that had survived the fire into "peace poles." He had already started telling potential donors that he could have a hundred kids out there every day shooting hoops instead of shooting people. "People want to donate," he told Miripol.

Terrance showed Miripol Prodigal Son's new strategic plan, which included Terrance's plan to use community development to fight gang violence, and the idea of an interim-use lease for the property. While long-term plans took shape, community efforts could be at the fore. Miripol was impressed. He told Terrance he was inclined to lease the property to him for one dollar a year—on one condition.

"You're in charge of the place," Miripol said.

"That's fine," Terrance said.

"Meaning, if anything happens, it's your responsibility."

"I got it," Terrance said.

"Anything," he said.

"You'll see."

WITH MIRIPOL'S SUPPORT, Prodigal Son got its first grant from the city. It was for a "community beautification project" at the Holly, for $65,000. The city would not release the money in advance, however; Terrance was required to show receipts. He felt offended. He had no way to front the cash. But Miripol agreed to advance him the money in pieces, and the work to install the courts and the peace poles began.

Terrance hired a construction company that worked exclusively with convicted felons. He found an executive at Kroenke Entertainment, which owned the Denver Nuggets, to donate premium glass backboards and send players to the opening.

As he rode around town, telling people about the redevelopment, he recognized the opportunity it had to bring positive energy to the neighborhood as well as something else. Community leaders around northeast Denver were telling him they were interested in a peace movement. As in LA, many of Denver's original gang leaders had been through too much. They were as tough as they came, and they couldn't take it anymore.

Terrance had begun wearing camouflage shirts and hats. In 2007, he'd spent two weeks in Haiti on a humanitarian aid visit. Some of the relief workers there wore camo. When he returned, Terrance found that the kids in Prodigal Son loved it and he had made it the organization's official colors. The peace-seeking gang members liked the camo too.

In the spring of 2010, along with a crew of community activists in predominantly Black neighborhoods, Terrance founded the Colorado Camo Movement. His team included Innerstate Ike in Montbello, a rapper who was confined to a wheelchair from a shooting; Gerald "Hoop Ride" Wright and Esi Juey, former top Tre Tre Crips (Gerald's son was in Prodigal Son); Namm, a rapper who was part of the New York–based Lama Squad rap crew; Kamao "Ktone" Martinez, one of northeast Denver's most prominent DJs; J Hood, a former Gangster Disciple who had moved from Chicago; Billy "Too Much" Wooton and his brother Chris "Lil Too Much," who were out of prison and wanting to change; and Bryan Butler, his childhood friend, among others.

Terrance designed camo shirts with the Denver skyline. The movement's leaders began to push into northeast Denver's neighborhoods the way the original Crips had, only this time it was in the name of peace and unity. They asked the young gang members what they were still in it for, and offered them the camo gear.

Soon, many of the older gang members they encountered began wearing the gear, as did some of the younger, active gang members. As the summer of 2010 approached, Terrance saw almost as much camo as he did red and blue. And they all noticed something else: shootings were becoming increasingly uncommon. Peace, they believed, was possible.

As the Colorado Camo Movement hit Denver's streets, undercover law enforcement operations in the city's gang communities were also on the rise. ATF informants stung more than a dozen gang members, including the recently released Ice Alexander on gun charges. Most of those ensnared were given a chance to help themselves stay out of prison by offering information about someone else. Some claimed to have information about the killing of Darrent Williams, the Bronco.

Nearly three years after Williams's murder, the Denver district attorney's office charged Willie Clark, a Crip, as the sole trigger man. Clark went to trial, where five witnesses, all of whom faced other charges, testified against him. He was convicted. The five witnesses had their own penalties reduced by a combined 150 years.

"There's one saying we go by," Mitch Morrissey, the DA, told Denver's Fox 31. "Crimes conceived in hell don't have angels as witnesses. There were some bad people around that night." Clark maintained his innocence, saying, "The evidence gathered should have excluded me, but somebody has to pay in order for the political pressure to cease."

THE UNDERCOVER OPERATIONS had also turned some high-ranking Bloods into informants. As their work began to ensnare others, accusations of snitching consumed the leadership of the Park Hill Bloods, and Denver began to see intra-gang violence rise.

One day, in a warehouse at the top of MLK Park, two of the Park Hill OGs, Pernell "P. Lok" Hines and "Ty Bud" Lockett, got into an argument that was believed by many to be about whether either of them was snitching. Pernell shot Ty Bud, who fell into a clothing rack and died. He was thirty-three. District 2 appeared on the scene quickly, and Pernell confessed. *Westword* described the case as "open and shut." Pernell, perhaps the most powerful Blood in the city, was looking at a mandatory life sentence.

But days later, without any media reporting, the district attorney declined to charge Pernell, whose criminal history was well-known to them, even for illegal possession of a weapon, an automatic prison sentence. Pernell walked.

The episode sent a chill through northeast Denver. Ty Bud was remembered by many as one of the youngest Bloods, who joined at age nine, his hat too big for his head. As was often the case after such a high-level inside job, a burst of traditional "set tripping" gang violence broke out as the OGs flexed their muscle and jostled for power. Katsina Roybal—the lone female Holly 9 Crip—was shot and killed on her sidewalk by two assailants on foot. The Bloods took losses as well, including nineteen-year-old Montea Tyree Davis, or Baby AD, who Terrance had spoken to in the Holly two years earlier about finding a job. Montea was killed by another Blood, during a robbery, around the corner from Ernestine's restaurant.

Terrance, dressed in camo, spoke at Montea's vigil and gave his mom a copy of the video his friend had shot of Montea in the Holly, in hopes it would be a testament.

THE FOLLOWING WEEK, Terrance led his first citywide anti-gang march, "Heal the Hood." Several hundred active and former Crips and Bloods in camouflage shirts and hats set off separately from Five Points and the Holly. They marched toward Colorado Boulevard, where they met at New Hope Church on the war's front line. It was the largest gang peace march Denver had ever seen.

Many of northeast Denver's leaders came out, including the civil rights icon Rev. Acen Phillips. Innerstate Ike's mom, the executive director of Families Against Violent Acts, signed on as a co-sponsor, as did Brother Jeff Fard, editor of 5 Points News. A Brooklyn rapper called Supa Nova Slom flew in.

When each side reached the church, they gathered under the shade of a tent in the parking lot. It was a hot summer day. Many hugged and cried. Terrance encouraged anyone who wanted to speak to take the mic. One talked about the food desert—"three hundred blocks without a supermarket"—in Northeast Park Hill.

Supa Nova Slom reminded everyone that Bloods was also an acronym for Brotherly Love Overpowering Oppressive Destruction, and Crips for Community Revolution in Progress. "If you ain't reppin' for Black power then you forgot what you should be reppin' for," he said to cheers and applause.

"Now I want you to hear from a brother that is *super* courageous!" Brother Jeff said. "On the front line. Who put his heart and soul not only into this gathering but you've seen him all over the community on the front lines, talking about peace."

"OG Terrance!" someone yelled.

"He's traveled into communities and neighborhoods where he's put his life on the line," Brother Jeff continued. "He's not just talking about it, he's being about it. Put your hands together for Terrance Roberts, Prodigal Son Initiative!"

Terrance stepped to the microphone to cheers. His muscled arms bulged from his camouflage T-shirt. He wore a camouflage baseball cap with a *P* for Park Hill.

"The first people I want to acknowledge," Terrance said, "are the OGs. These are the guys who can tear the city up, and they have done it. But they're here today for a peaceful gathering. When they do wrong, we need to tell them that, and I do. Let 'em do good. Today I honor you, brothers. Thank you, guys, for being so powerful today . . .

"This is the *movement*," he said, before pausing. "This is where the power is at."

People hollered.

"We gotta stop killing each other," he continued. "Just for them to use the word *violence*—that gives them the right to bring law enforcement into our community like an army . . .

"I remember a time," he said, going into a preacher's lilt the way he did at Mike Asberry's funeral, "I *remember* a time . . . when I could go to the projects. When I didn't know what a Crip or Blood was. When I was nine or ten years old. We could be in the Holly with the Kool-Aid Man. And nobody was at war."

Gang members and activists cheered and clapped.

"Now is the time, though," Terrance said. "We are *possessing* the land. Whether the Crips or Bloods like it or not, we are gonna be here! And just like they're here, I'm here. 'Cause I love the Crips and I love the Bloods—but I promise you, I am not gonna be afraid of *nobody*!"

"That's right!" someone yelled.

"I'm gonna go where I wanna go and I'm gonna *force* you to kill me," Terrance said, pounding his fist. "If you're set tripping I can't do nothing with that. But if you wanna come home, Prodigal Son accepts you 'cause we *all* comin' home. And we all possessing the land!"

"Terrance Roberts Healing the Hood," read the headline in *5 Points News.*

"When people think of prophets they often conjure up images or thoughts of the infamous Ms. Cleo, or some over the top religious zealot promising cars and new homes to everyone they meet," wrote Pastor Terrence "Big T" Hughes, a well-known northeast Denver parishioner. "With that being said, it is not hard to understand that when a real prophet such as Terrance Roberts arrived with a message that he had lived and now needed to share, the same Denver community he loves so dearly did not immediately embrace him.

"The prophetic message that he spreads locally, nationally and internationally is one of redemption, empowerment, and if you are in a gang, there are approximately 700 days until you end up in a grave or a wheel chair . . . I refer to Terrance as a prophet because he reminds me so much of the biblical prophet, Paul. Just like Paul, he was a committed warrior who took lives and was converted to a warrior that saves lives."

Denver's gang homicides in 2010 fell to an all-time low, officially only ten. The city had never seen so dramatic a downturn. While law enforcement efforts were also on the rise, many in northeast Denver credited the Camo Movement for affecting the attitudes of the youth. "It's like the Bible says, 'Where there is no vision, the people perish,' Michelle Wheeler, president of the Northeast Park Hill Coalition, told *5 Points News.* "I see [Terrance] preserving the people. He has the vision for today. I see the excitement."

Word of the Camo Movement spread. Aqeela Sherrills, who had become arguably the most well respected anti-gang activist in

America, invited Terrance to speak in Watts, describing him as "a rock star for the peace movement." To Aqeela, Terrance embodied the attitude of the 1992 peace movement, whose motto was "Nobody Can Stop This War but Us." The Camo Movement was a pure street movement, without law enforcement or other systemic funding. For many who had lived in gang communities, it was the only approach they felt they could trust.

Rev. Acen Phillips was inspired by Terrance's political awakening, but he also began to worry about him. Terrance reminded him of Lauren Watson, and he'd seen what happened to Black activists with large followings.

TERRANCE HAD HELPED stem Denver's gang violence at a time when most of America's gang communities were seeing an increase in gang activity. According to the FBI, between 2009 and 2011, gang membership soared by 40 percent.

The subprime-mortgage crisis, which disproportionately hurt low-income African American communities, hastened the expansion of America's gang war as gang-affiliated families left their neighborhoods for cheaper housing. Suburban areas, where gangs had not been as prevalent, saw more gang activity. In northeast Denver, bankruptcies and foreclosures rose alongside a decline in the city's African American population, many of whom left for Aurora and other Denver suburbs.

In cities like New York, Los Angeles, Philadelphia, Baltimore, Chicago, Oklahoma City, and Denver, among others, historic gentrifying neighborhoods were also the sites of police programs like Stop and Frisk and Broken Windows. Civil rights activists began filing lawsuits against police departments, saying the policies were based on racial profiling. The law professor Alexandra Natapoff questioned whether police departments were utilizing unregulated assets, such as informants, to weaken community opposition to objectives set by city hall.

For many gang members, the adversity their communities faced made more important their ties to their original neighborhoods. The sentiments were represented by a July 2010 music video by Waka Flocka Flame, a Blood-affiliated rapper, who launched his way to stardom in part with "Hard in Da Paint." The song venerated Baldwin Village, a famous South LA Bloods neighborhood known as "the Jungles." As if to underline the feeling of being forced out of one's own neighborhood, the music video, which was filmed in the Jungles, includes footage of the production's shutdown by the LAPD.

"Hard in Da Paint" inspired a wave of neighborhood rap videos by gang rappers, who posted to YouTube their own versions of the song, featuring their neighborhoods. Among those who participated were the Park Hill Bloods, who faced the threat of losing the neighborhood not only to gentrification but also to the Camo Movement.

Three of the Park Hill Bloods' best rappers co-wrote "Hard in the Hills," referring to Park Hill. "It's that motherfucking Hillside, till the day I die, red flags in the sky," a Blood called Wax raps. "I'm going hard from Quebec to the boulevard," another Blood called Tramp says. The video, professionally filmed and edited, features dozens of Bloods in the back of MLK Park, swaying to the beat and flashing gang signs. One is Hasan, who waves a red paisley bandana. At nineteen he had recently become a father. His rail-thin frame and hollowed eyes give him a wild look.

Three days after the video was shot, District 2 raided a Northeast Park Hill home where Hasan was napping. He had a small amount of crack in his pocket and was arrested.

TERRANCE PUSHED A big broom across the courts and emptied the trash. The first phase of what he considered his redevelopment of the Holly—the peace courts was finished. Three Denver Nuggets players had come to the opening and participated in a three-on-three basketball tournament. People from all over northeast Denver attended.

Terrance had seen the Bloods' "Hard in the Hills" video. Significantly, none of it was filmed in Holly Square. And he hadn't had a visit from the OGs since Pernell came to see him at his grandmother's restaurant. He believed he was going to be able to beat the Bloods on their own turf. To make the point that Holly Square was safe again, some days at dusk, Terrance pulled his truck onto the pavement and flipped on the headlights so that people could keep hooping.

One morning, Terrance got to the office to find John Arigoni of the Boys & Girls Club and two others waiting. Arigoni introduced his guests. They were Libby Anschutz, daughter of Phil Anschutz, and Ted Harms, executive director of the Anschutz Foundation.

Arigoni pointed to the drawing on Terrance's wall. "This is what it could look like over here," Terrance said. Anschutz and Harms looked at the sketch. Terrance had written "Boys & Girls Club" on the building.

"So what do you want to talk about?" Terrance asked.

Tell them what you told me, Arigoni said.

PHIL ANSCHUTZ, WHOSE net worth was $7 billion, was the wealthiest person in Colorado and one of its most influential residents. In 1992, he was a funder of a successful campaign to amend the Colorado state constitution, to bar gays, lesbians, and bisexuals from gaining protected status. (The Supreme Court later struck down the amendment.) Through his family foundations, he funded Christian conservative causes and think tanks, as well as the University of Colorado School of Medicine and the Denver police awards. But, aside from the purchase of Daddy-O Walker's KDKO radio station, which Anschutz closed down a year later, Anschutz had no known business dealings in northeast Denver.

Diminutive at five feet eight, with thick hair and large glasses, Anschutz, "the secretive billionaire," granted almost no interviews and was rarely seen outside of the church he attended on Sundays. According to a spokesman, he preferred anonymity due to concern for the safety of his family. His twenty-room central Denver home was guarded around the clock by off-duty Denver police.

Anschutz had moved to Denver from Russell, Kansas, in the 1960s with his wife, Nancy, a former flight attendant. He followed his father into oil prospecting and drilling, and bought up massive tracts of land in Kansas, Wyoming, and Utah. It was a high-risk industry, but Anschutz, according to Bloomberg News, "was known as a guy who could turn disaster to his advantage."

In 1982, he became America's youngest billionaire, at age forty-two. He used his oil profits to get into railroads. He bought and repaired the Rio Grande and Southern Pacific lines, along which he laid fiber-optic cable. In the early 1990s, he leveraged those to launch a telecom business, Qwest, which quickly became one of the nation's largest networks.

Qwest operated out of a Denver skyscraper that Anschutz owned. For nearly a decade in the late '90s and early '00s, the company's blue neon sign was a signature mark of Denver's skyline. But Qwest was soon under investigation by multiple regulators and accused of fraud.

Qwest's CEO, Joseph Nacchio, was hit with nineteen counts of insider trading. Nacchio believed that the charges were retaliation for his being the only major telecom CEO who had refused the NSA's request to conduct warrantless surveillance. Anschutz, who was chairman of Qwest's board, wasn't charged, but he did testify at Nacchio's trial. Nacchio was convicted and sentenced to six years in prison. After his release, Nacchio said he believed Anschutz and the federal government had set him up.

Anschutz changed industries again. He founded the Anschutz Entertainment Group (AEG), an events company that manages world-class venues and elite acts, such as Michael Jackson's final tour. (After Jackson's death while on tour, the Jackson family filed a wrongful-death lawsuit against AEG because Jackson's doctor, who was convicted of involuntary manslaughter for administering the fatal anesthetic, worked for AEG. AEG was found not to be liable.)

Anschutz also bought newspapers, including the *San Francisco Examiner*, the *Colorado Springs Gazette*, and the conservative political magazine *The Weekly Standard* (which he later shut down). He also bought LA's Staples Center, a controlling stake in the NHL's Los Angeles Kings, and six Major League Soccer teams; the MLS championship trophy is called the Philip F. Anschutz Trophy.

Members of the Anschutz family were prominent on various nonprofit boards. Libby Anschutz, Phil's middle child, who had shown up with Arigoni to Terrance's office, was on the board of the Boys & Girls Club. After getting agreement from Aaron Miripol, the Anschutz Family Foundation voted to approve a $5 million grant to Boys & Girls Clubs of Metro Denver, to pay for a new facility in the Holly. With the gift, the Anschutz family became the largest stakeholder in Holly Square.

AMONG THE DENVER Foundation, the Urban Land Conservancy, and the Anschutz family, some of Denver's wealthiest and most influential power brokers now led the Holly redevelopment. Meanwhile, the city's political leadership was about to undergo a major transition. In 2010, halfway into his second term, Mayor Hickenlooper announced he would run for governor when Bill Ritter, the former district attorney, said he would not seek a second term. Hickenlooper's decision paved the way for City Council President Mike Hancock to make a bid for mayor, the job he'd wanted since he was a kid with Mike Asberry in Rev Kelly's Red Shield program.

Under Hickenlooper, Denver's economy had prospered, but among the African American community, unemployment and poverty had not improved, and policing was a growing concern. Broken Windows had not been popular with many Black families in Northeast Park Hill. And police shootings and abuses began to spur civil lawsuits against the city of Denver. Paul Childs, Ismael Mena, and Frank Labato, another innocent victim of a botched Denver police raid, were all names many in northeast Denver would never forget. The Colorado ACLU believed that Denver police had shown a pattern of racial profiling.

Mike Hancock promised to reform the Denver Police Department, and Terrance, who had never gotten involved in local politics, decided to campaign for him, door to door. In June, Hancock was elected, becoming Denver's second African American mayor. The day he was inaugurated, District 2 responded to a call of suspicious behavior at the Denver Zoo in City Park. Alonzo Ashley, a Northeast Park Hill resident who was not armed, was tased. He went into cardiac arrest and died. He was twenty-nine. The Denver county coroner declared the death a homicide, but no charges were brought against the officers.

Mayor Hancock, in his first big test, denounced his police force and fired the police chief.

AFTER A NATIONWIDE search, Hancock hired Robert White, the former Louisville, Kentucky, police chief. White became the first person in fifty years from outside Denver's police department to lead it. Hancock and White would make a formidable partnership. Both Black and from gang communities (White grew up in Washington, D.C.), they were going to have the chance to helm a closely watched federal anti-gang effort: Denver had just been awarded another prestigious Project Safe Neighborhoods grant. Regina Huerter of the Crime Prevention and Control Commission had worked on Denver's proposal with funding from the Denver Foundation. The city's ambitions were high. Denver proposed to create a national model for fighting gang violence. With new regional headquarters of the FBI and ATF, the city had the ability to maximize resources, personnel, and intelligence. In northeast Denver, the target neighborhoods were Five Points and Northeast Park Hill

Getting Project Safe Neighborhoods grants had become more

competitive. Under President Obama, the program budget had shrunk from $133 million a year to $86 million. The Department of Justice had awarded Denver $2.2 million over three years, and added an additional grant to pay for an independent evaluation by some of the nation's top researchers. "The whole idea is to find a way to tackle what we call a hardened base of crime," said Jeffrey Butts, director of the Research and Evaluation Center at John Jay College of Criminal Justice in New York, who would lead the evaluation. In addition, the Centers for Disease Control awarded the University of Colorado a five-year, $6.9 million grant to study gang violence in Montbello and Northeast Park Hill. At a time of historically low gang violence in northeast Denver, the area would become the focus of the nation's leading federal efforts to counter it.

As Mayor Hancock and Chief White discussed plans, they realized they shared a favorite movie, *The Interrupters*, a 2011 documentary about an anti-gang program in Chicago. Directed by the award-winning filmmaker Steve James (*Hoop Dreams*), the film followed the "violence interrupters" in an anti-gang program created by the Chicago-based epidemiologist Gary Slutkin.

Slutkin's program, now called Cure Violence, used former gang members with street credibility to interrupt conflicts before they happened. The parties involved would then be brought into meetings with social workers and law enforcement in hopes of steering them onto a different path.

The program had notable successes, but in some cities its implementation had problems. In those places, gang members who were still criminally active managed to get hired, creating distrust and fear in the community among people who knew about these men's criminal activity. Steve James got close enough to encounter a similar situation while filming *The Interrupters*, but didn't include it in the film. The documentary premiered at the Sundance Film Festival and played on PBS's *Frontline*, and the success of the film helped Slutkin's model become the most widely implemented anti-gang program in the country. The DOJ had "encouraged" Project Safe Neighborhood cities to implement the Cure Violence/interrupters model. In Denver, Chief White and Mayor Hancock were determined to employ an interrupters-style approach.

THE METRO DENVER Gang Coalition meetings, run by Regina Huerter, filled up again. This time, they included mental health counselors, social workers, and even tattoo-removal specialists. Denver's model was to be a holistic approach to fighting gang violence. The city also needed an interrupter on the ground in Northeast Park Hill.

Huerter invited Terrance to meetings, but he didn't show. He had been proving he could do it without the city's help. He had just been named to NBC's Grio 100, the network's annual list of most influential African Americans. Others on the list included Attorney General Eric Holder, Michelle Obama, Oprah, and Jay-Z.

Huerter called again. Terrance told her he'd seen *The Interrupters*. In fact, he'd hosted the film's Denver premiere and the panel that followed. He said he didn't want to run an "interrupter"-style program. He did that work on his own; he wasn't interested in doing it as part of a law enforcement effort. He would lose any trust he'd built with his community.

Next, Paul Callanan came by the office. Callanan, a former probation officer, had been appointed by Mayor Hancock to be executive director of the Gang Reduction Initiative of Denver (GRID), which would succeed the Metro Denver Gang Coalition as the administrator of funds for the anti-gang effort. Aside from the DOJ money, funding came from the Denver Foundation and others.

Callanan told Terrance he wouldn't have to work with law enforcement or be an interrupter. He said he could get him a budget for two "outreach workers" at $50,000 per year, plus a $1,000-a-month organizational stipend for Prodigal Son. Terrance sent Callanan away, but he couldn't help thinking about what the money would mean, both for his efforts to fight gang violence and his own stability.

Despite his success, he couldn't afford any outreach workers. Fund-raising was a 24/7 job, and it wasn't easy. He didn't even have health insurance, and Gigi had just given birth to their first son, Judah.

He called Callanan back and agreed to take the grant.

A FEW MONTHS later, in December 2011, John Arigoni showed up at the monthly HARP meeting. He had a slide presentation of a proposed Boys & Girls Club. It had two hallways of office suites, a cavernous rec room, and two state-of-the-art community rooms for meetings and educational activities. Its construction, Arigoni said, was fully funded.

The HARP board, including Terrance, called for a vote, which was unanimously in favor. Terrance couldn't believe it. The Urban Land Conservancy's two-year visioning process had been quietly abandoned, and Terrance's dream of a youth center was coming true. Arigoni called him the next day and said he would make sure Terrance had an office in the new club.

The news immediately had an impact in the community. One day Terrance got to the office to find a blue-and-white sign going up across the crown of his building's entrance: "Mike Johnston State Senator," it said. Terrance got the muralist Dan Levinson to come over to paint a camo-colored mural on an exterior wall that faced the Holly. It included the Prodigal Son logo, which was a hand cupping the Denver skyline, and the words One Tribe, North East, and the neighborhood's zip code, 80207.

Two months later, in February 2012, Mayor Hancock hosted a press event at the Hiawatha Davis Jr. Recreation Center, formerly Skyland, across the street from Holly Square, to announce the new Boys & Girls Club. In attendance were Philip Anschutz and his wife, Nancy, for whom the new center would be named.

"Anschutz Gift to Help New Life Rise from Ashes," trumpeted the front page of The Denver Post. "We lived and grew up in central Denver and knew how badly a club was needed in the area," Libby

Anschutz told the paper. "Our foundation is dedicated to working with young people so this was a perfect fit for us."

Arigoni beamed. "This has been the most impressive process I have ever witnessed," he said. "The way the community came together—this is truly like a phoenix rising from the ashes."

Mayor Hancock began the program by walking to the podium, and looking puzzled. "First," he said. "Where is Terrance Roberts?" Guests looked around. "Well, when no one else listened or cared, he was there. We owe him a tremendous debt of gratitude."

Terrance was standing all the way in the back. He'd been left off the program.

Terrance didn't tell anyone about the slight. His pride ran deep. In the community he was still seen as a rising star. His office had become something of a community organizing headquarters. Activists from all over the state visited. Some took the Camo Movement back to their communities; others formed partnerships with Terrance to run workshops on nutrition and women's reproductive rights. Terrance and Alex Landau, who was twenty-three and had become an impassioned activist after being beaten nearly to death by Denver police during a routine traffic stop in 2009, began working on a petition to demand a civil rights investigation of the Denver Police Department (DPD).

But privately Terrance was concerned. He could see that the city was changing. Denver was one of the nation's fastest-growing cities. Five Points and Northeast Park Hill were two of its most sought-after neighborhoods. It appeared to Terrance that his advocacy wasn't what the powerful, new all-white leadership at the Holly wanted.

Days after he was left off the announcement stage, a ULC staffer had emailed him asking for help getting Deloris Wilson to sell the strip across the street from Holly Square. Terrance replied that they would need to find someone else to help, and went to warn Mrs. Wlison. At another meeting Terrance attended, someone asked about getting an inspector to look at her building. Terrance knew exactly what it meant. The Denver City Council was hearing arguments about declaring eminent domain over twenty-eight blocks of Five Points because of blight.

Terrance tried to talk about his concerns with Gigi, but the conversation didn't go anywhere. Terrance felt she only wanted to see him as the hero, lifting up the community. But he could feel the ground shifting under his feet.

In March, he was at the capitol, waiting to testify about a bill to reform the prosecution of juveniles, which he supported, when his friend Bryan Butler texted him. An article in *The Denver Post* had just posted. "Patience Helps Build Path to Boys and Girls Club" was the headline. The story chronicled the multiyear effort to redevelop Holly Square, which the reporter described as "something rare: authentic community engagement . . . Not a gathering of a select few to represent 'the community.'"

No mention of Terrance was made in the story.

He went back to his office and stared at the wall, feeling his anger swelling. He had tried to retrain himself not to react the way he had in the past. But when he felt disrespected, it wasn't easy. He was the founder of the Holly Area Redevelopment Project. He'd pitched the idea of a Boys & Girls Club to John Arigoni. He'd been working eighty-hour weeks at the site. He felt used.

He composed an email to Patrick Horvath of the Denver Foundation, which Terrance had learned was responsible for leaving him off the announcement program. "I feel that I am strategically being alienated because of the advocacy that my community asked of me to perform," he wrote.

Horvath replied late that night: "Please understand, Terrance that everyone here has only the best intentions regarding our work with you."

But Terrance didn't let it go.

"This is not a new thing Patrick, it has gone on for years, we are in fact bullied and hurt by YOUR community liaison . . . I promised GOD I would help children not join gangs and I would advocate for my community by any means necessary. We can all see you guys want Ceric Crimes and more manageable people to really be the voice, even though I have never disrespected the process one time . . . I want my people to get the respect we deserve and whether it is by us working together or me being that leader who can get 400 people to make sure it happens I am going to achieve that goal."

Terrance was also experiencing friction with Paul Callanan about the grant. He wondered if the tensions he faced on the Holly redevelopment were causing him trouble on the anti-gang grant. The Denver Foundation's Patrick Horvath also worked with Paul Callanan.

Eventually, his grant approval went through. Then Terrance's first choice for outreach worker, Gerald Wright, the former Crip and a Camo Movement leader, was disallowed because of his criminal record. Instead Terrance hired John "Qwest" Lewis, a former Crip affiliate who walked with a limp from a shooting. Qwest joined Bryan Butler, one of Terrance's oldest friends, as Prodigal Son's two full-time anti-gang workers.

Bryan and Qwest were charged with acquiring a caseload of twelve- to twenty-four-year-olds from Five Points and Northeast Park Hill who were already caught up in the system. Instead of doing interruption—intervening in ongoing tensions and disputes—they were to work more in the role of mentors and counselors, keeping youth on the right track and connecting them with other social services.

For Bryan, who still lived blocks from the Holly, it seemed like a dream job—until he got to the first meeting. He and Qwest were given questionnaires to fill out with information about their new charges, including the names of their associates. Just asking the question made Bryan and Qwest uncomfortable. In addition, once a month they were expected to discuss their cases during an Intervention Support Group meeting, with law enforcement present. Bryan felt duped. The city promoted GRID as a "faith- and community-based" program, but to him it felt like a law enforcement effort.

He and Qwest met with Terrance, who wasn't surprised. "Don't do anything you don't feel comfortable doing," he told them. The work was dangerous enough already. And it was going to become more dangerous still: though they were not privy to the plans, the neighborhood was about to become the site of an extensive undercover law enforcement operation.

CHIEF WHITE OF the Denver PD had not met Terrance, but his presence was virtually impossible to miss. After Trayvon Martin was killed in February 2012, Terrance had co-led a march to the state capitol. And word had gotten around that, at a recent GRID meeting, Terrance brought the conversation to a halt when someone asked what he, Bryan, and Qwest knew about some gang members recently released from prison. "We're not participating in this kind of word-on-the-street discussion," Terrance said. He got up and left.

Chief White left messages for Terrance, but they were not returned. Terrance's feelings about law enforcement were no secret. A prominent photo on his popular Facebook page depicted him on a bullhorn next to a sign that read, "The Police Are Denver's Most Dangerous Gang."

Chief White on the other hand quickly befriended Denver's other high-profile anti-gang activist, Rev Kelly, who ran a parole program for recently released gang members for the Department of Corrections. In June 2012, Rev and Chief White accompanied city council president Albus Brooks to the opening of Denver's Scientology Church. They went as guests of the Scientology head, David Miscavige, who'd bought a $12 million building in LoDo. Chief White, in his dress blues, gave a welcome speech that had been partially written by the church.

Chief White joined the board of directors of Rev's anti-gang organization. Rev, who reasserted his relationship with the new mayor, became a sounding board for Chief White, who made a series of personnel changes, most consequentially the promotion of

Captain Mike Calo of the gang unit to commander of District 2. Calo, who had worked with Rev for years, was now one of the top cops in Denver. Among other things, he would oversee the undercover operations at the Holly.

IN APRIL, TERRANCE flew to LA as a guest of Aqeela Sherrills, for the twentieth anniversary of the Truce of Nine-Deuce. Being among a community of sophisticated anti-gang workers was a welcome respite for Terrance. Years of trying to figure out how to fight gang violence had led LA's anti-gang workers to come up with a contract with the city, saying they would not be expected to work with law enforcement. It wasn't their job. Paramount to them was safety and community trust. Not that it was simple. The lion's share of available anti-gang funding came from law enforcement.

Terrance stayed with Aqeela in Watts, along with Ras Baraka, son of the activist writer Amiri. Ras was running for mayor of Newark. The weekend was sober, with a gang homicide the first day. The violence was a reminder that while their lives were defined by leaving the gang life, they could never completely escape. In fact, for the leaders of the anti-gang movement, the more success they had, the more dangerous the work became. Jealousy and pride were motives for murder in the gang world, as were power and politics.

Terrance received a certificate of honor from Congresswoman Maxine Waters, and he returned to Denver determined to test his resolve. Gang violence in northeast Denver had begun rising again. One day, Terrance watched a carload of Crips come through the Holly, shooting one youth in the face. Hours later, at City Park Jazz, the Crips and Bloods converged on each other. Celena Hollis, a District 2 officer, attempted to intervene, just as twenty-two-year-old Rollin "Boogie" Oliver, a Blood, fired his gun. Hollis, president of the Black Police Officers Association and a single mother, was hit in the head and killed. Her death made national news and put a rare spotlight on Denver's gang problem. "There aren't a lot of skiers and snowboarders in northeast Denver," Terrance told *The New York Times*. "We're talking about young men here who feel like they don't have any choices."

Terrance knew Boogie. He was one of the many neighborhood kids he watched become a Blood in the months after the Holly fire. Boogie was on the block all the time, limping from a gunshot wound.

He also knew Celena Hollis. She was one of the few officers he had trusted. He brought complaints to her because he knew she'd be fair. The day after Hollis's death, Terrance saw Commander Calo and felt a cold shoulder. Terrance wanted to show he wasn't against all cops. He got Mike Johnston to co-host a memorial for Hollis in the District 2 community room. "She was everything we advocated for in our community," Terrance said.

The next day, Terrance was on his way to Ned's candy shop when he passed some Bloods. "Service for the po-po but nothing for the homey?" one said.

THE PEACE COURTS were cracking and the paint peeling. With the Boys & Girls Club coming, Terrance was determined to repair and upgrade the recreation area. He met Terry Minger, CEO of the Piton Foundation, another well-funded nonprofit run by Sam Gary, the founder of the Urban Land Conservancy. Terrance convinced Minger to support the rebuilding plans.

Terrance, Bryan, and Qwest began cleaning and preparing the area. One day they were on the property with brooms when District 2 squad cars pulled up onto the courts. The officers got out and frisked a group of young men, arresting some of them. Terrance went over to one of the officers and gave him a piece of his mind. "This is private property," he told the cop. Terrance said he didn't allow gang members who were causing problems to be on the property. "I'm responsible for this property and I'm trying to make it a safe zone," he said.

His comment was met with a stare. To him, the Denver Police weren't giving him any reason to think a working relationship could be salvaged. Indeed, he almost wasn't surprised when, a few days later, one of the Bloods, Aundre "AD" Moore, told Terrance that during an arrest Moore had witnessed, a District 2 officer told him that Terrance was helping the police with evidence. Whether or not Moore's report was true, the level of danger Terrance had been living with had just ratcheted up.

THE NEW BASKETBALL courts were delivered on pallets. They were "snap" courts, to be installed in sections. Terrance had promoted a volunteer event to install the courts. Hundreds of community members showed up, many wearing camouflage. For two days they assembled two full-size yellow-and-black basketball courts, a futsal court, and green gazebos and tables. They also hung flags on the twelve "peace poles," made from the original shopping center stanchions, with images of leaders like Nelson Mandela, Martin Luther King, and Anne Frank. Sipio, the owner of the old auto garage on the south side of the Holly parking lot, let an artist paint his garage in camouflage.

Many who were there were moved. "This process has been an amazing experience," Eric Swan, a business development representative for the city of Denver, said. "It has served as a national model. It is inspiring other projects to do similar goals throughout the country." Terrance, who almost never cried, teared up.

THAT FALL TERRANCE heard that his old Blood friend Freddy "10-4" Johnson* had opened a new shop. 10-4 was one of the Bloods who had been generally supportive of the Camo Movement, but Terrance

---

* Not his real name.

had always been leery of him. A lot of Bloods claimed to give up the criminal life; many weren't able to.

Freddy's store was in a low-rent shopping strip between a Cricket Cellular and a Jiffy Lube on Colorado Boulevard. Terrance went by. When he walked in, a guy on a ladder was installing a camera on the ceiling. Terrance looked at him but the man quickly looked away. Terrance got a weird vibe. Almost nothing was on the shelves but some gum and a few candy bars.

But soon the store became a hub for neighborhood guys, including gang members. Terrance kept going because it was in the middle of everything and he could talk up the new courts and hand out camo gear to whoever wanted it. He always had a stash of hats and shirts in his truck.

One day he was standing outside the shop with Freddy when a gray sports car pulled up.

"What's up, Terrance? Freddy?"

It was Commander Calo. Terrance had never seen him in an unmarked car. He was surprised Calo knew Freddy.

Two of the regulars Terrance saw at Freddy's shop were Carl "Fat Daddy" McKay and Rodney "Big Rod" Jackson. They were both Blood OGs who Terrance had known for years.

Fat Daddy, who was in fact relatively slim, was now forty. He had a well-trimmed goatee and "Mafia" tattooed on his shoulder, short for Crenshaw Mafia Gangsters. He was a "baller," a drug dealer who dressed well. Rodney was more of the streets. He was a hulking guy, overweight, with a club foot from diabetes.

One day at Freddy's shop, Fat Daddy and Big Rod told Terrance they wanted the camo gear. They were "with the movement," they said. Terrance went to his car and got some shirts and hats, not believing them. Everything he saw suggested they were still deep in the game.

Another day, Carl and Rodney went with Freddy into the bathroom in what appeared to Terrance to be an obvious drug deal. Terrance waited, leaning against the counter, looking at the bare shelves and at the camera, wondering if the place could be a law enforcement storefront, run by informants to get intel on gang members.

TERRANCE'S FUNDRAISING SUCCESS had slowed to small checks here and there from community members. For months he had been trying to reach Ted Harms, the administrator of the Anschutz Family Foundation, in hopes of discussing funding. His private donor list was running dry. He had come to believe that the close-knit world of Denver's funding partners had decided he was out.

By Thanksgiving, he was in financial straits. Gigi was eight months pregnant with their second child. He didn't have enough money to pay their rent.

"I hate to be a pain in the butt to you gentlemen," Terrance began a November 29 email to John Arigoni, Aaron Miripol, Patrick Horvath, and Paul Callanan, four of the most powerful people in the redevelopment of the Holly. Horvath and Callanan also were key figures in the anti-gang effort.

"I am in probably the scariest and most desperate situation I have ever been in with a new born on the way. I have so much pressure to get funding I don't know what else to do. If you fellas know of any position I could possibly have with your connections I am pretty much begging you to help me so I can make ends meet, I am a hard worker and proven nationally known organizer."

Only Arigoni responded. He wished Terrance good luck.

"Yeah it looks like we organized for 4 years for everybody but ourselves to have a position over here," Terrance responded. "We're literally surrounded by millionaires and billionaires."

DAYS LATER, TERRANCE was at a friend's house when his phone rang.

"What's up, Freddy," he said. It was Freddy Johnson.

Freddy told Terrance he needed to talk about "the product."

"What?" Terrance said. Terrance hadn't been involved in drugs since he was a Blood. Freddy said they needed to go to LA to talk to a "Russian" about getting "the product."

"What the fuck you talking about, Freddy?" It sounded like a setup. Terrance hung up.

A chain-link construction fence went up in Holly Square. Tractors began digging a foundation for the new club. Alvin Jones, Nathan's brother, who still lived in his childhood home, went by to look. Changes were coming so fast to the neighborhood that Alvin had started calling it "reverse segregation"—a reference to the 1960s, when whites left in droves. Now it was Blacks who were leaving.

With home prices rising, many longtime Northeast Park Hill residents decided to sell. Among them was Ernestine. After fifty-three years in her home, she put it on the market, accepting an offer for $117,000. Four months later, after a renovation, it sold again for $301,000.

Most residents relocated to the adjacent city of Aurora or neighborhoods farther north, but not Ernestine. Then seventy-six, she had been accepted as one of the first residents of an affordable senior living home on the site of the old Dahlia Shopping Center. The redevelopment of the Dahlia was finally taking shape. The "Dahlia Campus" included a mental health center and a planned forty-thousand-square-foot garden that would offer free food to the community.

At a subsidized rate, Ernestine was given a small apartment with a balcony looking out over 33rd Avenue at the Red Bricks. She turned the volume up on her church programs to drown out the sounds of gunfire and sirens.

A few blocks away, Terrance sat outside his office in camouflage. He was adjusting to a shift in the neighborhood few had seen coming: with only six months to the opening of the Boys & Girls Club, Carl "Fat Daddy" McKay and Joel "Way Out" Alexander, who were both Park Hill OGs, had opened a new shop right in Deloris Wilson's strip. For the first time since the Holly Shopping Center burned down, the Bloods had a base right in the Holly.

The new establishment had literally opened with a bang. According to Fat Daddy and Way Out, they'd given the previous proprietors, who had alleged ties to the Crips, until sundown to clear out. The men did leave, but that night, in apparent retaliation, a Blood was shot in the leg behind the store.

Bryan Butler felt like he was back in the 1990s again, only the OGs were all in their forties. No matter, they still had their cliques of younger Bloods "up under" them, and they still believed that they were the self-appointed caretakers of the neighborhood. Terrance told Bryan he was going over to the new store. Bryan shook his head and watched Terrance walk over. This would be interesting, he thought.

The shop was at the far end of the strip, at the corner of 33rd and Holly. Terrance walked past the Horizon and Ned's and the hair salon. At the end was a small asphalt parking area in front of what looked like a former gas station or auto repair shop. It consisted of one car bay next to an office. There was no signage out front. Terrance opened the door. Carl was behind a desk in a camo hat.

"What's up, Fat Daddy?" Terrance said. "What's this about a shop?" The floors were oily.

Carl said it was a car detailing and computer repair business. On a table sat a few old PCs, the kind Terrance had used in prison. Carl said he was fixing them.

"How you learn to fix a computer?" Terrance asked.

Carl said he took a class. Terrance almost laughed. He was positive Carl didn't know how to repair a computer. To Terrance, the place was just as suspicious as the candy shop Freddy had. That one was now gone. Days after Freddy made the strange call to Terrance about a drug deal, Freddy himself had been taken down in a federal drug sting. There were a lot of strange things going on, Terrance thought.

"I appreciate you wearing the camo, Fat Daddy," Terrance said, "but can you tell me: if you're an activist now, how was it that you and Way Out ran the other owners outta here?"

Carl didn't answer.

"That's what I thought," Terrance said.

TERRANCE WASN'T GOING to let the Bloods take over the Holly on his watch. But he would have to resist them with limited resources. He'd recently posted some difficult news on his Facebook page.

> Looks like after eight years of programming for Northeast Denver underprivileged youth who nobody cared at all about we will be closing our doors due to the lack of support. We raised over 400 kids over some very hard and trying times and many of them are very successful to this day. We stepped into all out gang wars and stopped them cold. We resurrected an entire community where over 9,000 people live, 2,500 of them poor children! I am proud of my track record and that of my team! The Lord has used me to do unheard of before advocacy in this nation for my people and community! Thanks to everyone who has ever supported us! COLORADO CAMO MOVEMENT still in full effect!

Messages from all over the city came in. *Westword*, the city's alt weekly, wrote a story. "Terrance Roberts is one of Denver's great comeback stories," it said. "What's all the more painful is that the streets around the Prodigal Son Initiative . . . are finally making a comeback." The local CBS affiliate sent a reporter to interview youth from Prodigal Son. "I'd have nowhere to turn" without it, Ryan McCoy, who was twelve, said.

The publicity brought in several thousand dollars. More important for Terrance, his Facebook post sent a message that he knew his community, many of whom were on Facebook, would understand. Terrance was calling out the wealthy white interests behind the Holly redevelopment for a hypocrisy all too familiar to them. Rev.

Acen Phillips, who saw the post, wasn't surprised. *They pimped Terrance out to gain their own credibility*, Rev. Phillips thought, *then tossed him away now that he won't go along with the program.* Phillips and others came by Terrance's office with cash contributions. Terrance was upbeat. He wasn't worried, he told them. God had a plan for him.

He called Bryan and Qwest in for a meeting. He told them he would have to shut down Prodigal Son's after-school program, but he would keep their grant-funded anti-gang work going. "They're just waiting for us to fold," Terrance said. All he felt he got from city administrators was grief, but they had practically begged him to take the grant. Did they expect him to keep his mouth shut when he had strong opinions about what he was dealing with? Wasn't his expertise the reason they wanted him involved? Terrance suspected his issues with the anti-gang effort and the development of the Holly had collided, effectively blackballing him from the bulk of the city's funding opportunities. He confronted the Denver Foundation's Patrick Horvath about it by email. Horvath acknowledged his relationship with GRID's Paul Callanan, but denied that they spoke about Terrance.

Bryan and Qwest also felt they were getting a cold shoulder from city administrators, but they agreed with Terrance. Quitting wasn't an option. This was bigger than all of them. They saw themselves in a battle to save the Holly from control by the Park Hill Bloods.

Denver's gang violence sharply rose in the first half of 2013. Some of the shootings were classic set-tripping incidents—drive-bys carried out by the younger guys, typically on the orders of the OGs. Other violence was connected to an accompanying piece of the Project Safe Neighborhoods grant, one that Terrance wasn't privy to.

One afternoon Terrance was looking after his son Judah and playing chess outside his office when, across the street, gunfire erupted. A black Blazer screeched out of the Horizon Lounge parking lot as its back window was blown out. Terrance took Judah inside then went across the street, where several Bloods he knew stood. They told Terrance that the man driving the Blazer was Major "Magic" Clarkson.*

---

* Not his real name.

a Blood OG. According to the Bloods, Magic was an ATF informant. Needless to say, there was a green light on Magic.

No one bothered to pick up the debris in the parking lot, so Terrance got his broom and dustbin and swept up the glass and bullet casings as the Bloods watched.

THE TRACTORS BEHIND the construction fence dug. Terrance looked through the netting. He hadn't seen a single person of color at the work site. He did an art project with his final group of after-school kids. They painted wood placards in camouflage and hung them along the fence. With the camo-painted garage in the square and the camo wall on Terrance's office, Holly Square began to look like a game of color wars, with 33rd Avenue as a new border. Bloods to the south, Camo Movement to the north.

Gerald Hamel, a nonprofit fundraiser who knew Terrance's work and had seen his Facebook post, came to visit and quickly understood why Terrance told him he wanted to fight gang violence with community development. He saw Terrance talking to the younger Bloods about the courts and the youth center. "So long as y'all show respect," Terrance told them, "this is all of ours."

Hamel wasn't at all surprised Terrance was having problems with the establishment entities that had taken control over the Holly. Hamel wasn't sure Terrance would ever hold sway with them. He was way too rough around the edges. He suggested Terrance find another property that Prodigal Son could own and develop itself.

Together they drove around northeast Denver, scouting sites. One they both liked was the run-down East Side YMCA in Five Points, where Terrance had seen Mike Asberry for the first time. Terrance knew the guy who owned it. The next time Terrance saw Miripol, he mentioned his interest in the property. Soon, Hamel heard, the ULC was inquiring about it. The price rose out of Prodigal Son's range. Ultimately a high-end condo developer bought it.

Terrance's trust in the ULC's stewardship of the Holly redevelopment reached a new low at the next HARP meeting, when the Boys & Girls Club announced its first executive director for the Holly club, Jason Torrez, a Latino. Terrance emailed Miripol his resignation from HARP. "I don't desire to be a part of these processes," he wrote. Miripol asked him to reconsider and said he would hire a mediator. A staffer from the Boys & Girls Club wrote to offer Terrance two seats in its corporate suite at a Nuggets game.

THE NEXT DAY, Terrance ran into Hasan outside Ned's. Hasan was back on the block again too, often hanging out by Carl's new shop. "What are you doing tonight, Munch?" Terrance asked. He invited him to the Nuggets game.

Hasan was staying in the basement of a Northeast Park Hill home. When Terrance arrived, an unmade bed on a concrete floor was covered with clothing and diapers. Hasan, who was twenty-three, was now the father of two young children.

Hasan was showered and wore a pair of camo cargo shorts. On the ride over to the Pepsi Center, Terrance realized he might need to introduce Hasan. "What's your name, Munch?" he asked.

"Hasan."

"You been to the Nuggets before?"

Hasan said he'd never been to any kind of game.

When they got up to the box, Terrance told Hasan to take advantage of the perks. Hasan ordered chicken fingers, a cheeseburger, a beer, and a mixed drink. At halftime they walked down to the tunnel where the players went in. Hasan saw a woman he knew who was working at one of the food stands. "My big homey brought me," Terrance heard him tell her.

Hasan was the bellwether, Terrance thought. If the Camo Movement could win Hasan, it could have a domino effect.

On the way home, Terrance worked on Hasan. "Why you want to be claiming a Los Angeles street gang? You from *Park Hill*."

Hasan listened.

"You seen your dad?" Terrance asked him. Terrance was a member of the Community Corrections Board, which decided on applications for prison release into halfway houses. An application from Hasan's father, Ice Alexander, had recently come up. In his letter, Ice had falsely claimed he worked for Prodigal Son. Terrance decided to argue in favor of Ice's release anyway. Perhaps it would help Ice take a new path. By a single vote, Ice won his release. Terrance knew he should be in a halfway house by now.

Hasan said that Ice had pulled up a few days earlier behind Mrs. Wilson's strip, in a fancy car, with a wad of bills. *What?* Terrance thought. Hasan said he'd asked his father for a loan but that Ice responded, "Better get your hustle up," and pulled off.

Hasan told Terrance he'd done more for him than Ice ever had. "He ain't even really been my father," Hasan said.

Terrance dropped him off. "Come by the office," he said.

TERRANCE WAS DETERMINED to keep Prodigal Son afloat, and he had reached out to Freeway Rick Ross, the LA legend. Rick had gotten out of prison on an appeal. While inside, he had shared a cell with Xavier "Zayboo" Davis, a Montbello Crip and pioneer of Denver's hip-hop, who admired Terrance. When Rick was released in 2009, he had called Terrance to seek his advice on doing community redevelopment. Now Terrance asked if he would host a fundraiser in Denver for Prodigal Son.

Rick, who was fifty-three and thin, showed up in the Holly with a graying beard and a T-shirt with the phrase "The Real Rick Ross Is Not a Rapper." He was suing the rapper Rick Ross, who had assumed his name for publicity. Terrance showed him around Holly Square, where Bloods flocked around Rick. When they went back to the Prodigal Son office, Rick opened his rollerboard suitcase. He had dozens of T-shirts like the one he wore, which he sold for twelve dollars apiece. He was broke.

About a hundred people attended the fundraiser at the Jet Hotel downtown. Rick wore a black suit with a camo hat. Terrance posted photos on Facebook. He didn't net much after expenses, but the publicity, seen on social media from coast to coast, was priceless. Terrance felt the momentum had shifted back in favor of the Camo Movement. At the Kasbah nightclub in Aurora, which was popular with Northeast Park Hill residents, including the Bloods, almost the whole place wore camo. Then, one day, Terrance and Bryan were outside the office when Hasan and his crew pulled up. "We want the gear," they said. Terrance looked at Bryan then took Hasan and the young Bloods back to the storage room.

THE SHOOTINGS, HOWEVER, kept coming. One day it was an old friend of Terrance's known as Chucky B. A Crip shot him dead on the street over a girl. Another day, a Blood Terrance had never seen before approached him and said he was Lil ShowBizz. "You're my big homey," he said. For gang members it was considered an honor to have one's name passed on, but it unnerved Terrance. "I'm not your big homey," he said. "You're about to get yourself killed if you're not careful out here."

Bryan could see that Terrance's nerves were fraying. In addition to his financial uncertainty and the emotional toll of losing friends, Gigi had taken Judah and Jerusalem, ages three and one, and moved out, after seeing a woman drop Terrance off late at night. Terrance acted like it didn't bother him, but Bryan knew it did.

Terrance sensed danger lurking, but it was hard to know what was real and what was paranoia. One day, news broke about a "hit list" found by investigators looking into the March assassination of the Colorado prison chief, Tom Clements. Terrance had known Clements, a reformer who had enlisted Terrance as an informal adviser. Investigators believed Clements's murder may have been a hit called by leaders of the white supremacist gang the 211 Crew.

Terrance was quite familiar with them. The 211 Crew was founded by Benjamin Davis in 1995, after he was beaten badly by a group of gang members in Building 8. Each week, as a member of the Community Corrections Board, Terrance got parole applications from members of the 211s. Fearing he could be on the hit list, Terrance resigned from the board.

But the dangers Terrance faced in the Holly were inescapable. First, the Blood known as "AD" told Terrance that District 2 told him and other Bloods that Terrance was working with the police. Then, one day, one of the crackheads divulged to Bryan that he overheard the Bloods discussing the question of Terrance's relationship with the police. Terrance didn't take well to hearing about such news. "I've never been a snitch!" Terrance shouted at Bryan. "It wasn't honorable when I was banging—and it isn't honorable now."

Terrance went back to Carl's shop. He had his own theory about where that kind of information was originating.

"Thanks for wearing the camo, Fat Daddy," Terrance said, "but I can see you're on another movement."

You trippin, T, Carl said. He had a blunt and suggested they go outside to smoke it, because of the cameras.

"Those are *your* cameras," Terrance said. They had three white dots on the front, Terrance noted, like the ones at Freddy's shop.

Terrance had a joint of his own, and he lit it up in the store and walked to the security camera in the corner. Looking into it, he exhaled a smoke cloud and flipped it off.

TERRANCE'S BEEF WITH Carl was now on the record. At the candy store, Terrance felt as though the young Bloods were avoiding him, which they'd never done. "Anyone has a problem with me I'll be in the Holly at 9 am," he posted on Facebook.

Instead, many of Terrance's supporters showed up. It was clear things were becoming dangerous. Jason McBride, Ktone, Terrance's cousin DT, and J Hood, the former gang member who'd moved from Chicago, arrived. George came as well. Although they weren't in the Holly daily like Terrance, they were on Facebook and spoke to each other. For all of them it was a strange time in northeast Denver. Most of them knew Magic, the OG whose car was shot up in the Horizon parking lot. He was said to have been wearing a wire in the neighborhood. Terrance had already told them about Freddy's strange call to him about buying drugs. And *The Denver Post* was reporting that one of four gang members who had committed a quintuple homicide at a Colorado Boulevard bar had been an ATF informant. He was also the only one of the group not charged.

Terrance told his crew that he believed there was an undercover operation right on the block. "You know those cameras in Fat Daddy's shop?" Terrance said. "You know who uses those? I think Carl's working for the police."

The room went silent. In northeast Denver, informants were believed to have targeted everyone from real criminals to real activists. They knew Carl had been acting particularly cozy with the Camo Movement lately. None of the Camo Movement leaders believed Carl had left the criminal life, but he'd shown up for a Camo Movement photo shoot. They watched as Carl posed in a camo hat for the camera, and wondered what he was doing there. Like many inexplicable things in the Holly, Carl appeared to pose an existential threat to peace in the neighborhood, and possibly to Terrance.

George broke the silence in the room. "Terrance always said, 'If I have to be a martyr I'ma build this Holly back,'" George said. "'At least I'll die for a purpose, for a cause.'"

Terrance didn't let on that he was worried about his safety, but he was. Aside from a youth center, Terrance had had another vision about the Holly. Lately it had been coming back into his head. It was that he would have to shoot someone there. He hoped that wouldn't happen, but he also felt he needed protection. He made inquiries of some trusted contacts. As a convicted felon, it was illegal for him to possess a gun. But that no longer outweighed the danger he felt growing around him. For $300, he acquired a "pawnshop Nina," a used black 9 mm Jimenez pistol with a silver thirteen-round clip.

19

Terrance began to feel like he did when he was in the Bloods. Few people around him seemed to be who they claimed—not Aaron Miripol or the Denver Foundation's Patrick Horvath, not Rev Kelly or Commander Calo, and not Carl McKay.

One day, early in the summer, Terrance got a call from a producer who said she was from the National Geographic channel. She said she was doing a documentary about Denver gangs and wanted to feature the Holly. She asked if Terrance could help introduce her to gang members.

Terrance agreed. He needed media attention, and he had lost trust in the Denver media. He sought out Hasan. This was a big opportunity. Many of the Bloods wanted a voice. He found Hasan outside of Ned's and told him a crew was coming to film. "You could get on, Munch," Terrance told him. "Tell your story, talk about doing something positive. You're pushing a new movement now."

Hasan seemed interested and said he'd bring some guys. When the day arrived, Hasan and his crew showed up at the courts in Holly Square, where the interview was to be conducted. He and the others wore both red and camo as if they couldn't decide what they were repping. At first they acted tough, taunting the TV crew with gang signs and making an attempt to steal their equipment. The producer complained to Terrance. "I don't know what's going to happen," he told her. But he gave Munch a piece of his mind.

The young Bloods finally settled down at the gazebo and did the interview. Hasan talked about how Park Hill was a war zone but that they were ready for something better. He said that now he was with the Camo Movement.

Terrance looked around. Several other community members were watching, including Brazy. That was it, Terrance thought, the break he needed. The Bloods YG Regulator had just said he was leaving the gang for the Camo Movement. And it was going to be on national television.

In August, the construction fence came down, revealing the new centerpiece of Holly Square, the Boys & Girls Club. A heavy chain hung from its front doors. At the next HARP meeting, the room in the old Safeway building at the north end of Holly Square was full. Even though he'd resigned from the HARP board, Terrance attended. Gerie Grimes, HARP's new president and the mother of Brazy, ran the meeting. To Terrance, it was as if the Bloods and white people had taken over the Holly. Although HARP was supposed to be a body that represented the community, almost everyone who actually had a position of power in the redevelopment was white and didn't live in the neighborhood, from Commander Calo to Aaron Miripol to Patrick Horvath to John Arigoni and staffers from their organizations. The biggest funders, the Anschutz family, never attended meetings, that Terrance was aware of.

There was a sense of excitement that night. The Denver Foundation had already prepared a press release it would disseminate over a national wire service, entitled "A Community's Vision Realized." At the meeting, John Arigoni reported that the club was the "best and safest facility we've built in fifty-two years." A slideshow included a floor plan. Terrance looked closer but did not see Prodigal Son's name. At previous meetings, Prodigal Son was listed; Terrance even had a signed lease.

"What does this mean for the Prodigal Son office?" Terrance asked. The question was met with silence. Afterward Terrance waited to speak to Gerie Grimes. He asked her what happened to the office space he was promised at the club.

Gerie, who was sixty and was Bryan Butler's aunt, had known Terrance since he was ShowBizz. He and Bryan had been arrested on her lawn. She knew that Terrance was a firebrand, but he had also been responsible for much of the progress at the Holly, and he had been promised office space.

She emailed Arigoni and the club's new director, Jason Torrez, copying Terrance. "I would like to have a quick meeting with you all to give clarity to the question raised at last night's meeting," she wrote. "I felt strongly in a walk thru the [Prodigal Son] office space was there . . . I did not get the feeling at all last night . . . Let me also make clear, thank you to all for the hard work thus far on the community space. Don't confuse wanting clarity on the office space with the many accomplishments."

Terrance appreciated Gerie's email, but he didn't expect her gentle tone to get him anywhere; to him, that tone was the reason the new power structure at the Holly preferred her to be the face of HARP. Indeed, the club dragged its feet responding. With time running out, Terrance rounded up Gerald Hamel, the nonprofit fundraiser, and Haroun Cowans, the chair of his board, and asked them to go with him to Boys & Girls Club headquarters across town.

They were ushered into a wood-paneled boardroom. Arigoni and two staffers entered. Hamel had never seen Terrance so angry, but he didn't try to stop Terrance's tirade, as he couldn't help agreeing with the sentiment. "I brought *you* to the table!" Terrance shouted at Arigoni. "You're not even understanding or fulfilling the mission of the Boys and Girls Club." No one from the neighborhood, Terrance said, had been hired. Terrance's diatribe continued. He called Arigoni a "racist" and a "bigot."

When he was done, Hamel produced the lease that had been signed previously by a staffer at the club. A series of emails ensued. The club agreed to honor Prodigal Son's office lease in exchange for an agreement from Terrance not to make disparaging statements about the club.

As DAYS COUNTED down to the club's opening, Terrance began to feel like an enemy in his own country.

One day, Brazy pulled up to the office and asked him to go for a ride. Bryan couldn't believe Terrance got right into his cousin's car. Terrance and Brazy drove around talking about whether Terrance was a problem for the Bloods' recruitment. Terrance told Brazy that an LA street gang had no business being in control of their neighborhood. Brazy told him that they couldn't go backwards, this was how it was. When Terrance returned, he and Bryan acknowledged what was beginning to seem obvious: Terrance was about to be "in the hat." He'd left the gang and had never paid the price, yet.

Rodney Jackson, the OG who had worked for Rev Kelly, came by next. He told Terrance that he'd spoken to Booney, Terrance's friend who was still in prison. Rodney told Terrance that Booney had something he wanted to "hold on his heart," and that Terrance needed to contact him. The inference was that Booney was thinking about spilling some information about Terrance. Terrance blew up and threw Rodney out of the office.

That was it, for Terrance. He wasn't going to allow the Bloods to threaten him on the property he was charged with protecting. He called out to a group of Bloods across the street. "Stay off my property," he told them. "Don't be coming north of 33rd." A new neighborhood boundary had been drawn.

A few days later, Terrance was at the Kasbah with his friend DT. The bar was crowded with neighborhood guys. Carl was there as well. He approached Terrance and told Terrance he was taking things the wrong way. It was almost midnight and the music was loud. "Let's go outside," Terrance said to Carl. DT joined them. The air was damp from a summer rain. Terrance suggested they get into DT's truck and have a smoke.

Terrance, who sat in the passenger seat, lit a joint and passed it around. As they smoked, he turned to look at Carl in the backseat. "Fat Daddy, you already know, bro, I'm out here trying to do a positive thing, so I'm asking you, can you leave me alone, can you talk to the homeys—and if you are having conversations about hurting me or killing me, I'm gonna defend myself."

DT watched Carl through the rearview mirror as Terrance drew his gun from his waistband and held it up for Carl to see.

ON SEPTEMBER 15, the National Geographic documentary aired. The program was part of the channel's *Drugs Inc.* series, which had been criticized for its sensationalized inner-city stories. The show, which covered the city of Denver as a whole, did not include Hasan's discussion of the Camo Movement, nor any footage of Hasan or Terrance. It did feature stylized footage of automatic weapons and a scene in a nondescript location of two Denver gang members in balaclavas, voices disguised, doing a cocaine deal.

When Terrance and Bryan got to the office the next morning, Hasan was across the street, pacing and glowering. Terrance and Bryan called it his "Mad Guy Walk."

Terrance went over.

"Why you ain't put me in the doc?" Hasan said. "I got all the homeys."

"They left me out too," Terrance said. Terrance felt embarrassed that he believed the show would be an accurate representation of his community. When he got back to the office, Bryan said he was hearing reactions from others. Aaron Miripol and even the mayor were said to be upset about the portrayal of the city.

"Well, it ain't my show," Terrance said.

"They think it is," Bryan said. The Prodigal Son logo was shown at the end of the program. Terrance didn't remember being asked by the producer about that. He called her. "You took the most negative comments you could find," he said. He went across the street to the candy store, where Hasan and a group of Bloods moved away as he approached. "Snitch," Terrance thought he heard one of them say.

THE OPENING OF the Boys & Girls Club was less than two weeks away. Denver luminaries like John Elway were said to be coming for the opening ceremony. Terrance emailed friends and supporters about it, putting a positive spin on events. He also decided he was going to hold a rally. "Everyone's coming apart right when we need to pull together," he told Bryan. He would call it a peace-and-unity rally. Qwest designed the flyers. Terrance posted it on Facebook and walked around the Holly, passing out printouts. "This is a way to show we care for and support each other as people," the flyer said.

Bryan hoped a good crowd would show, but he wasn't sure he would attend, due to safety concerns. Bryan recognized the irony that he worked for an anti-gang effort but didn't feel comfortable reporting his fears to law enforcement. From his perspective, the police and developers would like nothing more than to see Terrance gone. He wondered if District 2 would even have a patrol car at the rally, as they usually did.

Terrance was determined not to cede any more ground to the Bloods. He'd been watching what was going on at the hair salon on the strip and accused Zenobia, the owner and the "baby mama" of Rodney Jackson, of letting the Bloods sell drugs there. Zenobia denied it and filed a restraining order against Terrance, saying he had threatened her. Bryan hadn't seen Terrance threaten her, but Terrance's temper had been on display. One afternoon a few days before the rally a kid on a skateboard was riding up on the benches next to the courts. Terrance asked him to leave, but he returned with his mother, and they all ended up in a huge argument. Someone called the police.

• • •

THE NIGHT BEFORE the rally, Terrance stayed late. He was playing chess outside his office when an SUV pulled up. "What you doing here this late?" came a voice Terrance recognized. It was Rev. "Man, you're working too hard," Rev said, walking over.

Terrance wasn't interested in Rev's advice and thought it was strange Rev was even over there. "I'm a grown man," Terrance told Rev. "I can do what I want to do."

"I know you're under a lot of stress," Rev said. "You could be home by now with your girl, the little ones."

"I'm *from* here," Terrance said, standing up. "I *live* down the street. This is *my* office. You're the one that lives all the way out in [the suburb of] Centennial. What are *you* doing here this late?"

THE NEXT MORNING was a busy one in the Holly. Preparations were being made for Senator Johnston's event as well as for Terrance's rally. Terrance arrived early to fix a net in the futsal soccer court. Aaron Miripol was on site as well. He was showing around Tony Pickett, a new vice president at the Urban Land Conservancy, who'd been hired to oversee the Holly Square redevelopment. Miripol had met him at a Ford Foundation event. Pickett was African American. It was his first day on the job.

Miripol tried to introduce Pickett to Terrance, but Terrance was on the phone, engrossed. He was talking to his father. George told him that his cousin had been beaten up overnight by a group of Bloods, including Hasan. When Terrance got off the phone, he went over to Miripol. That was when they saw two Black men, trying to get into the locked Boys & Girls Club. "Gentrifiers," the men shouted at Terrance and Miripol, after Terrance told them it wasn't open.

When Terrance turned to go back to his office, he saw Hasan. He and his crew were up early. More likely they hadn't gone to bed, Terrance figured. It wasn't even 9 a.m. and they were under the gazebo, smoking spice and drinking. He'd already told them they weren't allowed on the courts. The fact that they were there now, on the day of the rally, seemed to Terrance to be a statement. Terrance told them to leave; Hasan called Terrance a "snitch" and tugged his pocket, revealing what Terrance believed was the butt of a knife.

Terrance's conflict with the Bloods had just escalated. Not just because calling someone a snitch had to be acted upon, but also because Terrance believed that the OGs had to be behind this. Terrance wasn't a gang member anymore, but he had clout and favor in the neighborhood that guys like Hasan understood. Terrance didn't believe Hasan would come at him like this without the green light from the OGs.

Bryan called Terrance back to the office. He wanted to get them to Ikea. They already had their key to the Boys & Girls Club building. Ikea had same-day delivery. They would be moving their new furniture into the club that night.

BEING CALLED A snitch angered Terrance. He had risked his life and livelihood to put his community first. He had stood up against law enforcement abuses. One of those abuses, Terrance felt, was what Aundre "AD" Moore said: that District 2 had told him that Terrance was working for them. If it was true, the police knew such information would place him in danger.

A few hours later, when Terrance heard one of the Bloods make a crack about the camera on top of his building, he got the sledgehammer and climbed up on the roof. After knocking down the camera, he pushed it off, got down, and hauled it across the street to where Hasan and the Bloods stood.

There were at least a dozen of them. Terrance looked at each one. "If I'm such a snitch and a bitch," he said, "who's going to fight me? YT, you want to fight me, YT? I bet you I take your mouth to the turf."

Seconds went by. None of the Bloods had ever been challenged by Terrance this way.

"You guys supposed to be YG active Bloods?" Terrance said.

"When I was YG active we never let somebody we thought was a snitch come in the Holly. You know what we'd do? We'd *kill* 'em."

HOURS LATER, HASAN Jones lay on the ground, unconscious.

Terrance walked backwards over the courts, his gun in his hand. "I had to shoot that nigga!" Terrance yelled. "He pulled a knife on me. You would have shot him too. Fuck that nigga. I shot him for running up on me!"

"Drop your weapon!" came a voice. Terrance held on to the gun as long as he could, fearing a shot could come at him. He got on his knees. His face was pressed into the pavement, his hands cuffed behind his back.

New tonight, began the 10 o'clock news. *An anti-violence activist is in jail tonight, charged with shooting a man at a peace rally he organized.*

ACT III

20

I arrived in Denver a few months later. The outlook for Terrance's case seemed bleak. Terrance was arguing self-defense, but the Denver media was full of details that were hard to square with a self-defense claim. "He's been a ticking time bomb, telling everyone he owns all this [neighborhood]," a resident who was not named told *The Denver Post* of Terrance. The owner of what was said to be a cleaning company in the neighborhood, Carl McKay, was also quoted. "A person the neighborhood trusted has violated the trust of the neighborhood," Carl said. "That's never an easy feeling."

As a freelance journalist without an assignment, I hoped there was more to the story. But if the media reports were to be believed, there seemed to be little suspense about what had happened. I stayed at my mom's apartment in Lowry, the neighborhood built on the grounds of the old Air Force base, about ten minutes south of the Holly. On my way to meet Terrance at the International House of Pancakes, I reminded myself that Terrance's voice, oddly, was missing from the local media coverage.

I didn't know then why Terrance hadn't been interviewed by the Denver media, but soon after I sat down across from him I ruled out the possibility that he didn't like to talk. Terrance loved to talk. He was impassioned about a range of subjects from gang history to hip-hop to African American history to Denver. His fate and place in Denver's political landscape weighed on him. "Was I the angry activist?" he said in a southern-inflected accent. "Or was I the one that brought *you* to *my* community? Then they threw me to the side like Al Sharpton. I should be their friend. I don't want to be an activist anymore. I'm not trying to be. But there has to be some leadership."

Denver had become the fastest-growing big city in America, with one of its fastest-growing real estate markets and a ballooning demographic of young professionals, who were taking jobs in the city's growing tech, outdoor, and marijuana industries. Terrance said that it was the city's failure to protect low-income African Americans in northeast Denver that had made him become strident in his criticism of the city's gentrification. In 2012, the city council had moved quickly to declare eminent domain over a section of Five Points, he said, so that there was no time to organize opposition. "It's already done," he said of Five Points, calling it "the most gentrified black community in America."

We ate eggs and pancakes, and remembered Denver in the 1980s, which for me was a cow town with little racial integration, and for him was when a war that hasn't ended began. Eventually I decided to ask about his case. His demeanor changed. He seemed hurt and angry. "The Denver Foundation," he said, "used to tell me how to dress, how to run my events. They hated on me. Because they couldn't control me." He felt betrayed by Senator Johnston, whom he said had once been a friend. Since the shooting, he said, Johnston had visited Hasan but hadn't called him.

But his most vitriolic words were reserved for a group of Park Hill OG Bloods: Hasan's father, Isaac "Ice" Alexander; Carl "Fat Daddy" McKay; Joel "Way Out" Alexander; and Rodney "Big Rod" Jackson. He used their gang names. He called them "bitches" and "punks" and "snitches" and claimed that they had plotted to attack him on the day in question. He called them "Rev's guys," referring to the city's other high-profile anti-gang activist, Rev Kelly.

I didn't know what to make of it, but I was struck by how personal it sounded. He'd known them since childhood. Terrance told me how he'd been the deciding vote on the Community Corrections Board to spring Ice from prison just months before the shooting. "I'm trying to tell you, bro," Terrance told me. "They used me to bust out a snitch who sent his son to kill me."

As I continued to meet with Terrance, I found that he often said things such as that, which sounded startling but, at least to me, had no evidentiary basis and made little sense. I didn't know who "they" were, and I wasn't sure if he did. Terrance appeared to be in a state of extremis. He said he was living on the run, fearing for his safety from gang members. He'd been back to his house only once, in the middle of the night, to avoid reporters whom his neighbors had alerted him were waiting. His aunt Peggy had loaned him $3,500 to post bond. He was homeless, penniless, and unhirable, facing an almost certain prison term.

Oddly, the one person he was not upset with was Hasan. "Why would I want to hurt this young man?" he said. "I don't even think he wanted to assault me that day. I feel sorry for him. He was a pawn."

I DROVE TO the Denver Justice Center to get the case files. The $378 million complex, which opened in 2010, took up several city blocks along Colfax, just west of the state capitol. It was part of a transformation of the city's architectural stature since the turn of the millennium, which included a world-class art museum and convention center.

Two open cases were handed to me with Terrance's name. One was a restraining order, filed by John Arigoni on behalf of the Boys & Girls Club, the day after Terrance bonded out, barring him from coming near the Holly. The other, the shooting case, was thirteen pages and consisted mostly of a lengthy list of witnesses, submitted by the district attorney's office. They included Senator Johnston and Isaac Alexander, or Ice. Hasan was also on the list. For his address it said, "Unknown."

The probable-cause arrest report scantly described the scene when District 2's first car arrived, just after 6 p.m. A group of "suspected gang members" were present, including Hasan, who was "lying on the ground suffering from several apparent gunshot wounds."

Terrance, who was armed with a "semi-automatic handgun," was taken into custody. Officer Carl Sessions stated that he heard Terrance yell, "I had to shoot that nigga. He pulled a knife on me, fuck you all you would have shot him too, fuck that nigga I shot him for running up on me."

The report also included statements from two witnesses who said that Terrance had shot Hasan "while he was lying motionless on the ground." Due to the witnesses' "vulnerability to retaliation," the report said, their identities would remain shielded.

FOLLOWING THE SHOOTING, the Boys & Girls Club, officially named the Nancy P. Anschutz Center, for Phil's wife, had postponed its opening by a week. It appeared to me that a concerted effort had been made by the club and its partners to put the incident behind them. The Urban Land Conservancy had posted a blog one week after the shooting entitled "Holly Square Redevelopment Has Stabilized Northeast Park Hill." Two months later, in November, *The Denver Post* had run a front-page story, "Holly Square Blooms Again." The reporter had accompanied two hundred philanthropists on a tour of the Boys & Girls Club. "It's at the vanguard of what community development for the 21st century can look like," Chad Jones, executive director of the Community Investment Network, told the *Post*. "It's astounding how people from all over the community worked on this."

Again, Terrance was not interviewed, but the story quoted District 2 Police Commander Mike Calo. "We're not seeing as much gang activity, and there is no more open-air drug market," he told the *Post*. But, I soon learned, it had been years since the open-air drug market at the Holly existed. Calo also told the *Post* that the Boys & Girls Club had helped children "return to the neighborhood."

Many people from the community were wary about speaking to me about the shooting, but it wasn't hard to find residents who said that key details in the *Post* article were inaccurate. The club, which offered after-school care for youth, appeared to be running well below capacity; a surge in neighborhood shootings had left many parents worried about safety.

Terrance, with whom I'd stayed in touch, hadn't been back to the Holly, but one day he told me he was going and invited me. His friend Dub, who was thirty-eight and had a black SUV, drove. As we rode north through Park Hill, the neighborhood's renowned nineteenth-century Tudor homes, wide boulevards, and large trees disappeared as we crossed MLK Boulevard into Northeast Park Hill. Some lots were wildly overgrown; others had FOR SALE signs in the yard.

When we arrived at the area known as the Holly, 33rd Avenue bisected two very different-looking parts of the neighborhood. On the north side of the street was Holly Square, featuring bright yellow-and-black basketball courts, with glass backboards and nets, and the sprawling glass-and-brick Boys & Girls Club. Along the south side was Deloris Wilson's 1960s-era brick shopping strip. At one end the Horizon Lounge had a red neon sign and bars protecting the windows; in front of the old Ned's candy shop was a pay phone and a faded sign, Holly Food Market. Several of the shops seemed shuttered, including Zenobia's hair salon and Carl McKay's computer repair and car wash, which had closed soon after the shooting.

The city had joined the Urban Land Conservancy in asking Mrs. Wilson to sell the strip, but she refused. Instead, she renamed it the Park Hill Center and put in a new green-and-white sign that stood in a patch of brown grass that ran along the front of the shops.

We pulled into the Boys & Girls Club parking lot. Aside from the small public library building, Sipio's auto shop was the only other structure in the square not owned by the Urban Land Conservancy. Sipio was an old friend of Ernestine's. His entire building was painted camouflage. Outside it, two old men sat in salvaged car seats, surrounded by tires and car parts.

The Prodigal Son office was on the west side of the Holly, at the corner of 33rd and Hudson, catty-corner from the Horizon Lounge. It had been closed since the shooting. The city's anti-gang effort was in limbo. The city had cut off payments to Bryan and Qwest, who weren't sure what to do; they had more than a year left on their contract. The small building remained the official office of state senator Johnston, whose name was announced with a blue sign atop the building.

Terrance pointed to the twelve "peace poles" that ran along the courts, the only remains of the former shopping center. Each carried a small flag with a saying from a world leader, from Desmond Tutu to MLK to Anne Frank. "This is my art," Terrance said. "This is some of my life's work."

It was a weekday afternoon, but aside from the guys at Sipio's and two young white men playing basketball, the Holly appeared empty. The stillness felt unsettling. One of the white guys looked at Terrance as if he recognized him. "That's Terrance Roberts," Dub said to him. Jonathan Stalls came forward and shook Terrance's hand. Terrance knew his father, the longtime Denver activist Dave Stalls. "How's your dad doing?" Terrance asked him.

Dub and Terrance took the other court and started paying 21 while I wandered into the Boys & Girls Club. It was a huge building, with a multilevel meeting room and a cavernous rec room, where several seemingly unattended kids played pool. When I came back out, I heard a voice. "Is that Terrance?" A small woman in a blue windbreaker ran into his arms. Her name was Sherry.

"We were just sitting around the senator's office," she told Terrance, "saying it's a damn shame that ain't nobody in there since you been gone." Several others with soiled clothing appeared. "I miss you guys," Terrance said, hugging them. He later told me he'd known them since he was a kid; some of them struggled with drug addictions, he said.

A large man in a red sports jersey glowered at us from the sidewalk. "You left a body on the block, nigga," he hollered at Terrance. A howl of laughter came from the Horizon parking lot. Terrance and Dub stepped toward the man. "What have you done for the community, sir?" Dub yelled.

"A lot more than what the fuck you've been doing," the man said.

"How much money have you raised?" Terrance yelled.

"How much have *y'all* raised?" Dub echoed.

"We're trying to raise real money over here for kids!" Terrance shouted at the man. "You ain't doin' nothing but walkin' and talkin'."

Sherry shook her head. "They're shooting over here every day," she said. Terrance turned toward the car. "Let's get out of here before someone gets popped," he said.

AT LEAST TWO security cameras watched Holly Square. One was on the back of the library. The other, perched atop a streetlamp, was remotely controlled twenty-four hours a day from Denver police headquarters. At the time Terrance shot Hasan, it was pointed due east, along Deloris Wilson's strip. It appeared that no video evidence of the shooting existed.

Terrance gave me the names and phone numbers of two people he said had witnessed the shooting close up and would vindicate his self-defense claim. One was Reggie Fair, his "hot dog guy," who had lived in the neighborhood for decades; the other was his friend Kamao "Ktone" Martinez, who was setting up to DJ the event when the shooting began. But Reggie's number was no longer in service, and Ktone wouldn't return my calls. Terrance also put me in touch with Bryan Butler, but I gave up calling him after he stood me up twice. "People want to help me," Terrance said, "but they're afraid."

I wasn't sure what to think. Terrance was well-known to many of the most powerful people in the state. He'd worked with the mayor and the governor, shared an office with a well-connected state senator. Senator Johnston told me he thought about Terrance "all the time." Then-governor Hickenlooper told me he valued Terrance's ability to "bring together different views." But both of them sounded resigned to the idea that Terrance's activism career was over, despite his claim of self defense. "Just disbelief at how sad it is," Hickenlooper said, "That's the overwhelming emotion I come back to again and again. He was a really active force. Somebody who'd been through the worst, and paid for his crimes, and he was out there trying to make the community better. But it's not a hopeless setback to the Holly," he added. "The Holly's back."

THE MOST PROMINENT public figure advocating for Terrance was Rev Kelly, who appeared in virtually every news story about the case. "On the streets, it's about self-preservation," he told Denver's monthly city magazine *5280*. "There's an old saying: 'I'd rather be tried by twelve than carried by six.' Because of what he did, Terrance at least gets to have that trial."

Rev's support of Terrance appeared steadfast. It was hard to find anything about Terrance, including in *The New York Times*, that didn't cite Rev as Terrance's longtime mentor. So when Terrance insisted to me that Rev had "never done *one* thing for me," it gave me pause. As did something else Terrance told me. He said that the night of the shooting, Rev had come to see him at the jail. In a conference room, Terrance said, Rev "told me to stay out of the media and let him handle things behind the scenes." Terrance also claimed that Rev "admitted" to him that "he knew that the OGs sent Hasan and them Bloods to me," meaning the OG's had directed them to attack Terrance.

NORTHEAST DENVER'S GANG communities were bursting with "word on the street" information. Once I began to develop sources in the community, I was regularly in possession of it myself. One day Alvin Jones, Nathan's brother, took me to the spot where Nathan was shot in 1968. It was about forty feet from where Terrance shot Hasan. Alvin, who was sixty-four, had brought with him newspaper clippings. He wiped his eyes and told me about what he believed was a conspiracy between the Denver police and the local media to create a false story about Nathan being armed that night. "I found the gun right there," Alvin said of the toy gun Nathan had on him that fateful night.

Lauren Watson, the city's Black Panther leader, vetted me for more than a year before agreeing to an interview. He, too, believed the Denver police had "used" the media to undermine the city's civil rights movement, partly by framing Nathan. Watson, who was seventy-six and in a nursing home, said he didn't know what exactly had gone down with "Georgie's son," Terrance, but that when he saw the news it was clear to him that "a false story had been put out."

The word on the street about Terrance was that he was attacked. By whom wasn't clear. A former gang member who requested anonymity told me, "Terrance Roberts being gone is an opportunity for a lot of people."

I CALLED REV, who invited me to meet him in an old bus garage where he ran his after-school program two days a week. The building was in the Cole neighborhood, adjacent to Five Points, where industrial buildings were being scooped up by developers. On the next block was the new Urban Land Conservancy office, which was in a 95,000-square-foot former maintenance facility it had purchased. With the help of city funds, the ULC had turned the building into an "incubator," mostly for charter schools and other educational organizations. It also housed GRASP, the Latino anti-gang organization that received significant funding from the city.

Rev's building was accessed by a massive garage door that clanked open. Inside, elementary and middle school youths chased one another around a cavernous space. Rev, who wore jeans and an Open Door V-neck shirt, had dreadlocks and the physique of an NBA basketball player. He broke up an argument between two boys and waited while they apologized to each other. When we sat down he seemed apprehensive about talking to me and asked, in his deep bass voice, "what kind of angle" I had. He had a toothpick hanging from his mouth.

I told him I was interested in Terrance's story and putting the Holly in a historical context. "Holly has always been the hub," he said. "It's always been the target."

He seemed well aware of the unique vantage point he'd had to Denver's gang war. "After all the things Terrance went through and the battles that he and Michael Asberry had against each other and the battles that the Park Hill Bloods had with the Rolling 30's [Crips], it just grew, grew."

Rev's organization, which consisted primarily of just him, was based out of an office on the top floor of an old freight building on the downtown 16th Street Mall. Inside, every wall and surface was taken up by plaques or framed photos. In one he stood with the boxing promoter Don King. Framed letters from Colorado mayors and governors also were on display, including one from Governor Ritter in 2010, pardoning Rev's felony conviction.

Rev was a frequent recipient of awards, including from the police, and he began to invite me to events. He attended in bright-colored zoot suits and fedoras, posing for photos and playing up his exotic charm. If someone cursed, even mildly, he raised his extra-long finger. "Language," he would say.

I sensed Rev wanted me to know how closely connected he was to the city's power brokers. Once, when I was riding in his SUV, he contemplated aloud whether to call "Mike," the mayor, on speed dial. He referred to the district attorney, Mitch Morrissey, as "my good buddy." I'd read in *The Denver Post* that the mayor and the DA had roasted Rev two years earlier on his sixtieth birthday.

"I feel like Moses in his latter years," Rev told me, referring to the path he had forged in Denver's anti-gang effort. He said he thought Terrance was going to be "my Joshua," referring to the biblical figure God chose to lead Israel after Moses's death. He shook his head in seeming disbelief about Terrance's predicament. "This kid," he said. "I'm not so worried about the attempted murder as the gun charge." It was hard to see how Terrance could avoid being found guilty of possessing the gun. Rev's pardon enabled him to legally carry a gun, which he did. A small black pistol was holstered on his hip.

I told Rev that Terrance told me that Rev had visited him at the jail the night of the shooting. Rev confirmed it. "I told them to turn off the camera," Rev told me, referring to the jailers. I didn't ask why he would request such a thing or if he actually had such authority. I also didn't tell him that Terrance had claimed that during their meeting Rev acknowledged to him that there had been a plan by the Bloods to attack Terrance. Rev seemed to want to keep his conversation with Terrance between them. "We talked about some things," Rev told me. "I'm doing what I can behind the scenes."

21

Terrance had family all over the Denver area. Even for him it was hard to remember all their names. A cousin was married to a Blood called L Shady, who was among Hasan's closest friends. A half-brother on his mother's side, Chris, was a cop in Lakewood, a suburb west of Denver. But the only one Terrance kept in touch with regularly was his father, George.

George now lived in a 1940s housing project in the middle of Five Points. The seven buildings, each two stories high, were a nest of Crip-affiliated families in the middle of Denver's most rapidly gentrifying neighborhood. Bullet holes pocked George's front door, while across the street, condominiums under construction were listed for more than half a million dollars apiece.

George had lived there since 2011 when, after a divorce, he was broke and without a place to live. When he went to the city housing office, he said, his missing application for assistance was found behind an employee's desk. The employee was able to offer him the place and a lifetime rent of $25 a month.

The subsidized rent enabled him to quit his job fueling planes and focus on preaching funerals. He incorporated as the Church Without Walls Ministry, serving those who had no church or couldn't afford to pay for a funeral. Helping the dead get safely to heaven was what he told me he realized God had put him on earth to do. "The Bible means Basic Instructions Before Leaving Earth," he said. He didn't want to do anything else. "I'm blessed," he said. "I'm in service."

George had a wide freckled face and an easy smile. He shaved and ironed his clothing each morning and always smelled of fresh cologne. He sometimes worked a dozen funerals a week. On rare days off he wore a tracksuit with a large gold medallion around his neck. Without his platinum dentures, which he usually wore, he was missing a front tooth.

It was impossible to accompany George anywhere in northeast Denver without people calling out, "Pastor George." Though he was surrounded by death and mourning, he was possibly the most optimistic person I'd ever encountered. With a wink and a nod he would swing a playful jab at me whenever he saw me. He spoke with a preacher's lilt, often using the word *amen*. The way he said it, I was rarely clear if he was saying *a-men*, or *hey, man*.

His tiny one-bedroom apartment was on the building's second floor. In his cramped kitchen was an ironing board and several cardboard boxes, filled with funeral programs from services he'd led. He had no idea how many. "Thousands," he said. No one in the city had preached more gang funerals.

Like Rev's office, the walls of George's small living room were covered with framed photos. In one, he was in front of the famous Black Panther "white house" in Oakland, with Huey Newton. "People used to confuse us," he said. "Until I took out my teeth." The picture was taken a year before Huey's 1989 murder.

Another photo featured George with Muhammad Ali, whom he befriended when working security for a local promoter. In another, he had his arm around Lauren Watson, the Denver Black Panther leader. The photo, he said, "helps me remember where I came from." He said the Panthers had been his family growing up, at least for the two or three tumultuous years the group existed in Denver.

He also had several framed photos and newspaper articles related to Terrance. George was proud of his son. "No one else was marching in Denver against gang violence," he said. The day Terrance shot Hasan, he said, he was running late. On his way to the Holly he got a call. "Pastor," a friend said, "Terrance just killed a Blood."

"I pulled over and I spoke to the Lord. I said, 'Let that baby live, so he can be a testimony! That boy died three times that night," he said, of Hasan. "I got mad faith. That's why my life is so good. I pray for Munch, just like I pray for everyone else."

George told me God would take care of Terrance's case. But his perspective on what happened took me by surprise. He said he believed the Bloods were threatening Terrance, and that by doing so, they had "opened up Pandora's box. And Terrance might not agree with me but when they opened up Pandora's box, ShowBizz woke up. So when this happened, they weren't messing with Terrance Roberts. They opened up the door for ShowBizz to wake back up."

He looked at the ceiling. "Now I just pray to the spirit that that demon goes back into its tomb, that that demon goes back into its grave, that that demon *dies*, and goes back—*a-men*—to the pits of *hell* where it came from. And Lord, *resurrect* Terrance Roberts!"

FEW IN Northeast Park Hill wanted to talk to me about the shooting. Those who would seemed to be grappling with a larger sense of loss—the loss of the entire neighborhood.

Acen Phillips, who had once tried to buy the Dahlia Shopping Center and put it to use for the community, was put off by the Holly redevelopment. "Boys and Girls Club isn't a Black thing," he told me. "It's a white thing run by the system. It's a white thing sitting in a Black neighborhood, using the concepts generated by the mind of a Terrance Roberts." He said he had watched as the new powers at the Holly "pimped Terrance out," or used him to get the credibility they needed. "And right now," Phillips told me, "we are weak as water because we lost the voice of a Terrance Roberts. The same thing happened with Lauren Watson, the same thing happened with Malcolm X."

"I don't think the Holly will ever be the same," said Jason McBride, the former Blood turned activist who had worked with Terrance and the Camo Movement. "I mean, [Terrance] was our voice. He was the only one that really had the hood's back. It wasn't about him not accepting the new demographic—it was about him saying to that new demographic, 'This is who we are. And not only are we not ashamed of that, but we're growing into something different and we want y'all to be a part of it.'" He shook his head. "It's hurt us as a people and as a community, because they just expect us to kill ourselves."

McBride, who bore a resemblance to Suge Knight, had a glass eye from a shooting in his gang days. He remembered ShowBizz well. "Terrance turned around one-eighty degrees, man, but was doin' the same job," he said. "I don't think you could make it up. Them days when he was a younger cat riding around with a Mac 11 on his lap, *protecting* the hood, and then later still *protecting* the hood but just in two totally different ways. But two necessary ways, too, man. You never know how many people he kept alive."

McBride was planning to speak at the rally and was on his way to the Holly when he got word that "Terrance shot Munch." He didn't believe it. "Because it was a peace rally," he said. "It was *his* peace rally."

But McBride, who knew Hasan and had invited Hasan to help with his radio show, didn't second-guess Terrance for firing his gun. "Not at all," he said. "If it was me, I'm not stopping to ask questions. I'm gonna shoot, and I'm not just gonna shoot one. If there's four or five [gang members], I'm gonna make sure everybody catches something. I mean, you have to." He shrugged. "It's survival."

TERRANCE FINALLY TOLD me where he was staying, and I went over. It was a large home in south Denver, owned by the sister of a friend's wife. She had moved and was preparing to sell it. It was unfurnished but for two couches and a flat-screen TV in the living room. Terrance slept on the couch or upstairs on the carpeted floor, where in the closet was a stack of baseball caps with the decals still on, and vintage Chuck Taylors of all colors. They were among the only things he'd retrieved from his house when he'd gone in the middle of the night to avoid reporters. He presumed that he'd since been evicted; he'd missed at least four rent payments.

About half the time, his girlfriend, Bethlehem, whose parents were Eritrean immigrants and who worked at her father's liquor store, stayed over. Terrance had met her through volunteers who had helped move his office into the Holly. Bethlehem had recently given birth to their daughter, Ziahda. She was Terrance's sixth child. Except for Javon, his oldest, who was at a junior college in California, he typically saw his kids once a week, but it was harder now because he had no transportation. His car had been impounded on parking violations and he couldn't afford to reclaim it.

Terrance had found a $16-an-hour cash job doing home demolition for the same all-ex-con company that he had hired two years earlier to help clear the Holly. His back was often sore. Much of his free time was spent searching for rides to the construction sites.

He said only a few people knew where he was staying. Once when I was there he thought he heard something and told me to get down on the floor while he checked.

Many of his closest friends were former gang members who had supported the Camo Movement. Some were Crips who had shot at him back in the day. They still wore the camo gear, and when a shooting happened, they called Terrance. "There's only one person in Denver who can deal with that," Gerald Wright, who was a leader of the Camo Movement on the Crips side, told me.

Gerald believed Terrance had shot Hasan in self-defense. As did Aqeela Sherrills in Los Angeles. Aqeela told me that Terrance's role in the peace movement was so well-known that his case was being closely followed in gang neighborhoods on Facebook and on Streetgangs.com, a popular website run by the sociologist Alex Alonso, who was following the case.

GANG SHOOTINGS IN Denver had been coming in bursts. "You never used to see a rash of shootings like this when Terrance was around," McBride told me.

Terrance had barely been going out in public, but one night he agreed to meet some of his friends at a hookah bar to discuss the tensions. Eventually, the women in the group stayed inside and he and several former gang members and friends went to "politic" in the back alley. The conversation didn't get far before Terrance's frustration with both the rise in Denver's gang violence and his case overtook him. "I'm probably going to jail," he said, pacing up and down while the others looked on silently. "I got caught with my pistol in my hand. But *why'd I even have to live like this?*" He took off his hat and threw it on the ground. "If I was white," he shouted, "I'd be Captain America! But I'm Terrance from northeast Denver."

As a white man, I was never sure how I would be regarded. But the more time I spent in the community, the more people seemed to appreciate simply that I was paying attention. Soon, some of them joined Terrance in texting me after shootings. I got the sense it wasn't only to fill me in but to make the point that, at least in their view, nothing was being done about it.

Mayor Hancock and District 2 commander Mike Calo called the Denver Police Department a national model, which galled the activists I spoke to. One of the DPD's troubling deficiencies was its performance in solving homicides, which was well below the national average, and even worse in northeast Denver. Some believed that at least a portion of those murders were unsolved because they were committed by people who had police protection, presumably because they were working for law enforcement as informants.

Northeast Denver's gang world had at least one glaring case of this. It was that of the Fero's Bar stabbings, in 2012, when four gang members went into a bar on Colorado Boulevard and stabbed to death all five people inside. One of the assailants was an ATF informant. He was the only one not charged. That law enforcement would hire such dangerous men was bad enough in the eyes of community members; giving them immunity from their violent acts was, for many in the community, proof that law enforcement didn't actually care about the safety of the neighborhood.

One day, after another spate of shootings, I got texts informing me that the police had installed concrete barricades across 33rd Avenue in the Holly, blocking traffic. Terrance was irate and wanted to go but didn't want to risk violating his restraining order. When I arrived, the intersection at 33rd and Hudson, in front of Terrance's old office, was a scene of chaos. The barriers blocked the road; cars honked in protest. "Where's our senator, where's our congressman?" one woman said from an open car window.

Senator Johnston's office appeared shuttered. The Prodigal Son camouflage mural on the side of the building had been covered with a tarp.

Word on the street was that one of the shootings that had led the city to install the barricades was a drive-by, committed by Hasan Jones. "District 2 is looking for him *right now*," George told me. "But he ain't been seen, *nowhere*."

TERRANCE'S PUBLIC DEFENDER, Marshal Seufert, was the chief of the state's trial division. He was fifty and thin, with wire-frame glasses. In August 2014, I went to Terrance's motions hearings, where Marshal was going to argue that Terrance's statements at the scene—in which he appeared to admit to shooting Hasan—were inadmissible, because he had not yet been Mirandized.

The spacious courtroom was almost empty but for George Roberts and Rev Kelly, who sat on opposite sides. Rev and Terrance did not acknowledge each other.

Four police officers were scheduled to testify. The Denver police had determined that the case was not "gang related" and assigned a homicide detective, Randall Denison. Denison was heavyset and looked about sixty. He'd worked for the Denver PD for nearly twenty years, and had investigated a number of the city's most controversial cases, including the quintuple bar murder in which the ATF informant was not charged.

Denison testified that he was assigned to Terrance's case at about 6:30 p.m., which was less than half an hour after the shooting. Terrance had told me that when he was waiting in a holding cell at District 2, he had spoken to one of the arresting officers. Marshal wanted to see the video but had been unsuccessful and asked

Denison about it. Denison said that District 2 informed him that the recording didn't exist. "I don't know if it was mechanical or it wasn't on," Denison testified.

Marshal asked Denison about something else that Terrance had told me. While he was being booked, Terrance said he had inquired after Hasan. Denison remembered it. "He said, I think, 'How is that young man doing?'" Denison testified.

The first responders to the scene, the District 2 officers Antonio Lopez, Jr., and Carl Sessions, also took the stand. I'd learned that after Commander Calo took the reins of District 2 in 2012, he'd helped design a 911 call workaround, enabling District 2 to decide internally which car would be best suited to respond to emergencies. Lopez and Sessions had been chosen for this one, and from the documents I could find, they seemed well suited. At the 2013 Denver police awards, they had won honors for their work on the Project Safe Neighborhoods effort. The awards had been sponsored by *The Denver Post* and the Anschutz Foundation.

Lopez, who was twenty-seven and in his sixth year on the force, was the son of a legendary cop with whom Rev was close. Like all ambitious young cops, Tony Jr. worked with informants, including Northeast Park Hill gang members, according to my sources.

No police presence had been in the Holly at the time of the shooting. Lopez testified that he and Sessions were by the Dahlia when they received the call, at 6:03 p.m. They arrived within two minutes. Lopez said that as he ran toward the basketball courts, he saw a man in a brown shirt, holding a gun and shouting. He said he drew his gun and yelled "eight to ten times" for the man to drop his weapon. "That's the closest I've ever been to shooting someone," Lopez testified.

Lopez claimed he did not know who Terrance was, but he said he did recognize Hasan, who was on the ground, bleeding. "He hangs out in the Holly Shopping Center a lot. We've contacted him." A man was kneeling over Hasan, he said, "He was saying, 'Keep breathing, keep breathing, fight, fight, fight.'"

When Marshal tried to get Lopez to acknowledge that the scene was dangerous, Lopez became openly contentious. Lopez finally said it was "very hostile," with gang members, at least some appearing armed, threatening Terrance. "On Bloods, nigga, you're dead," he testified hearing them yell at Terrance. He said another officer was tasked with getting Terrance away from the area for his own safety. But, Lopez said, no one at the scene was searched.

"At that time, you were aware that Mr. Roberts was stating that he had to shoot," Marshal asked Lopez.

"Objection," Henry Cooper, one of two assistant district attorneys on the case, said.

"Sustained," the judge said.

Marshal rephrased. "At that point, Mr. Roberts is arrested and taken into custody?"

"Yes."

"But no one else is?" Marshal asked.

"Right," Lopez said.

"But if Mr. Roberts's statement is true, there wouldn't be any crime to arrest him for."

"Objection."

"Sustained."

THE STAND YOUR GROUND defense had come into the national spotlight in 2012 after George Zimmerman—a neighborhood watch coordinator in his gated Sanford, Florida, community—shot and killed unarmed Trayvon Martin, a seventeen-year-old African American who was visiting his father's fiancée there. Terrance, who had co-led a protest in Denver against Zimmerman, now hoped he could make a similar legal argument. He had shot Hasan on the property that his organization had developed. He had a lease with the Urban Land Conservancy to operate the property and was required to keep it safe.

Terrance's role as a peacekeeper was also recognized by more than just a neighborhood association. On the day of the shooting, Terrance's organization was receiving funding from the

The Park Hill Shopping Center, later renamed the Holly Shopping Center, just prior to its official opening in August 1955. Before the opening, Holly Square was just a field. (*The Denver Post* / Getty Images)

Denver Black Panthers founder Lauren Watson (second from right) with other Panthers in 1968 (*The Denver Post* / Getty Images)

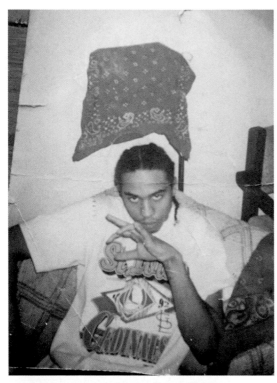

Terrance, age seventeen, soon after being "put on" the hood as an official Blood, flashing gang signs, circa 1993 (Courtesy of Terrance Roberts)

Terrance in Colorado's Fremont Correctional Facility in 2002 or 2003, serving a sentence for shooting at another Blood's car. He had already disavowed his gang membership and would be released in 2004. (Courtesy of Terrance Roberts)

Terrance's grandmother Ernestine Boyd, at home in the Dahlia Square Senior Apartments, 2017. Her restaurant, A&A Fish, was a neighborhood gathering spot for almost forty years after it opened in 1980. Ernestine died in 2019 at age eighty-three. (Julian Rubinstein)

Michael Asberry's mug shot, circa 2005. In 1985, Asberry co-founded Denver's first Crips gang. He was murdered in 2008 at age thirty-eight.

Rev. Leon Kelly speaks with gang unit captain Mike Calo (right) and another officer after Michael Asberry was killed. Asberry's death led nine Crips to burn down the Holly Shopping Center. (Brian Brainerd / *The Denver Post* / Getty Images)

Terrance leads a march to end gang violence through the neighborhood surrounding the Holly. The march occurred after nine Crips burned the Holly Shopping Center to the ground on the night following Michael Asberry's killing on May 23, 2008. (Karl Gehring / *The Denver Post* / Getty Images)

Denver mayor Michael Hancock speaks with Phil and Nancy Anschutz at the press conference announcing the Anschutz Family Foundation's $5 million grant to build a Boys & Girls Club in Holly Square, February 14, 2012. Terrance was left off the event's program. (Kathryn Scott Olser / *The Denver Post* / Getty Images)

(from left) Bryan Butler, Terrance, and John "Qwest" Lewis outside the office of Terrance's Prodigal Son organization. Bryan and Qwest were Prodigal Son's outreach workers funded by a federal Project Safe Neighborhoods grant.

(Anthony Camera)

Instead of moving into the Boys & Girls Club after the peace rally in Holly Square, Terrance was booked into the Denver Jail for shooting Hasan Jones, September 20, 2013.

Holly Square in 2016, with the Boys & Girls Club in the foreground and the mountains and downtown skyline in the background. Mrs. Wilson's strip is at the upper left, with the Horizon Lounge and parking lot at its end. Across the street from the "peace courts," left of the white-roofed building, is the small office Terrance and Prodigal Son shared with State Senator Mike Johnston. (Julian Rubinstein)

George Roberts shows the congregation the Bible he first learned to read while in jail at age thirty-eight. Easter 2014 in Five Points, Denver (Julian Rubinstein)

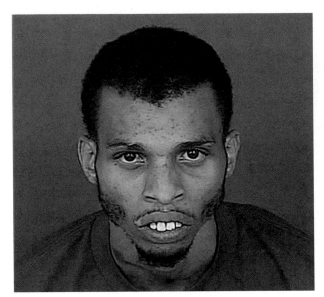

Hasan Jones is booked into the Denver Jail on August 18, 2014, on attempted murder charges involving a drive-by shooting that occurred after he was paralyzed. He was arrested at the Aurora, Colorado, apartment of his girlfriend, whose two-year-old daughter, Ny Ny, was dead. Hasan was found not guilty of the drive-by but pleaded guilty to child abuse resulting in Ny Ny's death.

Aaron Miripol standing on the "peace courts" in Holly Square, December 2014. Miripol is president and CEO of the Urban Land Conservancy, which bought the Holly in 2009, a year after the fire. (Julian Rubinstein)

ABOVE: Terrance takes the stand at his own trial,
October 1, 2015. (Julian Rubinstein)
BELOW: Terrance leads a counterprotest against the police during a
pro-police rally in Denver on July 19, 2020, two months after George
Floyd was killed in Minneapolis. (Reuters / Kevin Mohatt)

Terrance was a leader of the Justice for Elijah McClain movement, which gained more than 5.6 million signatures on Change.org and led Colorado governor Jared Polis to reopen an investigation into McClain's death. McClain, who was twenty-three, died at the hands of Aurora police officers in August 2019. (Philip B. Poston / *Sentinel Colorado* / Associated Press)

Terrance attends the signing of a police reform bill that banned chokeholds and made police officers personally and financially liable for violating a person's civil rights at the Colorado State Capitol on June 19, 2020. He was one of only two people thanked by name on the House floor when the sponsor introduced the bill. Terrance spoke after the signing, getting the crowd to do a Black Power salute. (Julian Rubinstein)

Department of Justice's premier anti-gang effort, Project Safe Neighborhoods.

But Colorado's Stand Your Ground law, which was called "Make My Day," specifically referred to protecting against someone entering one's "domicile." Marshal didn't think it was applicable.

Marshal also said he expected to lose the motion to suppress Terrance's statements, but he felt that the hearings had gone well in one important way. He was able to get a continuance. The trial was rescheduled for January 2015. Marshal's strategy for the moment was to stall. He had been able to confirm that there was in fact an arrest warrant out for Hasan. "Like you said," he told Terrance as we walked out, "I think Munch is going to cause problems. I think the longer it goes on, the better shape you're in."

Hasan's familial ties to powerful underworld figures seemed to complicate my effort to reach him. In the weeks after the shooting, his aunt Laquana Alexander had become the family spokesperson. She had short magenta hair and thick glitter glasses. "I'm sure Barack Obama felt threatened but he didn't shoot anyone," she told Denver's 7News. "They're both gang members, so at this point does it matter?" she added, suggesting Terrance was still a Blood.

I finally got Laquana's phone number, but when I introduced myself, she hung up on me. Eventually Sheria "Drettie" Hicks, an active Blood, who some described as the Bloods' "PR Man," offered to help me get to Hasan. Drettie, who was thirty-eight, was affable and appeared heartfelt in his hope to heal the wounds that the shooting had caused. He had known Terrance from the days when they were hatching schemes at the "Launching Pad," Ernestine's house, and said that Terrance's positive impact on the community had been significant. "I'm sorry it even had to happen," he told me. "This is homey on homey. This is all in-house business. We *all* from Park Hill."

One night, he called and said I should come to his condo, which was in a new development on the west side, because he had some guys who were willing to talk to me. I'd only been around him in public places before, but I didn't want to miss the opportunity. When I got there, Drettie was on the ground-floor patio in a Nuggets hat, with three younger men. One didn't want to meet me and left. The other two were Aundre "AD" Moore, whose "little homey" was Baby AD, the Blood who was interviewed by Terrance in the Holly about jobs before he was killed; and "L Shady," the husband of one of Terrance's cousins. Both were close with Hasan.

Aundre, who wore a Denver Broncos ski hat, was tall and slender with a broad face and soulful wide eyes. Shady, who was twenty-five, had a boyish face with big cheeks. He wore a red jean jacket and had red beads in his hair. Tattoo teardrops fell from his right eye. I recognized him from one of the Park Hill Bloods' music videos. In it, he stood next to Hasan and "Sneaky Boy Tramp," one of the Bloods' best rappers, on a front porch in Dahlia Gardens, the apartment complex recently purchased by the Urban Land Conservancy. In the video, the Bloods laugh as a District 2 patrol car sits thirty feet away on the street. "We see you Bloods . . ." an officer's voice can be heard calling out to them from a speaker.

We went inside and drank beer and shared a joint rolled with sweet tobacco paper. AD said he'd witnessed the whole drama between Terrance and Hasan the day of the shooting. "Man, they argued the whole day," AD said. He said he was trying to get Hasan to stop threatening Terrance but had to leave. "I come back"—he snapped his fingers—"he's on it again. Just like that."

AD and Shady seemed unable to grasp the events that ensued. "This really fucked us up," AD said. "Because Terrance was teaching us a lot." He said immediately after the shooting he had run over to Terrance, who was handcuffed and pressed to the ground, and that Terrance had said to him, "We're gonna learn from this, bro. We're gonna learn."

But he sounded frustrated, as if no further instructions had been left. "So now, what rules are you playing by then?" he said. "Are there any rules?"

"Where I come from, we just don't do that to people we love," Shady said of the shooting.

I asked about Hasan. "He's not doing too good, he's messed up," AD said. "I have to wheel him around." He said Hasan was "just a product of his own environment like we all are, trying to find a way out. He loves hard, all of that. Sleeping in spots with bedbugs and roaches—he's a good dude, straight up."

Shady and Drettie were a well-regarded Bloods rap duo that went by the name the Family Jewellz. They'd been working with AD on a new song, about the Holly. They let me stay as, one by one, they recorded their verses in a makeshift studio in the living room.

Shady rapped:

> *I ain't never scared when the funk is on*
> *Knowing damn well I might not make it home*

Afterward, Drettie went to a computer workstation off the kitchen and searched Google for news coverage of the Holly to sample as background. He found a 9News story from February 2012, announcing the Anschutz grant to build the Boys & Girls Club. As the anchor spoke, dramatic footage of the Holly fire played. "Flames lighting up the night sky—it's been nearly four years now since fire was set by gang members, devastating Denver's Holly Square," the anchor said. "Now there's a plan to reclaim it from crime and give it back to the community . . ."

"Echo that," AD said.

In a few seconds, Drettie had the last phrase of the anchor's words playing in a loop: *back to the community . . . back to the community . . . back to the community . . .*

"Ahh, that's gonna be hard," AD said, meaning good.

.   .   .

Nearly all of Denver's gang members were on Facebook. Most had set their privacy settings to public even though they used the platform for everything from seeing who was around to meet to making apparent threats. I finally found Hasan's page. After the shooting, he had changed his Facebook name to "Survivor B Blessed."

His profile photo depicted him seated in a wheelchair in a dimly lit kitchen. He wore black pants and a black button-down shirt over which hung a long gold chain. He looked up at the camera, his small features expressionless.

In another photo were three young boys, toddlers, sitting on a carpeted floor, smiling. "My sun looks like a mini me of me," Hasan commented on the photo. In another, he sat shirtless on a bed. His body was lithe and muscled. A long scar ran from below his navel up to his sternum. Over his left pectoral was a tattoo of the name Christine; on the right, colored in red over his pectoral, was a large "M," in the Minnesota Twins style. It was a common tattoo used by the Crenshaw Mafia Gangster Bloods.

I scrolled through his recent posts.

February 22
"The best thing waken up is to know that these niggas want me down"
"feeling super"

February 22
"Being Paralyze is a emotion of breaking up relationships"

February 22
"I need a woman that respects being tookn care of"

February 23
"Lol woke up felin like a million buCKs . . . $with cotton mouth"

"CK," in gang lingo, was short for "Crip Killer."

22

As a steady rise in Denver's gang violence continued, the city's federal anti-gang effort was conspicuously absent from public reporting. I couldn't find any mention of it since the prestigious grant had been announced in 2010. One night, I went to a public meeting of the Holly Area Redevelopment Project (HARP), held in the old Safeway building at the top of Holly Square. District 2 commander Mike Calo was there, in uniform. He had a broad chest and a high forehead. His black-and-gray hair was combed to one side. Afterward, he told me he'd be happy to discuss his work. "What we're doing here is a model for the nation," he said, and gave me his card.

Denver's policing had in fact become a model. Since the latest Project Safe Neighborhoods effort had begun, at least fifty cities had sent officers to Denver to train with District 2 and its primary partner in the effort, the ATF. The presence of law enforcement headquarters had given Denver access to resources such as the ATF's state-of-the-art ballistics lab.

I started going to public meetings the police held, often in the District 2 community room. At one of them, hosted by Commander Calo, an ATF agent said that Denver's law enforcement community had discovered that most of the city's crime was being committed by a small group of "trigger pullers." It was a variation on David Kennedy's findings about "impact players" in Boston. The same findings had been made in other cities, but Kennedy felt it didn't account for the fact that many of the "trigger pullers" were put up to the violence they carried out by the OGs. In Denver, according to the

ATF agent, law enforcement knew who the violent offenders were, and would bring them to justice.

I HAD STARTED collecting names of people who had been arrested in the neighborhood and was tracking a number of court cases that began to illuminate the otherwise invisible multi-agency law enforcement operations that were going on in Northeast Park Hill. That was how I learned that in 2012 and 2013, as part of Project Safe Neighborhoods, the ATF and District 2 ran a multi-task-force operation called "Operation Bleedout," which employed informants from inside the Bloods. One of them was Major "Magic" Clarkson. He was the Blood whose car was shot at in the Horizon parking lot while Terrance played chess with his son. Magic was outed as a snitch the way many snitches are. Freddy "10-4" Johnson, whom Magic had stung by wearing a hidden camera, learned of Magic's identity when Freddy got to see the discovery file in his case. Freddy was furious; Magic was one of his best friends.

Magic's story of becoming an informant for America's premier anti-gang effort was also common. According to court papers, sometime in 2012, he was in the Denver Jail facing his ninth felony. In exchange for going undercover as an agent of law enforcement, his charges were dismissed, he was paid $7,000 in cash, and his car was taken out of the impound lot. A few months later, he was escorted to a restricted area of District 2, where a technical team fitted him with a small camera under his shirt. On three occasions, he recorded one of his best friends, Freddy—who ran the shop on Colorado Boulevard—selling him a "zip," or an ounce of crack, which Magic told Freddy that he needed.

Freddy—who Terrance swore had tried to entrap him into talking about a drug deal with some "Russians"—was now facing a long federal prison sentence. Freddy decided to argue an entrapment defense. With no media coverage, the case went to trial in 2014, and Magic was required to testify. On the witness stand, according to transcripts I obtained, Magic admitted being an ATF informant and seemed to agree he thought Freddy had been entrapped. "I set up my friend," he testified. "I'm not accepted by Park Hill no more. My mom barely accepts me. I'm nobody," Magic testified. "I don't remember anything until I set up my best friend." He said someone who did that "deserves to die."

Freddy's defense team also raised questions about whether Magic's use as an informant may have violated DOJ guidelines. Magic had a previous conviction for a violent felony.

According to experts like law professor Alexandra Natapoff, the DOJ guidelines on informants were frequently violated. Most infamously, the Boston FBI used the Irish crime boss Whitey Bulger as an informant from the early 1970s into the 1990s. During that time, Bulger killed or ordered the killing of at least eleven people, including another informant. Still, no law exists regulating informant conduct; there are only the guidelines. Despite possible problems with the use of Magic as an informant, the jury convicted Freddy on all but one count. He is in federal prison.

In Denver, the 1,440 police officers on the city's force are expected to cultivate informants if they want to move up the ladder. Within the gang unit, informants are seen as vital to making arrests, because gang loyalty and the mistrust of law enforcement complicate efforts to get information on crimes.

An officer can become an informant's handler without even arresting them. Terms of the agreements vary. Most state that the informant will give his handler actionable information in exchange for the handler asking the district attorney's office to request leniency for the defendant in a pending case. But some informants may have long-term relationships with officers, particularly if they are higher up in a gang structure and in a position to consistently identify the players. All informants are paid in cash, disbursed by a district-level manager. They go by nicknames, which they are allowed to choose. Their real names are kept in a safe in Denver police headquarters.

Federal informants were also common in Denver, particularly in northeast Denver's gang communities. The FBI, DEA, ATF, and Homeland Security all had large offices in the city and dedicated gang agents, who relied on such relationships to do their work.

According to the law professor Natapoff, federal law theoretically allows any defendant to cooperate in any case, and many do. From 2010 to 2015, the DEA employed approximately eighteen thousand informants at a cost of $237 million per year, the ATF operated about two thousand informants per year at a cost of $4.3 million, while the FBI did not release numbers. Inspector General reports on the agencies showed that many of the informants had committed serious crimes.

Prosecutors and former cops I spoke to told me that using informants often requires an "ends justifies the means" approach. Many informants are useful precisely because they are criminals themselves. Natapoff's research corroborated what I was starting to see in Denver: while informants are not supposed to be immune from prosecution, they were often accorded significant favor. Aside from the ATF informant involved in the Fero's Bar stabbings, I also became aware of other violent men in Denver who had assault, domestic violence, DUI, or weapons charges dismissed and gone on to sting others in undercover operations.

Terrance believed they were their own subset of informants. He called them "goons" and "assassins." To him, they were the neighborhood's real "impact players," to use the anti-gang expert David Kennedy's term, guys calling the shots if not pulling the trigger. Yet they remained on the street and close to politically charged events, despite being the well-known authors of violent crimes. They were an invisible army inside the invisible war.

Their dangers were many. Nationally, informants were the leading cause of wrongful convictions in capital cases. Terrance and others I would soon meet believed they were also enlisted by law enforcement to undermine and intimidate activists.

. . .

IT WASN'T CONSIDERED safe to talk about informants in Northeast Park Hill. They were considered not just dangerous but also to be connected to powerful interests. One didn't have to be committing crimes to fear an informant. In a neighborhood like Northeast Park Hill, politics ran deep and generations of residents felt they had been unlawfully targeted for any number of reasons, from personal beefs to political disagreements to something indecipherable. For many in the neighborhood, getting arrested on any kind of charge could, at minimum, derail their life and cost them thousands of dollars they didn't have.

Those who would speak to me on the subject said most people from the community knew at least one person they suspected was an informant. In some cases their suspicion stemmed from that person's ability to avoid arrest themselves; in other cases it was because they had seen "the paperwork," usually a court document with the person's statement; in others, they had been stung by the person themselves.

All of them told me there was only one person who had been willing to speak out about informants. It was Terrance. Doing so, they said, had both distinguished him and quite possibly placed him in danger. "Calling out those forces is the most necessary and dangerous thing you could do," Hasira "H-Soul" Ashemu, a northeast Denver activist and the son of Lauren Watson, told me. "Think of the community as a body. Terrance is the immune system of the Black body. When there's a foreign entity that comes in and threatens the health of that body, Terrance is the one to say, 'Listen, this is inside, you know, we're sick because that.'"

Terrance spoke regularly with other anti-gang activists about the use of informants. In the gang world, a "snitch" could refer to anyone who'd spoken to law enforcement about a crime, including one they might have witnessed accidentally. To Terrance and other activists, "informants" were more specifically the people secretly working for law enforcement.

Alex Alonso, the sociologist and founder of Streetgangs.com, said that his research suggested a recent surge in the numbers of informants. Alonso, who lived in Los Angeles, believed that this was an untracked but leading factor in the rise of gang violence. He estimated that between 10 and 30 percent of gang homicides were connected to informants—either committed by them, or as revenge against their perceived presence. This was one important reason why intra-gang violence had surpassed inter-gang violence, and why gang violence statistics were often so off-base: the FBI and many municipalities, including Denver, defined gang violence as an action by a member of one group against another group. A member of the Bloods killing another Blood didn't count.

Alonso told me he was not surprised by Terrance's opinion that the growing presence of informants in Park Hill had helped stir up violence. Gerald Wright, the thirty-nine-year-old former leader of the Camo Movement, and the activist Alex Landau, who was twenty-five, and others told me they believed the problem went deeper. They believed the police used informants in northeast Denver to strategically undermine opposition to initiatives sought by city hall. To them, what happened at the Holly and to the Camo Movement was the most obvious example.

"Terrance wanted to save a neighborhood he came from and the city wanted to gentrify it," Alex Landau told me. "We've had plenty of people targeted for much less." He said that the group he worked for, the newly formed Denver Justice Project, had recently outed an infiltrator at one of its protests.

Denver law enforcement's record of illegal spying was not reassuring. Denver's FBI had illegally conducted surveillance on the Occupy movement in 2011, a year after the birth of the Camo Movement. And in 2002, Denver's "Spy Files" case was a scandal at the end of mayor Wellington Webb's administration, revealing that the Denver police had been conducting illegal surveillance on peaceful activists, including a police watchdog group that Denver police categorized as "criminal extremists."

Why would law enforcement want to undermine a successful

anti-gang activist? Commander Calo, who at first told me he was happy to speak to me, ultimately declined to be interviewed. I don't imagine he would agree with the premise. But for longtime anti-gang activists like the LA-based Aqeela Sherrills, the answer is clear. Sherrills saw the gang war as a critical piece of the multibillion-dollar-a-year criminal justice industrial complex. Gang communities across America were the targets of the biggest law enforcement programs, and sites of the most arrests. "Law enforcement is invested in the problem," Sherrills told me. In Denver, about one-third of the city's nearly $1.5 billion budget went to the Department of Safety, including the police, GRID, and other law enforcement programs. Gang violence comprised the bulk of the city's violent crime. Theoretically, in a world without gang violence, law enforcement stood to face severe budget cuts.

Whatever the truth of such views, in northeast Denver, many people believed that Terrance had become a target not because of his inefficacy but because of his success. For H-Soul, the northeast Denver activist, Terrance was the very prototype of a law enforcement target. "He's young, tenacious, fearless, intelligent, articulate, charismatic, and he knows how to use weapons and is not afraid to use them," H-Soul told me. Plus, he pointed out, Terrance was leading an unprecedented movement of unified gang members who wore camouflage and talked about "taking back the land" as northeast Denver began to rapidly gentrify and the FBI regional headquarters opened blocks away from the Holly. "We may not find out for thirty, forty years exactly how high up Terrance's name has traveled inside the halls of those that want to keep people of color oppressed," H-Soul said.

Terrance had insisted I watch a 1980 interview, now on YouTube, with a former FBI informant, Darthard Perry. In the late 1960s, Perry, who was African American, showed up at a burgeoning education and arts center in Los Angeles called the Watts Writers Workshop. Posing as destitute, he was offered a janitorial job at the center. He said that, on orders of the FBI, he secretly sabotaged equipment and made calls to members, asking if they were interested in buying a gun. Then, in 1973, as the center was preparing to grow again with a big grant and the opening of a theater, Perry says that the FBI told him to firebomb the building, which he did. The damage was so great that the organization never recovered.

In northeast Denver, several conspiracy theories surrounded the arson of the Holly Shopping Center in 2008. Some believed the police were involved. Some thought that the city was behind it, in order to wrest control of the area. Others, including Terrance, believed Rev Kelly was involved, which struck me as far-fetched, but one day when I was with Rev, he surprised me by sharing that he had been with the Crips late on the night that they decided to burn the Holly down. "They always said they would do it if Mike got killed," Rev told me. I had to wonder if he'd shared with them the information that might have stopped them: that the Bloods hadn't killed Mike. I had pulled the news coverage that showed Rev misleading journalists at the time, saying there was no connection between the fire and Mike's death. One thing Rev certainly knew was why the Crips were motivated to commit the arson.

EVENTUALLY, TERRANCE TOLD me something that I'd begun to gather he believed: that law enforcement had used gang informants to infiltrate the Camo Movement. He took me into the office of the house he was staying in, which was empty but for a desk, two chairs, and a desktop computer. He had stayed off Facebook, but his page—which had five thousand friends, the max—was live. It was the only place he had photos and videos of the events and actions he'd held. But this time he wanted to show me something about Carl McKay.

I understood that Terrance thought Carl's shop was suspect and seemed like a law enforcement storefront. And I had seen court documents showing charges against Carl that the district attorney had dropped. But that wasn't enough for me to know if Carl was working with the police.

According to people I spoke to, after Carl opened his shop in the Holly, he often acted like he was a supporter of the Camo Movement, but Terrance and others didn't believe him. In a neighborhood like the Holly, if you're "on the block," meaning still "gang banging"— or remaining involved in criminal activity—it is hard to hide. Carl's Facebook page, which I could see, didn't dispel the rumor. It featured a red car as its profile photo, and photos of him in a Boston Red Sox hat with the red B on the brim, indications of his self-identity.

Terrance told me that two months before the shooting, he had organized a Camo Movement photo shoot. Supporters came and took vanity shots in camo gear. Carl surprised them by showing up. Terrance pulled up the photos. In one, Carl, who was thin and had a trimmed goatee, posed holding the bill of a camouflage cap with a P on it, for Park Hill.

Then Terrance asked if I remembered what Carl had said in *The Denver Post*. It had been some time since I'd read the coverage, and I didn't know who Carl was then. Terrance clicked on the stories. In both of the *Post*'s big feature stories about the shooting, it was Carl who appeared as the voice of the community. He was identified as the owner of a cleaning company in the neighborhood.

Speaking to the *Post*, Carl criticized the Camo Movement, saying it sent "mixed messages" because people wore camo hats with letters on them for their neighborhoods. He also clearly intimated that Terrance had fallen back into criminal life. Hasan, Carl told the *Post*, "got a chance to witness two different individuals." Speaking of Terrance, Carl added: "When you're not firm in who you are, and you allow people to see a different side then, yeah, it's going to lead to questions . . . The way [Terrance] was feeling suggested he had forgotten what career path he had chosen. I had to remind him of that career path."

THE REDEVELOPMENT OF Holly Square was ongoing. Meetings of HARP were held bimonthly at the former Safeway building at the top of Holly Square. Aaron Miripol, who was forty-eight, kept a low profile, arriving in jeans and carrying a bike helmet. He sat in back.

Sixty-four-year-old Gerie Grimes, the HARP president, who wore business attire, ran the meetings. Usually between ten and twenty-five people attended, a mix of older longtime residents and white representatives of new projects under discussion. I did not see Commander Calo again, and I never saw Senator Johnston. For several months, discussion centered on a new charter elementary school, which was eventually approved. It would be built over the site of Terrance's peace courts.

Of all the places I visited in the community, I always felt most uneasy at these meetings, as if I was under scrutiny. One night, after a meeting an African American woman introduced herself to me and said she was interested in my work. She said she worked for a new "community news" network, called 60 Second News. I couldn't find its website. Eventually I found the LinkedIn page of one of its advisers, who had listed it as a project he oversaw before going to work for the Department of Defense. A former employee later told me he had quit his job there because he believed the company was operated by law enforcement, and that it wasn't a real news site.

At first, Miripol appeared interested in befriending me, insisting on taking me to dinner. He had told me that he was impressed with Terrance's work and "the energy he brought," but I sensed there was more. One afternoon he agreed to meet me at the Holly. It was cold and few people were around. He showed me the original Holly Shopping Center sign, white with purple lettering. It lay against a wall behind a fence.

I asked him about tensions between Terrance and others involved in the redevelopment prior to the shooting. "Terrance was pretty frustrated with a number of things and at times it came out," Miripol said. When I pressed him to be specific, he pulled out his phone and forwarded me March 2013 a group email from Terrance. It was a long email; Terrance sounded aggrieved, but, at least to me, his frustration seemed understandable. Terrance had written the email from the state capitol, where he was waiting to testify about a juvenile detention bill. He had just read *The Denver Post* feature that purported to tell the history of the Holly redevelopment, with no mention at all of Terrance. Terrance had emailed Miripol, the Denver Foundation staffers, and others and said that he felt he was being "strategically alienated." He added, "I am really hopeful we can have a dialogue about this before next week's meeting. I will come where ever I need to so we can address this."

Terrance had complained to me many times that he felt left out of prominent events and had been told he shouldn't seek media coverage without approval. Miripol seemed to suggest it was Terrance who stole the limelight. "If you look at coverage," Miripol told me, "it was 'Terrance saving the Holly!' 'Terrance doing all of these things!'"

He also brought up the documentary. "That mockumentary, that *Drugs, Inc.* thing, upset a lot of people," Miripol told me. "The drug warfare that's portrayed there—it wasn't giving a full picture. That's just saying it's a drug community."

It was difficult for me to understand how anyone would think that Terrance had had any real input on the program, even if the Prodigal Son logo appeared at the end of the show. I assumed Miripol didn't know that the material Terrance had in fact helped the producers obtain included the interview with Hasan and the Bloods, talking about leaving gang life behind.

When we stepped over a part of the courts, Miripol had me look down. A section was a different color. The night of the shooting, one of the police cars that had pulled onto the courts had left the scene so quickly that the car's wheels had torn out five pieces of the courts, which were later replaced. Recalling that day, Miripol became emotional. He said that upon getting a call about an hour after the shooting, he headed straight to the Holly. He said he'd spent most of the night there with Rev Kelly and dozens of other community members, in shock. "That questions all your work, Terrance," he said to me. "All the eight years you did to build this up—now to take it down by shooting someone. It felt very personal. I was very angry. We were going to lose momentum because of this. There was definitely some heartburn. But it made us stronger. One incident is not going to derail the work we've done."

On August 9, Terrance's thirty-eighth birthday, Michael Brown was killed in Ferguson. When I got to Terrance's place, he and George were watching the protests on CNN. Ferguson, Terrance said, was a Bloods community. He took me into the office and pulled up Brown's Facebook page, which included photos of Brown and his friends in red. Terrance began to follow posts of the activists on the scene. Many were gang members who had become politicized by the fight for justice for Mike Brown.

Denver was not among the cities that joined Ferguson in protest, but a shocking death in Aurora the following week changed the politics of northeast Denver's gang war. I didn't know whether to believe the news at first. According to Terrance, Hasan had killed the two-year-old niece of Pernell Hines, one of the top Blood OGs. "It's all over town," Terrance told me.

It hadn't been in the media, though, and I couldn't find Hasan listed as an inmate anywhere in Colorado.

The next day, George told me he'd been asked to do the baby's funeral. "The coroner has listed the cause of death as a *homicide* by blunt force trauma," he told me. He said that the baby, who went by Ny Ny, had wheelchair marks on her feet and cigarette burns on her body.

I finally found Hasan listed as an inmate not in Aurora's Arapahoe County, where Ny Ny died, but in the Denver County Jail. He was facing attempted murder charges for a drive-by shooting that had occurred blocks from the Holly on May 30, just before the concrete barriers were installed. But no other charges were attached to him. I would later learn that, in the three years prior to being shot by Terrance, Hasan had been arrested nearly two dozen times, including for child abuse, two drug possessions, and four assaults, none of which resulted in formal charges.

THE NEXT DAY, Rev Kelly told me he was going to visit Ny Ny's family, and I accompanied him. The apartment was in a large complex. Inside, three generations of women were around a kitchen table. Quisa, Ny Ny's mother, who was nineteen, wore a light green pajama shirt with a deer pattern. She had perfect skin and long braided hair. She seemed distracted and distant.

"It hasn't really hit you yet," Rev said to her.

"Nope," she said, looking down. "Probably hit me when I see her."

Quisa's mother, Nicolia, who was thirty-nine and heavyset, said she used to be a Blood. "We *ran* the Holly," she told me.

The apartment had a shag rug and leather couches and was the home of Ny Ny's great-grandmother, Sandra, who was fifty-nine. Sandra was thin and wore a black headwrap. She had clearly been crying and was still emotional. She said she often watched Ny Ny and her brother, who was four and was now running around the living room, oblivious.

The wall across from the kitchen table was full of framed photos of family members. Sandra grabbed my arm and took me to it. "He's dead," she said, pointing to an image of a young man posing next to a lowrider car. "He's dead," she continued. "He's dead. I don't know if I can take another."

Over the next few days, a picture of what had happened emerged. Quisa and the baby's father, Carnell Hines—Pernell's younger brother—had broken up about a year earlier. Quisa had since been dating Hasan, who was in a wheelchair and on the run from police for the drive-by. Quisa was allowing Hasan to hide out at her apartment. On the day Ny Ny died, Hasan had begun texting Quisa, demanding she come home from work, and threatening to hurt Ny Ny if she didn't. When Quisa got home, Ny Ny seemed sick, perhaps constipated. Quisa went back out to get prune juice, but when she returned Ny Ny's eyes were back in her head. She called 911, but Ny Ny was dead.

Carnell had allegedly been on a bender since getting the news, drinking and threatening members of Hasan's family. Rev raised the issue of security for the funeral. "I'll make sure the perimeter is covered so we don't have to worry about drama," he told the women. "You don't need to be worried about someone coming up on you."

THE TAYLOR MORTUARY occupied a double storefront at the far end of an Aurora strip mall. As I pulled into the parking lot, a group of people, drinking beer and smoking, eyed me. Inside, the mortician, Laquita Taylor, greeted me. She wore gold lipstick and purple fingernail polish on her extra-long nails. She had known George Roberts for decades and had served on the first board of Prodigal Son. She took me to her office, where Quisa and her family were seated at a round table, signing paperwork. When they were done, Laquita told them she had printed out the comments that friends and family had submitted about Ny Ny through the mortuary website. She asked Quisa if she wanted to read them aloud. Quisa, who was in a black dress, tried but began to cry. Laquita read them instead as the women held hands. "Her favorite activity was playing with her doll and pushing her cart. She also liked to color . . ."

I wandered into the adjacent chapel, which had several rows of chairs and, on the dais, a doll-sized open coffin. Inside was Ny Ny. Her cheeks were pudgy and her tiny eyes were closed. She wore a white wedding-style dress with a gold headdress. She looked like an African queen.

Relatives and friends were arriving in the foyer. I'd heard that Pernell, the baby's uncle, was outside, and I managed to get someone to introduce us. Laquita let me use part of her office to speak to him. He was about average height and wore a sweatshirt and glasses. He told me I could not record the conversation. Of Terrance's shooting case against Hasan, he said that if Terrance felt he was in danger, he was "within his right" to defend himself. I told Pernell that I assumed he felt the same way about facing Ty Bud in 2010, when I knew that Pernell had admitted to killing Ty Bud. Pernell went quiet and stared at me. "I don't talk about that," he said. The door opened, and Carnell, looking disheveled and acting drunk, entered and asked me if it was true that the coroner's report had declared Ny

Ny's death a homicide. I told him I had heard this—and then regretted trading in this word-on-the-street information, as he turned and stormed out with Pernell chasing after him.

When I got back to the chapel, George was gathering about two dozen guests in a circle, all holding hands. "We bow our heads and tear-stained eyes," he said. "Father of God, we ask you to touch right now this mother, touch her in a supernatural way. We ask in the name of Jesus that you touch everyone within this circle. We ask that you give us clarity that Ny Ny has made it home."

WEEKS CAME AND went with no charges or media related to Ny Ny's death. I called the Arapahoe County district attorney's office and was told that the case was "under investigation" and that the DA had sealed the coroner's report. It sounded strange that the district attorney's office would censor the report; I was not given an answer as to why.

One day Sandra called me to ask for help. "It doesn't make any sense," she said, that Hasan hadn't been charged. She said that Quisa had told her weeks before Ny Ny died that Hasan was abusing her. I managed to reach the Aurora police detective on the case, who testily asked how I got his number and referred me to the public relations officer.

Marshal, Terrance's lawyer, was not prone to conspiracy thinking, but even he shared the speculation that I heard from the community: that the Denver DA might have an interest in keeping its star witness in the Terrance Roberts case from becoming known as a "baby killer." Any communication between the Denver and Arapahoe County DAs' offices would be considered "prosecutorial misconduct," Marshal said, "but how do we prove it?"

The seeming imbalance of justice began to eat at Terrance. "What if I did kill Hasan?" he said to me one day. "That baby would be alive today." Another day he said, "Can you imagine what Hasan could do if he had two legs? But *I'm* a pariah."

Terrance rarely drank and didn't use drugs, aside from pot, which was legal. But his emotions swung wildly and I couldn't help but wonder about his mental health. One day he laughed at the thought of being back at the prison chow hall, and days later banged his fist on the table and said, "They're practically forcing me to rob someone just to stay alive."

He was desperately broke. He had quit his construction job because he was having trouble with one of the crew members. Terrance said the guy was provoking him to fight. Terrance knew he could be locked up before the trial if he got in any kind of trouble and didn't want to risk an altercation. He went weeks eating the same pot of rice and beans and spent much of his time working his phone, asking friends if he could borrow money.

He had also become mesmerized by the growing Black protest movement, which he followed on cable news and on Facebook. On November 24, St. Louis County prosecutors announced they would not pursue charges against Officer Darren Wilson, who had shot and killed Michael Brown. Ferguson, which had a strong Blood gang presence, exploded in protests that spread to other cities, as people marched and chanted, "Hands Up, Don't Shoot."

Terrance showed me the Facebook page of Deandre Joshua, whose brother had witnessed Michael Brown's shooting and who had been part of the protests. Joshua was found dead in a burning car. He had been shot in the head. Some in Ferguson believed that he had been targeted because of his activism.

While several cities joined Ferguson in protest, Denver, where the mayor and police chief were both African American, was not among them. Many I spoke to said that normally they counted on Terrance to organize such demonstrations. Brother Jeff Fard, the often-busy northeast Denver activist, had not organized anything. Instead a Blue Lives Matter demonstration, in support of police, drew several hundred people.

The next time I saw Terrance, his predicament seemed to epitomize the state of the city's protest movement. "I ain't really even focused on what you're saying right now, bro," he said. "I'm trying to figure out how to pay the heat bill or they're going to kick me out of this house. I don't even have any toilet paper."

Word got around that Terrance was in a bad way. People he hadn't seen in ages "inboxed" him on Facebook and arranged to meet him on the street to give him cash handouts. Drettie, from whom Terrance had largely stayed away because of his close connection to Bloods Terrance believed were involved in attacking him, spent several hours in a park trying to encourage Terrance. "Little old ladies over there are praying for you, and they know you shot this nigga down," Drettie told Terrance. "You got something else working on your side not anyone can touch. Like Martin Luther King and them niggas. Those dudes bustin moves, homey, they was doing shit. That's you, homey. You don't see it but that's what's going on with you."

But as the holidays approached, Terrance remained dour. Even George, who I'd never seen down, appeared dejected. "Someone told me a pastor got arrested down in Ferguson," he told me. "I said that's his problem. I'm worried about what's going on here in Denver. What about the young man they just found murdered in the alley? What about the baby? What about my son? Did anyone come and protest for us? Terrance told me, 'Pops, a gang war is coming.' I told Terrance, 'We ain't activists no more. That's not for us to deal with.'"

23

The Office of the Colorado Public Defender occupied two floors of a dark glass skyscraper a few blocks from the capitol. It was December, and Terrance's trial was only a month away, Marshal had called Terrance in. This time Terrance demanded that Marshal allow me to be present. "People need to see what's happening to me," he told him.

Marshal led us down a carpeted hall to his office, looking out at the *Denver Post* building. The "o" was missing from its white neon sign. It was a cold dying day and the sky glowed twilight blue. Marshal's desk was cluttered with three-ring binders from Terrance's case. One was open to the colorful flyer advertising the peace rally the night of the shooting. "One Love Black Unity Rally!" it read across the top. "This is NOT a gang or reactionary rally, this is a way to show we care for and support each other as people!" read the text below.

Marshal had important news. The DA had made a plea offer, for ten to twenty years. It didn't go over well. "I already told you I ain't taking a deal for shooting Munch," Terrance said, slapping his palms down on the sides of his chair. "On the day that this happened I was doing my job on my property."

"Well, you're not going to be able to take care of your family if you're in prison for more than a hundred years," Marshal said. He told Terrance that the DA's office had warned that it could still add "habitual criminal" charges to Terrance's case. As Terrance knew, the "big bitch" would significantly lengthen a mandatory sentence. Marshal said he thought he could get Terrance a better offer, but he needed to know what Terrance would consider taking.

About 95 percent of all criminal cases ended up in a plea deal.

Terrance made clear he didn't intend to be among them. "I'm *not* going to take a deal!" Terrance said. "The DAs don't want this trial to
happen. The police probably don't want this trial to happen. Let's see
if a jury of twelve thinks I didn't have a right to defend my life. And
I need you to do that. I need you to take me to trial and fight for my
life!"

TERRANCE HAD STAYED off Facebook since the shooting, but he
broke his silence that night:

> December 18, 2014
> The D.A.'s office offered me a 10–20 year cap my people, OR,
> they are also looking at filing the Habitual Criminal Charges
> on me. Because my advocacy has been "upsetting" to them
> and I'm such a criminal? . . . Where are all those political
> connections that called me all those years when dozens of our
> youth were getting killed in the streets and me and Well Done
> [Gerald Wright] were organizing Crips and Bloods to pause on
> the madness????
>
> Where is Reverend Leon Kelly, since the D.A. is his "best friend"?
> Do you see what has happened to a man who literally just
> wanted to put up playgrounds and youth centers for forgotten
> Black children in a forgotten community? They offered me a
> 10–20 over defending my life on property I developed and my
> company owned, against a man who was on a crime spree and
> pulled a weapon on me that day and tried to assault me. . . . A
> man who is incarcerated now for a shooting near Holly Square,
> a gang related shooting, and under investigation for murdering a
> 2 year old child? What if I was the Senator I shared my office
> with, how do you think this would have played out?
>
> My trial date begins January 27th my people, I hope some of
> you can join me.

Hundreds of people liked and commented on his post. In the morning Terrance posted again, this time specifically calling out the mayor and Rev Kelly, claims I could not substantiate.

> December 19, 2014, 10:06 am
> Denver—Have you all forgotten that the Denver Police worked with gang banger informants, who told Hasan & younger Bloods to hurt me . . . Have you all forgotten Mayor Hancock & "Rev" Kelly then hired these same informant goons to "shut up" Terrance Roberts . . . So if I say fuck the police, or the Mayor, or "Rev" Kelly, or them "gangstas" working for them, don't be surprised . . . And if you're hanging with any of them, Fuck You Too! . . . There goes some leadership for y'all. . . . Wishing you all a good weekend . . .

Two days later, Marshal called Terrance. The district attorney had added the "big bitch." If convicted, Terrance would die in prison.

I CALLED GEORGE. "The DA got Terrance's life in his hand right now," he said. Christmas was days away. He told me he was going to see Terrance later so he could drop off some toys he got at a church drive. Terrance had no money to buy presents for his kids.

George picked me up in his old white Lincoln Town Car, which could only be entered through the passenger-side door. "Rev is very interested in this case," he said as we drove. "He talks to the DA. He talks to the chief. I promise you he talks to the commanders. Reverend Kelly has the key to the city—*hey, man*—when it comes to politicians and people who have *authority* over Terrance's life. Rev Kelly can tell the DA *right now* what and what not to do."

He pulled his phone out of his pocket. "I'm calling him," he said.

"Georgie," came Rev's distinctive voice. I stayed quiet.

"Did you know that they're about to file the habitual criminal on Terrance?" George said.

"Man," Rev said. "When they saw what he was writing on the

Facebook thing—they weren't talking about no craziness, habitual and all that, until he got to just *blasting* folks. I tried to tell him: Stay off of that."

"There's a time to talk and a time to be quiet," George said.

Rev told George that he'd invited Terrance to his thirtieth-anniversary gala a couple months earlier. I'd been there. Mayor Hancock and the former mayor Wellington Webb sat at the head table. Both of Denver's African American mayors were close with Rev and the reality of Denver's gangs. Webb had his house shot up by the Crips as Mayor; a couple weeks before Rev's gala, Mayor Hancock's son Jordan was a passenger in a car from which shots were fired, hitting another man in the head. The mayor's office denied any gang connection, but witnesses told police they heard gang-related taunts exchanged at the scene. Jordan was not arrested.

Terrance had refused to go. "I know about the gala," George said. "Terrance just was trippin' because he knows that you know that Carl McKay and Rodney Jackson and all of them set it up so that Terrance was gonna get got that day."

I was stunned. It was a big accusation. There was a silence on the other end of the call. "Okay," Rev said. "My whole thing is . . . all this stuff has happened. I called him to invite him to this event . . ."

Rev went on and on without answering the question. We pulled up at Terrance's place. They hung up. Terrance let us in wearing shorts and a camo Broncos hat and walked straight back to the office, where he was responding to comments on Facebook. He was back, politicking from the only pulpit he had left.

George sat down across the desk.

"I talked to Rev," he told Terrance. "I know you wanna get your voice out there, but the DA and everybody's looking at it. That's what made them charge you, because of the Facebook things that you're saying."

"Nigga, I can get on Facebook if I want, my nigga!" Terrance shouted, smashing his hand on the desk.

"You're looking at life in prison—I'll shut this motherfucker down!" George shouted back. "And I'm a preacher telling you."

"I'm an activist, Pops," Terrance roared. "I should be able to say what I *want*, my nigga!"

"*After* the trial," George countered.

"*Before* the trial, how about that!" Terrance shouted. He stood up. "Everyone wants me *silent*, my nigga. Before I shot Hasan, the Bloods—'Shut the fuck up about the Crenshaw Mafia shit,' 'Shut the fuck up about the Camo shit,' 'Shut the fuck up about the violence.' My *words* are getting me prosecuted, *not* my criminal actions!"

"Then go to trial," George said.

"I'm not about to go to jail 'cause I'm on Facebook!" Terrance shouted.

"You called out the DA, man," George said, shaking his head. "That's crazy. That's suicidal."

"The DA has not charged these police officers—"

"That's not your business," George said.

"That is my business. I care about Ezell Ford [a twenty-five-year-old African American shot by police in Los Angeles in August]. I care about Michael Brown. I care about Eric Garner getting choked and saying he can't breathe. I care about that shit, Pops. It matters to me. Black Lives Matter, my nigga. One Facebook post and I deserve eighty years? 'Cause these niggas is powerful? Not to me they're not. I'm not afraid of these niggas, Pops. I'm not afraid of the DA's office. *Fuck* the DA."

"Don't say that," George said.

"Why not?" Terrance said. He stood up and held both middle fingers in the air. "Fuck him, fuck him! *Fuck him!*"

24

Mitch Morrissey, Denver's district attorney, was in his third decade as a prosecutor for the office. He was elected to lead it in 2005, and again in 2009 and 2013. He was a third-generation Colorado lawyer and public servant. His grandfather was the U.S. attorney for Colorado under Presidents Roosevelt and Truman. His father, who grew up in Park Hill, became a Colorado state congressman while still in law school.

Morrissey, who wore tailored suits and had silver hair parted down the middle, was a Democrat, like almost all elected officials in the city of Denver. His tenure had become increasingly fraught with criticism from citizens and public interest groups over his decisions not to charge any Denver police officers, even though the city had been paying out millions of dollars a year in civil settlements for excessive force and abuse complaints. Terrance's friend the activist Alex Landau was one of the victims who had won compensation for the nearly fatal beating he endured during a traffic stop. Landau's was one of many cases that civil rights lawyers in Denver thought should have resulted in charges against police officers. Now, Landau worked for the Denver Justice Project, whose goals included Mitch Morrissey's removal.

As an assistant district attorney, Morrissey had prosecuted gang cases and had developed a relationship with Rev Kelly. In 2001, Morrissey prosecuted a gang member for killing Rev's nephew, twenty-five-year-old Clarence Blaine, Jr. Morrissey had to hold back Rev's sister in the courtroom when she tried to lunge at her son's alleged assailant.

Morrissey had also known Terrance for many years. In 2006, he had visited the Prodigal Son office and given Terrance a community service award. He'd also praised Terrance's skills to the media in 2007 when the federal grant was awarded after Darrent Williams was killed. Terrance had twice been a guest on Morrissey's monthly public-access television program, *Dialogue Denver DA*, the last time in June 2013, only three months before he shot Hasan. "Terrance is one of the true community leaders we have," Morrissey said at the time.

Looking through Morrissey's programs, I found another episode in which Morrissey's "Legal Term of the Month" was *habitual criminal*. "These are professional criminals so we treat them differently," he explained. "These are people that are gonna keep committing crimes. They are career criminals." By that standard, Terrance was clearly not a habitual criminal. But prosecutors also regularly used enhanced charges to try to muscle defendants into taking a plea.

I called Morrissey's office to request an interview but was told that in order to ensure Terrance a fair trial, he could not comment until the case was over. So I called Rev.

"Man, Julian," he said, sounding exasperated. "My people over at the DA's office are just saying, 'Man, what's up with your kid?'" he said, referring to Terrance. "When you make the hood angry—all right, you can deal with that. When you start making public people angry over at the mayor's office . . ." He groaned.

"Has Mayor Hancock said something?" I asked.

"Yeah," he said. "People have called me, Julian—and it's not good. It's not good. If [Terrance] would have just did what I asked him to do. Just. Shut. Up. Be quiet. Let me handle damage control."

"He thinks people want to silence him," I said.

Rev laughed. "You want to challenge the system?" he said. "You *ain't* gonna win. It's like a chess game. You can't leave your valuable pieces unchecked. I said, 'Terrance, you're playing checkers, this is a chess game here.'"

I asked if he thought Terrance's Facebook posts had hurt his case.

"Hugely," Rev said. "Put it that way, hugely. Plus all the other stuff they've been watching him on is not good."

"What other stuff?" I asked.

"You know, when he was out there, he was going to these night-clubs," Rev said of Terrance. "He was smoking and drinking, doing other things. They had other people under surveillance and here he is in the same mix of it."

I wasn't sure what Rev was talking about, but I remembered Terrance telling me about the Kasbah, the nightclub where many from the Holly, including Carl, often went. It was there that Terrance told me he'd smoked pot with Carl before showing Carl his gun. I asked Rev if people were talking to him about the surveillance of Terrance.

"That's what I'm saying," he responded. "I've been having con-versations behind the scenes that nobody else knows publicly be-cause they're not going to say it publicly. But these are conversations that are being brought up and these are considerations that the DA and others have to entertain."

I DIDN'T KNOW what to make of what Rev said. It was possible he was inventing all of it, perhaps to undercut what Terrance had be-gun saying about him on Facebook. But if he wasn't making it up, he claimed to have inside knowledge of surveillance of Terrance that was damaging to him.

While I knew that some believed Terrance was a target of surveillance because of his activism, I also had to entertain the pos-sibility that Terrance was involved in something I didn't know about. About a month earlier, Marshal had received a request from the DA's office for a fingerprint from Terrance. Terrance had seemed nervous. Mitch Morrissey had made it a priority to solve cold cases. I had de-cided not to ask Terrance if he'd ever killed anyone, because there was no statute of limitations for murder and if such information ex-isted, I didn't want to be in possession of it. He'd given the sample.

A WEEK BEFORE Terrance's trial, Marshal was able to get another continuance until May, over the prosecution's objections. It seemed something of a mixed blessing for Terrance, who would have to figure out how to continue to survive financially. But the next time I spoke to him, he was euphoric.

He said that a Blood told him that he had been at a "B meeting" days before the shooting, at Carl McKay's shop. Terrance said the man, who I will call Amari, claimed to have witnessed Carl McKay and other OGs plotting to attack Terrance. According to Terrance, Amari was willing to come forward, to his lawyer and to me. "I told him, 'You better get ready to absorb a lot of energy,'" Terrance said he told Amari.

When I called Amari, he sounded conflicted. "I have a lot of people saying, be careful, you shouldn't do it, you shouldn't, you shouldn't," he said. "That's what puts me in a hard position. I know these guys. I know what they're capable of." But, he said, he felt obligated because the damage to the community had been too great.

We agreed to meet, but when the day came, I waited and waited. As I was leaving, he finally walked in. He said he'd been watching the entrance for the last hour. When I asked if he believed there was a plot to attack Terrance, he was unequivocal. "Wholeheartedly," he said. "I was there. I was sitting *right* there."

He said that days before the shooting, he was in "Way Out" and Carl's shop in the Holly. Rodney Jackson and others were also there. The OGs called Terrance a snitch and, Amari said, talked about the fact that "something needed to be done" about Terrance. My sources in the gang community, including Amari, said that meant Terrance was in danger of being hurt, badly. The Bloods' anger over the *Drugs, Inc.* documentary was a pretext, Amari said. They knew Terrance had nothing to do with how the show turned out and didn't care if it portrayed Denver as a drugs and gang capital. "I love those guys," Amari said. "But they're full of shit. I know 'em. I've known 'em all my *whole* life."

He believed the motive was mostly jealousy, of Terrance's media profile and of the perceived financial benefit from raising millions of dollars for the Holly. "A lot of people think there's money in it," he said, shrugging. But he said that for some of the OGs, there could have been another motivation, because they knew what Terrance had been saying. For example, Amari said, "Terrance was telling everyone like, 'Did you see those cameras? You know who uses those cameras?' He was like, 'Carl's working for the police.'" When I asked Amari if he believed it, he raised an eyebrow. "Sometimes it's just obvious," he said.

MARSHAL TOLD ME he'd also spoken to Amari and found his story credible. But he wasn't as bullish as Terrance about its impact on the case. Marshal had been a public defender for almost twenty years. Getting gang witnesses to show up for trial wasn't easy. He said he continued to be unable to reach Reggie Fair, the hot dog cook, who had been right in front of the shooting when it happened. He also told me that since an initial meeting, he had been unable to reach Rev Kelly.

Terrance's friend Kamao "Ktone" Martinez, who was Black, and had also witnessed the shooting up close, finally said he would speak to me. Ktone was thirty-two and lived with his wife and four young children in a suburban Aurora home. He made his living deejaying at events that were frequently attended by gang members, and seemed concerned about anyone seeing me visit. On my way over, he called to ask that I not park in front of the house.

A friend greeted me at the door and took me upstairs. Ktone, who was stocky and had a small mustache, was in his recording studio, which was a carpeted bedroom with two turntables on a desk and framed CDs on the wall. Ktone, who wore a gold watch and bracelet, said he'd grown up in Northeast Park Hill and remembered the heavy gang presence when he would go to sports practice at Skyland, a block from the Holly. "I just had this thing, I would just mind my business, mind my business," he told me. He had met Terrance at an event around 2010 and joined the Camo Movement. "He was a real leader," Ktone said of Terrance. "It was a tough job. They were waiting for him to slip up. They were waiting for it. But he just kept doing what he was doing, what he believed in. You can see the void now in that neighborhood."

I knew he was one of many who had been keeping Terrance afloat with small cash handouts. "We could never let him fall," Ktone said.

When I asked about the shooting, he became noticeably uncomfortable and spoke haltingly. He said that as he was setting up his equipment, a group of Bloods he hadn't seen emerged and began to surround Terrance. "They started coming four there, five there, three there, two there," he said. "Pretty aggressive."

He said he heard Terrance ask, "Why y'all brothers doing this to me?"

I asked if he was willing to testify if called, but instead of answering he moved his head in a circle. I didn't know what he meant. "That word," he said. *Testifying* meant "snitching" in the gang world. "I want to kind of stay away from that word." Ktone wasn't a gang member, but taking the stand against the Bloods had its risks. One witness in a recent Denver gang case was murdered the night before she was scheduled to testify.

TERRANCE MEANWHILE HAD uncharacteristically gone radio silent. When I did reach him, I learned that one of his cousins, Sharod Kindell, was shot multiple times by Denver police after he was pulled over in Montbello. One bullet went through his hand, which he had held in the air. He was in critical condition. And another cousin, Marlow Martin, had been killed in a drive-by shooting, by the Bloods.

Terrance sounded unhinged. "Like I've been telling you, Julian, we're talking about *murder*," he said. "Not one murder, not even two or ten. Many, my nigga. We've *known* these people. My cousin . . ." he said, trailing off. I'd never heard Terrance cry, but it sounded like he was fighting off tears.

Marlow was twenty-seven, a father of two. He was a Crip, known as Lil Ruff. The Denver police did not determine the case to be "gang-related," but Terrance pointed me to the Facebook pages of Bloods who were claiming credit for it. "Lotta mans down somebody pick em uph," one post said, the "uph" referring to Park Hill. The post included a photo collage of six young men, including Marlow, who were all murder victims.

Facebook taunts like this were often a driver of more violence, indications that the OGs had the green light on. A series of traditional set-tripping shootings between the Crips and Bloods got the attention of Denver's media. "The neighborhood has been getting nicer and nicer," a Northeast Park Hill resident, who was white, told *The Denver Post*. "Houses are getting sold and property values are going up. I didn't think Denver was a hot spot for gang activity but apparently it is more active than we all thought."

Two weeks later, four homicides in one weekend appeared to push the city over the edge. Mayor Hancock and Chief White stood together on the steps of city hall. "If you disrupt peace in our city, and you perpetrate violence like this in our city, we will find you and we will hold you accountable," Mayor Hancock said.

One of the four killed over the weekend was "Lil ShowBizz," Jeffry Starks, who had told Terrance that Terrance was his big homey in the months before Terrance shot Hasan. Starks was killed at a baby shower. He had stepped outside for a cigarette. His assailants were apparently hiding in the bushes. Starks was twenty-seven.

Terrance had been fielding calls from family and friends who had seen on Facebook that Lil ShowBizz had been killed on Pontiac Street, near Ernestine's house. But what had rattled Terrance, he told me, was that the next day, he'd gotten a call from a gang member he knew, asking Terrance if he needed a gun. Terrance hung up. He believed it was another setup.

THE RASH OF shootings prompted an emergency citywide meeting. Though not disclosed at the time, the meeting was the first of a series of such meetings held under the aegis of a new Project Safe Neighborhoods effort. The DOJ had just awarded Denver another grant.

The meeting was held at the District 2 police headquarters community room, three blocks from Holly Square. It was standing room only. Local television news cameras, uniformed police, and federal agents in sports jackets lined the side. About half of the attendees were African American. I didn't see Terrance.

Brother Jeff, arguably the most established African American activist in Denver, sat alone in the front of the room, in a Black Lives Matter T-shirt. "Many people asked why are we doing this event at police headquarters—you could have it at a church," he began by saying. "But I think it's important to have it here because law enforcement is an important part of the puzzle. They see what's happening on the ground daily. In many regards they see things we don't know about, we don't see."

I couldn't help thinking it was odd to see someone in a Black Lives Matter shirt praising the police while protests over police misconduct were raging around the country. I later learned Brother Jeff had an official role with the new anti-gang effort.

Brother Jeff invited to the table Chief White; Chief of Public Safety Stephanie O'Malley, who was the daughter of the former mayor Wellington Webb; Commander Calo of District 2; and, to my surprise, Rodney "Big Rod" Jackson, one of the OG Bloods who Amari said had called for Terrance to get beaten in the days before the fateful peace rally. I had never seen Rodney before. He was forty-eight and overweight. He had a wide face with large moles on it, and wore a baggy white T-shirt.

Commander Calo, who had arched eyebrows and graying hair, stood. "There is *too much violence* in our community tonight," he said. "We are going gray because bullets are still flying in the Holly Shopping Center. Why? *Why?*" He looked around.

Brother Jeff directed a question to Rodney about why he'd joined a gang and what should be done. Rodney spoke slowly. The Bloods, he said, were like family for many youth. "You would never understand it if you haven't been there." He suggested a new but unspecified approach. "We tried everybody else's strategy over the last twenty years," he said. "We think our strategy is better than everybody else's."

Rodney's comments lacked detail and didn't go over well with some in the room. An African American woman in a teal shirt came forward. "I've heard you talk, you and me have talked one on one," she said to Rodney. "Help us understand what your method is, because I haven't seen it yet."

Brother Jeff redirected the conversation to a thin man with a goatee. I recognized him from photos. It was Carl McKay. He was sitting in the second row in a gray T-shirt and a long silver necklace.

"I'm Carl McKay," he said, standing. "I'm from Park Hill. We keep losing our youth. And then it takes a couple of tragedies to happen for everyone to react. We're not being proactive, we're being reactive. Like Rodney was saying, if you want the solution, you go to the problem, and it doesn't seem like nobody's really reaching out to the problem. They're not solving the problem. So what we need and what we're asking for is for everyone to step out of the way and let us solve the problem."

I'd been studying anti-gang programs, and Carl sounded like he was reading from a script straight out of the Interrupters method championed by the Chicago epidemiologist Gary Slutkin. It was also the anti-gang program that I knew the mayor and police chief White both wanted to run. Terrance and Prodigal Son had been staunchly opposed to using it.

Calo came forward again. "I'm at a loss as to who can get control of these young men—*young* men—at this point in time, and bring them in collectively—without us. What I think we need at this point is for you to come forward, Carl, Rodney, and talk to these fellas. And bring them in—*no police*—and say enough is enough."

Hearing Commander Calo promise the police wouldn't be involved, while at a meeting at District 2 headquarters with the leadership of Denver's law enforcement seated at the front table, sounded incongruous. By then I'd become well aware that many of the city's "faith-based" and "community-based" efforts, as this one would be advertised, were actually funded by and significantly involved law enforcement.

Brother Jeff called on Rev, who was on a stool in back, in a brown baseball hat, with *REV* embroidered on the cap, turned backward. "This is a community issue, not a police issue," Rev said. "We go back twenty, thirty years. A lot of these youngsters are the offspring of some of the older ones." Rev spoke about the challenges in stopping gang violence, then began to talk about the shooting involving Terrance and Hasan. "You know, we had a situation about a year ago," Rev said. "Somebody's trying to do something for the community—people didn't like that. They come up on him because he's trying to do what he's trying to do—they didn't like it. Now, tell me it wasn't the older guys out there putting jumper cables on some of these youngsters, saying, 'Put hands on him.'"

I couldn't believe it. Whether to prove his street cred or otherwise, Rev appeared to have just publicly admitted that he knew Terrance had been attacked at the peace rally.

"Well, *say that*, then," came a voice. It was Gerald Wright, the former Crip and Camo Movement leader, who was standing in the back.

"*Tell that to my attorney*," came another, louder voice. It was Terrance. He walked toward the center of the room in a black shirt and a camouflage Broncos hat and turned to address Rev. "Tell my attorney you know they sent them Bloods to jump on me. Tell Marshal Seufert that, because you haven't done it for me, sir!"

Brother Jeff tried to regain control of the meeting but couldn't.

"I hate to be disruptive," Terrance said, turning to the front, "but we're talking about four murders yesterday. I'm not trying to be disruptive. I'm looking at life in prison, y'all, so I ain't got nothing to lose."

WHEN I REACHED Terrance by phone later, he was beside himself. He blamed the recent surge in gang violence in part on the Blood OGs, including Carl and Rodney. "We lost control of the gang war because of Carl and Rodney," Terrance said. "But now they're supposed to be activists." Rodney's lengthy criminal case file included two recent felony charges, for Schedule II drug possession of more than four grams, and for theft of more than $20,000. Both were dismissed by the DA in January 2013.

The fact of active gang members posing as anti-gang activists was nothing new. In Denver, it dated back at least to the mid-1990s when Mike Asberry and Orlando Domena had a brief and scandalous tenure as anti-gang workers. More recently I discovered that it had been a problem in publicly funded Interrupters-style anti-gang efforts in Chicago and Harlem. In 2014, a Harlem woman who worked for the program reported that active gang members were working as violence "interrupters" and had compromised the effort and frightened community members. She complained to the city that they were dealing drugs out of the office, and possibly more. "People's public safety is at risk," she told the Marshall Project. Simply reporting the information, she said, had made her a "snitch." She said she'd had to move and feared for her safety.

It wasn't clear to me yet what was going on in Denver, and the local reporting didn't offer any insight. I was also surprised that while nearly every local news outlet covered the emergency meeting, not a single story mentioned the meeting-stopping dispute between the city's two most prominent anti-gang activists over whether one knew the other had been attacked.

The next day I called Rev. For the first time, he sounded openly suspicious of me. "I know you're working with Terrance on this little book," he said. He called Terrance "paranoid" and "possibly bipolar." "All he's doing right now is just confirming the whole thing—that this is a guy who's a loose canon. All the things he was involved in, *man.* I can point out other things."

He didn't, but he did say that after the meeting he had spoken to both Chief White and Commander Calo about Terrance. "I was like, 'Terrance is cracking up. He's cracking up,'" he said he told Calo.

Rev denied that he'd avoided Marshal, Terrance's lawyer. "We sat right *there,*" he told me, referring to an initial meeting Marshal told me they had had. "I had them in my office, trying to come up with a strategy, come up with a game plan," Rev said. But, according to Marshal, Rev hadn't been returning his calls since.

I asked Rev if he thought it was possible that Carl and other OGs were involved in telling the younger guys to attack Terrance.

"I wouldn't be surprised," Rev told me. "The way Terrance was acting, I wouldn't be surprised." He added, "Terrance shouldn't be overly sayin' about his hatred or dislike about certain people in the neighborhood. They still got clout within the streets."

I asked Rev if he thought that what Terrance said at the meeting was a problem.

"It was like a death wish," he said.

Despite the DOJ's awarding Denver a new Project Safe Neighborhoods grant, its independent review of Denver's previous effort was
still unavailable. I did, however, find the DOJ-funded quarterly magazine *National Gang Center*, which devoted the bulk of its Spring 2015
issue to Denver. "Planning for Successful Summer Programs" was
the headline.

> In 2014, a community-led campaign dubbed "Safe Summer,
> Safe Holly" ensured a violence-free summer where children
> could learn, grow and play . . . During the 90-day period, not
> a single act of violence was reported . . . Based on this success,
> there are more plans for redevelopment in the area and, more
> important, a sense of pride among community residents.
>
> [Gang Reduction Initiative of Denver Director] Paul
> Callanan said it best: "These programs bring unity and
> a sense of welcoming to our communities. By fostering
> neighborhood connections, through safe activities for
> youth and families, by deterring violence, identifying
> and connecting families to needed resources. Ultimately,
> it inspires community pride and connectedness within
> neighborhoods."

I didn't recognize what I was reading. The summer of 2014 in
the Holly had been marred by a spike in gang shootings that caused
the city to block the main road through the Holly with concrete
barricades, sparking community outrage. The Denver police's own
publicly available statistics recorded fourteen violent crimes in

Northeast Park Hill between June 1 and August 31, the reporting period. One was a murder; eleven were aggravated assaults. That didn't include the drive-by shooting on May 30, blocks from the Holly, that the police alleged was committed by Hasan Jones.

The rise in shootings had led District 2 to implement the sonar ShotSpotter system in the neighborhood, typically used in war zones. Meanwhile, as if to announce their reclamation of the Holly, several OG Bloods recorded a gang rap video on the roof of Senator Johnston and Prodigal Son's building.

THE NEXT TIME I saw Terrance, he'd moved. He said too many people knew where he was staying. Now he was living in a suburban Aurora subdivision, in his mom's basement. He had put out some of his awards and trophies in the dark, carpeted room.

With northeast Denver's gang war sharply escalating, Terrance was determined to get involved. He called his own independent anti-gang summit, featuring several Crips and Bloods who had been working with the Camo Movement.

The meeting was held at Lowry Community Christian Church, on the Aurora-Denver border. Terrance hadn't been in touch with most of the participants since the shooting, and they hugged one another as they arrived. "I really miss you brothers," Terrance said. Some had complicated histories. "I've been shot by someone in this room," Gerald Wright, who had been a Crip, said. "I've been shot by a few people in this room," Terrance said, shaking his head. They all laughed.

They discussed what they could do to help the situation. "Can't none of us in here stop what's going on," Gerald said, "but us being older we have some influence on those younger cats. Just do something different. If you want to live, you have to do something different."

"They're too far gone for a program," another former gang member said. "They want to make some money. They need some employment."

"We can't stop nobody from banging, but we can set an example," Terrance said. Positive mentorship, they agreed, was critical.

The discussion ended with acknowledgments of their own struggles with PTSD. They resolved to start a men's support group.

Terrance also reached out to Aqeela Sherrills, in Los Angeles. Terrance, Aqeela, and other anti-gang leaders around the country were closely monitoring what was happening in Baltimore. The city's Bloods, Crips, and Black Guerrilla Family gang members had laid down their arms and banded together in protest against the police for the death of twenty-five-year-old Freddie Gray, Jr., who died in police custody. Baltimore's unified gang members had become a political force in the streets, demanding justice for Gray. Police had teargassed them and made arrests. Then, on the day of Gray's funeral, the Baltimore police announced that they had received an anonymous "credible threat" made by gang members, stating they were "teamed up" to "take out" police.

The allegation by the police raised eyebrows with anti-gang activists who recognized it as the same threat that the LAPD had claimed gang members made during LA's peace movement in the summer of 1992, and later in Newark and elsewhere.

Baltimore's gang members had refused to take the blame for making the threat. "We're not about to allow y'all to paint this picture of us," one told a local Baltimore TV station. Days later, the Baltimore police were forced to retract the claim. Though the retraction didn't make news outside Baltimore, gang communities spread it through social media.

ON APRIL 28, 2015, THE DAY after Gray was buried in Baltimore, Mayor Hancock appeared on the steps of city hall with two dozen of Colorado's highest-ranking law enforcement officers, including the attorney general, the Denver district attorney, the U.S. attorney, and members of the FBI, DEA, ATF, and Homeland Security. It was the official kickoff of Denver's new Project Safe Neighborhoods effort.

"We stand here together to announce a coordinated and multilayered approach to halting the gang violence that is playing in some of our northeast Denver neighborhoods," Mayor Hancock said. The previous day, a gang member was murdered as he left the funeral of another murder victim. "It has to stop, and we're gonna pull out all the stops to assure that it does." Some neighborhoods, Mayor Hancock said, would go under "twenty-four-hour surveillance."

Missing from the group at city hall was Rev Kelly, who was in his downtown office. When I arrived, he was on the phone, inquiring about adding names to an insurance policy for a van. A black pistol was holstered on his hip.

"Doing all this paperwork, man," Rev said when he hung up. He held up a packet. "Gang Violence Interruption Program—that's us," he said. He said it was his contract with the city. "Two hundred seventy thousand dollars," he said proudly. "Two-seventy."

Rev said he was going to be in charge of eight interrupters who would work in Five Points and Northeast Park Hill. He said he had hired four former Crips and four former Bloods who would make up a council. "We've never had a council as such," he told me, "a group of OGs who have been established in the neighborhood. And we come together and make *decisions* as to what needs to happen."

He said that on the Blood side his team was Carl, Rodney, Drettie, and Pernell. I tried not to blink. Not only did I believe that they were active and influential OG gang members, but Rev himself had told me that some of them had "probably" put the word out to the younger guys to attack Terrance. "The city saw the influence I had on them," Rev continued. He held up a long index finger. "There is one Reverend Kelly."

I asked how he got them on board. "There's things I've done personally with these guys that nobody else knows," he said. "*Nobody*. Sometimes I feel like the godfather. 'I'll grant you this favor but I may never need you in life again. But if it ever come a time that I *need* you'—he raised his finger again—'for whatever reason, I will call you. And I will expect for you to come.'"

The only inference I could draw was that he'd helped them on their criminal cases.

"We're going to be housed in Park Hill," he added.

"By the Holly?" I asked.

He raised his eyebrows. "We're going to be in Terrance's old place," he said.

It took all I had to get out of Rev's office without revealing my shock. I ignored a lot of calls from Terrance that week. I didn't want to be the one to relay the news to him that the people he thought had attacked him were among those about to take over his old office. Instead I attended Rev's weekly "Flippin the Script" program. As part of the Department of Corrections parole program, newly released inmates from Denver's gang community were required to come weekly, for lectures by Rev about peer groups and decision making. The meetings were held at the Church of Scientology.

The huge building occupied prime real estate in LoDo. So that I couldn't go elsewhere in the church, a staffer escorted me straight to the classroom, which had ivory busts along the walls and rows of student desks. In the back, a folding table featured bread and supermarket lunch meats and cheese, curled in rolls. Copies of a chapbook, *The Way to Happiness*, were also on the table. On its cover was an image of Rev, in a powder blue suit and black fedora, with the Denver skyline behind him.

The parolees—all men; most Black—stood around before the program started. Rev's interrupters—Carl, Rodney, Drettie, and Pernell—were all there. Carl drifted away from me every time I approached, so I introduced myself to Rodney, who was eating a sandwich.

"You been talking to the wrong guys if you're talking 'bout the Holly," he said. "*We're* the OGs." I told him I'd be happy to speak with him, and a few days later, I spent the day with Rodney and the other Blood interrupters as they moved into Terrance's office. Rev had billed the event as a "community cleanup" and invited *The Denver Post*.

Drettie wore a red hat and blue Chuck Taylors with red laces; in the gang world the style had a very specific meaning: Crip Killer. Cars passed by, with drivers and passengers hollering at them. One flashed gang signs and Drettie flashed them back. "Cut it," Pernell said, unaware I had seen the exchange.

Carl, who wore red jeans, shook my hand but continued to avoid me. Rodney made hot dogs and hamburgers on the grill on the patio. Pernell mowed the lawn.

"Wayski," I heard someone call. It was another knickname for Joel "Way Out" Alexander, who was close with Hasan, and had co-operated the computer repair shop with Carl. Joel was large and top heavy in black cargo pants, a black shirt, and a black baseball hat.

I walked over and introduced myself.

"You know who I am?" Joel asked me. He wore a diamond earring and a gold tooth. "Ninety-six indictment," he said, referring to the infamous racketeering case. He gave me a fish handshake.

I told him I was doing a project about the Holly and wanted to talk to him.

"You know Rev?" he said. "If Rev says it's cool, it's cool," he said. I wrote down my number, and he snatched the paper with his huge hand. As he walked away, he rolled it up in his fingers and tossed it over his shoulder.

When I got home I had several missed calls from Terrance. I didn't feel comfortable hiding what was going on any longer and called him back.

"What's the wiggle?" he said.

When I told him, he lost it.

"I told you I think Rev Kelly had something to do with what happened to me!" Rev's close relationship with the OGs who were in conflict with Terrance was clear, but I hadn't seen evidence that Rev was involved with what happened.

I had to hold the phone away from my ear as Terrance lost his temper. "They're a police-funded mob of Black murderers!" he yelled of the OGs. "Anyone hanging out with Carl McKay or Pernell, I'm not fucking with them. That goes for you, too, Julian. If they ever come near me, if I got a gun, I'm gonna shoot 'em, if I got a knife, I'm gonna stab 'em. If I got my hands, I'm gonna fight 'em."

. . .

SIX DAYS LATER, Carl McKay was arrested. Terrance was the first to tell me. The details seemed too outlandish to be true, but when I got the police report, I saw that they matched. At 2:15 p.m., Officer Derek Hancock of District 2 was driving westbound through the Holly in a patrol car, when he observed a white Buick driving erratically through the former Prodigal Son parking lot, then failing to fully stop at 33rd and Holly. Officer Hancock ran the car's plate and found it was a fake. He flipped on his lights and pulled the Buick over.

Carl was in the driver's seat; Rodney, whom Officer Hancock knew had previous drug arrests, was next to him. Hancock also saw an open beer and a bottle of Hennessy. He asked Carl to get out of the car so he could search it.

It was a Thursday afternoon in the Holly. When Carl got to the sidewalk, Officer Hancock sensed from Carl's body language that he could become combative or try to flee. He called for backup.

As people in the neighborhood watched, Carl was placed in handcuffs and a search of his car began. On the car's back seat, Officer Hancock found a bottle containing colorful balloons knotted in a way Hancock knew was common to packaging heroin. He also found a plastic bag containing what he suspected was cocaine, as well as bags of pipes and screens used for smoking crack.

The police report also contained the line that was coursing through the streets of northeast Denver. Soon after Carl was pulled over, he fumbled around looking to find his driver's license, telling Officer Hancock he must have left it at home. While doing so, according to the police report, Carl also "stated several times that he worked for [Commander] Calo."

CARL'S ARREST AND apparent admission that he worked for the police was a development that seemed to give credence to some of what Terrance and others had been saying. When I went to see Terrance, he was ecstatic. He posted on his Facebook page the photo of Carl posing in a Camo hat. "That's CAMO Carl to my right in the photo," Terrance wrote. "Do you all see how I was infiltrated by this guy? Open your eyes my people . . . He'll be at a night club near you now, trying to entrap you."

Gerald picked Terrance up and they rode around northeast Denver, stopping to see key people. "This is big," Alex Landau, the activist, said. "No one's talking about the role of gang informants, but this is part of the problem, not the solution."

Some wondered whether the drugs had in fact first been seized in police busts because they were packaged for small sales that normally wouldn't be made by someone of Carl's stature. I didn't have any evidence of that. But as a result, the incident resurrected rumors that the police were selling drugs through the OGs.

Even though the police report said that it was Carl's driving that got him pulled over, some questioned if Officer Hancock had been tipped off by someone close to Carl, because rumors of Carl being an informant had made him a liability.

It certainly seemed like a tangled situation. An anti-gang activist, arrested on drug charges, and thus seemingly still involved in gang-related activities, while also at least claiming to work for the commander of District 2.

Commander Calo referred me to the police public information officer, from whom I didn't get any answers. But activists, former police officers, and former gang members I spoke with both in and out of Denver said that there was in fact a reason that the police might want to use gang informants in an anti-gang program, and it was that law enforcement had control and leverage over informants. When Terrance was working for the Project Safe Neighborhoods grant, he didn't have to cooperate with law enforcement or give them any information, and his refusal to do so had caused major tensions. But an informant would already have a contractual relationship to help law enforcement.

The larger problem with informants, in the eyes of experts on informants like law professor Natapoff, was that their use in vulnerable neighborhoods and lack of regulation made it impossible to rule out that they were being deployed in other strategic ways, as they had in the past. In Black communities across America, allegations of activists being set up had given way to talk of a "New COINTELPRO."

I had no proof that Terrance was a target, but it was clear to me now that Terrance's prominent voice and inside knowledge made him a possible threat to some members of the police. According to Terrance and Amari and others in the neighborhood, despite Carl's involvement in the anti-gang effort, Carl was one of the people influencing younger guys to commit violence, not stopping them. A source I trusted told me that the Denver police's decision to use Carl and other active gang members as anti-gang activists had rankled some in the force. Two cops had come to blows over it, I was told.

As the Project Safe Neighborhoods effort rolled out, television commercials featuring the new anti-gang effort had begun to air regularly. "Together, we can show we have *zero tolerance* for crime," Mayor Hancock said, delivering the city's new slogan. Carl's arrest, I assumed, would be a major setback. In the neighborhood, it seemed like all anyone talked about. But day after day came and went with no charges and no media coverage.

Eventually, I called Rev. He sounded aggrieved. "It ain't no big thing," he told me of Carl's arrest. "People hear rumors and they put their own stamp on it. I'm on the *inside*. I hear what happens on the *inside*."

I didn't tell him I had the police report. "They pull anybody over for anything, whether they have an excuse or not," Rev said. "What was the probable cause for the search? That's the regular protocol they've been using on the east side and Park Hill. They get these guys, they put 'em in handcuffs."

Rev was suggesting that Carl's rights had been violated. It was the first time I'd heard Rev criticize the police.

"The small amounts of what they found and where they found it—it's not like it was in the console," he said. "It was in the back seat, so that could've been anybody's." I didn't correct him, but according to the police report, more drugs were found in a backpack on the back seat that also contained business cards with Carl's name.

Rev said Carl had been suspended "while the investigation takes place." Then he inartfully turned the subject. "Munch's dad is with me now," he said. "We're talking about all of this now."

I didn't understand why he was telling me this. Everyone I knew who knew Ice Alexander said he was one of Denver's most dangerous men. Many I knew also believed he had law enforcement protection. In 2010, he had federal gun charges against him dropped. Since then he had been arrested for aggravated assault, domestic violence, felony menacing, and parole violations but managed to stay out of prison. Several sources I spoke with reported that Ice had also called a younger gang member to tell him he needed a gun; when the young gang member arrived, he was arrested.

I asked Rev what he meant.

"Me and Isaac, Munch's dad," Rev answered, "he's up under my wing now. He's with my group, he's up under my umbrella. He's working with me."

I decided to ask him if Ice had a problem with Terrance.

"Well, he tried to kill his son," Rev said.

THAT WEEK, CARL changed his Facebook profile photo to an image of a chessboard. "This shyt chess not checkers," another Blood commented under the photo.

Terrance changed his profile photo to the image of the iconic Nickerson Gardens mural in Watts, from the original Truce of Nine-Deuce. "Nobody Can Stop This War but Us," read the inscription. Within hours more than two hundred people had liked it.

District 2, which had its own Facebook page, did not change its profile photo. It was a yellow sign bearing the slogan "Zero Tolerance."

Two weeks later, Hasan Jones went to trial. He faced the same charges as Terrance in the same courtroom, with the same judge.

When I arrived to the courthouse, Alex Landau was among a few dozen protesters in the Justice Center courtyard. They carried placards demanding the recall of district attorney Mitch Morrissey. I went up to the fourth floor, where George Roberts was in the hallway talking to two large African American men. One wore a white T-shirt that said "BIG SIKE" in blue, a memorial to Denver's Crips founder Michael Asberry. George later told me he was "Scarface," an OG Crip who was on Rev Kelly's "council." I asked George if they were there to check out Hasan's trial. George told me he got the sense they were there for Rev, to check me out.

Few spectators were in the courtroom, but among them were the assistant district attorneys Henry Cooper and Alma Staub, who were co-chairing Terrance's case. I had to assume they were aware that Hasan had finally been charged with "child abuse resulting in death," for Ny Ny. It carried a sentence of up to twenty-four years.

Hasan's family sat together on the defense side. I recognized some of them from their Facebook pages. His mother, Tisha, had small facial features like her son. She was short and stout and wore a brown patterned dress and hoop earrings. Hasan's aunt Lois, a cousin, and two sisters in their twenties, who wore their long hair in braids, sat with Tisha.

Several sheriffs appeared, and a heavy side door opened. In came Hasan in a wheelchair. He wore a salmon colored shirt and a tie. His thin face seemed much larger because of a tufty goatee. He acknowledged his family with a nod then gazed at me as if he wanted to say something. Through a loop of contacts, I'd been told that Hasan wanted to speak to me. Twice I'd gone to the jail on my own to visit him but, after long waits, I was told once that he didn't want to do it and another time that I couldn't speak to him for "security" reasons. After a long look at me, Hasan nodded and I nodded back.

The prosecutor, Zach McCabe, used his opening statement to paint a scene of a placid spring day in Northeast Park Hill just after a rain. Children were playing in the street. Suddenly it turned into a war zone, with semiautomatic gunfire coming from a moving van. Treylony Chambers, who was on the sidewalk in front of his brother's house, fell to the ground, bleeding. His brother dragged him inside, yelling for his kids to follow.

Chambers, who was twenty-eight, walked gingerly to the witness stand and once there had trouble containing his emotions. When McCabe asked if he recalled where he was on the afternoon of May 30, 2015, he said, "Yeah, I was on the floor bleeding."

Chambers said he'd just gotten off work at Walmart and had come to see his brother and sister-in-law and his new niece.

"What happened?" McCabe asked.

"This man to my left shoots me twice," Chambers said. "I see this dude in my dreams every night. I see him every night. Hasan Jones, to my left."

Chambers testified that he used to be a Crip. One of the effects of the gentrification of Five Points was that a number of Crip-affiliated families, including the Chamberses, had moved to Northeast Park Hill, where the smaller homes, farther from downtown, were less expensive. The micro-migration also flared gang tensions. The Bloods had attacked many Crip families who had moved to Northeast Park Hill.

Not long before Chambers was shot, a group of young Crips had taunted the Bloods with a group photo, taken in front of the Skyland Park sign, a traditional Blood stronghold, only one block from Holly Square. Law enforcement and community members I spoke to believed that the photo, which made the rounds on Facebook, caused a tit-for-tat shooting spree between the two gangs that happened to coincide with a visit from then vice president Joe Biden to Denver. Mayor Hancock and

Mitch Morrissey reportedly accompanied Biden to a fundraiser. Carl McKay had posted on his Facebook page, "Can you niggas please wait until the POTUS leaves to resume shootings in the Holly. Thanks."

Three days later, after Biden had gone, Chambers was shot on the sidewalk, a few blocks from the Holly. A few weeks after that, the concrete barricades went up on 33rd Avenue at Holly Square.

Chambers testified that he had had multiple surgeries and suffered from PTSD, depression, and back pain. Hasan looked straight ahead, expressionless.

I HAD MADE a point of introducing myself to Hasan's family, except for the few men, who didn't appear interested. When the trial broke for lunch the second day, I asked Tisha if I could eat with them. She agreed, and I accompanied the family to a food cart, which had hot dogs and burritos for $2.50.

We walked back to a garden on the side of the courthouse. Several young men in red shirts and shoes came by to say hello to Hasan's sisters. Hasan's public defender, who was nearby, rushed over. "The jury is walking by," he mouthed. The Bloods left.

Tisha wore a dark blouse, jeans, and silver hoop earrings. Her straight dark hair was cut short. She said she had taken off work all week from her job as a medical technician. She was nervous, she said. Just before the trial, she said, Hasan had been offered a deal for ten to thirty-two years, but declined.

She indicated that she believed Hasan was being framed, and brought up Terrance. "My son is in jail for a crime they can't even pin him to," she said. "And ShowBizz is free even though he admitted he shot my son. And you know why?"

I said I didn't.

"Because he's rich," she said of Terrance. Some in the neighborhood thought Terrance had cashed in on the $5 million Anschutz development gift to the Holly.

Tisha told me she remembered Terrance from his early days. "I knew ShowBizz," she said. "He was wild." She said she became close with several "original" Bloods when she met Isaac, or Ice, at school. They were seventeen. But she said people didn't realize that she had stopped dating Isaac by the time she got pregnant with Hasan. She said that Hasan's biological father was another OG Blood. Neither man was in Hasan's life growing up.

Her candor about Hasan's emotional struggles surprised me. She said he had "extreme anger problems ever since he was born," which was in 1991. Tisha said that Hasan was kicked out of multiple schools, for fighting and threatening people. She said she lost a job due to the disruptions his behavior caused her and that when Hasan was about 14, she told an Arapahoe County judge that she couldn't handle him anymore. He was ordered into foster care. Then a series of criminal charges as a juvenile led him into the youth correctional system. When he got out at eighteen, she said, his parole officer gave up on him. "Let the streets have him," she remembered the officer saying. She had agreed. "Some belong to the streets," she told me.

She hadn't been close with Hasan for years, but she said that the night before Terrance shot him, she had had a premonition that Hasan was dead. When she arrived at the hospital the following night, she said the doctor told her he was unlikely to survive.

The hospital waiting room was filled with OG Bloods, she said, some of whom she hadn't seen in years. As they waited, her phone rang. It was Mayor Hancock. She said she didn't know how he got her number. "Anything I can do, just let me know," she said the mayor told her. She asked him for more security. Within minutes, she said, security arrived.

AFTER THE TRIAL resumed, Special Agent Scott Eicher of the FBI took the stand. He brought with him a color-coded slide presentation that was put up on a large screen for the jury. It illustrated Hasan's movements on the day in question, which had been determined by the pings his mobile phone had made on cell towers in the neighborhood. Hasan had gone back and forth between two locations: the "Holly Shopping Center," which was how law enforcement continued to refer to the site six years after the fire destroyed it, and a residential home in Northeast Park Hill that was associated in court papers with Joel and Isaac Alexander, the primary targets of the 1996 takedown of the Bloods. According to its property records, the home hadn't changed hands until recently, when it went into foreclosure.

The prosecution's next witness was Dominick Salinas, a gang unit officer. My sources told me he worked with informants in the neighborhood. He had a wide face and thick chest. McCabe, the prosecutor, asked Salinas if he would recognize Hasan's voice and phone number and, oddly, if Hasan had called him the day after the shooting.

Salinas acknowledged that Hasan had in fact called him, from a number he recognized. I would later learn that Hasan had also been arrested on the day of the shooting but released. He hadn't been charged with the drive-by until three months later, when he was found in his girlfriend's apartment with a dead two-year-old.

Hasan looked at the floor. His lawyer, Greg Daniels, stood. "Your Honor, may I approach the bench?" he said. I strained to hear the heated conversation that followed. One interpretation as to why an active gang member would be in phone contact with a gang unit officer, according to my sources, was that Hasan was an informant. Salinas was likely Hasan's handler, according to a former Denver gang unit officer I spoke to on many occasions.

Judge Whitney sent the jury home for the day.

The following morning, the defense rested without putting on a case. Hasan did not testify. After closing arguments, I waited with Hasan's family outside the courthouse. Tisha was too nervous to speak. It seemed tough to say how the jury would vote. The prosecution had clearly shown that Hasan and another Blood, Darryl Dickerson, who was being tried separately, had stolen Darryl's mother's minivan. The minivan was identified by witnesses as the car from which gunfire came.

During his cross-examination and arguments, Hasan's lawyer had focused the jury's attention on whether witnesses could be sure that it was Hasan pulling the trigger, given that he would have been at a distance and in a moving car. Chambers's brother said he knew it was Hasan "because he looks like Bugs Bunny."

The jury reached its verdict in less than an hour. Hasan was wheeled in, and we took our seats. He was not guilty, on all charges. Hasan began to shake and cry. A guard wheeled him out as he mouthed "I love you," to his family, who hugged and wept. Hasan would be transferred to the Arapahoe County Jail, to face charges in the death of Ny Ny.

"Infamous Denver Gang Shooting Victim Acquitted in May 2014 Drive-by," read the headline of a short piece in *The Denver Post*. It made no mention that Hasan was still in jail, facing charges in the death of a toddler. I decided to call the reporter. Later that day, Colorado's paper of record reported on the killing of Ny Ny Hines, ten months after it happened.

THE NEXT TIME I saw Terrance, he was on the phone, talking about "Confidential Witness A" in his case, who had given a statement that he'd seen Terrance shoot a man twice while he was on the ground. When Terrance got off the phone, he showed me the court papers. An apparent clerical error had left the man's name unredacted on one of the pages.

Terrance told me he knew Dwayne.* He said that Dwayne had given the Bloods' "sa-whoop" alert call when Terrance had parked his car at the Holly just before the fateful peace rally. Terrance had made copies of the court papers and handed them out to key people in the community.

The revelation that Dwayne, a well-known Blood, was a confidential witness in the case made a splash in the neighborhood. To those who understood the inviolable rule gang members lived by, Dwayne's actions suggested that other forces were at work in the case. "It shows that what happened came down from a higher

---

* Not his real name.

source," Jason McBride told me, meaning from someone or something with leverage over Dwayne.

I checked Dwayne's arrest record. He had a couple of drug convictions and a slew of minor infractions, including an arrest for "jaywalking" two months before the shooting. I called the phone number listed on the police paperwork, but it was no longer in service. Word was that he'd left town, fearing retribution for his perceived snitching. I wondered if Terrance's actions amounted to witness tampering.

GANG SHOOTINGS CONTINUED to tear up northeast Denver, as did a massive law enforcement crackdown that was heavily covered by the local media. In a five-week span, Denver police said they made 2,168 contacts, 738 of them with gang members, and made 384 arrests. "Making Progress Against Gangs" headlined a lead editorial in The Denver Post. "Denver police are making a commendable effort to strike the right balance between an aggressive zero-tolerance campaign against gang violence that soared early this year and not harassing the innocent."

Despite the huge numbers of apprehensions, only one of the more than two dozen recent murders had led to any arrests. Brother Jeff continued to host public meetings about gang violence at District 2. When I walked into the meeting that followed Carl's arrest, I caught Rev's eye. He looked down. It was the first time that he had avoided me. I saw Pernell, Drettie, Rodney, and L Shady in the audience, though not Carl.

This time the meeting, which was promoted on the new social media platform Nextdoor.com, was attended by a mostly white crowd. The focus was on how to create better communication lines in the neighborhood. Commander Calo wanted more interaction among neighborhood groups, many of which had formed in the last two years, nearly all of them white. District 2 was promoting the use of Nextdoor.com.

About halfway through, Terrance's associate Gerald Wright

showed up and stood in the back. Commander Calo and Rev looked at each other. Rev went over to each of his guys, whispering in their ears. One by one they left the room, as Gerald held his hand high, waiting to be called on.

Finally Brother Jeff called Gerald by name. Commander Calo headed toward the back of the room and positioned himself only feet from Gerald, who seemed nonplussed. "Can we stop the gangs out here?" Gerald said. "I don't think so. You can slow it down, but you can't *have active gang members* working programs, *out here with these kids.*"

"Hey, Gerald," Brother Jeff said. "We're on *this* discussion." He held up a page with Venn diagrams about neighborhood associations.

"We already discussed that, brother," Gerald said. "My heart hurts. Because you can't have active gang members working with these little dudes who are gang banging. It's not going to work."

Another African American in his forties spoke up. He said he was a former Crip and had heard the same things about the city's new anti-gang workers as Gerald. "They're saying a lot of *those* cats are *still sending out hits*, calling shots, still active, so to speak."

"I want you to focus on this sheet," Brother Jeff repeated, returning the conversation to neighborhood associations. A white woman looked at the person next to her and shrugged.

After the meeting, I waited outside for Rev, who was doing a live interview with 9News. He left without speaking to me. It was suddenly dark and quiet, and I'd started walking toward my car when Pernell and Drettie appeared.

I shook their hands and tried not to appear startled. Drettie drifted away. Pernell patted me down, torso and back. "You better not be wearing a wire," he said.

He wasn't in a jovial mood, and he launched into an angry criticism of Terrance, whom he called a "coward." He said that he had invited Terrance to talk in person, but instead Terrance was "throwing bombs" on Facebook. Terrance had told me he had met with Pernell soon after the shooting but didn't feel safe meeting him again.

Pernell spoke to me like he expected me to be the go-between.

I nodded along in hopes of deflecting what seemed to be a test of whether my loyalties lay with Terrance. I told him I agreed that Terrance "talks in circles."

"What did Terrance really do over there?" Pernell said. He said Terrance never got anyone a job. "It's not hard to get people jobs," he said. That was what his team was going to do, he said.

An SUV pulled up across the street. Pernell walked toward it. I retreated toward the entrance to District 2 and waited for their car to drive away. I took a roundabout way home, eyeing the rearview mirror.

I HAD PROMISED to give Terrance a ride to do an errand the following morning, and when we got to the parking lot at the Cherry Creek mall, he didn't get out. "So you think I talk in circles?" he said. Before I could answer, he cut me off. He said that Drettie had put him on the phone with Pernell late the previous night. Obviously Pernell had relayed some of what I'd said.

"I told you if you're fuckin' with them guys we're done," Terrance bellowed at me. He pounded his fists on the console. "I'm not playin' a game, bro. You're gonna get yourself killed out here."

I tried to explain that Pernell made me feel I had no choice but to distance myself from Terrance, and that Pernell had acted like he wanted me to be the messenger.

"And what'd he say?" Terrance asked me.

"He said you were a coward because you wouldn't go talk to them."

"I fucking told you I already did, Julian!" he bellowed. He emphasized how dangerous they were. "You know I haven't told Rev Kelly where I lived for eleven years? Why do you think that is? I told you if you're fucking with those guys, we're *done*!"

Finally Terrance calmed down. "Pernell said he don't like you, bro," Terrance told me. "I don't think you're safe."

I tried to spend some time away from the community but found it difficult. The story had become all-consuming. I'd moved back to Denver and into my mom's apartment just to stay on top of it. I had come to trust Terrance and admire his fearlessness, but at times I wrestled with feelings of bitterness toward him. Sometimes he was the awe-inspiring peacekeeper; other times, it seemed, he was the reason my life could be in danger. Or was he?

So much had become hard to make sense of. I felt like I'd been living in an alternate universe, an invisible Denver. Most people I encountered outside the community told me they didn't know Denver had a gang problem. One night I went to a party celebrating the release of a documentary about Colorado's first year of marijuana legalization. The film was being promoted as "How Pot Saved Journalism," due to the success of *The Denver Post*'s new section "The Cannabist."

The Denver Post was the most trusted news source in Colorado. In 2013, it had won a Pulitzer Prize for its coverage of the Aurora *Batman* theater shooting. The judges had cited the paper's expert use of social media in its reporting. I could only assume its reporters weren't following the city's anti-gang effort on social media. It had an official Facebook page—called POTS, for Part of the Solution. On it, the group posted photos from its events, including one of young teens flashing gang signs. In another photo, Pernell looked on in red pants. To me and to others I spoke to in the community, it was as if the new "anti-gang" team was winking to other gang members on Facebook who might be wondering if they had really left the gang. On Facebook one could also find the new profile photo of Carl McKay, the erstwhile "anti-gang" activist. After being busted with drugs and leaving the program, he posted a selfie in a red jacket and a Boston Red Sox hat with the red B on the brim. "Feeling like myself again. God is Great!" he wrote.

Everything about Denver's "zero tolerance" anti-gang effort seemed upside down. Men whom the community feared were in charge of waging peace, while the man whose success at reducing gang violence had been historic was out. The results were alarming. In the first year of the program, the city was on pace for a significant increase in gang violence; even more troubling was that some of the people allegedly responsible for committing it appeared to be working for the police. Many of the murders committed during this period remained unsolved.

I started to get text messages from active gang members who were at odds with Terrance. Drettie, whose apartment I'd been to, wanted to get together. L Shady, whom I'd met at Drettie's apartment and a community meeting, texted to ask advice about a camera. Aundre "AD" Moore left a message. I no longer trusted their motives.

Rev was rarely the one who called me, but one day he reached out to invite me to a POTS event. I told him I'd go, but I didn't feel safe and stayed home. When I checked the group's Facebook page later, one of the few photos posted of the event depicted Rodney Jackson with his arm around another man. "Look who came thru" was the caption.

It was Ice Alexander. He was about average size, with a stubble goatee and an oversized T-shirt. On his head was a red Kansas City Chiefs hat. The intertwined "CK" logo conveyed a clear message to anyone with a basic knowledge of gangs: Crip Killer.

Terrance went to Walmart and got an air pellet gun. It shot BBs and he could legally possess it. "This thing will fuck you up," he said, brandishing it. He put it in a backpack that he carried everywhere, along with a switchblade knife. He and Gerald and others told me that I better get a "whopper," a gun. "This ain't a game, bro," Terrance said. I had to think about it.

TERRANCE'S NEW TRIAL date was two months away, in September, and Marshal indicated it was unlikely he could get another continuance. He started calling Terrance in to prep. Usually, he sat Terrance down in a conference room with a large table. Marshal wanted him to go through his discovery, which was contained on a laptop and in several boxes. Inside them were ballistics tests, photos, and, it turned out, a video.

Part of the shooting had been captured on a camcorder by a community resident, Ronald Washington, who had attended Senator Johnston's event that night. Washington, who was fifty-five, considered himself a chronicler of the neighborhood. He was interviewing Gerie Grimes, the president of HARP, outside the Prodigal Son office.

"Mrs. Grimes," Washington said from behind the camera, "I remember you last year at the opening day of the [courts]; you were so moved by that as all the community was. Now I see people playing and the community thriving again, but more significant is a building that was once an empty lot. Tell me about that."

Grimes, who wore a patterned scarf, stood with her back to the Holly. "It's official now," she said. "The goal is definitely being accomplished . . ."

She didn't finish because gunfire erupted from the Holly, behind her. About a second later the video stops.

If examined carefully, the scene behind Grimes's head and shoulder depicts Terrance walking to the back of his black SUV and appearing to get something before leaving the frame. Seconds later three audible pops can be heard as people run in both directions behind Grimes's head. One appears to be Hasan, in a white shirt. As others keep running, he drops to the ground as the video abruptly ends.

Terrance seemed unable to watch it or even sit still. He and his mother had had a fight, and he was now staying in his dad's tiny apartment, in the heart of Crips territory. Terrance, who had been sleeping on the couch, seemed irritable and distracted.

Whenever Marshal came by, Terrance made sure Marshal knew how he thought the case should be run. "Reverend Kelly, Carl McKay, and Commander Calo need to get on the stand and say what happened to me," he said. "Marshal, I'm telling you, these niggas tried to plot on my life and they work for the police. They have said they work for the police."

The elephant in the room was always the supposed five shots. It was a lot of times to shoot someone who was running away from you. Terrance himself had said he'd shot Hasan five times, in an on-camera interview a few months after the shooting with the gang historian Alex Alonso for Streetgangs.com.

According to the case's discovery file, the police discovered only four bullet casings. Terrance told Marshal that he didn't think he could have possibly shot Hasan more than three times. The pistol, he said, was small and squirrelly, and he hadn't had time to aim. He explained that at the time he'd done the Streetgangs.com interview, he had read so many media reports that said he'd shot Hasan five times he assumed it was true.

Marshal had a plan to tackle this issue. Terrance said that Hasan was telling people he wasn't going to show up at trial. If that was the case, Marshal said, he believed Hasan's medical records should be inadmissible, protected by HIPAA, the health privacy law. Hasan had presumably not signed any waiver giving the DA's office the right to his medical records. "I didn't see a shooting," Marshal said, in a lighter moment. "Did you see a shooting?"

But just as the DA's case could hinge on who showed up to testify, Terrance's defense had the same concerns. Amari, the witness who said he'd been in Carl McKay's shop when Carl discussed getting the younger Bloods to attack Terrance, had changed his phone number. Reggie, Terrance's hot dog cook, still could not be located. That left Terrance's friend, the DJ Ktone, as the sole eyewitness for the defense. But Ktone, Marshal said, hadn't been returning his calls.

Upon hearing this Terrance immediately called Ktone and learned why. According to Ktone, Ice Alexander's girlfriend had just opened an office across the hall from Ktone's wife, in an Aurora office park. No one I asked about it believed it was coincidental.

Terrance perceived other efforts to intimidate him and his

supporters. One day, he and Gerald were warned by someone I knew and trusted that there was a green light on Gerald, and this time there was money attached.

Gerald, who had made a very public series of accusations against the city's anti-gang effort, began wearing large hats as a disguise. When I asked if he was afraid, he scoffed. He said he was on a mission to make sure what he saw as corruption in the city's anti-gang effort became known. "God put it on my heart to let the people know the truth and that's what I'm gonna do," he said. Plus, he said he'd had hits on him before. "Several," he told me. But, he noted, there had never been money involved.

WITH TERRANCE'S PERMISSION, I managed to copy most of his cases' discovery documents onto a thumb drive. Among the materials was the audio of Detective Denison's interview with Hasan, conducted three weeks after the shooting.

"This is Friday the tenth," came the dry Boston-sounding accent of Denison, "and it is now 4:06 p.m. and we're at Denver Health Medical Center with Mr. Hasan Jones." The interview was also attended by Alma Staub, the assistant district attorney assigned to the case.

Denison asked Hasan to start where he wanted. Hasan began with the *Drugs, Inc.* documentary. "Okay, well, first, Terrance started this drug incorporation video thing like, for the community," Hasan said. It was first time I'd heard Hasan's voice. It sounded calm and confident.

"When I was interviewed [for *Drugs, Inc.*] it was about some positive stuff so when I seen the show, all the positive stuff got canceled and it was nothing but negative stuff about the community, so I didn't really feel it too much," he said. "I just remember telling [Terrance] like, I don't want to deal with you, I feel like you're lying to the community about everything. I just don't understand it 'cause like, me and Terrance, we was cool like, I did my little gangbang thing before all this happened, like I'm done with now."

"Yeah," Denison said.

Before the documentary, Hasan said, he had "no problems" with Terrance. "He done did stuff with me that I never did with nobody," he said. "Like the Nuggets game. He took me to the suites. Like, and I was in the suites with people like that played professional football. Like, standing right next to professionals and stuff like.

"I thought he was more like, one of the people that like, was tryna help people like me who was like, in the gangs and was tryna get out. So I open my arms to him. To try and see what he had to offer me. And when I seen the video and all the negative stuff, I just felt like everything was a lie."

Denison asked Hasan if Terrance was part of the *Drugs, Inc.* production. Hasan said he didn't know. In fact, he said he'd never actually seen the documentary. "I just seen bits and pieces on people's either phone or computer," Hasan said.

Hasan recalled being surprised to see Terrance with a gun. "I can just remember swerving on my bike," Hasan said. "I looked at him—boom—jumped off my bike and tried to get gone." He said he felt Terrance had targeted him. "And that's because I knew the truth as far as the video."

Some of what Hasan told Denison and Staub didn't sound remotely credible. Hasan said that Terrance "threw a gang rally that day, it was a gang rally." When Denison asked Hasan if he had a knife or weapon on him that day, he said, "The police, everybody knows I don't walk around with no knives or anything like that." Yet a lengthy report of police contacts that I obtained for Hasan shows that as little as two weeks before the shooting, Denver police described him as a "known criminal."

Denison's twenty-four-minute phone interview with Dwayne, the gang member who had called the confidential police TIPS line days after the shooting, was also in discovery. To protect Dwayne's identity, only Denison's voice appears on the recording. Presumably Denison found Dwayne's account credible. "This just makes no sense what [Terrance] did to Hasan," Denison said to Dwayne. "If you know of anybody that might speak to us too about this.

Regardless of how people feel about the police up there and stuff, we are working for Hasan and for the people who live around there. Because, you know, we don't want this guy getting off and saying that it's self-defense." Terrance was never interviewed.

As concerned as I was becoming about the investigation, Denison's interviews also revealed two potentially problematic details for Terrance's case that I had not been aware of. According to both Dwayne and Hasan, Terrance was wearing a glove on his shooting hand. And, after Terrance shot Hasan, Dwayne alleged that Terrance took a knife out of his pocket, wiped it down, and placed it in Hasan's hand. Hasan said he was on the ground when Terrance "was like, tryna put something in my hand. I just kept trying to swat it away like, 'What are you doing?' And then next I heard another shot and that was it."

I wasn't looking forward to asking Terrance about this.

ON AUGUST 9, the anniversary of Michael Brown's death in Ferguson, Terrance turned thirty-nine. When I went to see him at a park, he was in a reflective mood. "I was thinking how MLK and Malcolm X died at thirty-nine," he said.

Gerald, who continued wearing large hats to disguise his appearance, showed up to smoke. He also had an update for me. Derrick "Lil Crip" Wilford, whom Terrance had fought in the Denver Jail and who had later turned Terrance on to the Bible group in Building 22, had told Gerald he was willing to speak to me. My interview request had been under consideration for some time and, Gerald said, would reveal even bigger problems with the anti-gang effort. Lil Crip's brother "Shaq" was on Rev's council on the Crips side. Like those on the Bloods side, Shaq was an active gang member. I told Gerald I was available to meet Lil Crip anytime. But the interview never happened. Two days later, Lil Crip was dead.

LIL CRIP'S MURDER rocked invisible Denver. The Wilfords were one of Denver's legendary original Crip families. The oldest Wilford,

Christopher, had been killed in 2006. Derrick, or Lil Crip, was shot in the head on the street in Five Points. He was thirty-six.

Laquita Taylor's mortuary in Five Points handled the memorial. On the day of the service, hundreds of mourners clogged the streets surrounding the church, many wearing blue silkscreen T-shirts featuring Lil Crip's image. Ropes made from blue bandanas hung across the road, blocking traffic.

Several District 2 police cars watched from checkpoints blocks away while an unmarked gray SUV sped around the perimeter. At the wheel I saw Commander Calo. I didn't see Rev, who had known the Wilford family for decades. "He knows he's not safe here," Gerald, whose tears were visible behind his sunglasses, told me.

Inside, the church was full. George Roberts stood at a podium in a double-breasted gray suit with a purple breast-pocket handkerchief. Next to him was a casket, which was closed. A bouquet of white roses sat on top.

In the front row, Derrick's ex-wife clutched their four-year-old daughter, Kayla. Shaq, the only remaining Wilford sibling, went to the podium. He was tall and wore a matching blue paisley vest and tie, which he tugged on as if for support. "This is not gonna break me," he said, shaking his head back and forth. "I know that's what they want—it's not going to happen." Some applauded. Two women in blue ran to his side; he put his arms around them. "Been doing this since I was ten," he continued. "I'm thirty-five. You do the math. I'm still right here."

Derrick's ex-wife went to the front, holding Kayla in her arms. "I hope all you guys go home and look at your kids," she said, as tears streamed down her cheeks. "The hardest thing is to tell your kid her daddy ain't never comin' home again."

Terrance didn't feel safe attending and waited in a park ten minutes away. When I found him, he was on the phone with Shaq, whom he'd known since his gang days. When he hung up, he turned to me and said, "It's all comin' to a head."

· · ·

THE FACEBOOK PAGES of most of the community members I followed urged peace or war in Lil Crip's name, and a few weeks of multiple shootings per day began.

"What is going on!!!!" one white resident posted on Northeast Park Hill's Nextdoor.com page. "5–6 blocks of Montview barricaded with police! Police helicopter above!"

The body count wasn't restricted to homicides. Among the dead was Christopher Swain, the older brother of Cameron Smith—the first Northeast Park Hill casualty of the gang war in 1988. Christopher, who was thirty-nine, had put a bullet in his own head, at his brother's grave site. Terrance said Christopher had texted him only a few weeks earlier to wish him luck with his case.

Racial tensions and gun violence had continued to occupy a major part of the national conversation, and I wondered if the explosion of Denver's gang violence would garner any national media attention. Instead, on September 7, CNN covered news of Denver area law enforcement going on "high alert" after an anonymous call to the police that threatened, "It's time you guys know that we are no longer playing around with the police departments. Aurora and Denver, we are about to start striking fear, shooting down all cops that we see."

Given what I was experiencing, I was surprised this was the story out of Denver that broke through. Not only was it based on what police said was an anonymous phone call, but it also sounded to me like the false threat Baltimore police had attributed to gang members a few months earlier. Nonetheless, the story was picked up by dozens of national outlets.

I checked who had first broken the news. It was a local TV journalist Terrance had been telling me about, Whitney Wild. She was a criminal justice reporter for 9News, Denver's top-rated station. Terrance said Wild had introduced herself to him after the community meeting in which he had yelled at Rev. I'd been with Terrance when she texted with him about getting together. Terrance had also told me several times that she kept asking him what I was working on. He found it suspicious, he said.

I looked her up. She was thirty-four, a Northwestern University journalism graduate. I found an online wedding registry that listed the name of her husband, Christopher Amon. It sounded familiar. I went to the stacks of court files I'd copied and found it. He was the ATF agent who had arrested Ice Alexander in 2010 on federal gun charges that were dropped.

WITH TERRANCE'S TRIAL looming, the pressure seemed to be wearing him thin. He and his father weren't getting along, and Terrance had moved again, this time into the Dahlia senior living home, with Ernestine. Her third-floor balcony looked directly at the Red Bricks, where he had grown up. Terrance entered and left wearing hats and sunglasses to disguise his appearance. He didn't feel safe living only blocks from the Holly.

Ernestine was eighty-one but looked twenty years younger. She wore colorful blouses and earrings and moved around using a scooter. Diabetes had rendered one of her legs useless. She spent much of the day baking cakes and watching televangelists.

After thirty-five years running A&A Fish, she had recently retired. She and Terrance never discussed his case, but her friends, who included prominent neighborhood activists, came to see Terrance and express their support. "I thank you to this day for the fact that the last five years I was there because of your help in the community," Hazel Whitsett, co-founder and former executive director of the Northeast Women's Center, told him one day. "You worked with the young people, but you also helped me work with their parents. Because if the parents don't have it together, they can't help the children. We had to deal with housing, food, clothing, education, everything."

"The problem with the Holly wasn't that I did crappy work like some young thug," Terrance said. "It was that I did work that they've never seen a young Black man do. And then when I did it, they didn't want me to be the face of it. If the Holly was burned down by Black kids from Five Points, then a Black man should be running that youth center, then Black developers should be over here. And Black people like yourself should be the voice of the community."

"We need some kind of system like you had," Whitsett said, "that collaborated and coordinated activities."

MARSHAL SEUFERT, TERRANCE'S public defender, remained non-committal about whether he would run a conspiracy defense, as his client was insisting. He did get his office to assign him a full-time law school intern, Knicky Van Goetz, whom he put to work analyzing the police HALO camera footage. While it didn't capture the shooting, it did record the scene along 33rd Avenue leading up to it. The tape, which was in color, indicated a large presence of young men in red. It also showed that about five minutes before the shooting, a car pulled up outside Zenobia's hair salon in the middle of Mrs. Wilson's strip, just south of the peace courts. Five men got out and looked around then got back in. They sat in the car until moments after the shooting, when they quickly pulled away.

Terrance told Marshal it looked like a classic "chaser" car, used to follow someone from a scene if needed. He said that was the reason he didn't just get in his car and drive away when he felt the attack coming, which was what Rev had recently suggested to me Terrance could have done. "The most dangerous place you can be is in a car," Terrance said. He named Tupac and Biggie, who were both killed in cars, as examples.

Marshal also reported that two key police officers were not likely to show at trial. He said that Officer Lopez, the first to arrive on the scene, might come under unwanted scrutiny if he testified. The other was Commander Calo. He would be away at the FBI Training Academy in Quantico, Virginia. Marshal was trying to arrange for his video testimony.

. . .

TERRANCE SPENT HIS last week visiting friends and the four of his children who lived in northeast Denver and Aurora with their mothers: Trinity (nine), Judah (five), Jerusalem (two), and Ziahda (two). Javon, who was twenty-one, still lived in Sacramento. Terrance had recently learned of another son, Shiheim, who lived in Vallejo, California. When I asked Terrance if it was hard for him to have so many kids, he said, "I can't even imagine not having them. That's *my* tribe." He longed for a place of his own so that they could stay over, but for now he relied on rides to their mothers' homes, where he played games with them.

I accompanied him a few times. The kids didn't fully understand that it could be one of the last times they saw their father again outside a prison visiting room. The habitual criminal charge meant that, if found guilty, Terrance would not have a sentencing hearing. He would go straight from the courtroom into custody.

For me, this was a difficult vision. I'd tried to maintain my journalistic neutrality, but seeing Terrance go to prison seemed like a tragedy on top of a tragedy. I'd been recording much of my reporting, including the District 2 meeting in which Rev appeared to say that he knew that the OGs had put "jumper cables" on the younger guys to go after Terrance on the day in question. Because it had happened in a public meeting, I decided to tell Marshal about the footage.

Marshal wanted to see it. He said that if any law enforcement agents had witnessed Rev's statements, they would have been required to share the evidence. The so-called Brady Rule, named for a 1963 Supreme Court case, required prosecutors to turn over any potentially exculpatory evidence to the defense. I told Marshal that virtually all of Denver's top law enforcement officials had witnessed Rev's statement, including Commander Calo; the police chief, who also sat on Rev's board; and Stephanie O'Malley, the city's director of public safety, who was in charge of the police.

"Are you willing to testify?" Marshal asked me. He said I could be needed to vouch for the authenticity of the video.

Taking the stand wasn't something I'd considered. He suggested I get a lawyer. "I don't want to have to subpoena you," he said.

TERRANCE SPENT HIS final days before trial in Denver and Aurora public parks, where friends came through to politick and almost always to smoke. Everyone I met in the gang community smoked huge amounts of pot. They said it helped their PTSD. Many had a medical card, which made purchases about a third cheaper than recreational pot, and they were barely taxed. Terrance said that in prison it was always calmer when the inmates had pot. One day we were alone at a picnic table, and I asked him about the glove and the knife.

Terrance said that right after Dwayne made the sa-whoop call to his fellow Bloods, he saw a rotisserie chicken in a plastic tray on the ground. A folding knife was stuck in it. He said that when he looked closer, he saw a note was pinned to the knife. "Snitch ass nigga, Bitch ass nigga," it read, according to Terrance. He picked up the knife, assuming it was Hasan's.

He said that after he shot Hasan, he walked over to him and found him not just conscious but speaking. "He said, 'Don't kill me, Blood, I'm boo,'" Terrance told me. In Blood lingo, *boo* was "cool." Terrance told me he took the knife out of his pocket and threw it down on Hasan. "I said, here's your shit," he told me he said.

Regarding the glove, there wasn't much of a story. He said his hands were sweating when he'd gone to his car, so he put on the glove, which was next to his gun.

When he returned from his SUV to the spot near the gazebo where Ktone and Reggie Fair, his cook, were setting up, Hasan rolled back toward him on his bike, flanked by a group of Bloods. Several were guys he knew, in their twenties who looked like they were ready to fight. They were maybe ten feet away, he said, and moving toward him fast. Terrance had been in similar situations before. He knew people who had died in such situations. He said he had only seconds to react.

ON THE EVE of his trial, Terrance met up with the activist Alex Landau, who had followed Terrance's case closely and was determined to help bring attention to it, and the issue of the lack of accountability around informants.

"A lot of people don't want to wrap their minds around these kinds of things," Landau said. To him, as progressive as Denver claimed to be, the city's white population had not shown much interest in the realities facing the Black community. He said law enforcement infiltration of activist movements had become a basic reality, everything from undercover cops joining a march and being the ones to throw rocks at police to fake accounts on Facebook undermining people's reputations.

He felt the circumstances of Terrance's case were particularly egregious, and he had told Terrance he was ready to do what he could to bring the case to light. He had already arranged for his wife and kids to be out of town, for their safety. "I can't take chances with them," he said.

Fall had arrived, but they sat on the back patio in the cool night air. Alex had his laptop. Whenever a dog barked, Terrance looked in the direction of the sound. He seemed nervous for the first time. "There's nowhere I've been going where people know where I'll be," he said. "But tomorrow is the first time where people do know where I'm at."

Alex showed Terrance a Facebook event page he was creating for people to follow the trial. He planned to update it throughout the proceeding. "Folks need to understand how deep this is," he said.

"I think we need to start seeing if there are any senators or reps who got the balls to make a state law saying that active gang members should not be able to work for any law enforcement agency, never ever," Terrance said.

Alex typed. They decided to discuss the issue at a press conference in front of the courthouse at 8:30 the following morning, before Terrance's trial began. The media would likely be there already. Alex had a list of a few dozen local TV, print, and radio reporters. They drafted a media advisory. Time was getting late, and the air chilly. Alex hit SEND.

"How are you feeling?" he asked.

"I'm ready," Terrance said.

Alex proposed a toast, but they were out of beer. They hugged and Terrance left.

I couldn't sleep and got to the courthouse around 7:30 a.m. About a dozen activists and homeless people were scattered around the courtyard. One handed me a pamphlet that read "Jury Nullification." It described a little-known Colorado statute that jurors could use to acquit a defendant if they felt the charges were unjust.

Mostly white street activists, some of them homeless, had recently started the pamphleting effort, saying they had been targeted with petty arrests to disrupt their lives and their advocacy. Their Jury Nullification effort had made national news a few weeks earlier when Mitch Morrissey, the district attorney, had charged many of them with "jury tampering" and banned them from passing out information at the courthouse. That move prompted the City of Denver to take the rare step of suing its own district attorney for violating the protesters' rights to free speech. The case was tied up in appeals, and the activists had returned to the courthouse. I couldn't help but wonder if any of the pamphlets would end up in the hands of Terrance's prospective jurors, who were due to arrive in thirty minutes.

I spotted Terrance, who was in a dark suit and gray tie he'd bought at Walmart. Behind him were Gerald, Alex, and J Hood, another former Camo Movement leader, who was loaded up with boxes of Dunkin Donuts and coffee. "Let's occupy this square," Terrance said, pointing to the middle. He said he wanted to make it a gathering place for anyone needing food or drink. "Danishes over here, brother," he said to one of the homeless men

Gerald went to talk to some people who were waiting near the courthouse entrance. When he came back he told me they were

Crips, there to support Dexter Lewis, who would be sentenced in a few hours for his role in the Fero's Bar quintuple murders that involved the ATF informant.

Along with Terrance's case, the Fero's Bar saga had gripped the city's gang community for the last two years. The fact that the ATF informant had never been charged was, for some, the latest piece of evidence that working for law enforcement meant having immunity, even for murder. The case was also significant because Dexter Lewis was the son of a legendary gang member, Dexter Lewis Sr., a Crip who ran with Asberry but was shot and killed at twenty-three. Rev told me that after Dexter Sr.'s death, he had become a second father to Dexter Jr. He said that Dexter Jr. had come to see him after the stabbings. Rev told me he had urged him to confess.

Instead, Dexter fought the case. At his trial, all three other assailants, including the ATF informant, cooperated with law enforcement and testified against Dexter. Now Morrissey sought the death penalty for Dexter, which had never been applied before in Denver.

George arrived, wearing a double-breasted suit, as did several other supporters of Terrance, some of whom were on their way to work. Soon a small crowd formed. A short, unkempt thirty-something man approached me and asked what I was working on. "If you need anyone to work on the really dangerous missions," he said, "I'm your guy." Terrance took poorly toward him and asked him to leave. Alex Landau later told me he recognized him as an undercover Denver police officer.

By 8:30, only one reporter had shown up, a woman from Channel 7, with a cameraperson. Terrance and Alex decided to begin the press conference. Gerald and J Hood fanned out like security guards, keeping watch.

"Active gang members are getting paid from money that's supposed to go to keeping our city safe," Terrance said. "And our city is not safe. I don't think anyone in the northeast sector of town feels safe right now. But yet the mayor just freed up five hundred thousand dollars and we have a federal CDC grant and we have GRID, fresh off of a million-dollar grant. But still we're dealing with a youth war in this city, a war that never would have had to happen, had active gang members not worked for the Denver Police Department and plotted to remove me from my position over political reasons."

Alex stepped forward. "We need oversight of informants in northeast Denver," he said. "Since Terrance has been removed we have an all-time high for gang-related shootings and violence. When you don't have any kind of accountability over informants, that creates more immunity for individuals, it promotes crime—it's the same kind of thing that we've seen law enforcement engage in in this community for decades."

"Active gang members should not be able to work for the Denver Police Department," Terrance said.

He was late and hurried into the courthouse. When he got out of the elevator on the fourth floor, news camera operators flocked around him. I hung back with George. As we walked past another courtroom, he pointed to the information plate on the door. Kindell, it read. Terrance's cousin Sharod Kindell, who had been shot by police in his car and was still in jail, was due in court for a motions hearing.

Terrance's courtroom was at the end of the hall. It had six rows of wooden benches on two sides. When I got inside, it was about half full. The judge's wood-paneled bench ran across the front. Terrance took a seat at the defense table, which was on the right, across from the jury box, now empty. Marshal, who had shaved his beard, sat next to Lisa Arnold, another public defender, who had come on to co-chair the trial.

The district attorneys sat to the left of a central podium at a table with a silver nameplate, PEOPLE. At it sat Henry Cooper, who was African American, and Alma Staub, who was white and had long blond hair. Cooper, who was tall with a shaved head, had prosecuted the last criminal case against Terrance, in 2001, for shooting at Kelly Glasper's car. Detective Denison, the investigator on this and the Fero's Bar murder case, sat between them.

Much of how Marshal was going to run the trial was still unclear. But as the morning proceedings began, some of the case's previously unseen issues became plain, though without the jury's presence. One was that the question of Rev's impartiality was at issue. "Part of our hesitance in calling Rev Kelly is the reality that he is so close to this," Marshal addressed the judge as a pretrial discussion began, "and the reality that he has factored in a number of ways that create a lot of tension. It's our belief that he's a friend of Mr. Cooper's. We are aware that there is a lot of pressure on him."

Marshal also reminded the judge of HIPAA, the law prohibiting Hasan's medical records from being introduced without his permission. "He has yet to be heard from," Judge Whitney said of Hasan, sounding annoyed.

In the row in front of me I recognized one of the *Denver Post* reporters. The paper had lost more than one-third of its newsroom staff since its takeover in 2010 by a New York–based hedge fund; a media columnist for *The Washington Post* wrote that the *Denver Post*'s owner was "seemingly intent on destroying local journalism."

That morning, the front page of the *Post* carried a two-year-old photo of Terrance from a court hearing days after the shooting. His slumped posture and gloomy expression practically screamed, *I'm guilty*. It seemed a strange choice for the opening day of his trial. I struck up a conversation with the *Post*'s reporter and decided to ask her why she thought the paper's coverage of Terrance had seemed so negative. "When you go and shoot someone at a peace rally," she told me, "you can't exactly expect much sympathy."

A few hours later, the Channel 7 report from the journalist who had attended Terrance and Alex's press conference aired. It was about thirty seconds long and offered the basics about Terrance's case; nothing from his press conference made it in.

But on social media, support for Terrance began to appear. Elizabeth Epps, a lawyer and well-known African American activist in Denver, tweeted: "Mitch Morrissey head of @DenverDAsOffice refuses to ever indict cops for near-lethal brutality, but for Terrance Roberts he seeks 102 years?"

Fidel "Butch" Montoya, who was the city's director of public safety under Mayor Wellington Webb, posted on Facebook:

"Terrance, more than ever we need the leadership you can provide to calm our streets. It seems like the city leadership is not involved in creating a safe city. It must come from street leadership. Praying for you."

By the end of the day, the jury of six men and six women—including one Black man and one mixed-race woman—had been selected.

THE NEXT MORNING, at 5:36 a.m. Carl McKay posted on Facebook: "Woke up with something on my heart . . . God is good, Terrance Roberts I truly pray that God shows up for you in that courtroom, regardless of our differences in the way we see things one thing we do agree on is that we're losing to a corrupt system who would rather see us turn on one another than grow together."

I wondered if Carl felt he'd been used by the system, or if he wanted to come clean about anything. Only two months earlier he'd proudly declared himself a Blood again on his Facebook page. I got a message to him but received one back that he wasn't interested in talking. On the way to the courthouse I spoke to Terrance and I asked him what he thought of Carl's post. He was totally unmoved. He called Carl a "Sambo," a character from *Uncle Tom's Cabin* who beats his fellow slave Uncle Tom on orders from their slave owner.

A FEW HOURS later, Terrance's trial began with the prosecution's opening argument. "The Holly," assistant district attorney Alma Staub said, looking at the jury. "The Holly is part of the Park Hill neighborhood. It's been in the news for many reasons over the past decade. And more recently it's been part of urban redevelopment . . ."

"You will hear from Hasan Jones," she said. "You may not like him. But liking him is not relevant to the fact that he was unarmed, he was walking away and then running away from Terrance Roberts, who had a gun. And he shot him as he was running away and then walked up to Hasan Jones, who was lying on the ground bleeding, and shot him again—and then threw a knife down on top of him."

When she finished, Marshal walked slowly to the podium and nodded to the jury. Then he turned and walked behind Terrance, putting his hand on Terrance's shoulder. "We expect to show you that Mr. Roberts is very happy to be here, in front of a jury," he said. "Because the reality is that Mr. Roberts expected to die that day . . .

"Absolutely there's a shooting. Absolutely there's a knife," Marshal said. "No contest here . . . But you can't see or know what Terrance Roberts saw."

Making the invisible become visible to the jury would not be easy, Marshal hinted. "We don't know who's going to make it here or not," he said, "but we do believe you're going to hear witnesses who were there during the earlier encounters."

He told the jury that Terrance had risked his life to try to rebuild Holly Square and rid the neighborhood of gang violence. I had never seen Terrance cry, but tears streamed down his face. Lisa handed him a box of tissues and he wiped his eyes.

THE PROSECUTION'S FIRST witness was Officer Carl Sessions of District 2, who, along with his partner, Tony Lopez, was first to arrive at what he called "the shopping center." Despite Terrance's ubiquitous associations with the site and its importance to District 2's law enforcement efforts, Sessions stated that he'd never heard of Terrance.

Alma handed him a sealed evidence box and asked him to verify its contents. Inside was the black 9 mm pistol he had confiscated from Terrance. It was tiny, with a silver metal clip. Sessions said that when he and his partner approached, Terrance seemed "upset, enraged" but that Terrance did not resist arrest. On cross-examination, Marshal got Sessions to acknowledge that the scene was dangerous enough that his partner, Lopez, had pointed his gun at a group of gang members to keep them back.

"Any of these people stopped and searched?" Marshal asked.

"I did not," Sessions said.

"Is it fair to say that you don't have any idea if they were armed?"

"I do not."

THE PROSECUTION'S NEXT witness was Ronald Washington, the resident who had been videotaping an interview with the HARP president, Gerie Grimes, when the shooting happened. Washington wore a cream suit and thick black-framed glasses. Staub's questioning began with an acknowledgment that Washington had a felony conviction, for attempted theft, and was still on probation.

Aside from the short video Washington took of his aborted interview with Gerie Grimes, he said he had taken a number of other photos and short videos in the following minutes "out of journalistic obligation." Staub had him confirm they were his as she exhibited them on a jumbo screen and entered them into evidence.

The most damning one appeared not in fact to have been taken by Washington. I saw that it wasn't in his batch of photos in the discovery file. Terrance said he heard it was taken by a woman who was afraid to appear in court. Yet the photo would remain on the screen for much of the prosecution's case. It was taken from perhaps twenty-five feet away from Terrance. Terrance's camo baseball cap, checkered button-down, and designer jeans were visible. Terrance leaned over Hasan's supine body, as if yelling something at Hasan. It was a chilling photo. I found it hard to get out of my mind. I looked at Terrance. His gaze was down at the table.

Washington's other videos were short but showed a chaotic scene in the moments after the shooting, with a number of people in red, angered and yelling. Washington's brief interview with Gerie Grimes was played multiple times. "It's official now—the goal is definitely being accomplished," Grimes said, before three short pops promptly suggested otherwise. Staub stopped the video and used a pointer to draw attention first to Terrance and then to the figures running away from the shooter, who was blocked from view by Grimes's head. Staub drew the jury's attention to one of the figures racing toward 33rd Avenue, in a white shirt. By slowing the play-back, the man can be seen collapsing to the ground as the video abruptly ends. "That is Hasan Jones," she said.

THE DISTRICT ATTORNEY next called Anthony Grimes, a distant rel-ative of Gerie's, who had in the weeks before the shooting started working with Senator Johnston. Grimes, who was thirty-one, ap-peared visibly shaken on the stand. He said he knew and respected Terrance but hadn't spoken to him since the shooting.

Grimes said he was co-hosting Johnston's event and had just got-ten outside when he heard gunshots. After helping people take shel-ter inside, he said he went back out. Across the street, he said he saw a man standing over someone on the ground, before firing a shot into him. Grimes said he ran to the victim and found him uncon-scious and bleeding from the neck and torso. He said he didn't know initially who the gunman was.

It was damning testimony, and it was accompanied by the photo on the jumbo screen of Terrance hovering over Hasan.

On cross-examination, Marshal got Grimes to talk about Ter-rance and about the neighborhood—"a violent part of town," Grimes put it. Grimes also confirmed Terrance's heavy promotion of the peace rally, on social media and with flyers. Marshal also asked Grimes if he was sure, before he reached Hasan's body, that Hasan had been shot. Grimes acknowledged he couldn't have been positive until he was standing over Hasan. It was a point Marshal would return to, as it raised the question of whether Terrance would have known that any threat from Hasan was over until he, too, was standing over him.

WHEN GRIMES STEPPED down, a small commotion broke out in the courtroom. Judge Whitney asked the jury to leave. Greg Daniels, Hasan's lawyer, appeared at the podium, just as the courtroom's large side door slid open. In rolled Hasan, in an orange jumpsuit. He had gained weight since his own trial and had grown a bushy, full beard. A sheriff directed him to stop at the defense table, about two feet to Terrance's right. Terrance and Hasan snuck glances at each other.

"Your Honor," Daniels said. "Mr. Jones does not want to testify. He was prosecuted by this office, as Your Honor witnessed. And he's being prosecuted by Arapahoe County, and he does not feel it appropriate to cooperate with folks who are trying to imprison him."

Judge Whitney looked exasperated. "Mr. Jones, you're here in court today, called as a witness," he said. "Are you aware that it could be a sentence of up to six months for not testifying?"

"Yes, sir," Hasan said.

"That doesn't change your decision?"

"No."

"I will find he is in direct violation of an order, and find him in contempt," Whitney said. He sentenced Hasan to six months in jail. Daniels went over to Hasan, who gave his lawyer a fancy handshake then wheeled himself back out. One person had now been sentenced in the case.

The jury returned. The day ended with two more witnesses, both women who happened to be in the area at the time. They both said that they had witnessed a man shoot another man who was on the ground. As they testified, the prosecution again placed the photo of Terrance hovering over Hasan on the jumbo screen. It appeared to me a difficult start for Terrance, and on my way out I avoided him.

THE FOLLOWING MORNING, Terrance had a fresh scab on the right side of his head, from shaving. He looked down and scribbled on a legal pad as the day's first witness became the fourth person to testify that he had shot Hasan on the ground.

The next witness was Dr. Andrew French, head of the emergency trauma unit at Denver Health hospital, who took the stand over vehement objections from Marshal. Dr. French spoke from memory of the night Hasan had been brought in by ambulance, because Dr. French was not allowed access to Hasan's medical records.

Dr. French testified that when Hasan came in, he was at "substantial risk of death." A breathing tube was inserted, he said, and his team performed an emergency thoracoscopy, to open his chest cavity. "We found that there was essentially a hole in his heart," Dr. French said.

Staub produced a Denver police "Serious Bodily Injury" form that Dr. French had filled out that night. On it, he had written that Hasan had suffered "multiple gunshot wounds."

Marshal's cross-examination of Dr. French focused on the volume of gunshot cases Dr. French saw and whether he could recall the details of this one from memory.

"Do you have permission from Mr. Jones to talk about his medical condition?" Marshal asked.

"Objection," Staub interjected.

Judge Whitney sustained it.

In Colorado, juries are permitted to ask their own questions of witnesses, which they do by passing them to the judge. Terrance's jury wanted to know how many times Hasan had been shot, and where. Dr. French could only say it was at least twice.

GERALD HAMEL, the nonprofit adviser, was called next, a reluctant witness for the prosecution. Terrance hadn't spoken to him since the shooting, and Hamel had told me he wanted to wait to speak to me until after the trial.

Hamel was forty-five and had a goatee and glasses. He seemed pained to be on the stand. He said that he had spent much of the day at the Holly and had witnessed what looked like an argument, out of his earshot, between Terrance and the Bloods earlier in the day. Later, he said, he had gone to Johnston's event. He was concerned about Terrance, and when that event ended, he went straight across the street and asked Terrance if he could help.

"He seemed to me kind of agitated, something was going on. It wasn't normal," Hamel testified. He said he walked away. Seconds later he heard three shots. Hamel said he looked and saw Terrance "go after the man that was shot."

"Did you see what happened when Mr. Roberts walked up to the person on the ground?" Staub asked.

"There were more shots fired," Hamel said. "I was praying they were shot into the ground."

Hamel appeared traumatized not only by the shooting but by what happened immediately afterward. "There were people gathered in front of Mrs. Wilson's [shopping strip] in prayer," he testified. "Just a moment of trying to be calm, what happens in the Holly, the way that you deal with things. And I came over to be part of that because that was something in that moment I definitely needed. There were probably thirty to fifty people in front of the convenience store. Some of the people pointed to me and said I was with Terrance . . . Ms. Grimes walked over to me and said, 'You need to leave.'"

THE PROSECUTION'S FINAL witness was Senator Johnston, whom I'd spoken to several times. He'd had nothing but positive things to say about Terrance and told me he thought about him all of the time. As he settled into the witness stand, his wife, Courtney, who was an assistant district attorney and was seated behind the prosecutor's table, sighed deeply.

Johnston, who wore a suit, testified that he had a dual role as both the elected state representative for northeast Denver and the head of a nonprofit organization that offered summer internships for college students on issues of social justice. This was something I'd heard about many times from Terrance. Terrance said it was one of the reasons he had fallen out with Mike. According to Terrance, for a few weeks each summer a group of Ivy League students took over the office and treated him like he was their busboy, leaving plates and garbage around that he had to clean up. Terrance had also told me that part of the reason he started calling his office the Park Hill Community Center was because Mike had asked him what he thought of calling the building the Mike Johnston Community Center. Terrance said he'd told Johnston he didn't like it.

Johnston testified that he wanted to open a community center in his district and chose the Holly because the elevated levels of poverty and crime demonstrated a need, and because he was "inspired" by the community's activism. "I asked Terrance to come join us," he said.

His work, Johnston said, was "seasonal"—half the year he was at the capitol, but in summer and fall he was in the Holly "all the time." This contradicted what multiple people had told me, that Johnston was rarely there.

Of Terrance, Johnston said, "He had built a strong relationship particularly with Commander Calo." This may have been the official police stance, but everyone I spoke to who worked with Terrance said that his relationship with the police, including Calo, had severely deteriorated well before the shooting, because of Terrance's outspokenness against police tactics in the Holly and his refusal to run the type of anti-gang program the city wanted.

Johnston said he didn't witness the shooting but that in the moments after the gunshots, he came outside and saw Terrance holding a gun. "I was originally relieved," Johnston testified. He said it had not occurred to him that Terrance could be the shooter. In the Holly, Terrance was the peacekeeper.

Cooper pressed Johnston about whether he had noticed a change in Terrance's behavior: "In the days leading up to this, did Terrance express frustration where he had to deal with Anschutz and politicians?"

"Yes," Johnston said. "I think he had an increasing amount of frustration that he had done a tremendous amount of work on the courts and the development of the Boys and Girls Club and I think he was frustrated that he didn't feel like he was receiving fair treatment from those folks."

"Did you see frustration rise to a level that he was not acting like himself?"

"There were definitely a couple incidents in those last few weeks that were unlike anything I'd seen before, disagreements with community members, elevated temper."

"Would he talk to you as an office mate?" Cooper asked.

"We were close friends," Johnston said, "so we would share those things." Terrance did not look at Johnston. I knew he disagreed. Terrance told me he had once considered Mike and his wife to be friends, but that he had come to believe that Mike had used him to get credibility in the neighborhood.

On cross-examination, Lisa Arnold was able to get Johnston to recall the day he and Terrance had their grand opening barbecue. Terrance had to run out front because Hasan was trying to force someone into a car.

The prosecution rested its case at the end of the second day. It had called fourteen witnesses. Counting another woman who had been on her way to the post office that day, a total of five people testified that they saw Terrance shoot Hasan on the ground. Prosecutors had also planted the seeds of a cover story—that Terrance had thrown the knife down on Hasan to make it look like Hasan had come after him. A police crime lab technician had testified that DNA found on the knife matched Terrance but not Hasan, calling into question whether Hasan had ever possessed it.

To me, the prosecution had presented a potentially persuasive case, but it also stood out for who had not appeared, notably Hasan; Dwayne, the original confidential witness; Officer Lopez, who arrived first on the scene; Commander Calo; and Rev.

Terrance's friend Ktone, who had been setting up to DJ the event when the shooting happened, had been subpoenaed by Marshal and was waiting in the hall. Marshal was concerned he might not return, so Judge Whitney allowed the defense to begin its case before finishing proceedings for the day.

Ktone wore black pants and a black button-down shirt. He walked slowly to the stand as if thinking about every step. With effort and over continuous objections by the prosecution for hearsay, Lisa Arnold managed to get Ktone to say he saw "about fifteen" Bloods appear around Terrance just before the shooting. Ktone's barely audible answers spoke of the discomfort he felt. He said that Terrance asked the Bloods to leave, but that the Bloods responded that it was their neighborhood.

The prosecution had no questions for Ktone, and Judge Whitney sent the jury home for a long weekend. I met up with Terrance at a park, where others showed up to hear about the case. Whether genuine or not, Terrance seemed upbeat. "The doctor said he was only shot twice," he said. He also seemed buoyed by support on social media. I managed not to say how it looked to me. Because of the habitual criminal charge, he was going to do a mandatory seven years just for possession of the gun.

THE JUDGE HAD set the following morning for motions. The courtroom was virtually empty; the jury was not present. Marshal made a motion for acquittal, arguing that the prosecution had not shown deliberation or intent, which was required for an attempted murder charge. Judge Whitney said he had seen "enough evidence that there was a second event, going over to a person on the ground and shooting them again," from which he said a jury could "reasonably infer" premeditation. He denied the motion.

Judge Whitney then turned to Terrance. "I have to talk directly to you," he said. "Your right to testify is your right, it cannot be waived by anybody but you." He described to Terrance the "pluses and minuses" of his taking the stand in his own defense, which included that he would be subject to cross-examination. His past criminal record would be fair game. "Are you thinking clearly today?" he asked Terrance.

"Yes, sir."

"Under the influence of drugs?"

"No," Terrance said. "At this time I think I should testify."

Marshal also asked for an update on the accommodations to allow Commander Calo to testify by video phone from FBI headquarters. "We'll figure out how to get it into court," Judge Whitney said.

When I got up to the fourth floor the following morning, Amari, the witness who had described the plot in Carl McKay's shop, was lying supine across a bench outside the courtroom, breathing deeply. I asked if he was okay. He nodded unconvincingly.

I could only imagine the stress he was under. Marshal had informed me that he didn't plan to call me to testify. He had decided against showing the clip from the community meeting. Rev's comment that appeared to suggest he believed the older Bloods had put the younger guys up to jump Terrance had been interrupted by Terrance's aggravated retort. It made it a risk to show it, Marshal said. That was not the way he wanted the jury to see Terrance. I knew Terrance wanted the material introduced, but, for me, not having to step into the witness box was a relief.

There were other developments over the weekend. Terrance told me that the DA's office was preparing to call for a mistrial because it had discovered that Terrance was Facebook friends with one of the jurors, the only African American. Terrance said he hadn't said anything because he wasn't even sure they'd ever met.

Inside the courtroom, the assistant district attorney Staub was at the podium, flipping through printouts of Facebook pages. The juror had even commented on Terrance's Facebook post about the peace rally. Staub appeared barely able to control her anger, and Judge Whitney seemed to share it. During jury selection, the juror would have lied about questions regarding his knowledge of the events or Terrance.

Judge Whitney called the juror into the courtroom and curtly dismissed him. He was replaced by an alternate. The discovery that

Terrance was Facebook friends with one of the jurors was a media hit, making the city's afternoon news programs.

Before the proceedings could begin, there was yet another issue to deal with, and it was that Marshal was now planning to call Rev Kelly as an expert witness for the defense. Assistant District Attorney Cooper, who had worked many times with Rev in that capacity for the prosecution, objected. "My biggest issue is that they're calling Reverend Kelly to talk about tensions in the community, things like that, which I don't think are allowable if he's called as an expert," Cooper said.

"I think all parties are aware, Mr. Kelly is in the audience here," Marshal said. Rev looked on from the fourth row. He wore a tan button-down shirt. His long dreadlocks fell around his chest.

"Is he going to be called as an expert or is he a fact witness?" Judge Whitney asked.

"I think he's both, and I think he can testify to both," Marshal said. "Mr. Kelly knows Hasan Jones, knows Mr. Roberts, and is intimately connected to the players in the case."

Cooper stood. "Mr. Seufert said [Rev Kelly] would talk about tensions in the community. That's the ultimate in hearsay, Judge."

"I don't know how Reverend Kelly is going to testify," Judge Whitney said, "but if he became aware of the tensions in the community . . . it's relevant."

The jury was brought back, and Rev was called to the stand. He settled his long frame into the box, where he'd been dozens of times. Marshal asked him to explain what he spends his time doing.

"Helping kids make better choices," Rev said.

"And are you just involved with youth or are you involved with older people and law enforcement?" Marshal said.

"With law enforcement, community of faith, schools, guys, kids on the streets, really the oldest gang program in existence in the state of Colorado," Rev said.

Marshal moved to have him admitted as an expert. With the jury present, Cooper didn't object.

Marshal got Rev to talk about how he'd known Terrance and his grandmother for decades. "I've found that I've become a surrogate dad to many," Rev said. "One of those kids was Michael Asberry . . . I had the two Mikes. Mike Asberry, creator and originator of the Rollin 30 Crip gang. And Mike Hancock, now the mayor of our city. I had both the kids up under my wing."

"What was Terrance's involvement with the Holly?"

"That was his neighborhood," Rev said. "His turf. Back in the days."

"After the Holly is firebombed, what is Mr. Roberts doing—is he taking revenge, fighting back?" Marshal asked.

"No, when I met Terrance coming back from prison . . . we spent quite a bit of time together. I felt like I was Moses in the latter years. I was looking for little Joshuas to come along to take this duty on," he said. "And [Terrance] was the closest thing to a Joshua that I felt."

"Is there naturally tension between an anti-gang activist and a gang?" Marshal asked.

"I've been doing this for thirty years," Rev said. "When I say that we're the only program that still exists—there have been so many who have come and gone. Many got out because of the concerns they have, the number one being safety."

"What are we talking about here?" Marshal asked. "Your foot getting hurt?"

"Everything from a beating to the loss of one's life," Rev said.

Marshal turned to the National Geographic *Drugs, Inc.* documentary. "I wouldn't have done it," Rev said of Terrance's helping the show, "because as I explained earlier: concerns about safety." Rev said that when the show aired, "it didn't sit well, certainly with some of the older guys in the hood." He said that it caused him "to have a lot of concerns."

"About what?" Marshal asked.

"About the safety of Terrance," Rev said.

"Did you think something was going to happen to him?"

Cooper objected. Judge Whitney sustained it.

"Do you know of a time the community became concerned or believed Mr. Roberts was a snitch?" Marshal asked.

"Oh, yeah," Rev said. "Yes."

"Does that give license for members of the Bloods to do anything against Mr. Roberts?"

"A snitch is a title you don't want to have," Rev said.

"Why?"

"Because it can do you a lot of harm. If you are, you have to be dealt with."

"Is it fair to say a younger Blood like Hasan Jones wouldn't call out someone like Mr. Roberts unless had the blessing of OGs?"

With the other witness waiting outside the courtroom, it appeared Marshal was beginning to build a conspiracy defense. But Cooper objected again and Judge Whitney sustained it.

Cooper stood and began his cross-examination by acknowledging Rev.

"One of the things you've criticized [Terrance] for as an antigang activist was that he never really removed himself [from the gang] because of where he hung out, correct?" Cooper said.

"Difference was that even though he was housed in the beehive, he took a stance there," Rev said. "He was determined to make a change in that neighborhood."

"So he stayed in the neighborhood," Cooper said.

"There were times I'd go through—he'd be sitting out there on the tables. He feels that this was his home," Rev said. "He was one of the ones who just stood for what he felt was right. He has always been the type that took a stand. He wasn't one to just back down."

"If you're a gang member and you're an OG, the one thing you cannot let happen is you cannot let the little Gs disrespect you, right?" Cooper said.

"In the gang," Rev said, "but outside the gang—"

"But I'm asking, in the gang, you put in all this work, someone calls you a name, you can't let him get away with that," Cooper said.

"If it was still a true gangster OG, yes," Rev said.

"Right," Cooper said, "and you'd have to do something. You'd have to beat him down, kill him, anything, because you can't let any of the other gang members see this gang member disrespect you . . .

Let me ask: You've been doing this thirty years. How many times you've been called a snitch?"

"Oh, man . . . ," Rev said.

"A hundred, a thousand? You ever shot five times any of those people who called you a snitch?"

"Maybe if I wasn't a pastor," Rev said. "If I had a different frame of mind, I may have thought of it. But then to actually follow it . . ."

"I'll take that as a no."

"I never shot, no."

Rev got down from the box. It was persuasive testimony in Terrance's favor. Even if Rev had turned against Terrance, he had little to gain by being dishonest on the stand. As he'd said to me, Terrance already seemed headed for prison for the gun charge.

AFTER A BREAK, Lisa Arnold said that the defense would call Terrance. He sprung from his chair, nearly spilling water from a foam cup. He wore a gray shirt and a checkered maroon-and-gray tie, with no jacket.

Lisa asked him to spell his name and say where he worked.

"I work for a friend's moving company. Moving furniture." Terrance had picked up some work on a truck run by a former Crip, Lumumba Sayers, for $15 an hour plus tips.

"How about in September 2013?" Arnold asked.

"I was executive director of Prodigal Son Initiative."

Arnold took Terrance back through his teenage years as a gang member. "At that time, almost everyone in that community were either actively gang members or they will become gang members or sympathized with the gang members," Terrance said.

"Can you tell the jury about what your life was like?"

"It was a very dangerous time," Terrance said. "I was beaten quite a few times. I was gunned down twice. Then you had moments when you had barbecues and everyone was supposedly family and friends."

"What was your job?" she asked.

"It's not that organized a structure."

"How did you earn money?"

"I sold drugs," he said.

"And when you were in the gang, did you carry a gun?"

"Yes, ma'am."

"Did other gang members carry guns?"

"Every gang member I knew that was at least a little bit serious about it had to carry a gun," Terrance said. "They had to."

"And why did they have to?"

"Because you'd be killed even possibly by your own friends, depending on what was going on. You just didn't know what could happen at any moment."

When he got out of prison, Terrance said, he was a changed man. "I just wanted to be a part of something positive for the community," he said. "That's kind of why you became a Blood when I was a kid because I wanted to help the community. That's what I thought we was doing."

When he started Prodigal Son, he said, "My goal was to literally take away recruitment numbers from the Bloods. Northeast Park Hill was nine thousand people, roughly twenty-five hundred kids, and there was nowhere for them to go after school. So they would hang out with the Bloods in Holly Square, smoke weed, fight, the same things I did when I was a kid. So I just wanted to provide them with a safe place to go . . .

"Sometimes there were fifty Bloods in the Holly," he said. "We let them come in to use our phone or use the bathroom."

Lisa put up an overhead shot of Holly Square and had Terrance show the jury where the fire had destroyed the old shopping center. "It was disgusting," he said. "It was a huge mountain of rubble. It kind of sat as an empty lot for maybe a year."

She asked how he funded Prodigal Son.

"Oh, I wrote grants, got donations," he said. "Sometimes it wasn't funded very well. You know, we have to survive on fundraisers, just like any other 501(c)(3) nonprofit."

"When did you move into Holly Square?"

"After the bombing," he said, referring to the fire. "Me and Senator Johnston renovated the space."

"Did you ever witness gang violence at the Holly?"

"Yes, ma'am."

"Is there ever a time that you were accused of providing evidence to police?"

"Yes, ma'am."

"Can you tell the jury about that?"

Terrance told the story of the day the Bloods shot at Magic. "There was a shooting of a man who these Bloods thought was a informant," he said. "Some Bloods shot his truck and there was a bunch of glass everywhere and a bunch of bullet shells. We waited for DPD to clean it up. I didn't think they were ever going to come clean it up. There were people walking into the parking lot, barefoot. Kids were getting out of school, so I went and swept up the glass and the bullet shells. I put it in a huge bag and I threw it away. But the Bloods were telling people that I provided the bullet shells to the Denver Police Department to get the Bloods arrested."

Lisa asked Terrance to describe the shops along Mrs. Wilson's strip. Terrance named the candy store, the Laundromat, the cleaner's, as well as Zenobia's hair salon. "There was also a supposed fix-it shop," he said, referring to Carl McKay's shop, "that the Bloods ran that was on this last corner right here." He pointed to it on the screen.

"That was a known Blood hangout right there?"

"Yes, ma'am."

In the early summer of 2013, Terrance testified, he got a call from a producer from National Geographic. He said he thought it could help the community. He said he told law enforcement, activists, and gang members alike, but was disappointed with the end product. "It was sensationalized," Terrance said.

In the aftermath, he said, tensions in the neighborhood rose. That was partly why he wanted to do the rally.

"Tell the jury what, how were you feeling around the time that you start planning that peace and unity rally?"

"I was afraid, of course," Terrance said. "I used to be a Blood.

I know how dangerous they can be. I personally know some of the guys. I grew up with them. I was anxious, nervous. But we just wanted to get people together, not just to talk about gangs—to talk about development, talk about whatever they would like to discuss. We were going to feed them and play music and have a good time, I guess."

He said he was "legally obligated" to make sure that the courts were safe but the first thing that happened in the morning suggested to him that the tensions had become dangerous. He described speaking to Aaron Miripol near the front of the Boys & Girls Club when "two guys started yelling at us that we were gentrifiers, asking us who built the building and saying that we ruined Park Hill."

He said he walked away from that encounter into his first of several with Hasan, who was under the gazebo with several other gang members, smoking spice, which was illegal.

"I said, 'Bro, can I talk to you?'" he testified, referring to Hasan. "And he got up like, 'Get the fuck out of my face, fuck you, you're a snitch, you're a bitch.' . . . I told him if I'm such a bitch and a snitch then you guys are no longer allowed on my property. You can call me a bitch or snitch from across the street . . . When I took another step toward him, he reached into his pocket and pulled what I believed to be a knife out of his pocket."

Bryan Butler called him back to the office, Terrance said, but Hasan's actions left him facing a new reality. "I knew that these guys were going to have a confrontation with me," he testified.

He said he got in a car with Gerald Hamel and Bryan Butler. They went to Ikea. "We were moving into the Anschutz Center after the rally," he said. When they returned, "about twenty" Bloods were under the gazebo, Terrance said. They were yelling that he was a snitch and pointing to the cameras on top of his office.

He described getting the sledgehammer and climbing to the roof as the Bloods yelled, "Tarzan!" "It was a spectacle," Terrance said. He smashed the camera and pushed it over the roof, then dragged it across the street to where the Bloods stood.

"I asked Hasan and those Bloods to get off the property," Terrance testified. "'You're not allowed here. You already know we have a function.' And they pretty much were laughing at me, calling me a snitch." Again, Bryan Butler called him over and he left.

He went home to shower, and returned at about 5:40. On the ground near the gazebo was a chicken in a tray with a knife sticking out of it. Pinned to the chicken was a note: "Snitch ass nigga, Bitch ass nigga."

"I put the knife in my pocket," Terrance said. Soon afterward, he said, Ktone pulled up and asked Terrance if he could help unload his speakers, but just then Hasan appeared on a lowrider bicycle. "I asked Hasan, 'Why are you doing this to me?'" Terrance said.

"His answer," Terrance testified, "was because I was a snitch." Terrance testified that Hasan told him, "On Bloods he'd be over in a minute to fuck me up."

Terrance testified that he saw Hasan pedal over to a truck, where he stopped at the driver's window and looked back at Terrance, laughing. Terrance decided to go to his own truck to get his gun. His hands were sweating, he said, so he put on a glove.

Terrance said that minutes later "between twelve and fifteen" gang members came toward him from the 33rd Avenue side, about twenty feet away, calling him a bitch and a snitch and holding their sides as if to indicate they were armed. "Some of them I knew personally," Terrance said.

He said he saw a "car full of Bloods" to his right, where a small road led from 33rd Avenue into the Holly Square. He heard Hasan ask someone where he was. Then, "About four guys with Hasan surrounded me," Terrance said. He said they were "acting like they were going to try to grab my legs or attack me." Terrance said he had to act quickly. "I pulled out my gun," he said, "and I shot at them."

For many, those shots marked the end of an era. For Terrance, the scene was still active. He said he thought he had fired "three or four" times. He said that he saw Hasan fall. "I walked over to Hasan and I thought I was going to talk to him a little bit," Terrance said. "He was leaning up and he was saying, 'Blood, you're stupid.' He was coherent. And I shot him."

I wasn't sure if I'd heard him correctly. Terrance appeared to admit shooting Hasan while he was on the ground.

"He laid back," Terrance continued. "I put my gun in my left hand, I threw the knife on him, and he said, 'Blood, don't kill me.' And I said, 'I'm not going to kill you. You're going to lay here and shut the fuck up.'"

Terrance said that he backed away, holding the gun out so that it could easily be seen. He said he didn't want to drop it because he felt the scene was still dangerous. "There was a bunch of Bloods who were pretending to return fire, so I just wanted to make sure I could defend myself if someone started shooting."

"Why did you throw the knife on him?" Lisa asked him.

"I don't know," Terrance said.

ASSISTANT DISTRICT ATTORNEY Henry Cooper, who wore a suit with a pink shirt, stood to begin his cross-examination. "You were a Blood gang member," he said to Terrance. "I guess your name was ShowBizz, right?"

He went through Terrance's past felonies then came back to the day in question. "Let's talk just a little bit about some of the choices you made that day," Cooper said.

One, he said, was to do nothing.

"Some of these guys are about your height and weight," Terrance said. "Could have been fifteen of them that could have kicked me in my head and killed me."

"I don't want to cut you off, but just answer my questions," Cooper said.

"I thought I was answering the question," Terrance said. "I apologize."

"You said that it's shooting the gun that scared everybody away," Cooper said. "How about shooting in the air? Fire off a few rounds, scare everybody?"

"There's a young girl who was in my program who was just killed on Colfax because she walked into a room, shot a gun in the air—they shot her and killed her," Terrance said.

"So shooting a gun in the air to scare Hasan and the others was not as good an option as trying to kill Hasan Jones, right?"

"I wasn't trying to kill Hasan. *You* keep saying that, but I just wanted to make sure he couldn't hurt me," Terrance said.

"Let's get to that, then," Cooper said. "You had another option. You could have shot him once, right?"

"Yes, sir. I thought I did only shoot him once."

Cooper reminded Terrance of his own previous statement to Streetgangs.com that he had shot Hasan five times.

"I thought I shot him five times because that's what his family was saying to the media and I didn't have all the facts. So I repeated that erroneously," Terrance said.

Lisa Arnold had already asked Terrance why he didn't just get in his car.

"These guys were all over," Terrance had responded. "I didn't feel like for one I could get in my car safely. That's not the best place—you're getting assaulted or shot at. For two, I had DJ Ktone there and I had the guy cooking my food. I didn't know how many people were going to collapse on the area and maybe our Prodigal Son kids." Their safety was his responsibility.

Cooper continued his questioning. "There's absolutely no question that you shot Hasan Jones, he went down, you stood over him and shot him again," he said to Terrance.

"I was walking up to him and he was talking to me," Terrance said.

"Is that a yes or no? That you shot him on the ground."

"Yes, sir," Terrance said. "I didn't know he wasn't a threat until I got close enough to him to see that he was down."

"The only other weapon recovered at the scene was your knife, right?" Cooper asked.

"Me and my father were told about other weapons recovered but that person was afraid to testify," Terrance responded.

Cooper turned back to questions about the ownership of the Holly itself.

"You say you own the hoops, the gazebo," Cooper began. "But

the understanding was it was public, people didn't have to come ask you for permission. It was like a park, right?"

"No," Terrance said, "I think the community understood that it was for the community, but it was actually privately owned."

"My question was if people didn't have to come ask you for permission," Cooper said. "They could just go. They didn't have to come ask."

"No, they didn't, but for special events they did have to come ask us because it's a privately owned property," Terrance responded.

"So you're telling this jury that anytime anybody played basketball they came and knocked on your door and said, 'Can we go play basketball on the courts?'"

"No," Terrance said. "I said that people do *not* have to, but if someone had a special event then yes, because per our insurance we had to get special permission or I had the right to say you don't have a right to be here, it's private property."

Terrance stepped down.

THE JURY WAS given a break. I went into the hall. For the first time it seemed to me that Terrance had a chance. He passed me on the way back from the restroom. "They can't reach Calo," he told me. "He isn't calling back." The defense had only a few witnesses left, including Amari, who was still in the hall.

Marshal next called a community member who worked at the library. She testified that she saw a man who did not fit Terrance's description, with a gun. Marshal then announced that they were "still waiting for Commander Calo," so he called Detective Denison to the stand.

Marshal played for Denison the police HALO camera footage and asked Denison to describe the shops at Deloris Wilson's strip. After Denison mentioned a few of them, Marshal asked, "Is that the same auto shop at the end that Rev Kelly essentially referred to as a front?"

Denison looked startled. Rev hadn't mentioned anything about a front, at least on the witness stand. "I'm not clear," Denison finally said. Marshal moved on.

Next the defense called Knicky Van Goetz, the law school intern who had analyzed the video from the HALO camera. Van Goetz brought a color-coded presentation made from images from the video. She showed sixty-seven separate people on the street who appeared to be wearing red in the thirty minutes before the shooting. At one point, two of them approached each other and appeared to furtively exchange something.

Marshal also walked her through the strange case of the car that pulled up to the curb along the strip about five minutes before the shooting. Five men got out, looked around, then got back in. They remained inside the car until just after the shooting, when the car quickly pulled away.

Commander Calo remained unreachable. Marshal and Lisa made a last-minute decision not to call Amari, perhaps betting that the pendulum had swung in their favor and that it might be better not to introduce a new defense theory. To win on the main charges, they needed only to show that Terrance felt his life was in danger. The defense rested.

TERRANCE AND OTHERS gathered at a friend's house. The mood was optimistic until someone saw the 9News coverage that had just posted online.

"Anti-gang activist Terrance Roberts took the stand Tuesday in his own defense and admitted to planting the knife," the story began. The accompanying TV spot ran on the five and six o'clock news.

I hadn't seen the reporter in the courtroom and wondered if her source was the DA's office. It was certainly not what Terrance had testified. Nonetheless the story was picked up by wire services and published in newspapers around the country, under the same headline, "Anti-Gang Activist Admits to Planting the Knife." Terrance's phone began ringing. Relatives from Texas who'd seen the story called, as did a friend in New York, in tears, asking if it was true.

．　．　．

CLOSING ARGUMENTS BEGAN the following morning. Marshal began by standing behind Terrance, with his hand on his shoulder. "Bitch," he called out. "On Bloods you're gonna get yours in a minute. We're gonna fuck you up. We're taking over."

He looked at the jury. "There's only one question in this case," he said. "Did the prosecution prove Mr. Roberts was not afraid?" He put up a text card on the big screen: "No one has proven Mr. Roberts did not need to defend himself," it read. He also displayed an image from the HALO camera, of the car that had pulled up before the shooting. "No one gets out," Marshal said, suggesting more answers about what happened remained out of reach.

Cooper stood and began his closing argument. "Mr. Seufert sat up here for forty minutes," he said. "One thing that they didn't talk about because they have no explanation: Why did you plant the knife? Why did you gun a man down, throw a knife on him, and make up a story to the police that he ran up on you with a knife? It's called a guilty conscience.

"This wasn't the case of a young G, as they call them, trying to get respect. This was the case of an old G trying to keep respect. This wasn't Terrance Roberts shooting Hasan Jones. It was Show-Bizz shootin' Munch," he said. "Ladies and gentleman, reach a verdict that says, this is not a war zone in the Holly Shopping Center. It's not Afghanistan. It's not South Central LA. It's Northeast Park Hill. They have a gang problem. That doesn't mean the laws don't apply there. That doesn't mean that in the Holly Shopping Center you can walk up to a man lying on the ground paralyzed, not a threat to you at all and—BANG—shoot him again. No. Reach a verdict that says in Denver, Colorado, that's a crime."

TERRANCE HEADED OUTSIDE. It was a mild, sunny day. George and others, supporters and homeless people, gathered around Terrance as if holding a vigil. But five o'clock came with no verdict, and the following day came and went as well.

On Friday morning I went to see Terrance at a friend's house.

When I arrived, he was talking to Ernestine. "All right, Granny," he said. "I love you, and no matter what, if I do gotta go to jail, you know I love you and thanks for helping me to get to this point."

When he hung up, he told me his lawyers expected a verdict. Soon the call came. I waited while Terrance got dressed. Instead of his dress shoes he put on a pair of Nike high-tops. He knew he could be in custody within the hour. "I don't want to be in jail in penny loafers," he said with a laugh. "I might have to fight someone."

I got in the car with him for the short ride to the Justice Center. Terrance was reflective. "No matter what happens," he said, "we did a lot of work, we saved a lot of lives, we had a good time—we touched the sky."

When we arrived, local TV trucks were parked along the street. The courtroom filled. I caught George's eye. He nodded. I wondered if Terrance's friends and other members of his family were aware that Terrance's trial had come to an end. A group of bailiffs streamed into the room, taking positions behind Terrance and along the aisle of the public seating. The jury foreman handed a paper to Judge Whitney, who examined it. I felt my heart pounding. It had been an intense couple of years with Terrance. It was hard to imagine never seeing him again outside prison walls.

"All rise," Judge Whitney said.

He declared Terrance not guilty—on both the attempted murder and assault charges. Terrance, who looked straight ahead, wiped his eyes. Gasps and several cheers were audible. Judge Whitney banged his gavel and asked the lawyers to approach. Marshal had gotten Judge Whitney to bifurcate the case, meaning the gun charge against Terrance would be considered separately by the jury. Because it was a charge for being a convicted felon with a gun, Marshal had not wanted to prejudice the jury about Terrance's criminal history, in case Terrance decided not to take the stand.

The lawyers huddled at the bench, their conversation inaudible to the courtroom. Marshal asked Alma Staub, the assistant district attorney, to drop the gun charge. The jury had just found that Terrance had used the weapon to lawfully defend his life. Staub agreed.

Judge Whitney banged his gavel. "You're free to go," he announced to Terrance. "Justice!" someone yelled. Others stood and cheered. George remained in his seat, crying. "Thank you," Terrance said to the jury, many of whose members also were crying. Then Terrance got up and pushed his way through the crowded aisle and out the courtroom door. He ran down the back staircase to avoid the media.

Epilogue

The verdict appeared to stun most of Denver. The reporting on how Terrance had "admitted to planting" the knife on Hasan, and the long-held view that Terrance had shot Hasan five times, including twice "while he lay motionless on the ground," made it difficult for anyone who had followed the media coverage to understand how Terrance got off.

To me, the shock was seeing Terrance walk without any prison time for possessing the gun. Perhaps Terrance's increasingly obvious community support, and potential questions about the way the case was investigated, helped the DA's office decide for the first time to back down. Anti-gang work, they knew, was dangerous. The two-years-long ordeal resulted in no convictions (excepting Hasan's for contempt) and was a high-profile loss for the DA's office. The public defender's office threw a party for Marshal and Lisa.

I didn't know how to explain the discrepancy between Terrance's testimony and that of others regarding how many times or in what manner Terrance shot Hasan. Nor did I know what to think about the notion that Terrance had been pushed to the point of becoming his former gang self, ShowBizz. I consulted the psychiatrist Dr. Frank Ochberg, an expert in PTSD. Ochberg told me that given the heightened tensions and Terrance's past experience of being shot, he believed it was likely that Terrance was in an altered state by the time he started shooting. His past was literally staring him in the face. One of the Bloods standing next to Hasan was Kelly Glasper, the last person Terrance had shot at, thirteen years earlier.

Terrance told me he didn't think he'd reverted to his earlier self. Neither did some of his friends I spoke to, who suggested that someone in a gang state of mind would have shot Hasan in the head.

I sensed that what clinched the jury's decision was the vivid testimony from the city's two most prominent anti-gang activists about the mortal dangers of anti-gang work. Rev Kelly testified that he had become aware that Terrance was being called a "snitch" and that because of it, he believed Terrance was in grave danger. Terrance's own testimony about a lifetime spent on the front line of Denver's gang war—where he'd been shot and nearly killed—was powerful. His description of the events preceding the shooting sounded credible and was also refuted by no one. Hasan Jones conspicuously never appeared on the witness stand despite the district attorneys' promise in their opening argument that the jury would hear from him. And Ktone's unnerved description of the seconds before the shooting strongly supported the defense's theory that Terrance was being attacked.

A local TV reporter got a jailhouse interview with Hasan after the verdict. Hasan said he regretted not testifying and that he planned to sue Terrance. When asked if he thought Terrance would be safe in the neighborhood, Hasan said, "I don't think so."

Terrance's emotions in the weeks after the verdict ran from exuberant to agonized. He had been exonerated but not vindicated, at least in the eyes of the general public. He still wasn't even allowed to go to the Holly, because of the Boys & Girls Club's restraining order. He bounced from couch to couch, penniless. He applied for service, sales, and construction jobs and got several interviews, only to fail the background check. The shooting of Hasan remained on his public record despite his acquittal. Any Google search of his name turned up dozens of articles that would give any employer pause.

Terrance's reputation also suffered from the continuing media coverage of the anti-gang effort, which people I knew outside the community felt undermined Terrance's credibility. A month after the trial, *The Denver Post* published a feature about Rev Kelly's new anti-gang team at the Holly. No mention of Carl's arrest was made nor of the community's outrage over the city's use of active Bloods as "anti-gang" activists. No mention was made either that Denver's effort was funded by a federal Project Safe Neighborhoods grant, a program that was having similar problems in other cities. Regarding Terrance, the *Post*'s story stated that the city had recently "learned a hard lesson when it trusted a reformed gang member to help Park Hill."

If the city had learned anything from trusting Terrance to help Park Hill, it was not evident to anyone in the community who wanted to defeat gang violence. "The Denver Post Needs 2 go away and die," Gerald wrote on Facebook. The year ended with fifty-four homicides, a majority of them gang related, most unsolved. It was a 75 percent rise, and the most in nine years.

I WAS FINALLY able to get hold of the DOJ's independent review of Denver's Project Safe Neighborhoods effort. It was released nearly three years behind schedule. In the interim, the report's lead author, Jeffrey Butts of John Jay College of Criminal Justice, had been named to the Science Advisory Board of the DOJ's Office of Justice Programs. The 167-page report made no mention that the executive director of the grant's lead organization in northeast Denver had shot someone during the grant period and faced life in prison. In fact, it did not mention Terrance or Prodigal Son at all.

The acknowledgments listed thirteen people. Only two appeared to be African American, including the prominent activist Brother Jeff Fard, who had become the program's conspicuous booster at the same time many in the community believed it had become indefensible. Incredibly, neither Bryan nor Qwest nor Terrance appeared to have been interviewed. The report's main conclusions were hard to decipher. Some things worked and others didn't, it seemed to say. "It was hard to get good data," Butts told me by email.

As I CONTINUED my research, I moved out of my mom's apartment into a small house in East Colfax, a northeast Denver neighborhood that abutted Park Hill on one side and Aurora on the other. Like Northeast Park Hill, my neighborhood's small brick homes were built in the late 1940s, and it, too, was undergoing an obvious transition. FOR SALE signs were on every block; almost every new resident was white like me. Shootings were also regular. As the Park Hill Bloods were being squeezed out of Northeast Park Hill, they had begun to battle with an Aurora Crips set over control of my neighborhood, which sat between them. District 2 was my police district.

One day I awoke to find a white police tent in the yard two doors down, where the legs of a man were visible. I'd heard gunshots the previous night but didn't call 911 because, according to posts I saw on Nextdoor.com, two neighbors already had. District 2 did not come until morning, by which time a twenty-seven-year-old member of the Crips had bled out while crawling to my neighbor's door for help.

Another night my dog's barking awakened me. Flashlights swooped through my yard. It was District 2. They wouldn't speak to me, but in the morning Terrance told me there'd been a murder at a Colfax motel, two blocks away. The assailant had fled down my alley. The deceased was a female Blood I had met. She was one of Hasan's friends, who went by Nay Nay. She was twenty-three.

In the Holly, tensions between new and old residents were rising, in large part because of the violence. On Nextdoor.com, white residents posted racist-sounding comments and openly called for the closing of the Horizon Lounge, where shootings were not uncommon.

Meanwhile, Holly Square was about to undergo another major phase of redevelopment. The Urban Land Conservancy had brought on a new partner, Roots Elementary, to build the charter school originally envisioned in the city's 2000 Neighborhood Plan, before the Holly burned down. It would be constructed on the spot of Terrance's peace courts, swallowing most of the Holly's remaining open space. Community gathering space had been unanimously favored by residents in the ULC's 2011–2012 Visioning Process.

The day that the courts were to be ripped up, I went to watch. Other community members came as well. Free coffee and boxes of doughnuts were on the table under the gazebo. Near me was an older man in a leather jacket and a baseball hat that said on the bill, "I'm Fair." As I hoped, it was Reggie Fair, Terrance's hot dog cook on the day of the shooting, who had eluded investigators and me, until then.

Fair had lived in the neighborhood a long time and said he couldn't risk testifying. But he said he felt a "big relief" when he heard the verdict. He said he'd watched the entire shooting happen. Terrance had only one chance to act, he said. "It was kill or be killed," Fair told me.

We watched in silence as white volunteers carried pieces of the basketball courts to a truck. "We were told to do this," a woman called out to the group of African Americans I stood with, seemingly ashamed. Tractors were already parked on the site. With the addition of the new building, Holly Square was about to become unrecognizable to what it had been only a few years earlier.

Changes were coming quickly across northeast Denver. The city used a "nuisance abatement" law that enabled it to seize properties for which complaints had been filed. In 2018, one of those places, the Platte Valley Projects, where George Roberts lived, was slated to be mostly demolished. George was given three weeks to move. He accepted relocation to a building on the I-70 corridor, in the most polluted zip code in the country. Meanwhile, real estate in Five Points boomed. The old Rossonian Hotel, which sold in 2006 for $800,000, was purchased for $6 million by a group of investors, who hope to turn it into a jazz club.

TERRANCE —WHO IN 2016 became the father of his seventh child, Divinity—was determined to get into the real estate business. He found a patron willing to loan him money for his training and certifications to become a home inspector. The first time Terrance called me from a rooftop, he was giddy like a kid. He had built his own website, bought his own tools, and had a phone app to take photos and make his reports. It was impressive. But business was slow. Some people continued to fear being around him because they believed his life was in danger. And key referral sites such as Home Advisor wouldn't allow his business to be listed due to his criminal record.

He continued to use Facebook for his activism. He called out what he saw as corruption in the city's anti-gang effort and in its misuse of informants who he believed were responsible for unsolved shootings and homicides. His voice commanded high respect in the Black community and had considerable reach. He kept his Facebook settings public and had thousands of followers. Many believed Terrance's continued berating of the city for employing gang members as "anti-gang" activists led to the quiet departures from Denver's federal anti-gang program of Drettie Hicks, who pleaded guilty in 2017 to possession of controlled substances with intent to distribute, and Rodney Jackson. Only Pernell Hines remained.

Pernell, who continued to appear in Blood rap videos on the roof of the building and to show up at Blood functions decked out in red, kept working out of the old Prodigal Son office. His organization, Impact Empowerment, which was actually Prodigal Son but renamed, got city grants to support his "anti-gang" work. Many people I knew feared him, but not Terrance, who continued to hector him and the city on Facebook about what he and others felt was a scandalous and seemingly unchecked federal anti-gang effort.

Seeing himself as a whistleblower, Terrance created a new nickname for himself, T Rob Tha Realest, and he began to sign all his Facebook posts with it because, he wrote, some posts that he had not authored and didn't agree with had begun appearing under his name in comment threads. Then, one day, his page completely disappeared. He was unable to get a response from Facebook. His political platform, along with all his personal photos and videos, and five thousand supporters, was gone.

IN BLACK COMMUNITIES around the country, talk of a "new COINTELPRO" was growing. Activists and protesters linked to the emerging Black Lives Matter movement reported that they believed they were being undermined, intimidated, and arrested under false pretenses. Fueling the speculation were the deaths of six activists in Ferguson; two of them were shot and left in burning cars, including Deandre Joshua, the Ferguson protester who Terrance had been following on Facebook. In July 2015 in Raleigh, James Elvin Austin III, a twenty-three-year-old former Blood turned anti-gang activist, was shot and killed hours before a peace rally he helped organize.

Many prominent activists whose efforts placed them in the greater Black Lives Matter movement lost their lives in its first few years. The activist Erica Garner, the daughter of the Staten Island police choke-hold victim Eric Garner, died in December 2017 of a heart attack at twenty-seven. Three of the six deceased Ferguson protesters appeared to have died by suicide. Seeking justice took a toll in many ways.

In 2017, leaked FBI documents revealed that as the Ferguson pro-tests grew, the FBI had begun tracking activists. Methods included the use of informants as well as Geofeedia, a social media location tool funded in part by the CIA. The Black activists who the Department of Justice were concerned about had been given a designation, Black Iden-tity Extremist. It applied to African Americans whose views the DOJ believed made them a threat. During a November 2017 House Judiciary Committee oversight hearing, then attorney general Jeff Sessions was asked whether Black Lives Matter was considered to be a Black Identity Extremist group. "I'm not able to comment on that," Sessions said.

I was able to get hold of an FBI file with Terrance's name. It was updated enough to include the fact that he was "bald," which he hadn't been until he'd become an activist. The file's otherwise bare readout showed that he had another "local" file in the Denver field office, but I was not able to access it. While it no longer seemed far-fetched to me that law enforcement could have been well aware of the tensions in the Holly involving the Bloods and Terrance, I couldn't find any smoking gun that connected the Bloods' attack on Terrance to anyone outside the gang.

What was striking was that in the year and a half preceding the shooting, Terrance had fallen out with all the powers at the Holly. His own temperament and the stress he was under, financially and with regard to his own safety, were likely factors. Equally striking was how interconnected the influential new players at the Holly were, how few of them were from the neighborhood, and the extent of their ties to law enforcement.

The Denver Foundation and the Anschutz Foundation, two of

Colorado's most powerful nonprofits, had supported the neighborhood's anti-gang effort and were regular supporters of Denver's law enforcement efforts. The Anschutz Foundation sponsored the District 2 police awards in which the two first responders to the scene of Terrance's shooting received top awards the prior year. Patrick Horvath, the Denver Foundation's point person for the Holly, and Paul Callanan, the director of Denver's anti-gang effort, were in regular communication. Months before the shooting, Terrance had accused Horvath of conspiring with Callanan to delay his GRID contracts and to undermine his reputation. Horvath denied it, and I assumed Callanan would too. Horvath and Callanan were also recipients of Terrance's desperate plea for financial aid in late 2012.

Carl McKay and Hasan Jones, both Bloods who my reporting suggested were involved in an attack on Terrance that day, also appeared to have developed relationships with law enforcement. A Colorado Open Records Act request provided me with a startling report on Hasan. Though he had only the 2010 drug possession charge on his official record prior to the death of Ny Ny, he had been arrested nearly two dozen other times without facing charges. In 2014, on the day he was alleged to have committed a drive-by shooting, he was also arrested and released. Gang officer Salinas testified that he spoke to Hasan by phone the following day.

One former Denver cop with experience in this area told me that Hasan's record appeared to be a clear case of an informant getting favor from the department. Hasan was later found responsible for the death of a two-year-old. Ny Ny had cigarette burns on her body and tire tracks on her feet.

As for Carl, records available are less clear, but the file I was able to obtain listed multiple aliases and charges that were dropped, as well as police contact for possession of an illegal weapon, which did not result in charges. His admission of working for Commander Calo came in 2015, nearly two years after the shooting.

I tried filing open records requests to law enforcement agencies, looking for possible information about Carl's shop, but came up empty. Experts told me that even if the shop was a storefront, little or no such paperwork about it would be open to public view. The ATF's improper use of storefronts in other jurisdictions had led to an Inspector General report in 2016 that criticized the agency's training and management of such operations. In St. Louis, ATF agents set up a storefront six hundred feet from a Boys & Girls Club, potentially endangering children. In Milwaukee, a 2012 *Milwaukee Journal Sentinel* investigation revealed, a fake gun shop was so poorly disguised that residents said they could tell it was fake and robbed it.

I don't know the business purpose of Carl's shop, but none of my reporting suggested that Carl knew how to repair computers. My reporting did suggest that the shop was the place from which a plot against Terrance emanated. If Denver's law enforcement was not aware of this, it would not speak highly of its intelligence capacity. The attack took place while a premier multi-agency task force employing informants in the neighborhood was aiming to stem gang violence. Every single person I spoke to who was on the ground in the Holly told me that tensions between the Bloods and Terrance were evident. Bryan and Qwest were afraid to attend the peace rally. Rev Kelly testified that he became aware that Terrance was being called a "snitch," at least as early as when the *Drugs, Inc.* program aired, five days before the shooting. Rev, who also had significant connections to law enforcement, testified that he feared for Terrance's safety.

But, if law enforcement didn't become aware of the Bloods' plan to attack Terrance before the peace rally, they had good reason to learn about it later. At the emergency gang violence meeting at District 2 in 2015, Rev Kelly spoke about the matter in front of Commander Calo and Police Chief White. The Denver media appeared not to have understood what they had just heard, but I didn't find it plausible that the police missed it. Terrance's reaction to hearing Rev's statement had brought the meeting to a dramatic halt.

It was equally concerning to me that the DA's office would charge Terrance as a "habitual criminal" when it had been thirteen years since he had been charged with criminal activity. Terrance didn't even fit the habitual criminal description—"a career criminal"—that the DA Mitch Morrissey gave on his own program. If Morrissey had added the charges just to gain leverage over Terrance, or in retribution for his scathing criticism on Facebook, as Rev told me, it seemed to me like an abuse of power. I had to assume that the surveillance video of Terrance that Rev referred to did not in the end depict criminal activity, or perhaps even exist, as it never surfaced.

Was Terrance overly paranoid about the danger? I found his nerves understandable. By the time he decided to hold that fateful peace rally, he was isolated from the new powers in his own community while in the midst of a gang war and an undercover operation, both of which had contributed to rising tensions. Like tens of thousands of Black men in communities like the Holly, Terrance didn't trust the police to protect him. Despite the fact that his felony record prohibited him from carrying a gun, he decided to get one. That the gun would eventually go off was something even Terrance, the anti-violence crusader, had prophesied. The irony wasn't lost on him.

"I got caught with my gun in my hand," he said to his friends months later. "But why'd I even have to *live like this*?"

In 2018, President Trump hailed Project Safe Neighborhoods "one of the most effective crime prevention strategies in America." He credited it with prosecuting 15,300 defendants for federal gun crimes in one year, 20 percent more, he said, than the previous record. But in Denver, where Project Safe Neighborhoods funding had been re-upped again, the gang war had only continued to grow.

In the spring of 2019, Terrance's old friend Jamaica "Bounce" McClain, a Blood, was shot dead in the Horizon parking lot. Another Blood, Aundre "AD" Moore, whom I'd met several times, was charged with the murder. Five days later, the popular Crip-affiliated rapper Nipsey Hussle was killed in Los Angeles. AD's case is proceeding, but both murders appeared to come after the deceased had made accusations about gang members working for the police. Anger about gang informants was growing; speaking out against them remained dangerous.

Terrance hadn't organized an event since the rally at which he shot Hasan. He decided to do another "Heal the Hood." A couple hundred people gathered in City Park.

Many peace-minded community members aired their frustration with Mayor Hancock's record of fighting gang violence and his attitude toward his own community. In 2016, Hancock had used his MLK Day speech to say, "We not only celebrate Black lives, we celebrate all lives." He was loudly booed. At another speech, he said, "Black men need to examine our own biases toward police and the role we play in being hurt by police." While Hancock's race made many in Denver assume he had the support of the Black community, a significant segment of Denver's Black community was determined to stop his reelection to a third term.

Jamie Giellis, a white woman who worked in community development and was running against Hancock in the June election, attended the Heal the Hood event. Terrance and H-Soul, the son of Lauren Watson, became high-profile supporters of her campaign. Terrance had built up a new Facebook page. He and H-Soul both reported that during the mayoral campaign they were smeared online by fake social media accounts. In June, the election results were a mixed bag. Terrance and the activists successfully helped Candi CdeBaca defeat the city council president Albus Brooks, the African American who represented northeast Denver and who had favored eminent domain in Five Points. Brooks, who was seen as being groomed to succeed Hancock, lost. But Mayor Hancock won reelection by 12 points, giving him a third term as Denver's chief executive.

TWO MONTHS LATER, Lauren Watson died, at seventy-six. The Black Panther leader's death occurred in the midst of another record streak of gang violence in Denver. One of the dead was Ngor Monday, a young Blood gang member I had been mentoring for the past three years. He was nineteen. His family were refugees from Ethiopia, where factional fighting had endangered them. Ngor, who was tough and smart and whose gang name was "Trouble," had fit right in with the street gang in his apartment projects, which housed low-income Americans and other refugees. He told me he wanted to get out of the gang and we were talking about his plans. He was interested in the army. One day his mother, Susannah, called me sobbing. Ngor had been hit by a single bullet in a gang shootout that followed an argument over the sale of a gun. He died in the ambulance on the way to the hospital.

Funeral services for Lauren Watson were held at Shorter AME on Colorado Boulevard, where Terrance's first Heal the Hood march had taken pace. The occasion drew a crowd of northeast Denver's activists and clergy. Acen Phillips spoke. George Roberts officiated. Terrance was one of the pallbearers. He wore a black beret and gloves.

H-Soul used his eulogy to talk about the violence. "Just three or four days ago I walked into Pipkin to make services for my father," he said. "They have screens of the people who have services coming soon and I expected to see middle-age Black and brown people. What I saw was thirteen-year-olds, fifteen-year-olds . . ." The audience began calling out, "Yes!" "Seventeen-year-olds"—*Yes!*—"Nineteen-year-olds"—*Yes!*

"We are right now in a war with ourselves."

"Truth!" someone shouted.

"We had a solution to that," H-Soul said. "Terrance Roberts was that solution. But because he didn't belong to the Black leadership class, because he was not a Stepin Fetchit type of person . . . Because he didn't do that, right now we have our babies murdering each other, right as we speak."

George's eulogy was about the Black Panthers' breakfast program and the need to educate and mentor Black youth. "They can shut down the Black Panthers, but the government can't shut down the Ku Klux Klan!" George called out. "Can't shut down the Bloods and the Crips!" People applauded.

Among them in the church that day, George said, was the FBI. "Lauren told me, 'At my funeral, the FBI is gonna be there.' For reals. The FBI will follow you till you're dead and they're gonna make sure you're dead." He looked out at the audience. "If you're here, I pray you get saved today, *ayy-men!*"

FOUR DAYS LATER, in Aurora, twenty-three-year-old Elijah McClain was walking home from the grocery store around dinnertime when he was stopped by Aurora police. Elijah was the cousin of Jamaica "Bounce" McClain, Terrance's friend who'd just been murdered in the Horizon parking lot. Elijah's mom had left northeast Denver for Aurora years earlier to escape gang violence.

Elijah, who was a massage therapist, was a sensitive young man. He had taught himself to play violin, and liked to play for kittens in animal shelters. He was anemic and got cold easily; on this night he wore an open-faced ski mask. A 911 call reported someone looking "sketchy." Four Aurora police officers stopped Elijah on the street. One of the officers told another, "He reached for your gun, dude." The officers forced Elijah to the ground, where for the next fifteen minutes he was beaten while pleading for mercy. "I don't even kill flies," he said. "I don't eat meat. But I don't judge people. That's my house. I have no gun. I will do anything. I just can't breathe." His last words were "Please help me." Paramedics administered a large dose of ketamine. Elijah went into a coma three days later and died three days after that.

Terrance got in touch with Elijah's family, and soon he and another activist, Candice Bailey, were organizing rallies at the Aurora police headquarters, demanding the release of the police body cam footage, and that the four officers be charged with Elijah's murder. At the rallies, Terrance wore a full ski mask over his head and paced in front of teams of officers in SWAT gear. "It's okay to wear a ski mask *on your face*," he raged at them. "If I am breaking the law, right now, I am saying the Aurora police should come across the barricade and do me like they did Elijah. *But they won't!*"

"You can't teach that kind of talent," H-Soul told me. "That's what makes the white racist establishment so afraid of Terrance, because you can't defeat that kind of courage. There's a lot of ShowBizz inside of T Rob, just like there was a lot of Detroit Red inside of Malcolm X."

The Aurora police eventually released the body cam footage, showing one of the cops telling others to turn off their cameras. Terrance and Candice drafted a police reform bill banning chokeholds and requiring police cameras to be public, among other things, and took it to State Representative Leslie Herod, who was African American. Herod, a Democrat, told them she could never get the bill passed. Then, six months later, George Floyd was killed by police in Minneapolis.

For six days, central Denver was shut down as thousands of protesters, most in masks to protect from COVID-19, gathered at the capitol for speeches and marches. Carrying his "lifesaving gun"—the bullhorn he kept on a shelf in his bedroom—Terrance was in the center of it all, drawing some of the biggest crowds with his impassioned speeches about the unchecked gentrification and gang violence in northeast Denver. He wore camouflage hats with red and blue to demonstrate gang unity.

At night, he was home, but the protests continued, including looting and rioting that was met with tear gas, and triggered curfews that were disregarded. Cops in riot gear faced off against protesters. Dumpsters and cars were set on fire, store windows smashed; the capitol building and dozens of others were vandalized with spray paint. Denver's government buildings and businesses along Colfax were boarded up for months.

As had been the case in the late 1960s, for many of the protesters, affordable housing was a pressing issue. A report by Freddie Mac showed that the percentage of affordable housing units in Colorado had dropped more than in any other state between 2010 and 2016. Terrance, who was leading marches about twice a week, led hundreds through Five Points one day. "Liar, Liar, Gentrifier," he had everyone chanting. "I don't even want to be called an activist," he told me. He said he believed "activism" in Denver was limited to causes the city and its most powerful foundations and allies approved. "Call me a revolutionary or don't call me nothin'," he said.

Representative Leslie Herod became the sponsor of a police reform bill banning chokeholds, mandating body cam footage be public, prohibiting law enforcement from shooting at fleeing suspects, and holding them personally accountable for their actions. Before the House vote, Herod thanked only two people by name: Terrance and Candice.

After the bill's signing, Terrance was among the speakers at the capitol. Colorado was the first state in the nation to pass police reform following the killing of George Floyd. The media and supporters of the bill gathered. Terrance wore a camo Nuggets hat and a dark button-down shirt. "My name is Terrance Roberts," he said, from the capitol steps. "I'm from a historical African American community called Northeast Park Hill. My whole life, I've never known what it's been like for a community to have good relations with policing . . . This bill did not come soon enough. But this bill means that those lives lost are not in vain. They did not die for nothing." He got the couple dozen people behind him, as well almost everyone in the crowd, to do a Black Power salute. "This is just the beginning, Colorado!" he said.

The media didn't seem to know what to make of Terrance. Few of the stories mentioned anything about his past. His life had indeed entered a new phase. He finally had landed his first real job. He was in charge of all the local home inspectors for Zillow, which was betting big on Denver's real estate and making cash offers for homes. Terrance was able to get a small one-bedroom apartment in south Denver, where he hosted his kids for sleepovers every weekend.

Terrance had been working sixty-hour weeks at Zillow, but after George Floyd was killed, he told his boss he couldn't work more than a regular schedule anymore. He spent what seemed like every other waking hour organizing. He and others co-founded the Frontline Party for Revolutionary Action, FPRA, which became one of the biggest protest forces in the Denver area, drawing thousands to its rallies. In a matter of two months, the Justice for Elijah McClain movement became one of the biggest in the nation. Celebrities flew in for events. The Change.org petition asking for the arrests of the police officers registered nearly six million signatures. Terrance's face, looking out from behind a mask that read "I can't breathe," appeared on news sites around the country.

As Terrance became one of the most prominent Black Lives Matter organizers in Denver, he also faced some familiar challenges. Two gang members he hadn't heard from in years began posting on his Facebook page that he was an informant. Terrance in turn posted photos of court documents he argued showed that they were actually the ones with ties to the police. The men's intimidation stopped.

The Frontline Party's events became dangerous as well. At one, a Jeep sped through the crowd, injuring protesters who had to dive out of the way. To the anguish of many of those who were there, the driver was not charged. Later, a bullet struck the person standing next to Terrance in the head. Terrance held the man as they waited for the ambulance. The man survived.

Terrance played down what many around him feared—that the bullet was meant for him. Activists across the country increasingly claimed they felt they were endangered. In November 2020, Hamza "Travis" Nagdy, known in Louisville, Kentucky, for his leadership and his bullhorn at events demanding justice for Breonna Taylor—killed by Louisville police in her apartment—was himself shot and killed. Nagdy was twenty-one. In January 2021, the well-respected Baltimore anti-gang activist Dante Barksdale, whose uncle was the inspiration for Avon Barksdale's drug trafficking character in *The Wire*, was shot and killed. Dante, who was part of a federal Project Safe Neighborhoods effort, was forty-six.

Terrance began arranging for friends to guard him at events. He told me he had become suspicious of a young Black man who kept showing up openly carrying a long rifle and urging attacks on the police. Terrance had a confrontation with the man, asking him to leave. He also had problems with a group calling itself the Night Crew, who began showing up to his rallies and agitating for violence. "Make your own flyers and organize your own events," he told them.

Terrance wondered about their connections to law enforcement. Across the country, rumors of agitators and agents provocateurs were the talk of protests. In Fargo, North Dakota, the deputy police chief was found to have disguised himself and joined protests, yelling, "Fuck the police!" In New York City, an informant accompanied a twenty-four-year-old protester, Jeremy Trapp, as he cut the brakes on a police vehicle. Trapp's subsequent arrest worried criminal justice advocates like Michael German, a former FBI agent. German said that past behavior of informants suggested they sometimes act "not as listening posts but as agents provocateurs."

In Aurora, undercover police were among those at the Elijah McClain rallies. After one rally, sponsored by Terrance's organization, the Aurora mayor, in a tweet he later deleted, referred to the organizers as "domestic terrorists."

TERRANCE WAS FRUSTRATED. He wasn't as radical as he was made out to be. As some activists across the country called for abolishing police forces, Terrance favored reforms but opposed moving policing to community control. The rise in violent crime, he said, demonstrated the need for good policing. Homicide was sharply up nationally in 2020. Denver was on pace to post its sixth straight year of increased homicides. One day in July, five people were shot and two killed in the parking lot of the Horizon. Among the dead were Pernell Hines's little brother Leland, "Lil T Blood," and Ice Alexander's little brother, Dewan, "Baby Ice."

Multiple witnesses to the shooting told Denver police that the shooter was Ice Alexander himself. Ice was not arrested. Anger again grew inside the community, and many looked to Terrance, whose understanding of the "impact players" and "trigger pullers" in Denver was deep. Terrance believed that many of the city's most dangerous men were being protected by law enforcement. Ice, he believed, was one of them. In 2016, Ice had charges for DUI, drug possession, and illegal weapons possession dismissed. For two domestic violence assaults in 2018, he received probation, which he had violated at least twice.

I was able to obtain a video that showed a Denver police detective interviewing Ice, or Isaac, about the Horizon double murder. The detective acknowledged to Isaac that witness accounts pointed to him as the shooter, but the detective said he wanted Isaac to know that the Denver police believed Isaac's claim that he was not the gunman. The double murder of the two well-known Park Hill Bloods was not classified as gang related and remained unsolved.

It was unclear to me what conclusions the DOJ or the City of Denver had drawn from their efforts to stop gang violence. Between 2010 and 2019, Denver received approximately $16 million in DOJ and CDC funding to fight and study gang violence. During that period, the city's gang violence, which began at an all-time low, climbed each year to new heights. Analysts appeared no closer to answers. "There's still an uptick in gang violence so we're still trying to figure that out," David Bechhoefer, a project director of the CDC-funded effort in northeast Denver, told *Denverite*, an online news outlet.

Rev Kelly continued to be the anti-gang activist that Denver's establishment trusted. In 2016 he received a prestigious My Brother's Keeper award from President Obama's foundation. "Our situation in Denver [regarding gangs] is not nearly as bad as it is in other parts of the country," Mayor Hancock said, "and that's due to the work of an individual by the name of Leon Kelly. Everybody—no matter where they walk from in relation to gangs—trusts this individual."

My reporting suggested that wasn't true. For me, Rev was perhaps the most complicated figure I encountered. He was at times hard not to like. He was smart and charismatic and often I sensed the pain he'd lived through. But his credibility, at the least, was questionable. Despite his long-claimed assertion that he had gone to prison on drug charges, the only record of his incarceration in Colorado that I could find was for three years beginning in 1979 on two robbery charges. Between 1972 and 1978, Rev was arrested for or charged with aggravated robbery, aggravated assault, four narcotics possession charges, a DUI, and forgery charges—all of which were either dismissed by the district attorney or dropped by the police. And despite Rev's claim that his organization ran community- and faith-based programs, his ties to law enforcement were significant, including key members of his organization's board who were active or former law enforcement. He also had close ties for years to the OGs who my reporting suggested were behind the attack on Terrance. And his declarations to me that Ice Alexander was "up under my wing" were deeply concerning. In 2019,

I was shown a minute-long video on Instagram of Rev at a shooting range with two young gang members, wearing an ammunition belt, Rev stood behind one of them, adjusting his posture as the young man fired an assault rifle.

Meanwhile in the Holly, Pernell Hines continued working out of Terrance's old office, where a vigil for his and Ice's brothers was held. While Pernell had apparently convinced someone in Denver's public safety office that he was no longer a Blood, that was not something I found credible. In January 2019, Pernell was charged with eight counts, including two drug felonies. All but one felony drug possession charge was dropped, and for that he received eighteen months' probation. He was also stopped for a DUI but no charges were filed. In 2020, he was charged with third-degree assault and violating his probation. In addition, all of my best sources in the neighborhood, including Terrance, told me that Pernell and his brother Leland, recently deceased, had made it clear that they still controlled the "car," meaning they were in charge in the Holly. Yet, somehow, Pernell not only stayed out of prison but continued to do anti-gang work, and to receive support from the activist Brother Jeff. Pernell's record fighting gang violence, though unchallenged, spoke for itself. On his watch gang violence in the Holly had exploded, with his own brother among the victims.

Hasan went to prison, after pleading guilty to child abuse resulting in the death of Ny Ny. He received a sentence of twenty years. Carl McKay was eventually charged with four felonies for his 2015 drug arrest in the Holly. He pleaded guilty to two charges of possession, his sixth and seventh felony convictions. Though he could have been sentenced to several years in prison, he got a year in a halfway house.

Two prominent Denver civil rights lawyers who were interested in drafting a law creating oversight and accountability for the use of informants began to speak to Terrance, and me. Terrance had begun talking about what he called the "urban war industrial complex," an industry that had brought millions of dollars to Denver's law enforcement. The misuse of informants was a critical piece of it, and the more he educated people in his community about it, the more they agreed it needed to be addressed.

It was hard to fathom that no such law existed. During the 2003 congressional hearings concerning the Boston FBI's misuse of informants, including Whitey Bulger, Representative Dan Burton of Indiana called the FBI's misconduct "one of the greatest failures, or the greatest failure, in the history of federal law enforcement." My reporting suggested that similar relationships between law enforcement and violent gang members were not uncommon, at least in African American communities, where America's most well-funded law enforcement efforts and a disproportionate share of its violence take place.

AROUND LUNCHTIME ON Thursday September 17, 2020, Terrance was going for a walk in a Denver park when several police cars pulled onto the grass. He was told to put his hands in the air. He was arrested as part of a sweep that included five other Denver protest leaders who were members of the Party for Socialism and Liberation, which had joined forces with Terrance's party for the Justice for Elijah McClain protests. At forty-four, Terrance was the oldest of the arrestees.

He called me from jail. He said that one of the Denver police officers who arrested him told him that they had been following him "for weeks." George told me a cop who'd visited him at home had told him the same. Terrance's charges stemmed from two Elijah McClain rallies that took place months earlier. They included a felony count of "inciting a riot," and six misdemeanors.

Thousands had attended Terrance's rallies, including me, and had witnessed his calls that there be no violence or vandalism. Activists and even elected officials were alarmed by his arrest. "If you've ever wondered what it was like to watch fascists snuff out a people's movement, you are living it," Candi CdeBaca, the new city council member representing northeast Denver who had beaten former council member Albus Brooks, wrote on Facebook. "My friend [Terrance], a community leader who has defended his community and fought tirelessly for justice was arrested today for using his VOICE!"

Straightforward media coverage of Terrance's arrest appeared in a new daily publication begun only weeks earlier, the *Denver Gazette*.

The new online-only Denver newspaper launched with the aim of reaching people who feel disenfranchised by the local media. It was owned by Philip Anschutz.

Terrance's charge of inciting a riot was for a Justice for Elijah McClain rally on July 3, at the Aurora police District 1 station. That was where the officers who apprehended Elijah worked. The protests were getting national attention, and about a thousand people had attended. Terrance led the most incisive chants, his anger and energy charging up the crowd. Hundreds stayed as the sun fell, surrounding the police station and banging drums. The young African American Terrance didn't trust was there, openly carrying a rifle. Terrance had another argument with the Night Crew, whose faces were hidden behind masks and hats and glasses that looked to Terrance like they wanted to be anonymous. He didn't want to be there any longer, and left. Some of those who stayed ended up wiring the doors to the police building shut. Day eventually came and they left; no one was hurt.

"It's crazy," Terrance told me when he got out of jail the next day. "On the seven-year anniversary of me shooting Munch, I am facing charges again, but for my lifesaving gun, not an actual gun." He said the police would not give his phone back because it was part of an "ongoing investigation." He said a lawyer who visited him at the jail told him he was under FBI investigation.

Two days later, the New York–based Party for Socialism and Liberation helped organize a demonstration, demanding the charges against the "Aurora 6" be dropped. A few hundred people gathered in a socially distanced fan around a makeshift stage a few blocks from the capitol. Terrance was scheduled to speak. Before him, his friend Lindsay Minter, in a red FPRA shirt and a camouflage hat and pants, spoke about the Black Panthers in 1969, "assassinated, imprisoned, publicly humiliated, and *falsely* charged," she said, as people cheered. "We are watching history repeat itself!"

Helicopters hovered above. Terrance climbed onto a ledge on the sidewalk, and led the crowd in a series of chants. He wore a red FPRA shirt and Ray-Ban sunglasses. "What side are you on, what side are you on?" he said, holding the mic to the crowd for response as drums beat. "This is a rev-o-lu-shuuunn!" he yelled to cheers.

"Make no mistake, this is political," he said of the charges. "Let me tell you why. We have been embarrassing the Aurora police all summer and DPD. You know why? Because they're *murderers!*"

The crowd clamored. "We are not afraid!" Terrance said. "We are swelling. We are getting deeper. The message has *not* changed. We want those officers charged . . . In closing, we need to practice unity. *They* are organized," he said, pointing to the police, who wore riot gear, on the edges of the group. "*They* are not arguing. We need solidarity!"

The group began marching behind Terrance. As they rounded a corner and headed back toward the capitol, the young African American who had been bringing a gun to the rallies began yelling that they should "tear down a fence" and "attack" some police. Terrance abruptly stopped the march. He called out to the man using his bullhorn. "Are you a cop?" he said. Terrance walked straight toward the man as others watched. "Why you always disrupting us?" Someone held Terrance back, and he went back to the front, shaking his head.

H-Soul, the activist, was there, in all black. "There's a Chinese proverb: He who mounts the tiger can never get off," he told me. "Terrance can never get off. But he's built to be on. And his voice is coming back to relevancy because we're in critical times, and in critical times people want a fighter, and that's what Terrance is."

"At least it's not like last time," Terrance told me later. "I'm not facing life in prison. I'm not going to be unhealthy and stressed out. That's not what I'm going to do. We are going forward." The felony charge for inciting a riot, the same charge Lauren Watson faced in 1968 for the Dry Cleaner Riot, carried a sentence of one to three years. If the DA's office added the "habitual criminal" charge, it would be twelve years. There was also the question of the FBI investigation. Terrance was ready to go to trial.

"I'm not worried, because I have nothing to hide," he told me. "I never told anyone to break something or hurt someone. But if I have to march from prison, I'll be marching on the yard. I'll march on the chow line."

A Note on Sources

When I began reporting this book seven years ago, I started with what I thought was a basic question: Why did Terrance shoot Hasan? It wasn't long before I understood that an answer wouldn't come easily.

I interviewed more than a hundred people. They included elected officials, developers, prosecutors, defense attorneys, criminal justice advocates, cops, former cops, and activists. They also included gang members, former gang members, victims of gang violence, clergy, and other residents and former residents of northeast Denver.

Inside the community, where many of the important keys to understanding what happened lay, a lot of fear surrounded the case. Only later did some of my sources tell me it may have helped that I was white. Mistrust among Black men in the community was high.

Several people agreed to speak to me on the condition that their name not be used. I evaluated everyone with the same caution and skepticism. For every significant character in this book, I pulled court and police records. I also filed Colorado Open Records Act (CORA) requests for additional materials, including police reports and emails, some of which I got while others were denied. Particularly glaring was the city of Denver's refusal to turn over detailed budget information about its anti-gang effort. I was able to piece most of it together from other available public information as well as documents I was able to obtain from other sources.

Significant details and scenes in this book are possible because of the trove of videos, photos, letters, and emails I was given by members of the community. Once I began reporting, I also recorded video and audio of many of my interviews and encounters. They proved to be an important record as critical events began to happen in front of me.

Key details about activism in Denver's civil rights era were preserved in Mayor Currigan's papers at the Denver Public Library. I was also fortunate to interview some of that era's major players, including Bishop Acen Phillips and the Denver Black Panther founder Lauren Watson, who I spent several days with in his south Denver nursing home. Watson hadn't spoken to a journalist in years. I was fortunate to be the last one to interview him.

Many of the primary characters in this story were involved in events chronicled by the media. At times, critical discrepancies existed between their accounts and those of the media, which I felt was important to point out. In some cases the misperceptions of the neighborhood and of the anti-gang effort contributed to further problems.

Most of the people I came to know in reporting this book I came to trust; others I came to fear. I agreed to give one of my sources who spoke freely about what he witnessed an alias, which is noted in the text. I also decided to use aliases for two other people who I never met—one an informant, the other a Blood he testified against—because unlike others in this story, they hadn't sought coverage or been part of a publicly funded effort. I discovered most of their details through court papers; the rest checked out with multiple sources.

The rest of the names and all of the events are real. I tried to evaluate what I could about the truth and present it fairly. Some of what I discovered was disturbing, and I have been made well aware that some people in this book would rather not see it come out. I hope it will shine a light on issues that have been hidden for too long.

Notes

PROLOGUE

8 *"After Violence Interrupts Progress, a Struggle Ensues in Denver"*: Dan Frosh, "After Violence Interrupts Progress, a Struggle Ensues in Denver," *The New York Times*, Sept. 27, 2013.

8 *"I swept up the glass"*: Frosch, "After Violence Interrupts Progress."

CHAPTER 1

19 *The Dahlia, owned by the local businessman Bernard Bernstein*: Phil Goodstein, *Park Hill Promise* (New Social Publications, 2012), p. 472.

19 *It had a department store*: Goodstein, *Park Hill Promise*, p. 473.

20 *President Lyndon Johnson, during a visit*: Barnet Nover, "Negro Homes Impress LBJ," *The Denver Post*, Aug. 28, 1966.

20 *One flyer warned that Park Hill was becoming "Dark Hill"*: S. A. Gonzales, "CALM Stands for 'Be Cool, Man!':"A Black Citizen's Patrol in Denver, p. 4.

21 *The Watts Riots of 1965*: Alex Alonso, *Out of the Void: Street Gangs in Black Los Angeles* (NYU Press, 2010).

21 *Soon after LBJ's visit, Currigan*: Greg Pinney, "Group Charts Racial Peace in Denver," *The Denver Post*, Aug. 3, 1967.

21 *According to a report*: Commission on Community Relations: Dahlia Center Area, December 14, 1966. (Letter to Mayor re Dahlia.)

22 *new federal Model Cities*: Art Branscombe, "Troubled Model Cities Idea Viewed Still as Sound," *The Denver Post*, Oct. 25, 1970.

23 *Huey Newton, the group's co-founder*: Summer Burke, *Community Control: Civil Rights Resistance in the Mile High City* (Psi Sigma Siren, 2011), p. 16.

24 *Like other Black Panther chapters*: Burke, *Community Control*, p. 16.

24 *On Saturday, July 29, as a city-sponsored*: S. A. Gonzales, "CALM Stands for 'Be Cool, Man!,'" p. 1.

24 *"Disturbances are becoming"*: Doug Huigen and Chuck Green, "Police Disperse Rock-and-Bottle Hurlers," *The Denver Post*, Aug. 1, 1967.

25 *"About fifty youths"*: Huigen and Green, "Rock-and-Bottle Hurlers."

25 *Another tried to photograph*: Doug Huigen and Chuck Green, "Negro Leaders Charge 2 in Brutality Incidents," *The Denver Post*, Aug. 2, 1967.

25 *By night's end, three youths*: Huigen and Green, "Rock-and-Bottle Hurlers."

25 *The Group of 15*: Doug Huigen and Chuck Green, "Three Stores Lose Windows," *The Denver Post*, Aug. 2, 1967.

25 *"Dozens of private cars"*: Huigen and Green, "Three Stores."

26 *"Denver is at the crossroads"*: Greg Pinney, "Group Charts Racial Peace in Denver," *The Denver Post*, Aug. 3, 1967.

CHAPTER 2

27 *Around 1 a.m., when a skirmish*: "Officer Testifies on Shooting," *The Denver Post*, Jan. 16, 1970.

28 *"Civil rights!"*: S. A. Gonzales, *"CALM Stands for 'Be Cool, Man!,'"* p. 15.

28 *The night came to an end*: "Officer Testifies on Shooting."

29 *One had gone through his*: Richard O'Reilly, "DA Receives Shooting Data," *The Denver Post*, June 25, 1970.

29 *W. Gene Howell, of Denver's NAACP*: "NAACP Asks Shooting Probe," *Rocky Mountain News*, June 25, 1968.

29 *"The lack of sufficient"*: "NAACP Asks Shooting Probe."

30 *"This is the most serious"*: Ed Pendleton, "Thornton Calls for More Jobs," *The Denver Post*, June 23, 1968.

30 *"This demonstration is to show"*: "Here's Text of Speech on Negro Pledges, Demands," *The Denver Post*, June 26, 1968.

31 *"I would assume that the police"*: John Morehead, "Mayor OKs Firm Police Reaction," *The Denver Post*, Sept. 30, 1968.

32 *charges of assault with a deadly weapon*: "Officer Testifies On Shooting," *The Denver Post*, January 16, 1970, page 11.

33 *Watson branded Caldwell*: Goodstein, *Historic East Denver*, p. 215.

33 *The Black Panthers, Hoover*: "Black Panther Greatest Threat to US Security," *United Press International*, July 16, 1969.

35 *Mayor Currigan unexpectedly left office*: Leighton Whitaker, "Social Reform and the Comprehensive Community Mental Health Center—The Model Cities Experiment: Part II," *American Journal of Public Health*, 1971, p. 217.

36 *Director Hoover of the FBI*: Eric Dexheimer, "Fade to Black," *Westword*, Sept. 20, 1995.

36 *According to reports, the Dahlia*: Goodstein, *Park Hill Promise*, p. 474.

37 *In 1974, a fire*: Goodstein, *Park Hill Promise*, p. 476.

CHAPTER 3

40 *A 1974 study commissioned*: Charles F. Cortese, "The Park Hill Experience," 1974.

43 *to turn down an Olympic Games*: Jack Moore, "When Denver Rejected the Olympics in Favour of the Environment and Economics," *The Guardian*, April 7, 2015.

43 *remained a particularly segregated one*: David Rusk, "Denver Divided: Sprawl, Race, and Poverty in Greater Denver" (Denver University thesis, 2003), p. 7.

45 *purchased the Rossonian Hotel in the hopes of refurbishing it*: Danika Worthington, "Rossonian Hotel Changes Hands Again as Five Points Neighborhood Changes Up," *The Denver Post*, Sept. 13, 2017.

45 *a staff nurse told Denver's alternative weekly newspaper*: Alan Prendergast, "To Die Inside," *Westword*, Dec. 19, 2002.

48 *"We morphed into"*: Amy Goodman, "A Conversation with Death Row Prisoner Stanley Tookie Williams from his San Quentin Cell," Democracy Now, Nov. 30, 2005.

49 *By the late 1970s, Denver police were tracking a few dozen street gangs*: Tom Coakley, "Groups in Flux, Resurge After Summer's Lull," *The Denver Post*, Dec. 11, 1983.

51 *"You all keep saying, Gang, gang, gang"*: Coakley, "Groups in Flux."

CHAPTER 4

55 *"I feel I'm the only one who has rapport with the Crips"*: Ann Carnanan, "Preacher Devotes Sunday to God, Rest of Week to Crips," *Rocky Mountain News*, June 29, 1986.

57 *Archduke Ferdinand in the war*: Dan Baum, *Smoke and Mirrors: The War on Drugs and the Politics of Failure* (Little Brown and Co., 1996).

57 *"from being cops to being crooks"*: Freeway: Crack in the System (documentary), Marc Levin, 2015.

58 *City Park that ended only after police in riot gear arrived*: Luke Turf, "The Transformers," *Westword*, Feb. 22, 2007.

CHAPTER 5

60 *"Police in Denver and elsewhere have offered a variety"*: William Overend, "Crips and Bloods: L.A. Gangs: Are They Migrating?," *Los Angeles Times*, April 3, 1987.

60 *"Be cool, don't do nothing"*: Karen Bowers, "Gang 'trying to get along with society,'" *Denver Post*, Feb. 8, 1987.

60 *according to* Newsweek: "Number One with a Bullet," *Newsweek*, June 30, 1991.

61 *squeezed the trigger of his gun*: Kevin McCullen, "Drive-By Shooting Tied to Gang Wars," *Rocky Mountain News*, July 26, 1988.

61 *The Bloods opened fire*: Tony Pugh, "Violence Shatters NE Denver Unity," *Rocky Mountain News*, Sept. 18, 1988.

61 *This time the gunman was an undercover police officer, Bernard Montoya*: Associated Press, "Police Officer Shoots Teen; Second Death in 24-Hour Period," July 15, 1988.

62 *was not charged or reprimanded*: "Witnesses, Cops Vary on Shooting," *Rocky Mountain News*, July 15, 1988.

62 *Smith, who was a high school senior, lived in Northeast Park Hill*: Colleen Barry, "Church Leaders Offer Crowd a Plan to Fight Gang Problem," Associated Press, Nov. 13, 1988.

62 *Raibon called Smith*: M.C. Moewe, "The Original Gangster Rap," *West-word*, Jan. 4, 1995.

63 *Peña said*: "Deadly Street Gangs Now Plague Denver," *Deseret News*, Dec. 5, 1988.

65 *"It's not a crackdown on gangs; it's a crackdown on blacks"*: Dirk Johnson, "2 of 3 Young Black Men in Denver Listed by Police as Suspected Gangsters," *The New York Times*, Dec. 11, 1993.

65 *"If it walks like a duck and talks like a duck"*: Bill McBean, "Police Anti-gang Efforts 'Backfire,'" *The Denver Post*, Dec. 6, 1991.

CHAPTER 6

71 *Several hundred young men were murdered every year*: Jesse Katz, "County's Yearly Gang Death Toll Reaches 800," *Los Angeles Times*, Jan. 19, 1993.

72 *Nation of Islam leader Louis Farrakhan*: Charisse Jones, "Farrakhan to Speak to 900 Gang Leaders to 'Stop the Killing,'" *Los Angeles Times*, Oct. 6, 1989.

72 *"When you're underrepresented"*: Mike Comeaux, "Farrakhan Speaks Out On Gangs—Blames Society for Rise in Violence," *Los Angeles Daily News*, Oct. 9, 1989, p. N4.

73 *according to their account*: Stephanie Chavez and Louis Sahagun, "Slaying by LAPD Becomes Rallying Point for Activists," *Los Angeles Times*, Jan. 5, 1992.

74 *Hyde told the Judiciary Committee*: Hearing Before the Subcommittee on Civil and Constitutional Rights of the Committee on the Judiciary, House of Representatives, Serial No. 78, June 26, 1992.

74 *"Give us the hammer and the nails, we will rebuild the city"*: Luis J. Rodriguez, Cle Sloan, and Kershaun Scott, "Gangs: The New Political Force in Los Angeles," *Los Angeles Times*, Sept. 13, 1992.

75 *Holmes told the* Los Angeles Times: Jessie Katz, "Gang Truce Leader: From Peacemaker to Prisoner," *Los Angeles Times*, Dec. 6, 1992.

76 *Denver radio host Alan Berg*: "Jury Told of Plan to Kill Radio Host," *The New York Times*, Nov. 8, 1987.

76 *KKK and White Aryan Nation members disrupted the traditional*: Associated Press, "Klan Supporters Attacked," Jan. 21, 1992.

77 *"teetering on the edge of a murderous abyss"*: Ken Hamblin, "Where Are Our Leaders as Denver Dies?," *The Denver Post*, Aug. 5, 1993.

77 *"Under Siege: Living with Barbarians at the Gate"*: Clifford May, "Under Siege: Living with Barbarians at the Gate," *Rocky Mountain News*, Aug. 8, 1993.

77 *"to pray that we will be violence-free"*: "As Papal Visit Nears, Denver's Crime Surges," *The Washington Post*, July 31, 1993.

CHAPTER 7

83 *"He's charismatic"*: Harrison Fletcher, "The Buddy System," *Westword*, Nov. 5, 1998.

84 *"national leader in the fight"*: Peggy Lowe, "When A Community Prays Together," Associated Press, December 11, 1993.

84 *"We're taking our own lives"*: Tracy Seipel, "A Battle over 'The Holly': It's Residents vs. Drug Dealers for Control," *The Denver Post*, April 24, 1994.

85 *lyrics that Quayle said threatened law enforcement*: John Broder, "Quayle Calls for Pulling Rap Album Tied to Murder Case," *Los Angeles Times*, Sept. 23, 1992.

85 *"What we're doing is using our brain to get out of the ghetto any way we can"*: E! interview, 1992.

86 *Clinton called him out by name*: President Clinton, "Remarks on Signing the Violent Crime Control and Law Enforcement Act of 1994," Sept. 13, 1994.

86 *police officers on the streets of America's cities*: U.S. Department of Justice, "Violent Crime Control and Law Enforcement Act of 1994."

87 *and most were not significant dealers*: Human Rights Watch, "Drug Arrests and Race in the United States," March 2, 2009.

CHAPTER 8

97 *"maximum harassment"*: Mark Obmascik, "Race Issue Enters Election, Despite Denials It Has Key Role," *The Denver Post*, June 1, 1995.

98 *Both of Denver's daily newspapers endorsed DeGroot, but Webb narrowly won*: Deborah Mendez, "Wellington Webb Wins Second Term as Denver Mayor," *The Denver Post*, June 6, 1995.

CHAPTER 9

99 *President Bill Clinton, May 13, 1996*: President Clinton, "Remarks Announcing the 'Anti-Gang and Youth Crime Control Act of 1996,'" May 13, 1996.

99 *The violent crime rates had been steadily dropping since 1993*: Jeffery Butts and Jeremy Travis, "The Rise and Fall of American Youth Violence: 1980–2002," Urban Institute Research Report, March 2002, p. 6.

99 *before President Clinton's remarks*: "US Clinton Juvenile Crime," AP Archive, May 13, 1996.

100 *based on evidence obtained by informants within the gang*: George W. Knox, "Impact of the Federal Prosecution of the Gangster Disciples," *Journal of Gang Research*, 2002.

100 *"DA Slams Bloods Gang"*: Sue Lindsay, "DA Slams Bloods Gang," *Rocky Mountain News*, Nov. 13, 1996.

100 *"to go after a street gang"*: Howard Pankratz, "Gang Leaders Indicted. Racketeering Charge DA's New Weapon," *The Denver Post*, Nov. 13, 1996.

103 *"For the better part of a decade"*: Gary Webb, "U.S. Policy Helped Start Crack Plague. Drugs Sold to Gangs; Profits Funded CIA's Contras," *San Jose Mercury News*, Aug. 21, 1996.

103 *Lt. Colonel Oliver North indicted*: "Oliver North Guilty of Tricking Congress," *The Guardian*, May 5, 1989.

103 *The CIA eventually acknowledged*: "The CIA-Contra-Crack Cocaine Controversy: A Review of the Justice Department's Investigations and

Prosecutions," USDOJ/Office of the Inspector General Special Report, Dec. 1997.

103 *"troubling aspects"*: Warren Richey, "CIA Under Pressure to Divulge Info on Contras," *Christian Science Monitor*, Sept. 20, 1996.

104 *He was sentenced to life*: "Dealer Alleging CIA Drug Link Gets Life Term," *The Washington Post*, Nov. 21, 1996.

105 *"This might save my life"*: Charlie Brennan, "Gang Members Probation Blasted. Judge Dumps Problem on California, Cop Says," *Rocky Mountain News*, Sept. 7, 1995.

108 *"It's not the sentences we had hoped for, to be sure"*: Kieran Nicholson, "Reputed Bloods Get Day in Court. 3 of 10 Indicted Sentenced So Far," *The Denver Post*, June 7, 1997.

109 *"Who among us truly believed the Asberry saga would end differently"*: Bill Johnson, "A hanging judge passes sentence," *Rocky Mountain News*, Dec. 6, 1996.

110 *"by a gang without a gun"*: Howard Pankratz, "Ex-Gang Leader Asberry Gets 4 Years After Flunking Probation," *The Denver Post*, Dec. 3, 1999.

110 *"I can't make no excuses"*: James Meadow, "Crips Founder Gets 4 Years. L.A. Parole Violation Lands Asberry in Colorado Prison," *Rocky Mountain News*, Sept. 15, 1996.

CHAPTER 10

112 *Ceasefire reported a 67 percent drop in shootings*: "Who we are," Project Ceasefire website.

112 *"what I call 'happenstance homicides'"*: Bob Kemper, "Law Leaves Criminals Gun-Shy: Richmond's Bad Guys Don't Want to Carry," *Chicago Tribune*, March 26, 2000.

113 *crimes involving guns plummeted 65 percent*: Michael Janofsky, "Fighting Crime by Making Federal Case About Guns," *The New York Times*, Feb. 10, 1999.

113 *Richmond public defender's office decried Exile as racist*: Dominic Perella, "VA Crime Crackdown Called Racist," Associated Press, May 30, 1999.

113 *Attorney General Janet Reno and Robert Rubin*: Associated Press, "Clinton Orders Tighter Federal-State Reins on Gun Violence," March 21, 1999.

115 *1999 National Conference of Black Mayors*: Bob Jackson, "Million Man March Threatens Local Protest," *Rocky Mountain News*, April 18, 1999.

116 *the deadliest school shooting in U.S. history*: "Terror in Littleton: The Community; Columbine Students Talk of the Disaster and Life," *The New York Times*, April 30, 1999.

116 *Webb won a third term as mayor with a record 81 percent of the vote*: Brian Bergstein, "Mob Defense Lawyer Leads in Las Vegas; Denver Mayor Wins Third Term," Associated Press, May 5, 1999.

116 *USA* Today *deemed Colorado "a new ground zero for gun control politics"*: Patrick O'Driscoll, "Rare Alliance Against Guns: NRA and Its Opponents Back Crackdown in Denver," *USA Today*, March 7, 2000.

118 *led his team into the wrong house*: Alan Prendergast, "Unlawful Entry," *Westword*, Feb. 24, 2000.

118 *"Project Exile has transformed our court into a minor-grade police court"*: David Holthouse, "Living in Exile," *Westword*, March 21, 2002.

122 *"I don't know what will happen now"*: Martin Luther King, Jr., April 3, 1968.

122 *Less than twenty-four hours later, King was assassinated*: Earl Caldwell, "Martin Luther King Is Slain in Memphis; a White Is Suspected; Johnson Urges Calm," *The New York Times*, April 5, 1968.

CHAPTER 12

132 *"Prodigal Son Leaves Jail, Starts Nonprofit for Kids"*: Myung Oak Kim, "Prodigal Son Leaves Jail, Starts Nonprofit for Kids: Former Gang Member Wants Students to Hope," *Rocky Mountain News*, Feb. 6, 2006.

133 *The New York Times called*: Michael Janofsky, "Denver Election Is a Model of Civility," *The New York Times*, May 25, 2003.

133 *Paul was hit four times and died in front of family and neighbors*: Sean Kelly, "Cop Recounts Slaying of Teen," *The Denver Post*, June 7, 2005.

134 *the City of Denver to pay $1.3 million to the family in a civil suit*: Michael Roberts, "A Brief History of Denver's Police Shootings and How Much They Cost," *Westword*, April 23, 2018.

134 *the demolition of the Dahlia Shopping Center*: Kristi Arellano, "Dahlia Demolition Underway at Last," *The Denver Post*, Sept. 21, 2005.

134 *the policing strategy that Hickenlooper had championed*: Christopher Osher, "Profs Debunk 'Broken Windows,'" *The Denver Post*, March 6, 2006.

136 *One of them hit twenty-four-year-old Darrent Williams*: Mike Klis, "Indictment in Slaying of Bronco Darrent Williams," *The Denver Post*, Oct. 8, 2008.

137 *district attorney's office to hire more gang investigators*: Melanie Asmar, "Denver's Plan to Cool Down Gang Violence," *Westword*, July 3, 2012.

137 *Governor Romer's anti-gang bill ran out*: Tina Griegio, "Anti-Gang Group Struggles Against Violence, Frustration," *Rocky Mountain News*, Nov. 5, 2007.

139 *"Hold up a second"*: Luke Turf, "Metro Denver Gang Coalition: Beyond Darrent Williams," *Westword*, Oct. 11, 2007.

140 *Michael Asberry was dead*: Christopher Osher, "Crips Founder Unable to Flee Trouble," *The Denver Post*, May 19, 2008.

CHAPTER 13

145 *Denver's assistant fire chief*: Eli Stokols, WB2 Denver Late News, May 18, 2008.

147 *The Denver Post quoted*: Carlos Illescas, "Gangs Ruled Out in Slaying," *The Denver Post*, May 21, 2008.

148 *He called for a march*: Jeremy Meyer, "Call for Peace Echoes in Marchers' Footsteps," *The Denver Post*, May 25, 2008.

149 *Terrance walked toward a young girl*: Meyer, "Call for Peace."

151 *The meeting was held in*: Arthur Rosenblum, "Fire at Holly Center Fires Up Neighbors," *Greater Park Hill News*, June 19–July 15, 2000.

151 *She referred to Bullock*: Rosenblum, "Fire at Holly Center."

151 *Terrance proposed building*: Rosenblum, "Fire at Holly Center."

151 *"The Holly is the hub"*: Rosenblum, "Fire at Holly Center."

153 *As Obama clinched the historic*: Michael Booth, "Resounding Cheers Roar Across State, into Future," *The Denver Post*, Nov. 5, 2008.

154 *One of the kids in his program*: Tina Griego, "Looking at Obama, These Kids See Themselves," *Rocky Mountain News*, Nov. 6, 2008.

154 *"That is one of the older"*: Howard Pankratz, "Gang Members Charged in Holly Street Arson," *The Denver Post*, Dec. 19, 2008.

CHAPTER 14

155 *As the charges against the Holly 9 were announced, the American Planning Association*: "Greater Park Hill: Denver, Colorado," American Planning Association.

158 *"There's a lot of motivational"*: John Zwick, "Shopping Center to Face Wrecking Ball, Renewal," *The Denver Post*, April 23, 2009.

158 *What had happened at the Holly, Hickenlooper*: Bill Johnson, "Empty Lot Is Full of Promises," *The Denver Post*, May 22, 2009.

159 *Steel and other building*: Kirk Mitchell, "New Denver Justice Center Stresses Security and Convenience," *The Denver Post*, Feb. 10, 2010.

CHAPTER 15

168 *"these one million individuals account for upwards of 80 percent"*: I.A.C.P. "Annual Conference Denver, Colorado," speech by Robert S. Mueller III, FBI, October 6, 2009.

169 *"I'm not going to knock the prosecutors"*: Dave Krieger "Krieger: Trial a Teaching Moment," *The Denver Post*, March 11, 2010.

170 *Coverage of the "visioning process" appeared in the* Greater Park Hill News: Patrick Horvath, "Holly Fair Draws Big Crowd," *Greater Park Hill News*, May 20–June 16, 2010.

174 *"There's one saying"*: Zapollo and Friends, Fox 31 KDVR, March 14, 2010.

174 Westword *described the case as "open and shut"*: Jef Otte, "Pernell Hines, No. 7: Suspect Turns Himself in After Shooting Man in Argument," *Westword*, June 16, 2010.

175 *The following week, Terrance led his first citywide anti-gang march*: Bianca Davis, "Bloods, Crips, Walk in Solidarity Against Violence," *The Denver Post*, Aug. 1, 2010.

175 *"If you ain't reppin' for Black power then you forgot what you should be reppin' for"*: Davis, "Solidarity Against Violence."

CHAPTER 16

177 *"When people think of prophets"*: Terrence "Big T" Hughes, "Terrance Roberts Healing the Hood," *5 Points News*, Feb. 2011, p. 3.

178 *left for Aurora and other Denver suburbs*: Kurtis Lee and Jeremy Miller, "Aurora's Growth Reflects that African Americans Are Finding Base in Denver 'Burbs," *The Denver Post*, March 24, 2012.

181 *according to Bloomberg News*: "Qwest: What Did Phil Know?," *Bloomberg News*, Nov. 3, 2002.

181 *said he believed Anschutz and the federal government had set him up*: Andy Vuong, "Unrepentant Joe Nacchio Blames Feds for Qwest's Financial Collapse," *The Denver Post*, May 27, 2014.

182 *the Anschutz Family Foundation voted to approve a $5 million grant*: Anthony Cotton, "Holly Square Revitalization," *The Denver Post*, Feb. 15, 2012.

183 *The Colorado ACLU believed that Denver police had shown a pattern of racial profiling*: Michael Roberts, "ACLU Wants Department of Justice to Investigate Denver Police," *Westword*, Jan. 12, 2012.

184 *"encouraged" Project Safe Neighborhood cities*: Kathleen A. Tomberg and Jeffrey A. Butts, "Cross Site Evaluation of the OJJDP Community-Based Violence Prevention Demonstration Program," *John Jay Research and Evaluation Center*, Sept. 2016, p. 5.

186 *"Anschutz Gift to Help New Life Rise from Ashes"*: Anthony Cotton, "Anschutz Foundation's $5 Million Gift to Help New Hope Rise from Ashes of Holly Square," *The Denver Post*, Feb. 14, 2012.

CHAPTER 17

189 *"Patience Helps Build Path to Boys and Girls Club"*: Tina Griego, "Patience Helps Build Path to Boys and Girls Club," *The Denver Post*, March 7, 2012.

191 *After Trayvon Martin was killed*: Brother Jeff, "I Am Trayvon Martin," *5 Points News*, April 2012.

191 *gave a welcome speech that had been partially written by the church*: Eric Gorski, "PR Makeover—Church of Scientology Takes Higher Profile Across US and in Denver, Where It Just Opened a New Facility," *The Denver Post*, June 23, 2012.

192 *Oliver, a Blood, fired his gun*: Jessica Fender, "Cop Killing Returns Spotlight to Street Gangs," *The Denver Post*, July 1, 2012.

193 *"There aren't a lot of skiers and snowboarders in northeast Denver"*: Dan Frosch, "Officer's Death Reminds a City of Work to Be Done," *The New York Times*, July 2, 2012.

194 *"This process has been an amazing experience"*: Ronald Washington, "The Holly Center is Reborn" (video), 2012.

CHAPTER 18

200 *"We raised over 400 kids over some very hard and trying times"*: Colleen O'Connor, "Fading Lights?," *The Denver Post*, March 1, 2013.

200 *"Terrance Roberts is one of Denver's"*: Joel Warner, "Terrance Roberts' Anti-Gang Initiative, Prodigal Son, Faces Potential Shutdown," *Westword*, Jan. 24, 2013.

207 *one of the group not charged*: Matthew Nussbaum, "Fero's Bar Massacre: Shadowy Federal Informant at the Center of Trial," *The Denver Post*, July 26, 2015.

CHAPTER 19

209 *"best and safest facility"*: "The Nancy P. Anschutz Center Opens in Northeast Park Hill—A Community's Vision Realized," *PR Web*, Aug. 27, 2013.

CHAPTER 20

219 *a resident who was not named told* The Denver Post *of Terrance*: Sadie Gurman, "'Role Model' Facing Charges," *The Denver Post*, Sept. 22, 2013.

219 *"A person the neighborhood trusted"*: Sadie Gurman, "Residents Struggle with Unanswered Questions," *The Denver Post*, Sept. 26, 2013.

221 *The $378 million complex*: Christopher N. Osher, "Denver Need and Cost for Jail Annex Sparks Debate," *The Denver Post*, Nov. 16, 2013.

222 *"Holly Square Redevelopment Has Stabilized Northeast Park Hill"*: Christi Smith, "Holly Square Redevelopment Has Stabilized Northeast Park Hill," Urban Land Conservancy, Sept. 28, 2013.

222 *"Holly Square Blooms Again"*: Colleen O'Connor, "Holly Square Blooms Again."

222 *"astounding how people from all over the community worked on this"*: O'Connor, "Holly Square Blooms Again."

222 *"We're not seeing as much gang activity, and there is no more open-air drug market"*: Colleen O'Connor, "Revitalization of Holly Square Moves into New Phase After Shooting," *The Denver Post*, Nov. 13, 2013.

226 *"On the streets, it's about self-preservation"*: Robert Sanchez, "The Rise + Fall of Terrance Roberts," *5280*, Feb. 2014.

228 *the mayor and the DA had roasted Rev*: Colleen O'Connor, "Anti-Gang Icon Leon Kelly's 60th Birthday Marked by Golf Game, Roast," *The Denver Post*, July 10, 2013.

CHAPTER 21

235 *One of the DPD's troubling deficiencies*: Wesley Lowery, Kimbriell Kelly, Ted Mellnik, and Steven Rich, "Where Killings Go Unsolved," *The Washington Post*, June 6, 2018.

CHAPTER 22

245 *Bulger killed or ordered the killing*: "A look at the 19 murder victims in Bulger trial," *The Associated Press*, Aug. 12, 2013.

246 *the DEA employed approximately eighteen thousand*: "Use of Confidential Informants at ATF and DEA," Hearing Before the Committee on Oversight and Government Reform House of Representatives, April 4, 2017.

248 *Denver police had been conducting illegal surveillance on peaceful activists*: ACLU of Colorado, "ACLU Calls for Denver Police to Stop Keeping Files on Peaceful Protestors," March 11, 2002.

251 *what Carl had said in* The Denver Post: Sadie Gurman and Colleen O'Connor, "Terrance Roberts Shooting Arrest Leaves Park Hill Divided, Bewildered," *The Denver Post*, Oct. 6, 2013.

258 *On November 24, St. Louis County*: Monia Davey and Julie Bosman, "Protests Flare After Ferguson Police Officer Is Not Indicted," *The New York Times*, Nov. 24, 2014.

258 *Joshua was found dead in a burning car*: Jack Healy, "Another Killing in Ferguson Leaves a Family Grappling With the Unknown," *The New York Times*, Dec. 1, 2014.

258 *Instead a Blue Lives Matter demonstration*: Kirk Mitchell, "Hundreds Gather in Denver's Civic Center to Show Support for Police," *The Denver Post*, Dec. 27, 2014.

CHAPTER 23

260 *95 percent of all criminal cases ended up*: Lindsey Devers, "Plea and Charge Bargaining: Research Summary," Bureau of Justice Assistance, Jan. 24, 2011.

CHAPTER 24

265 *the city had been paying out millions of dollars a year in civil settlements*: Michael Roberts, "A Brief History of Denver Police Shootings and How Much They Cost," *Westword*, April 23, 2018.

265 *activist Alex Landau was one of the victims who had won compensation*: "After A Traffic Stop, Teen Was 'Almost Another Dead Black Male'," NPR, Aug. 15, 2014.

270 *Sharod Kindell, was shot multiple times*: Joel Warner, "Denver Police Kept Pulling Over Sharod Kindell—and the Last Time They Shot Him," *Westword*, Feb. 3, 2015.

271 *"but apparently it is more active than we all thought"*: Jesse Paul, "Gang Tensions Grow 'Hot' in Some Denver Neighborhoods as Bullets Fly," *The Denver Post*, Feb. 25, 2015.

271 *"we will find you and we will hold you accountable"*: Jesse Paul, "Denver Police: 3 of 4 Recent Slayings Were Gang Related; 8 This Year," *The Denver Post*, March 16, 2015.

275 *She complained to the city that they were dealing drugs*: Simone Weichselbaum, "Gangs of New York," Marshall Project, April 3, 2015.

CHAPTER 25

277 *"Planning for Successful Summer Programs"*: National Gang Center Newsletter, Spring 2015.

277 *The Denver police's own publicly available statistics*: Northeast Park Hill Reported Offenses, Denver Police Department, 2014.

278 *ShotSpotter system in the neighborhood*: Noelle Phillips, "Denver Police Want to Expand Shot Spotter Gunshot Detection System," *The Denver Post*, Dec. 4, 2015.

279 *gang members had laid down their arms*: Baynard Woods, "Baltimore's Uprising: Rival Gangs Push for Peace After Freddie Gray's Death," *The Guardian*, April 27, 2016.

279 *Baltimore police announced that they had received an anonymous*: Justin Fenton, "Baltimore Police Say Gangs 'Teaming Up' to Take Out Officers," *The Baltimore Sun*, April 27, 2015.

279 *"We're not about to allow y'all to paint this picture of us"*: "Police: Gangs Team Up to 'Take Out' Officers," WBAL-TV 11, April 28, 2015.

CHAPTER 26

287 *It carried a sentence of up to twenty-four years*: Colorado Legal Defense Group, *CRS 18-6-401 - Colorado Child Abuse Laws*, August 15, 2020.

292 *"Infamous Denver Gang Shooting Victim Acquitted in May 2014 Drive-by"*: Jesse Paul, "Infamous Denver Gang Shooting Victim Acquitted in May 2014 Drive-by," *The Denver Post*, June 12, 2015.

292 *reported on the killing of Ny Ny Hines*: Jesse Paul, "Hasan Jones, Denver Gang Shooting Victim, Accused in Toddler's Death," *The Denver Post*, June 12, 2015.

293 *"that soared early this year and not harassing the innocent"*: "Denver Police Making Progress Against Gangs," *The Denver Post*, June 10, 2015.

CHAPTER 27

296 *In 2013, it had won*: "Details on the 2013 Pulitzer Prize Winners," *The Denver Post*, April 13, 2015.

302 *Two days later, Lil Crip was dead*: Michael Roberts, "Derick Wilford ID'd as Victim in Stout Street Homicide, Still No Suspect Info," *Westword*, Aug. 17, 2015.

304 *"shooting down all cops that we see"*: Elizabeth Hernandez, "Aurora Police Receives Threatening Message Sunday Night," *The Denver Post*, Sept. 7, 2015.

CHAPTER 28

311 *violating the protesters' rights to free speech*: Noelle Phillips, "Denver Judge Dismisses Charges Against Jury Nullification Activists," *The Denver Post*, Dec. 16, 2015.

312 *quintuple murders that involved the ATF informant*: Matthew Nussbaum and Noelle Phillips, "Dexter Lewis Found Guilty of Stabbing Five People to Death in Fero's Bar Massacre," *The Denver Post*, Aug. 10, 2015.

314 *"seemingly intent on destroying local journalism"*: Margaret Sullivan, "Is This Strip-Mining or Journalism? 'Sobs, Gasps, Expletives' over Latest Denver Post Layoffs," *The Washington Post*, March 15, 2018.

314 *Terrance from a court hearing days after the shooting*: Noelle Phillips, "Terrance Roberts Attempted Murder Trial Opens in Denver Court," *The Denver Post*, Sept. 30, 2015.

CHAPTER 29

337 *"admitted to planting the knife"*: "Anti-Gang Activist Admits to Planting the Knife," 9News, Oct. 6, 2015.

339 *declared Terrance not guilty*: Jesse Paul and Noelle Phillips, "Denver Jury Finds Anti-Gang Activist Terrance Roberts Not Guilty," *The Denver Post*, Oct. 9, 2015.

EPILOGUE

342 *"I don't think so"*: "Jury Finds Anti-Gang Activist Terrance Roberts Not Guilty," CBS4 News, Oct. 9, 2015.

343 *"a reformed gang member to help Park Hill"*: Noelle Phillips, "Original Gangsters Paid to Stop Violence in Two Denver Neighborhoods," *The Denver Post*, Oct. 31, 2015.

345 *that enabled it to seize properties for which complaints had been filed*: Revised Municipal Code Ord. No. 41–97, §3, adopted Jan. 13, 1997.

345 *a group of investors, who hope to turn it into a jazz club*: Danika Worthington, "Rossonian Hotel Changes Hands Again as Five Points Neighborhood Changes Up," *The Denver Post*, Sept. 13, 2017.

346 *"new COINTELPRO"*: "The New Cointelpro? Meet the Activist the FBI Labeled a 'Black Extremist' & Jailed for 5 Months," *Democracy Now!*, May 23, 2018.

346 *including Deandre Joshua*: Lois Beckett, "Ferguson Protest Leader Darren Seals Shot and Found Dead in a Burning Car," *The Guardian*, Sept. 8, 2016.

346 *in Raleigh, James Elvin Austin III, a twenty-three-year-old*: Thomasi McDonald, "Former Gang Member Turned Neighborhood Activist Shot Dead in Southeast Raleigh," *The News & Observer*, July 3, 2015.

347 *died in December 2017 of a heart attack*: Vivian Wang, "Erica Garner, Activist and Daughter of Eric Garner, Dies at 27," *The New York Times*, Dec. 30, 2017.

347 *Three of the six deceased Ferguson protesters appeared*: Jim Salter, "A puzzling number of men tied to the Ferguson protests have since died," *The Chicago Tribune*, March 18, 2019.

347 *Geofeedia, a social media location tool*: Lee Fang, "The CIA Is Investing in Firms That Mine Your Tweets and Instagram Photos," *The Intercept*, April 14, 2016.

347 *given a designation, Black Identity Extremist*: "Leaked FBI Documents Raise Concerns About Targeting Black People Under 'Black Identity Extremist' and Newer Labels," ACLU, Aug. 9, 2019.

347 *"I'm not able to comment on that"*: "Lawmaker Asks Sessions Why There's an FBI Report about Black 'Extremists' but Not One About Those Who Are White," *PBS NewsHour*, Nov. 14, 2017.

349 *ATF agents set up a storefront six hundred feet*: The Editorial Board, "Editorial: Botched ATF Sting Endangered St. Louis Residents," *St. Louis Post-Dispatch*, Sept. 18, 2016.

349 *a 2012 Milwaukee Journal Sentinel investigation*: Raquel Rutledge, "ATF Sting in Milwaukee Flawed From the Start," *Milwaukee Journal Sentinel*, Sept. 12, 2016.

350 *15,300 defendants for federal gun crimes in one year*: "Remarks by President Trump at the 2018 Project Safe Neighborhoods National Conference," White House Briefings, Dec. 7, 2018.

350 *was charged with the murder*: Saja Hindi, "Denver Coroner Identifies Man Shot and Killed in Northeast Denver," *The Denver Post*, March 26, 2019.

350 *Nipsey Hussle was killed in Los Angeles*: Eric Leonard and Doha Madani, "Nipsey Hussle Murdered After Snitch Remarks, Grand Jury Transcripts Say," *NBC News*, Jan. 27, 2019.

351 *giving him a third term as Denver's chief executive*: John Ensslin and Ernest Luning, "'This Is the People's Victory': Hancock Wins Third Term as Denver Mayor," *The Colorado Springs Gazette*, June 4, 2019.

351 *Lauren Watson died, at seventy-six*: Michael Roberts, "Denver Black Panthers Legend Lauren Watson Dies," *Westword*, Aug. 9, 2019.

351 *One of the dead was Ngor Monday*: Aldo Svaldi, "Victim in Double Shooting Last Week Is Identified," *The Denver Post*, Sept. 13, 2019.

353 *A 911 call reported someone looking "sketchy"*: Colleen Slevin, "A Year After Elijah McClain's Death, Activists Want Charges," Associated Press, Aug. 23, 2020.

354 *For six days, central Denver was shut down*: Tynin Fries, "Denver Protests Live: Updates from June 7 Demonstrations Following the Death of George Floyd," *The Denver Post*, June 7, 2020.

354 *Representative Leslie Herod became the sponsor of a police reform bill*: Alex Burness and Saja Hindi, "How Colorado Found the Political Will to Pass a Police Reform Law," *The Denver Post*, June 19, 2020.

356 *At one, a Jeep sped through the crowd*: Andrew Villegas, "No Charges for Man Seen Driving Jeep into Aurora Protest," *Denverite*, Sept. 23, 2020.

356 *The man survived*: Shelly Bradbury, "Arrest of Suspect in Shooting of 2 Protestors in Aurora Deepens Distrust of Police," *The Denver Post*, July 28, 2020.

357 *"not as listening posts but as agents provocateurs"*: Justin Rohrlich, "Informant on NYPD Payroll Drove Protester to Attack," *The Daily Beast*, Aug. 5, 2020.

357 *referred to the organizers as "domestic terrorists"*: Michael Roberts, "Mike Coffman Tweets Like Trump About Aurora Elijah McClain Protest," *Westword*, July 27, 2020

357 *five people were shot and two killed in the parking lot*: Shelly Bradbury, "Five people shot—two killed, three wounded—in Park Hill shooting," *The Denver Post*, July 26, 2020.

358 *"we're still trying to figure that out"*: Allan Tellis, "Youth Violence Researchers Hope to Deepen Neighborhood Ties with Montbello Event," *Denverite*, Dec. 3, 2018.

360 *"inciting a riot"*: Elise Shmelzer, "Protestors, Demonstration Leaders Arrested in Connection to Rallies in Aurora," *The Denver Post*, Sept. 17, 2020.

Acknowledgments

First and foremost, thanks to Terrance Roberts, an extraordinary person, who opened up his life to me. I hope his voice carries far and wide. It needs to be heard. His father, George Roberts, was also an inspiration, for his honesty and his ability to help people, including me, through some of the hard times this book took me through. Father and son are both powerful testimonies to why people deserve second chances in life.

Extra special thanks to my mother, Diane Rubinstein. It's not always easy when a child in their forties moves back into your apartment, much less to work on a gang story. This book wouldn't be possible without her support and understanding. Same goes for my dog, Sophie.

Thank you, Dale Maharidge, for always being there, for your advice, journalistic integrity, and editorial input.

This book was not easy on me, or on those in my life. Julia Haslett was there with me when it was rough. Dr. Katie Dawson of the Traumatic Stress Clinic at University of New South Wales in Sydney, Australia, took me into a study for PTSD for journalists. Our weekly telecom sessions helped me back on my feet. Others who helped: Ronnie Shaw, Jay Carlson, and Matt Case.

In New York, Alan Chin, Christina Voros, Marie-Hélène Carleton, and Micah Garen. Mark Binelli, thank you for your understanding, friendship, and excellent notes. Ditto Lara Santoro.

At Columbia, Bruce Shapiro and Todd Gitlin met with me when the crap hit the fan in Denver and I didn't know what to do.

For their time and expertise on key parts of this book, thank you to Alexandra Natapoff, David Kennedy, Alex Alonso, Cle "Bone" Sloan, Aqeela Sherrills, Bishop Acen Phillips, Lauren Watson, Jahsasamut, Alvin Jones, Tyrone Glover, Steve Laische, Dan Rubinstein, Ed Cope, and Frank Ochberg.

For their friendship, understanding, and notes on the manuscript, thank you to donnie l. betts and Hasira "H-Soul" Ashemu, as well as his son, Aingkhu Ashemu.

In Denver, solace and support when it was most needed came from Rachel Sturtz, Liz Yarnell, Sheila Kaehny, Todd Vitale, Dave Fulton, Doug Vaughan, Johnny Klein, Tryg Myhren, Erik Myhren, Chris Christmas, Britta Erickson, Zack Armstrong, Mike T, Jared Jacang Maher, J Hood, Max Potter, David Sirota. Special thanks to Sara Rosenthal for being there while working the ER in a pandemic.

Thank you to Colorado College and to Lynn Schofield Clark at University of Denver, for offering resources that helped my research, and to Stefanie Henson, Zachary Van Stanley, Brian Krapf, Ellen Wen, and Nicole Barker, as well as Joe Purtell, who was with me on this project for much of the way. Thank you to Maxyne Franklin, Lisa Chanoff, Xan Parker, Sarah Dowland, Dia Sokol Savage, Rachel Raney, Tony Hardmon, Lana Garland, and the Denver Film Society for supporting my visual documentation of this story.

Peter Alson offered spot-on feedback and asked astute questions, as did Diana D'Abruzzo, Mary Silva, and the estimable Denver journalists Alan Prendergast, Diane Alters, and Joel Warner.

At Farrar, Straus and Giroux, I was lucky to have Alex Star as my editor. He pushed me to get to the heart of the questions at stake; this book is far better for it. Thanks to Ian Van Wye, for keeping things organized and on track.

Special thanks to my agent, Zoë Pagnamenta, who saw the potential in this story from the beginning and whose expertise made everything about this long and arduous process better.